Baseball Play and Strategy

Baseball Play and Strategy

Ethan Allen

Third Edition

ROBERT E. KRIEGER PUBLISHING COMPANY
MALABAR, FLORIDA
1982

Original Edition 1959
Second Edition 1969
Third Edition 1982

Printed and Published by
ROBERT E. KRIEGER PUBLISHING COMPANY, INC.
KRIEGER DRIVE
MALABAR, FL 32950

Printed in the United States of America

Library of Congress Cataloging in Publication Data

Allen, Ethan, 1904-
  Baseball play and strategy.

  1. Baseball. 2. Baseball coaching. I. Title.
GV867.A387 1982   796.357′2   81-17177
ISBN 0-89874-450-4   AACR2

PUBLISHER'S NOTE

In bringing out this revised edition, corrections have been made to the
text. Accordingly, varieties in the density of type may be noticed.

About the Author

Ethan Allen attended the University of Cincinnati in the mid-1920's and then went directly from the college campus to major league baseball, beginning with the Cincinnati Reds and after that the New York Giants, St. Louis Cardinals, Philadelphia Phillies, Chicago Cubs, and St. Louis Browns. After retiring in 1938 with a lifetime .300 batting average, he was the National League's Director of Motion Pictures for several years before going to Yale where he coached baseball until retiring in 1968.

He is the author of *Baseball Techniques Illustrated* and *Winning Baseball* (series): *Batting and Base Running; Pitching and Catching; Infielding;* and *Outfielding and Coaching,* and creator of *All Star Baseball, All Star Baseball, Hall of Fame Edition,* and *Play Ball,* three scientific games based on Major-League batting records. He has also photographed and narrated ten instructional sound films about baseball.

On January 11, 1970, he was elected to the American Association of College Baseball Coaches Hall of Fame; and to the initial class of the University of Cincinnati Hall of Fame, February 28, 1976. To be eligible for the University of Cincinnati Hall of Fame, nominees must have earned letters in two varsity sports or two letters in one sport. Allen was a three-letter man in baseball, basketball, and track. In his senior year he was an All-Ohio guard in basketball, being high point man on a championship team and high point man on the track team, scoring a record total of 18 points in the final conference meet. His 1926 batting average of .473 is still the highest in the University of Cincinnati baseball history.

Foreword

Ethan Allen's new, complete book on baseball makes an invaluable contribution to the game. The book complements the author's other baseball publications and offers significant material to all who are concerned with the great American game, whether they be coaches and players, physical education teachers, or merely lovers of the sport.

The author is extremely well qualified, both as a player and as a teacher, to write authoritatively about baseball. As an outstanding major-league player for many years, he acquired a thorough knowledge of baseball in its most technical phases. His book sets forth this knowledge completely and concisely. Because it is based on experience and high technical skill, it should prove to be of great benefit to coaches and players now and for many years to come.

Further, Ethan Allen's professional training in education and his more than twenty years of experience as head coach of baseball at Yale University, have combined to make this publication an excellent text for the men and women in the teaching world who need technical information as a basis for instructional flexibility in their classes and supervisory work.

The baseball-conscious public also will find in this book a wealth of interesting information. The specialized knowledge which Ethan Allen presents and the clear manner with which his teaching experience enables him to express it will give to the average fan a detailed and comprehensive understanding of the game—an understanding which is bound to make his enjoyment of baseball richer and more complete.

It is for these reasons that I am delighted to introduce *Baseball Play and Strategy*. In my judgment, it is a book which deserves a prominent place in the literature of our profession.

Commissioner of Baseball

Preface

The Third Edition and revision of this established and successful book has been prepared as a comprehensive instructional guide which attempts to include every aspect of baseball under one cover. It is intended for physical education instructors and students, players, coaches, managers, and fans.

The beginning baseball player who carefully studies this book and supplements it with practice and personal instruction should acquire a thorough understanding of the techniques of the game. The more seasoned player who reviews the materials can expect to perfect his playing skills and to learn more about baseball strategy. Coaches and managers will find valuable teaching tips, practice drills, strategy aids, and signal systems to help develop winning baseball teams. Every fan of the national sport will derive fresh knowledge about the intricacies of the game.

The more than 500 illustrations and diagrams are an integral part of the book and complement the text. Sequence shots throughout demonstrate the various skills of expert baseball effectively. Each series of shots is accompanied by descriptions of the skill or play. Thus the reader will be able to understand even the most complicated maneuver because he can see it as he reads about it. The numerous drawings include diagrams of twenty-five practice drills with detailed legends so that each movement can be followed step by step.

In addition to the descriptions of the techniques and skills of play and the explanations of the fine points of offensive and defensive baseball, the book contains an analysis of an actual World Series game which pinpoints the strategy of managers, coaches, and players during each inning of the hotly fought contest and includes the complete scorecards of the game; a method of scoring games and determining percentages; diagrams of the official diamond layout and of batting tees and other practice aids; and minor refinements in the playing rules.

Discussion Questions and True-False Questions and Answers have been provided at the end of most of the chapters where appropriate, and a series of Sample Tests appears in the Appendix which may be used in the classroom or for self-testing.

Finally, extensive discussions of team organization and preseason training are included in the Appendix.

The Author is grateful to the Commissioner of Baseball, for the preparation of the Foreword, to *The Sporting News* for permission to reproduce the layout of the official baseball field; and to the many baseball players, coaches, managers, and officials for their cooperation during the preparation of the original manuscript and subsequent revisions.

Ethan Allen

Contents

I. DEFENSIVE BASEBALL

II. OFFENSIVE BASEBALL

III. PRACTICE TECHNIQUES

IV. GAME STRATEGY

APPENDIXES

DEFENSIVE BASEBALL

1

Basic Fundamentals

Every player must be able to field and throw the ball with some degree of accuracy. In order to do this adequately, it is necessary to take the proper defensive position before the pitcher completes his delivery, so that the fastest possible start can be made to field the ball, cover a base, or perform some other assignment related to the action. Although individual players possess varying degrees of running speed, all players should be able to make a fast start. This, combined with a fair amount of skill in fielding the ball and executing the proper throw, makes a player a real asset to his team.

THE STANCE

The stance of all players, with the exception of the pitcher, is a crouched position with the legs comfortably spread, the feet directly opposite each other (some catchers have the left foot several inches ahead of the right foot), and the knees slightly bent. As the ball is pitched, the body is leaned forward and the weight is transferred to the balls of the feet. Outfielders keep their hands on their knees until the ball is hit or passes the batter. Infielders stand similarly or bring the hands forward in front of the knees from the same position. The catcher forms a target with his hands in front of his body between the knees and shoulders. The follow-through position of the pitcher resembles the stance for other positions, except that the body is turned slightly to the opposite side from which the ball is thrown, and the foot from which the pitcher throws is usually planted just ahead of the stepping foot. (See Fig. 1-1.)

3

a. Outfielder: hands on knees.

c. Catcher: hands in front between knees and shoulders.

b. Infielder: hands forward in front of knees.

d. Pitcher: follow-through of arm and body.

Fig. 1–1.   Stance.

START FOR THE BALL

The position of the ball in relation to the player determines his footwork for the start for the ball (Fig. 1–2). When the ball is hit directly in front of a player, the first step, of course, can be made either with the left or with the right foot. If the ball is in front and to the right of a player, the first step is made with the left foot. The first step is with the right foot if the ball is forward to the left. When the ball is in back and to the right of a player, the first step is to the rear with the right foot. The first step is to the rear with the left foot if the ball is back and to the left. In retreating, a first step is followed by a crossover step to get into position to field both fly balls and grounders. The above footwork is also used for starts in performing duties such as covering and backing up bases. Short steps are taken first, and the stride is gradually increased until maximum speed is attained, or until the desired defensive position is reached. The arms are swung at the sides, and no effort is made to reach for the ball until the time of the catch.

CATCHING THE BALL

A player tries to keep his body directly in front of fly balls and ground balls. The hands are cupped and the eyes remain centered on the ball until the catch is completed. On some hard smashes a retreat is first made toward the path of the ball to attain a better throwing position. This, however, normally excludes retreating directly back.

FLY BALLS

In catching fly balls the feet are approximately in the normal walking position. (A right-hand thrower catches the ball with his left leg forward, and a left-hand thrower with the right leg forward.) If the ball is caught above the belt, the body is erect and the hands are held either with the thumbs together and fingers up or with the thumbs out and fingers up (Fig. 1–3a, b). The latter method offers an advantage in both vision and throwing. When the ball is caught below the belt, the trunk is bent forward slightly and the hands are held with the thumbs out and fingers down (Fig. 1–3c). (The hands are held much as in Fig. 1–3a and c in catching thrown balls and line-hit balls under the same conditions.) Most catches

a. Ball forward right: left foot.

b. Ball forward left: right foot.

c. Ball back right: right foot.

d. Ball back left: left foot.

Fig. 1–2. Start for the ball.

a. Above the belt: thumbs together and fingers up.
b. Above the belt: thumbs out and fingers up.
c. Below the belt: thumbs out and fingers down.

Fig. 1–3.   Position of the hands for catching fly balls.

a, b. The glove hand is used to block out the sun until just before the catch. (The bare hand can be employed if the sun is on the opposite side.)

Fig. 1–4. Position of the glove hand to shade the eyes from the sun to catch a fly ball.

are made about forearm's length from the body. The hands are extended beyond this point prior to the catch, but move back toward the body as the ball goes into the glove. This action continues until the hands part for the throw.

When a player is sure he can catch a fly ball, he yells loudly and insistently, "I have it" or "I'll take it." In response, a teammate calls the player's name. "Take it" is avoided because it may be construed as "I'll take it." "No, no" and "Plenty room" are guides where there are obstructions. (The bench and bull pen can help on fly balls along the foul line.) In pursuing such balls it is advisable to get to the obstruction as soon as possible.

If a fly ball goes near the sun, the player keeps to the side of the ball and shades his eyes with his glove or bare hand to make the catch (Fig. 1–4). If the sun is to the right, the eyes are shaded with the right hand, and when it is to the left, with the left hand. It is often possible to look away when the ball goes near the sun and still make the catch. This is particularly true on high fly balls. Many such balls are caught even though the sight may be temporarily impaired by following the ball into the sun. A glance toward the ground is used in this case to restore normal vision. The previous explanation also applies to lights when night games are played.

GROUND BALLS

In catching ground balls the body is kept low and controlled so that the weight can be shifted to meet any change in the course of the ball. When possible, an advance toward the ball is made with the arms hanging loosely at the sides. The ball is caught at the maximum height of a bounce or just after a bounce occurs. If you have to go back and to the side to get in front of a grounder, first take a short step back and to the side with the foot nearest the ball, then a cross-over step.

Most grounders are fielded with the legs in approximately the normal walking position and with the weight on the balls of the feet. The knees and hips are bent, and the ball is caught opposite the front foot with the thumbs out and the fingers down (Fig. 1-5). A right-hand thrower has the left foot forward. The hands are extended slightly beyond the point where the ball is caught but move back toward the body as the ball goes into the glove. This action is continued until the hands part for the throw.

Fig. 1–5. Position for fielding a normal ground ball.

Because many hard-hit balls might elude a player if fielded in this manner, the path of such balls is blocked. This is done in one of two ways. In one method the heels are placed together so that the feet form almost a right angle. The ball is then caught where the heels meet, provided, of course, it rolls on the ground (Fig. 1–6a). In the other method one knee is placed on the ground and the ball is caught where the knee and foot meet (Fig. 1–6b). (A right-hand thrower places the right knee against the heel of the left foot, and a left-hand thrower the left knee against the right foot.) The ball is not always handled cleanly when fielded in this manner, but if it is dropped it usually falls in front of the fielder and can be easily retrieved and possibly the batter or a base runner retired. In some instances the blocking of the ball prevents further advancement and additional scores. The former method of blocking is preferred because it permits a quicker recovery if the ball is missed.

A fumbled or free ball is generally picked up with two hands. The technique in this case corresponds to that described and illustrated under "Fielding Ground Balls" in Chapter 3, unless the ball has stopped rolling. Such balls are pursued with no attempt to watch runners.

b. One knee on ground.

a. Heels together.

Fig. 1–6. Positions for blocking hard-hit balls.

Fig. 1–7.   Grip for throwing.

It is important to refrain from throwing the glove, cap, or mask at a ball because a penalty is incurred if the ball is hit. In this case base runners advance two bases if a thrown ball is hit (the ball remains in play), and three bases when a batted ball is hit. (There is no penalty for the defense if the ball is missed.)

THROWING THE BALL

In throwing, the ball is gripped toward the ends of the first two fingers and thumb with only moderate finger pressure (Fig. 1–7). The ball is more likely to travel straight with the fingers across the widest separation of seams, as shown in the illustration. This is particularly true on overhand throws. There are many times when it is impossible to grip the ball with the fingers across the seams, especially if a hurried throw is necessary. However, unless a very short snap throw is required, the fingers can be shifted to this position as the hands come back after the catch. After a little practice it is possible to do this without actually watching the ball.

An overhand throw (Fig. 1–8) is made by shifting the weight to the throwing foot and making a moderate step with the free foot toward the direction of the throw. A right-hand thrower shifts the weight to the right foot, and a left-hand thrower to the left foot. The arm is bent through the first part of the throwing action and is whipped to an extended position as the weight is transferred to the front foot. A short hop in place or toward the direction of the intended receiver frequently adds momentum to the throw. The

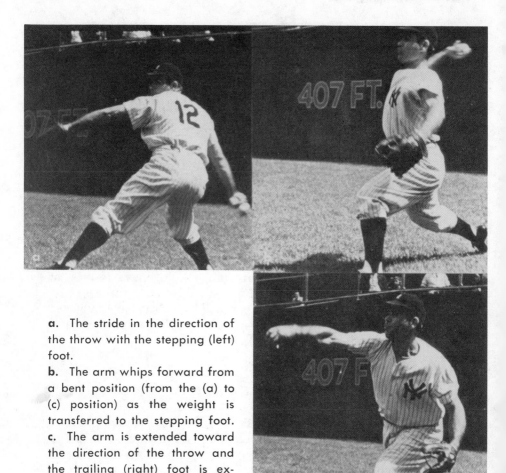

a. The stride in the direction of the throw with the stepping (left) foot.

b. The arm whips forward from a bent position (from the (a) to (c) position) as the weight is transferred to the stepping foot.

c. The arm is extended toward the direction of the throw and the trailing (right) foot is extended in the opposite direction for a good follow-through.

Fig. 1–8. Overhand throw.

hop is forward to the left if it is necessary to reach to the left for the ball. This brings the body to a good throwing position. The right arm is extended toward the direction of the throw, and the right leg is extended in the opposite direction. This conforms to the theory of opposition and is a good balanced position for all overhand throws.

An overhand throw from an erect body position is generally used because it achieves greater speed and accuracy. This is especially important on long throws. Many short throws, wherein an infielder can catch the ball in a stationary position or stop after making the catch, are similarly made. However, in situations where time is an element it is often necessary for the pitcher, catcher, or infielders to throw without raising the body to any great extent. This frequently happens when the ball is caught close to the ground on both hit and thrown balls. A sidearm throw is then effective.

All throws are aimed to reach the receiver above the belt on force-outs and below the belt when a runner must be tagged. The throw is direct to the bag except when the ball is fielded between the pitcher's mound and the plate and the play is to first base. (The pitcher sometimes throws slightly to the side of second base.) In this case the throw is to the second-base side of the bag.

A player must consider at all times where he will make his throw if the ball is hit to him. The strength of his throwing arm, the speed of the opposing players, the position of the infielders, the score, and the stage of the game affect his decision. A player must also anticipate adjustments that may have to be made if the ball is hit or thrown to another player. Infrequently a player not involved in making the catch can glance at runners on the bases and tell the player fielding the ball where to make the throw. This often makes it possible to play for an advanced runner instead of merely throwing to a base ahead of one less advanced.

If a balk is immediately followed by a pitch which the batter hits and permits the batter and each base runner to advance a minimum of one base, the balk is ignored and the ball does not become dead. All defensive players have to be alert in this situation because runners may attempt to advance more than one base.

SUMMARY

1. Lean the weight forward as the pitcher releases the ball so that you are ready to move in any direction. The pitcher's weight should be forward at the completion of his follow-through.
2. Step first with the foot farthest from the ball in starting forward and to the side. Step to the rear with the foot nearest the ball in going back.
3. Get in front of fly balls and ground balls. Break toward the side for hard-hit balls which are hit to your left or right.
4. Catch fly balls above the belt with the thumbs together and fingers up (also thrown balls) or thumbs out and fingers up. Catch balls below the belt with the thumbs out and fingers down.
5. Call decisively for balls—"I have it" or "I'll take it"—once you are sure you can make the catch, and watch the ball into your glove.

6. Help each other by calling "No, no" and "Plenty room" where obstructions such as fences and stands may interfere with the catch.
7. Play to the side of balls near the sun, or lights in a night game, and shade the eyes with the hand—the glove hand, if possible.
8. Maneuver on ground balls so that the catch can be made at the maximum height of a bounce or just after a bounce occurs. Keep the body low—knees and hips bent.
9. Block hard-hit balls with the feet together or one knee on the ground.
10. Pick up a fumbled or free ball with two hands, unless the ball has stopped rolling.
11. Refrain from throwing the glove, cap, or mask at a ball because a penalty is incurred if the ball is hit.
12. Step toward the intended receiver on long (overhand) throws. Bend the trunk forward and swing the arm down. Keep the elbow bent at the start of the throw and extend the arm as the weight is transferred to the stepping foot.
13. Make throws so that the ball reaches the receiver above the belt on force-outs and below the belt when the runner must be tagged.
14. Think where the throw should be made, or if a throw should be made, when a ball is hit toward your position or is thrown to you.
15. Anticipate adjustments which may have to be made if a ball is hit or thrown to another player.

HINTS TO PLAYERS

1. Run to and from your position and play hard regardless of the score.
2. Try to overcome weaknesses.
3. Study the strong and weak points of your opponents.
4. Subordinate individual performance to team play—never alibi if you make a mistake.
5. Have confidence, but do not underrate the opposition.
6. Follow instructions to the best of your ability.
7. Avert controversies with umpires (let the captain do any talking).
8. Arrive at the park at least a half hour before a practice session or before your batting practice starts for a regular game. Circle the field upon reporting and warm up before batting and fielding practice.
9. Determine the condition of the field, the type of sky, and the speed and direction of the wind.
10. Bathe slowly and dry thoroughly. Avoid drafts when not in action.
11. Eat lightly before playing—drink very little water during the game.
12. Obtain plenty of rest. Abstain from tobacco and alcohol.

13. Keep the fingernails clipped short, and do not wear jewelry.
14. Rest muscle injuries, and consult a physician on serious physical disabilities.
15. Remain loyal to the coach and players of your team.
16. Disregard remarks by spectators and members of the opposing team (this includes comments and advice by defensive players when you are at bat or on base).
17. Refrain from blocking the base lines, and do not fake or bluff a catch to force players to slide. Inform the runner when it is not necessary to slide by raising the hand and calling "Stay up."
18. Be a good sport—keep a level head—know the rules.

TIPS ABOUT EQUIPMENT

1. Buy shoes which fit snugly. Clean, brush, and oil (water-repellent) your shoes regularly.
2. Select a glove that fits your hand, preferably with medium-length fingers. Long fingers may affect your vision when catching balls above the belt. (Use a golf-type of glove for batting, if practicable.)
3. Apply grease or oil sparingly on your glove. Petroleum jelly or saddle soap is best.
4. Handle the rosin bag lightly with the fingers when your hands become moist (or the tar cloth, if one is provided for batters).
5. Choose light catching equipment—a comfortable glove, easy to handle.
6. Wear a light glove or place a thin piece of sponge rubber in your catching glove if pitches sting your hand.
7. Use clean undergarments—try to look neat and always appear on the field in full uniform. Wear a long-sleeved shirt when it is cold.
8. Avoid the use of strong rubber bands around the legs, for they frequently cut circulation.
9. Roll long stockings in and pull the trousers on in regular fashion.
10. Always wear sliding pads or pants in regular or intrasquad games.
11. Use a cup supporter if you pitch, catch, or play the infield.
12. Employ a protective helmet when you step into the batter's box or stand at the plate during a pitcher's warm-up.
13. Rub the bat with a bone or bottle to harden the hitting surface.
14. Store bats where it is not too dry or too damp.
15. Obtain a pair of sun glasses if you play the sun field (infielders as well as outfielders)—practice using them, and have them available for all games.

16. Keep the spikes free of mud on damp days.
17. Hang all equipment in orderly fashion in the locker room.

DISCUSSION QUESTIONS

1. Describe the position of the pitcher after the ball has been delivered. In what way may the stance of an infielder differ from that of an outfielder?
2. How does a player use his arms and legs in starting and running from the crouched defensive position?
3. Why is a player's name, rather than "Take it," called to inform a player he has the right of way on a fly ball?
4. Discuss the technique for catching fly balls above and below the belt. When is it advisable to turn the head away from high fly balls near the sun and where is the logical place to look?
5. What two methods are employed to block hard-hit balls? Which of these is preferred? Give the reason for your answer.

TRUE–FALSE QUESTIONS AND ANSWERS

T   F   1. The base runners advance two bases if a defensive player hits a thrown ball with his glove.
T   F   2. In starting forward and to the right, a player steps first with his right foot.
T   F   3. Fly balls that result in easy catches may be caught with the thumbs together or thumbs out.
T   F   4. Infielders try to catch ground balls at the height of a bounce or just after the bounce occurs.
T   F   5. An overhand throw is more likely to travel straight if the ball is gripped with the fingers across the widest separation of seams.

ANSWERS

T   T   T   F   T
5   4   3   2   1

2

The Pitcher

A good fast ball is the main asset of a pitcher. Poise, endurance, and control are other assets. The ability of the pitcher to outsmart a variety of batters is usually the decisive factor in the final score of a game. To do this effectively a pitcher must have a knowledge of opposing players and be able to perform the many tactical and strategic maneuvers the pitching position demands. In addition the pitcher must know himself, because unless he applies himself in relation to his natural talent he may never reach his peak as a pitcher. This may involve his method of delivering the ball and the type of pitches he employs—and how each is released—either of which might have a bearing on his control and consequently his effectiveness.

Pitchers are usually classified according to their method of delivering the ball, the assortment of fast balls, curve balls, and so on, that they pitch, and whether or not they have control. The classification as to method of *delivery* depends on the plane through which the pitcher's arm passes in releasing the ball. There are three ways of delivering the ball: overhand, sidearm, and underhand. The majority of pitchers falls into the overhand group and pitches with what is known as a three-quarter overhand delivery. This is not only a more natural way to throw, but breaking balls are more effective when pitched from this delivery because they break down.

A great many pitchers, and successful ones, too, do not restrict their pitches to one delivery, but often resort to a combination of overhand and sidearm deliveries. Leading pitchers, however, generally use only one style. They develop their assortment of fast balls, curve balls, slow balls, or whatever it may be, from their one delivery to the greatest degree of efficiency in regard to speed, break, and control of the ball. Pitchers who resort to a variety of

17

deliveries do not approximate this perfection with any single delivery, principally because there is not enough exercise of one delivery. Walter Johnson, Christy Mathewson, Cy Young, Grover Alexander, and many other immortals were exponents of "one delivery." In the more modern era Dizzy Dean, Bob Feller, Carl Hubbell, and Lefty Grove reached top ranking with the employment of one delivery.

There are a few pitchers who have physical assets that enable them to overpower batters. This does not necessarily mean muscular strength, but rather muscular adaptation. Sandy Koufax and Early Wynn, for example, were big men; but they did not derive their effectiveness from their bigness, but from their ability to control the muscles used in pitching. Undoubtedly the stamina which enabled them to pitch at full speed throughout a game can to a great extent be attributed to their size; but much of it can be credited to their faculty of putting something on the ball without apparently making a maximum effort. They presented perfect pictures of grace on the mound, and delivered the ball to the catcher with such freedom and ease that they expended much less energy than other pitchers of similar proportions who apparently do not know the meaning of the word "relax."

The classification relative to the *assortment of pitches* varies with individuals. Pitchers with good fast balls can frequently overpower batters. They have little need for control except to get the ball over the plate. Normally such pitchers rarely possess another pitch that is worrisome to the batter, and consequently they must rely mainly on a fast ball. However, it would be futile to expect a batter to be fooled if fast balls of approximately the same speed were continually pitched. Therefore, this type of pitcher commonly employs a mediocre breaking ball or slow ball, and attempts to pitch it just close enough to the plate either to tempt the batter into swinging at it or at least to make him think it was pitched for the purpose of hitting.

Control of the muscles is not confined to the large muscles, but includes those of the wrist and fingers as well. For this reason a number of pitchers, either small or frail of stature, have achieved records that are equal to those of larger men. Most of them are famous for especially good curve balls. Dolph Luque and Herb Pennock are so characterized. Occasionally this type of player possesses an unusual fast ball. Lefty Gomez was such an exception. Tommy Bridges was unique because he had both a good fast ball and a curve ball. Bobby Shantz, weighing less than 140 pounds and measuring only 5 feet 6 inches, can be classified with Bridges.

A few pitchers become successful because they perfect some odd pitch. Carl Hubbell is known for a puzzling screwball, Jim Bunning a slider, Bill Lohrman a sailer, Elroy Face a fork ball, and Hoyt Wilhelm a knuckle ball. These pitchers, however, did not rely on such pitches as power pitchers Koufax and Wynn relied on fast balls, but they did attempt to make the batter hit their favorite pitch when a hit was likely to prove damaging.

The classification with regard to *control* likewise varies with individual pitchers. Young pitchers usually have more problems with the batter's strike zone than do older ones. Some experienced pitchers with only ordinary "stuff on the ball" are past masters of control and are able to keep the ball pitched to the batter's weakness consistently. The batter never seems to get the ball he wants to hit. Even with the count two balls and no strikes, three balls and one strike, and occasionally three balls and no strikes, the ball sometimes just ticks the corner of the plate for the most doubtful kind of strike, and often the pitch is a curve or slow ball instead of a "fat" fast ball. Most of these pitchers have developed control through experience or because of a need to compensate for a loss of "stuff on the ball" late in their careers. In other instances it has been the result of not having enough strength to pitch hard throughout an entire game.

TECHNIQUE

POSITION ON THE RUBBER

The stance of a pitcher depends on the number of runners on base. For example, if only third base, second and third bases, all the bases, or no bases are occupied, the pitcher takes a position facing the plate so that he can take a windup. In all other situations he stands sideward to the plate in a set position. The body is erect in both stances and the shoulders are level. Both feet are planted on the ground with the foot from which the ball is pitched in contact with the pitching rubber. This foot is placed in the center of the rubber by some pitchers so that the shoulder and hand of the pitching arm are directly in line with home plate.

It was formerly necessary to keep the stepping foot behind the rubber in a windup stance, but now it may be to the side, thus making it possible for the pitcher to place his pitching foot on either end of the rubber. This does not apply to a set stance which requires the stepping foot to be in front of the rubber.

Windup Stance. When the stance is taken facing the batter, the feet are comfortably spread and slightly angled toward the side from which the ball is thrown. The spikes on the ball of the pitching foot extend over the front edge of the rubber, and the stepping foot rests on or to the rear of the rubber. A right-hand pitcher has the right foot forward, and a left-hand pitcher the left foot. The arms hang at the sides with the ball in the pitching hand just to the rear of the thigh. This prevents the batter from seeing the ball (Fig. 2–1A, a). If the bases are unoccupied, the pitcher centers his eyes on the spot where he intends to pitch the ball. When only third base, second and third bases, or all the bases are occupied, he must watch the movements of the runner on third base once the windup is started. A recommended procedure is to start the delivery while looking toward the runner, then concentrate on the batter once it appears the runner does not intend to break for the plate. In bringing the arms overhead for the windup, the back of the hand is held toward the plate to keep the ball hidden from the batter (Fig. 2-1A, b). To get the proper traction in a windup, the pivot foot must be slightly turned at the start of the delivery.

Set Stance. In the set stance the feet are also comfortably spread and angled toward the side from which the ball is thrown. In this case some pitchers extend their pitching foot over the front edge of the rubber in a manner similar to the position used for a windup, whereas others rest the outside edge of the foot against the front edge of the rubber. A right-hand pitcher has the right foot in contact with the rubber, and a left-hand pitcher the left foot. Both arms are bent, and the forearms are usually extended inward above the waistline so that the hands meet in a comfortable position between the belt buckle and the middle of the chest. The hands are cupped, and the ball is pocketed in the glove with the pitching hand holding it (Fig. 2–1B, c). The pitcher usually lifts his arms (to loosen the undershirt and baseball shirt around the shoulders and elbows) then brings the hands down to the set position (Fig. 2–1B, a–c). (The hands must be stopped momentarily in the regular pitching position before the ball can be delivered.) An exception occurs with first and third bases occupied in situations wherein the runner on third might attempt to steal home. In this case it is advisable to bring the hands up quickly to the set position; otherwise a balk might be committed. This is also a good tactic to combat an early break by the runner from first base.

In taking the set position, a pitcher stands with his body turned slightly to the left if he is watching a runner on first base. When watching a runner on second base, the position of a left-hand

A. Windup stance.

a. The hand rests behind the thigh so the batter cannot see the ball.
b. Position of hands at the top of the arm
swing.   The back of the glove is toward the
plate, again hiding the ball from the batter.

a, b, c. The hands are brought down to a comfortable position in front of the chest(c). There must be
a pause in this position before pitching.

B.   Set stance.

Fig. 2—1.   Pitching stances.

pitcher is also toward the left, but that of a right-hand pitcher is to the right. These positions mean that only a slight turn of the head is necessary to watch the runner. By making such observations, it is possible to catch runners straying too far from base as well as to prevent steals. When the pitcher is ready to deliver the ball from a set stance, it is usually advisable to have the eyes on the target of the catcher. However, it may be necessary to vary this procedure occasionally with second base occupied. This is done by starting some pitches with the eyes on the runner. A right-hand pitcher may also look toward third base and a left-hand pitcher toward first. (The runner on first base is disregarded because his actions are controlled by the runner on second.) Pitching quickly after pausing in the set position one time, then delaying the delivery of a subsequent pitch another are additional tricks.

Other tactics involving stance include pitching from a windup position with no arm swing (hands set in front of the body) and using a set position in some normal windup situations (to combat a squeeze play).

It is important to have possession of the ball when stepping on the rubber; otherwise a balk is committed. Thus if some infielder attempts a hidden ball trick, it is advisable to fake having the ball and stand far enough from the rubber so that the umpire will not construe that the feet are in a legal pitching position.

Stepping from the Rubber.   If time has been called by the umpire, it makes no difference how a pitcher steps from the rubber; but if play has not been terminated he must back from the rubber before breaking his hands. This is very important when a runner, anticipating a pitch, runs before the pitcher starts his delivery. In this situation the pitcher steps back from the rubber, because if the runner is on first base and any indication is made to throw in that direction prior to backing from the rubber, the ball, of course, must be thrown to that base. (If the ball is thrown to first base, the runner is more likely to beat the throw of the first baseman to second base than if the pitcher makes the throw.) The pitcher steps back by lifting his back foot over the rubber (Fig. 2–2). A throw to any base is then permitted. If a runner on first base attempts to start for second base in the above manner, the pitcher turns to the left after stepping from the rubber so that the runner can be watched. If the runner stops, the pitcher runs directly toward him and tries to drive him back to first base, at the same time being alert for an attempt to score in case there is a runner on third base. In fact, some teams have a specific play with first and third bases occupied. In this case the runner on first purposely takes a big lead or starts for second base to draw a throw from the pitcher, thus making it possible for the runner on third base to score. On some teams the pitcher turns toward third base after stepping from the rubber to thwart such a play. However, a left turn and fake throw to the second baseman seems to work best, in which case a right-hand pitcher continues his pivot toward the glove hand to catch the runner off third or attempting to score. A left-hand pitcher also turns toward the glove hand, but the opposite way. If the runner on third base does not try to score, the pitcher, of course, again transfers his attention to the other runner.

The above defensive measure can also be executed when the offensive team is not attempting a specific play. In this event the pitcher goes through the same routine, first backing off the rubber, then faking a play to first base and throwing to third. This can be a preplanned play with the pitcher and third baseman using the same signals that are employed for a pickoff play at second.

It is also advisable for the pitcher to back off the rubber if the batter uses excessive time to take his position in the batter's box. If there is an appeal play and "Time" has been called, the pitcher must obtain the ball and come to a legal position on the rubber (to put the ball back in play), then back off before making his throw.

a. Set stance.

b. The step back with the hands stationary.

c. Watching the runner.

Fig. 2–2. Stepping from the pitching rubber.

a. Position of feet to take windup stance.

b. Position of feet to take set stance.

Fig. 2–3.   Taking the sign.

TAKING THE SIGN

The pitcher is required to take the catcher's signal from the stance with which he expects to deliver the ball (feet as in Fig. 2–3). This gives him the option of using a windup or set stance (with the arms hanging naturally), or he may take the windup stance and hold his hands in a set position in front of the body.

With the bases unoccupied it is important to immediately take the windup position because a pitch must be delivered within 20 seconds after the ball is received—to avoid delaying the game. The pitcher may, however, back off the rubber in which case he is then free to use either the windup or set stance.

The cleverness with which a pitcher is able to combat base running is very important. This includes the actual taking of the signal, bringing the hands to the proper stop position, watching the runner, or at least giving the runner the impression that he is being watched, and pitching or attempting to catch the runner.

It is often said that in pitching, the pitcher's greatest asset is the batter's imagination. An excellent example is the pitcher who has the batter thinking he can get perspiration on the ends of his fingers to throw an illegal spit ball, even though one is never thrown. The same rule can be applied to holding a runner on base.

A pitcher's main objective is, of course, getting the batter out. He does not necessarily have to watch the runner but only turn his head far enough to make the runner think he is being watched. This combined with other tricks enables a pitcher to keep most base runners under control.

The pitcher must remember that he cannot take a pitching position facing the batter on, astride, or near the pitcher's plate without the ball. This constitutes a balk.

The pitcher watches the complete sign series of the catcher instead of getting ready to pitch as soon as he has seen the actual signal. This is especially important with second base occupied; otherwise the runner might easily determine the set of signs used, and relay the information to the batter. The pitcher usually accepts the first signal of a reliable catcher. However, he may decline the sign by shaking his head or by wiggling his glove. The pitcher may decline the sign because of an inexperienced catcher. He may do this with some experienced catchers even though he is satisfied to make the pitch signaled. This delay frequently captures the batter's imagination and prevents him from correctly guessing the judgment of a catcher who gives signals methodically. A smart catcher usually repeats his original signal since he knows the pitcher declined the first sign as part of battery strategy.

Prior to taking the sign, the pitcher notes what bases are occupied so that he will know whether to use a windup or to pitch from a set stance. He often pitches from the set stance with two out, all the bases occupied, and the count three balls and two strikes on the batter, because this delays the start of the runners. He also makes sure the defensive players are in their positions. This is likewise important after a throw to a base to catch a runner or, as is frequently the case, when an infielder has driven a runner back to the bag. Wide openings in the defense are avoided by this means.

GRIP OF THE BALL

A pitcher decides on one specific grip of the ball and develops his fast ball, breaking ball, and slow ball from it. The opposing team is then unable to detect that perhaps a fast ball is held one way, a curve ball another, and so on. A successful pitcher ordinarily combines fast balls and curve balls of various speeds to foil the batter. Since, in most cases, either the fast balls or the curve balls are more puzzling, the ball is gripped so that the fingers can propel

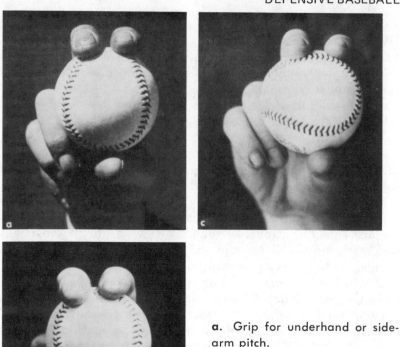

a. Grip for underhand or sidearm pitch.
b. Grip for knuckle ball pitch.
c. Grip for overhand pitch.

Fig. 2–4. Normal grips.

the ball at the greatest possible speed or cause it to curve in the
most proficient manner.

Fast balls are rolled from the ends of the index and middle
fingers, and curve balls from the inner surface of the middle finger.
It is therefore necessary to hold the ball so that these portions of
the fingers may grip the ball firmly. One method to ensure such
contact is to place the fingers along the seams of the ball where
they are narrowest. The inner sides of the fingers thus rest on the
rough portion of the ball (Fig. 2–4a). This grip is used by underhand and sidearm pitchers. A second method is to grip the ball
with the fingers across the seams, either at the point where they are
narrowest (used by knuckle ball pitchers) or where they are widest

(used by overhand pitchers). The latter grips are illustrated in Fig. 2–4b and c. The thumb is tucked in more for a curve.

Some pitchers who use the second method move the fingers over on the ball when they want to throw a curve so that the middle finger rests on or against the seam. (A left-hand pitcher grips the ball with the seam to the outside of the middle finger.) Sidearm and underhand pitchers usually prefer to grip the ball along the seams because the majority of their pitches are sinking fast balls, and the ball sinks more when two seams are revolved toward the batter. Most overhand pitchers, however, favor the grip across the seams where they are widest, because their most effective pitch is often a rising fast ball, and the ball rises more when four seams are revolved up and toward the batter. Thus, in the former instance the least amount of resistance is desired and in the latter the greatest amount. For the same reason, some overhand pitchers prefer to throw a curve from the normal sidearm grip because it enables them to revolve four seams down and toward the batter. A pitcher who throws a great many knuckle balls generally grips the ball across the narrow seams, since this type of pitch is usually made by placing the ends of the index and middle fingers between these seams. In gripping the ball to throw a fast ball or curve use only the fingers, not the back of the hand.

PITCHES

Pitched balls are classified as fast balls, breaking balls, and slow balls. Breaking balls include curve balls, screwballs, knuckle balls, fork balls, and palm balls. Slow balls generally involve a variation in speed of a fast ball or curve. Fast balls may be pitched high or low, but breaking balls and slow balls are only effective low, and preferably away from the batter. A pitcher, of course, cannot have all pitches at his command. The majority of pitchers employ a combination which includes a fast ball, a breaking ball—preferably a curve ball, since it is easier to control—and a slow ball. With such an assortment he can very effectively cope with batters by varying both the speed and action of the ball.

Fast Ball. The path of any pitch depends primarily on the delivery used to make it. Thus, if a fast ball is thrown from a directly overhand delivery, it rises slightly, and if from a three-quarter overhand delivery it rises and goes toward the side from which it was pitched. If a sidearm delivery is accompanied by a sideward follow-through, the ball goes toward the side from which it was thrown, and if by a downward follow-through it sinks toward the same side. If a semiunderhand delivery is employed, the ball sinks toward the side from which it was thrown, and if a full underhand delivery is used, it sinks. Consequently, overhand pitchers are often considered high-ball pitchers, and sidearm and underhand pitchers low-ball pitchers. Some overhand pitchers, however, become effective low-ball pitchers by holding on to the ball a trifle longer.

The amount of break on a fast ball is ordinarily not visible. Pitched chiefly for speed, the ball is rolled from the ends of the index and middle fingers with a natural forward break of the wrist. The wrist is given a decided snap as the pitch is released, thereby propelling the ball with a tremendous amount of speed. If there is enough speed, an overhand pitch may rise with a hop. A fast ball, aside from being an effective pitch, is easier to control than other pitches; therefore it is the basis of good pitching.

There are exceptions to the fast ball described above. For example, some overhand pitchers can throw a sinking fast ball because they rotate their arm and wrist inward as they release the ball, thereby causing downward spin. Then some right-hand pitchers can consistently make an overhand fast ball sail or glide toward a left-hand batter and away from a right-hand batter, and left-hand pitchers vice versa. They grip the ball with the index and middle fingers along the seams where they are narrowest. The first and second joints of the fingers rest on the smooth part of the ball where the seams are widest, but as the pitch is released they raise the index finger. They throw the ball at approximately three-quarter speed. Any new ball that is thrown from an overhand delivery with moderate speed will sail to the opposite side from which it is thrown if gripped so that the fingers conform to the seams of the ball; that is, the ball must be held so that when it leaves the hand two narrow seams will revolve toward the plate. Some overhand pitchers release a fast ball in such a way that it slides or moves to the side like a curve (slider). It is thrown with an off-center grip (pressure: on middle finger-off index finger). The ball is slid over the side of the index finger (wrist rigid) instead of from the tips of the fingers. The slide effect can also be obtained by releasing the ball with about a quarter turn of the wrist. There is very little arm rotation. The slider is often called a nickel curve since it moves to the side and breaks but not in the explosive fashion of a curve. It can be a very effective pitch but it requires practice and not every pitcher can perfect it.

The action of the fast ball of one pitcher may differ from that of another because of the pitcher himself. He either possesses some unusual physical trait or traits, applies his ability at the start of his career in an unusual manner, or, as is often the case, develops a dif-

ference through experience. An excellent example of the first of
these is Mordecai Brown, who became a great pitcher even though
he had only three fingers.

Curve Ball.   A curve ball is thrown with an outward rotation of
the hand and arm. The stride is less and emphasis is on shortarm
action. The ball is spun from the hand between the thumb and
forefinger with the middle finger and wrist providing the spin. For
this reason more pressure is usually applied to the middle finger.
Though the curve starts like a fast ball, once the arm becomes even
with the body the wrist is snapped about a half-turn outward and
in, thus giving the ball a tremendous amount of down and in spin.
A curve ball thrown in this manner always breaks toward the opposite side from which it is thrown. It goes down from an overhand
delivery, up from an underhand delivery, and parallel to the ground
if thrown from a sidearm delivery. Some pitchers can make a curve
ball break almost straight down from a directly overhand delivery
by eliminating arm rotation. Similar results can be obtained by
turning the back of the forearm toward the batter and letting the
ball roll from the ends of the fingers.

There are various applications of the curve. For example, one
pitcher may throw an effective curve with the ball held loosely in the
hand, while another may get corresponding results with a decided
grip. Similarly, one pitcher may throw a good curve with a great
expenditure of energy, and another with a mere flip of the wrist.
You can get the feel of a curve by snapping the wrist from a standing or sitting position. Employ short forearm action to do this,
using a soft one-half roll of the wrist.

Screwball.   A screwball, or reverse curve, is held in the same
manner as a fast ball or curve, and is thrown with an inward rotation
of the hand and arm. It is spun out of the hand between the
middle finger and the fourth and fifth fingers, with the middle
finger and wrist providing the spin. The screwball also starts like
a fast ball but, unlike the curve, the wrist is snapped a quarter-turn
inward. It is usually pitched from an overhand delivery and breaks
down and toward the side from which it is thrown with less speed
and break than a curve. Carl Hubbell derived his effectiveness with
the screwball from the ability to break his wrist forward more than
the average pitcher, thus causing a greater downward break. Hub
Pruett, who gained fame by his ability to strike out Babe Ruth,
threw a similar screwball, but used stiff arm action. This proved
a strain, and perhaps prevented him from becoming a great
pitcher.

Knuckle Ball. A knuckle ball usually breaks in the same direction as a curve. It is thrown either from an overhand or sidearm delivery, and the break depends on the resistance of the air or wind against the seams of the ball. For this reason a wind toward or across the path of the ball gives a better break. A good knuckle ball floats toward the plate, then breaks abruptly a few feet in front of the batter. Ordinarily these pitches are inconsistent in their break because the cleanliness of the seams varies.

There are a number of ways to hold a knuckle ball, but most pitchers use one of two methods. In one method the first joints of the index and middle fingers rest against the ball between the seams where they are narrowest. The thumb and fourth and fifth fingers encircle the ball and hold it tightly (Fig. 2–5a). As the ball leaves the hand, the bent fingers are extended, thereby giving the pitch additional speed. Freddy Fitzsimmons employed this method. The other method that is favored by most pitchers is similar except that the tips of the fingers or fingernails rest on the ball (Fig. 2–5b). There is also less pressure on the thumb and fourth and fifth fingers. The former method requires a decided amount of wrist snap as the ball leaves the hand. This plus the extension of the index and middle fingers revolves the ball slightly. In the latter method the fingers and wrist remain stiff. The ball rarely revolves when thrown in this manner.

Fork Ball. A fork ball breaks in the same manner as a knuckle ball. It is held with the index and middle fingers apart. It is thrown with a forward wrist snap, and the ball is slid from the hand between the spread fingers. The middle finger is placed on the lowest seam of the right side of the ball where the seams are narrowest; the index finger, between the seams where they are narrowest on the left side (Fig. 2–5c). Jim Weaver was an unusual exponent of the fork ball. Normally the movement of the arm and hand of a pitcher throwing a knuckle ball or fork ball coincides with the same movement used when a fast ball is thrown, granted like deliveries are employed; but Weaver's arm and hand moved through the last half of the delivery in a position that corresponds to the final position of the hand when a curve is pitched. He rolled the ball from his middle finger, permitting it to slide from the index finger. For this reason he applied resin to the middle finger and kept the index finger smooth. The ball has greater spin when thrown in this manner, and breaks down more.

Palm Ball. A palm ball is usually thrown from an overhand delivery, and breaks down slightly. It is held with all the fingers

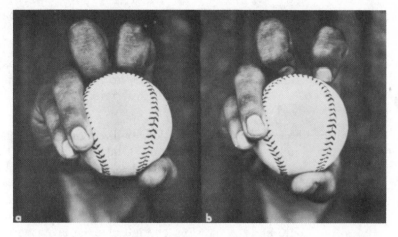

a. Knuckle ball: joints of fingers on ball.

b. Knuckle ball: ends of fingers on ball.

c. Fork ball.

d. Palm ball.

Fig. 2–5. Specific pitches.

on and around the ball. The fingers are spread a little, and the ball lies against the palm of the hand (Fig. 2–5d). This type of palm ball is slid from the thumb and palm with little wrist action. The fingers rest very lightly on the ball, and act more or less as guides. For this reason the ball revolves very little, and floats somewhat like a knuckle ball or fork ball but much more slowly. A palm ball can also be pitched with the normal two-finger grip. Pressure in this case is on the second joints of the fingers or toward the back of the hand. The ball is slid from the fingers with the palm to the side as in the delivery of a curve (a slip pitch), or down as in the delivery of a fast ball. In both of these releases there is little wrist action involved.

Slow Ball or Change of Pace. The slow ball, or change of pace, is not a specific kind of pitch. It is usually a fast ball or curve that is thrown with less effort and consequently less speed. It is pitched for speed deception, and may be approximately three-quarter speed, half-speed, or the slowest possible speed. A medium-speed change of pace is more effective. One of faster speed resembles the majority of pitches too much, and a very slow change of pace often permits the batter to recover his balance after being fooled by the start of the pitch. Generally speaking, a loose grip and moderately stiff wrist (lazy wrist) are characteristics of a good slow ball. The emphasis is on finger-tip control. In a second method the two fingers are raised as the ball is released. This action may be likened to inserting the fingers in the ring of the cord and pulling down on a window shade.

Although it is usually advisable to make the arm leg, and body actions the same as for other pitches, some pitchers throw a very effective slow ball by dragging the trailing foot instead of swinging it around quickly (Fig. 2-8). Taking a longer step with the front foot is another variation in footwork. In bringing the arm forward, lead with the elbow (let the forearm lag).

DELIVERY AND PITCH

The arm, leg, and body actions in making a pitch vary according to the stance from which the ball is thrown and the delivery used. When the ball is pitched from a set stance, the pitcher begins his delivery from a stationary position. Just prior to the start of the pitch, the weight is shifted to the ball of the back foot. The forward or windup position permits the pitcher to take one step backward with the rear foot prior to stepping to deliver the ball. One or two arm swings may accompany the delivery, and most pitchers employ a combination of the two for deception. An arm swing also enables a pitcher to develop rhythm and momentum in his delivery.

Before reading the discussion below regarding leg and arm action on delivery and pitch, first study the actions portrayed in Figs. 2–6 to 2–9. In sequence these photographs show techniques em-

a. The trunk bend forward and arm swing to the rear.

b. The weight is transferred to the rear foot as the hands meet overhead.

c, d. Delivery begins by transferring the weight to the front foot and pivoting the body away from the batter.

e, f, g. The transfer of the weight to the stepping foot.

h, i, j. The release of the ball and follow-through.

Fig. 2–6. Arm and leg action with a windup (fast ball).

a, b, c. Start of the delivery from a set position (a right-hand pitcher keeps the stepping leg lower).

d, e, f. Transfer of the weight to the stepping foot (the front knee is slightly bent).

g, h, i. Release of the ball and follow-through (the left leg around and the left foot is planted slightly ahead of the right foot in the final position).

Fig. 2–7. Arm and leg action from a set position (fast ball).

ployed by right- and left-hand pitchers, and the accompanying captions describe the actions.

When a pitcher uses a windup, he begins his delivery by shifting the weight to the front foot, meanwhile bending the trunk slightly forward and swinging the arms to the rear of the body. The weight is then shifted to the rear foot and the body straightened. During this action the arms are swung forward past the hips and joined overhead (Fig. 2-6a, b). The pitcher may repeat the windup or he may transfer the weight to the front foot and start to pitch. Most pitchers pivot away from the plate before releasing the ball to add both momentum and deception to the pitch. An overhand pitcher often gets this effect by tilting backward on the foot from which he pitches and raising the stepping foot high in the air (Fig. 2-9a, b).

Leg Action. There is little similarity of arm and body movement in the different deliveries, but the action of the legs is almost the same once a pitcher steps to pitch, except when a cross-fire delivery is used. With that one exception, the step is always a natural stride toward the plate. The elevation of the foot, of course, makes no difference when a windup is permitted unless the runner on third base is attempting to steal home; but if the ball is pitched from a set stance, the foot is generally passed close to the ground to prevent base runners from gaining an advantage. A left-hand pitcher can raise the leg higher because the start of his leg action is the same for pitching as for throwing to first base (Fig. 2–7b). When a cross-fire delivery is used, the fundamental foot and leg actions are the same, but the step is made toward a point between first or third base and the plate. A right-hand pitcher steps toward the third-base line and a left-hand pitcher toward the first-base line. In all pitches the back leg, or leg from which the pitcher throws, follows around quickly and is planted a considerable distance from the foot already on the ground and slightly in front of it (Fig. 2–7h, i). A right-hand pitcher has the right foot forward, and a left-hand pitcher the left.

Arm Action. The arm is bent at the start of the delivery and is whipped to an extended position at the completion of it, regardless of the type of pitch or delivery used (Fig. 2–8). As a general rule the leg, arm, and body actions are the same for all pitches because such sameness prevents the batter from anticipating a certain pitch. The arm action is a smooth, free movement with little muscular tension. If the muscles of the wrist and arm are properly relaxed, the weight of the ball will pull the pitching hand inward

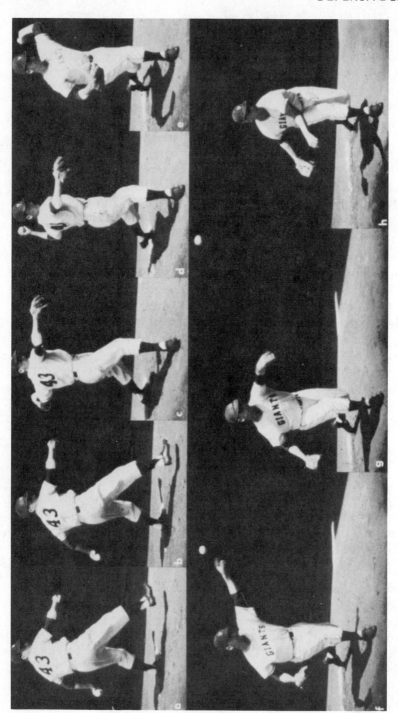

a, b. Start of the delivery.
c, d, e. The relaxed arm in the first part of the action
(elbow bent).

f, g, h. The extended arm in the last half of the action
(the back-toe drag is one method of throwing an effective slow ball).

Fig. 2-8. Arm and leg action (slow ball).

as the arm goes back for the pitch (Fig. 2--8a, b, c). When the arm is swung forward, the wrist bends again and the hand is pulled outward for the same reason (Fig. 2--8d, e). The wrist is bent once more by the actual throwing of the ball (Fig. 2--8f, g). The pitcher attempts to snap his wrist at this point because therein lies the secret of "stuff on the ball." Without relaxation of the muscles prior to this attempt, maximum wrist snap will not be possible. Swinging the pitching hand too near the head may cause tenseness.

The previous explanation is further illustrated by the down swing of the arm in the three overhand deliveries (Figs. 2--10 and 2--11) and the lower swing of the arm in the sidearm delivery (Fig. 2--12). Because these are the two basic deliveries, it is well for young players to study the arm, leg, and body actions. These pitchers push off from the rubber, driving their weight forward and the trunk down. The pitching arm lags behind the stride and the step is slightly to the left of a direct line to the plate, if the pitcher is right-handed; to the right, if he is left-handed. This opens up the hips for a well-coordinated pitch. Actually, a pitcher throws against his stride the same as a batter swings against his stride. The weight lands on the ball of the stepping foot and the toe points toward the batter. These are fundamentals of pitching which help to give a smooth, well-coordinated delivery.

Normally the leg and body action is slightly lower in a sidearm delivery because the arm passes parallel to the ground. The wrist action is also different in the two deliveries. In the three overhand deliveries, the wrist is snapped forward and down (Figs. 2--10 and 2--11); in the sidearm delivery it is rotated inward (Fig. 2--12e, f). This, of course, spins the ball toward the ground and makes the pitch sink. Sidearm pitchers usually employ a deep swing of the arm and thereby attain maximum leverage for the pitch.

It was previously stated that the three-quarter overhand delivery is favored by most pitchers, and it may be concluded that this method is best for the average player. On the other hand, the sidearm delivery is used successfully by many pitchers. It is a particularly effective pitch when a right-hand pitcher is pitching to a right hand batter, or a left-hand pitcher to a left-hand batter. In fact, some overhand pitchers use it as a strike-out pitch when they have the batter in the hole under these conditions. In this case the ball must be over the outside edge of the plate to be effective. If it is inside, the batter may be fooled by the delivery yet fall right into the pitch. If the sidearm and overhand deliveries are combined, it is important not to confine a specific pitch to a

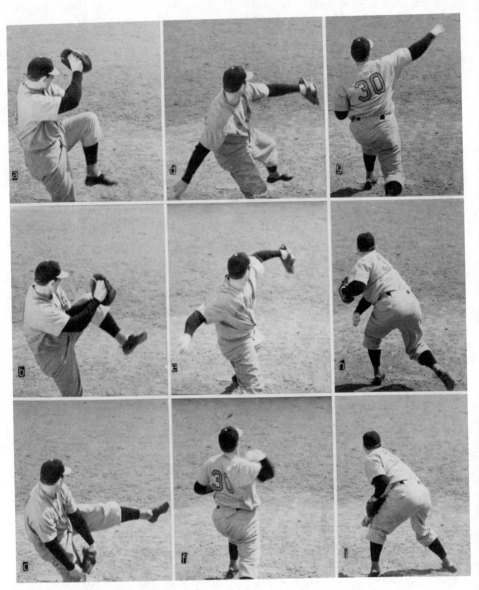

Fig. 2—9. Arm action (curve ball).

a, b, c.   The pivot away from the plate. The weight is directly over the rubber.

d, e, f.   The step is slightly to the left of a direct line to the plate. The foot hits the ground just before the release of the ball.

g, h, i.   The completed pitch and follow through. Observe the arm snaps forward from a bent position (f) to an extended position (g). Outward and down wrist snap accompanies the release of the ball.

certain delivery, because the opposing team may take advantage of this practice.

PITCHING TO THE BATTER

Control is unquestionably the greatest factor in pitching. In a general sense it means the ability to throw the ball into the strike area, when the occasion calls for it, without variation in the normal pitching effort. To define it more specifically requires a thorough knowledge of hitters' weaknesses and strengths and offensive tactics, and a careful consideration of the number of runners on base, the number of outs, the score, and the stage of the game.

Batters are classified as pull hitters, opposite-field hitters, and straightaway hitters. Pull hitters include right-hand batters who hit early and pull the ball into left field most of the time and left-hand batters who pull the ball into right field. Opposite-field hitters include right-hand batters who hit late and drive the ball more often to right field, and left-hand batters who hit the ball to left field. Straightaway hitters include both left- and right-hand batters who hit the ball according to the location of the pitch and who therefore drive the ball consistently in the area between the left and right fielders.

PITCHING TO WEAKNESSES

The classification of hitters alone indicates that some players are weak on inside pitches and others on outside ones. In addition, some batters are unable to hit low pitches as well as high ones, and the reverse is true of others. The vulnerable points of batters are therefore the four extremities of the strike area, which, as defined by the rules, is the space above home plate between the batter's arm pits and top of his knees when he assumes his natural position (Fig. 2–13). The more consistently a pitcher is able to reach these extremities with his pitches, the more successful he is likely to be. He must in addition, though, analyze each batter because some players are considered good fast ball hitters whereas others are known for their ability to hit breaking balls and off-speed pitches.

The stance in the batter's box, the manner the bat is gripped prior to the pitch, and the leg, arm, and body actions in the swing at the ball reveal batting weaknesses. The manner a player grips his bat usually determines his stance. A player who grips the bat on the end normally stands away from the plate, whereas one who

a, b. The inward break of the wrist at the start of the arm action.

c, d. The outward break of the wrist as the step is made (slightly to to the right of a direct line to the plate to open up the hips).

e, f. The body pivot as the arm whips forward to release the ball.

g, h. The body pivot as the arm whips forward and down to a good follow through.

Fig. 2—10. Three-quarter overhand delivery with a windup (fast ball).

employs a choke grip with the hands two or thee inches from the end stands close to the plate. The former may step forward, in , or away, and usually favors a low ball; the latter normally steps forward, and is more likely to prefer a high ball. The step with the front foot generally reveals the weakness of the batter. If the step is toward the plate, the batter is likely to be weak on inside fast balls and quick-breaking balls that break in toward the knees. When the step is away from the plate, an outside fast ball, breaking ball, or slow ball will be difficult to hit. A batting weakness may be revealed by the way a player stands or holds his bat. Players

a, b, c. The windup and pivot of the body-weight directly over the rubber, knee slightly bent (c).

d, e. The natural stride toward the plate and push from the rubber.

f, g, h. The arm swing down-shoulder and body follow through (stepping foot pointed toward batter).

Fig. 2—10. *(Continued)*

who stand erect usually prefer a high ball, and those who crouch, a low ball. Players who control the bat from a high position are also likely to be high ball hitters and those who control it from a low position, low ball hitters.

Then some players take full swing whereas others employ shorter arm action. The hitter who grips the bat on the end usually

a. Ready to pitch—eyes are on the plate.

b. Delivery is started by pivoting slightly to the right. The stepping foot is kept low to prevent steals.

c, d, e. The arm follows the stride (note the knee of the stepping foot is bent).

Fig. 2–11. Three-quarter overhand delivery from a set position (fast ball).

takes a decided swing, and the choke hitter tries only to meet the ball. This, however, may be reversed. Swing hitters are more easily fooled, and since they are generally distance hitters, most pitchers attempt to make them hit medium-speed breaking balls or slow balls. They are thus forced to use their own power and consequently get less distance on their drives than if fast balls are pitched. This particularly concerns the player who takes a long stride and lunges at the ball. A player who stands with his feet spread and employs a very short stride is less likely to be fooled on such a pitch even though a hard swing is taken. The late swinger is also a distinct type as well as a player who sweeps at the ball. Inside fast balls are more effective against these players.

The mannerisms of a player may also disclose flagrant batting weaknesses. For example, many players are exceptionally nervous. The pitcher delays his pitches to this type of batter. Conversely, fast action may affect a player who is casual in the batter's box. Similar pitching strategy often finds a player who continually swings his bat unready to hit.

In addition, other valuable information may be divulged by the batter. Very often a player will indicate his intention to hit or take the next ball. Then again he might disclose a hit-and-run

f. The pitch is released just after the transfer of weight. (Observe good technique of stepping to left of direct line to plate and hitting ground with ball of foot; also wrist is bent down in (c) and back in (e).)

g, h. Follow-through of shoulder and body, bringing pitching hand to a point near left knee.

Fig. 2–11. *(Continued)*

sign, a desire to bunt, or an inclination to pull the ball or hit it to the opposite field. A wide pitch is advisable if a hit-and-run sign is discovered, and a high inside fast ball if a bunt is likely, unless the catcher has already signaled for a curve-ball pitchout to try to catch a runner off base. The ball is pitched outside to a left-hand batter and inside to a right-hand batter when an attempt is likely to be made to hit behind the runner. (Hitting behind the runner is explained in Chapter 12.) A pitcher rarely permits a left-hand batter to hit a slow ball or breaking ball in this situation because such pitches can be pulled. This is particularly true when a right-hand pitcher is on the mound. The above tactics are slightly altered if a right-hand batter steps back from the plate to be able to hit inside pitches to right field. In this case a low outside pitch is occasionally made because it will be difficult to reach. If the batter indicates he will attempt to pull the ball, the pitch is aimed outside.

If a pitcher is at bat, all pitches are kept low and no slow balls are pitched. Because the pitcher is ordinarily a weak batter, he is more likely to hit high pitches and slow balls. This also concerns other weak batters. Low balls are also effective with runners on base because such pitches are usually hit on the ground. This is

a, b. The right shoulder dips and the arm swings deep behind the back.

c, d. The arm is extended to the rear (elbow slightly bent) as it accompanies the pivot of the body.

e, f. The pitch is released just after the complete transfer of the weight, and the wrist rotates to give the ball downward spin.

Fig. 2–12. Sidearm delivery (fast ball—sinker).

particularly true of curve balls. Low pitches are likewise effective in parks with short fences or when there are overflow crowds. On the other hand, if the park has plenty of outfield territory, high pitches work to advantage in some situations because most high pitches are hit in the air. However, high pitches are avoided with third base occupied and less than two outs unless your team has a commanding lead or the batter is a good low-ball hitter.

THE FIRST PITCH

Very few pitchers possess sufficient control to begin to pitch to a hitter's weakness on the first pitch without getting in the hole. Thus in most situations a pitcher puts plenty of stuff on a fast ball for his first pitch and attempts to get it over the plate for a strike. There are very few good first-ball hitters, so a pitcher is playing the percentages if he can get his inital pitch over. This is particularly true with the bases unoccupied, and also when the opposing team is several runs behind and the batter does not represent the tying or winning run. When the first pitch is a strike, the batter is more likely to swing at the following pitch even though it is outside the strike are. On the other hand, if the pitcher attempts to pitch to the batter's weakness with his first pitches, and gets in the hole (two balls and no strikes, three balls and no strikes, or three balls and one strike), it is very likely that the batter will get the ball he wants to hit. By the same token it is advisable to get the initial pitch over if the previous batter was retired on a first pitch because the following batter is usually instructed to take.

There are exceptions, such as the intentional pass or attempt to make the hitter offer at a wide pitch when a base on balls will not be damaging. A base on balls is often good strategy with the winning run on second base or on third base with second base occupied and first base unoccupied. But generally speaking, it is best to try for a strike on the first pitch. In fact, it is important for the pitcher to get ahead and to keep ahead of batters as much as possible. This saves energy and instills confidence in the defensive players. For a similar reason the pitcher remains on the pitching mound after delivering the ball unless a specific duty has to be performed as a result of the pitch. This prevents unnecessary delay and keeps the game moving. If there is no play after you have completed your delivery, take the catcher's return throw in the follow-through area (don't walk toward the plate) then immediately go to the pitching rubber. This prevents unnecessary delay and helps to speed up the game. It will also conserve energy.

The majority of pitchers are usually too cautious about getting the ball over the plate. In other words, they overpitch. This frequently occurs with the count one ball and two strikes. Failure to fool the hitter with a bad pitch at this stage invites trouble because a count of two balls and two strikes, of course, improves the batter's chances of getting a walk or hit. Some pitchers attempt to retire the batter on a maximum of three or four pitches. This is a good rule for all pitchers. Other pitchers try to throw only strikes below the belt. This is also a good rule for most pitchers, since low pitches are normally the most difficult to hit.

Lack of Control. The pitcher is often wild to either side of the plate. He shifts to the left or right on the rubber as a corrective.

The strike area is the space above home plate between the batter's arm pits and top of his knees when he assumes his natural position.

Fig. 2–13. The strike area.

High or low streaks of wildness are also problems. If the pitcher is wild high, he releases the ball later (or shortens his stride)—if he is wild low, he releases the ball sooner (or lengthens his stride). In some instances the control of the pitcher is affected by the failure of the catcher to stand directly behind the plate. The catcher is requested to move if this seems to be the reason for the pitcher's failure to reach the strike area. Another factor that might cause wildness is the ball. This may be overcome by obtaining another ball from the umpire. If so, it is important to request that time be called before asking for the change.

Some pitchers reduce the speed of fast balls to overcome the problem of control. However, a successful pitcher always throws his stuff on the ball if the catcher signals for a fast pitch. In fact, failure to do so often results in a lack of control and, of course, improves the batter's chances of hitting the ball.

PITCHOUT

The pitchout is a ball pitched for the purpose of permitting the catcher to throw to one of the bases for runners who take long leads or, as is often the case, when an attempted steal, hit-and-run play, or squeeze play is anticipated. It is usually a shoulder-high fast ball that is pitched either far enough from the plate so that the hitter is unable to reach it, or inside so that he will have to drop down or fall back from the plate to avoid being hit. An exception occurs when a bunt is in order with first or second bases occupied and a right-hand pitcher facing a right-hand batter, and with second base occupied and a left-hand pitcher facing a left-hand batter. A sidearm curve can then be thrown low outside. The batter often leans over the plate for such a pitch, leading the runner to think the ball will be bunted. The pitch must be kept wide of the strike zone in this situation because the player covering leaves his position unprotected. If there is to be a throw to first base, the pitch is usually away from a right-hand batter and inside to a left-hand batter. The opposite is true if the throw is to third base. When the throw goes to second base, the pitch is always away from the batter. The same is true for an intentional pass. In this case the ball is delivered from a set position with only second base occupied.

Because of a variety of pitchout situations, the pitcher may not know to which base a pick-off throw is to go. In such cases the catcher indicates with a flat hand whether he wants the pitchout inside or outside.

If a squeeze play is anticipated (see Chapter 13) the pitch is away from left-hand batter and toward a right-hand batter. When a fast ball is not signaled the pitcher may switch to a medium-speed fast ball (by a previous arrangement with the catcher). The same holds true on an attempted steal with less than two strikes on the batter. In this case the pitch is low since the runner must be tagged. If two strikes are charged against the batter, an attempt is made to throw a strike because a hard swing usually cannot be taken at the ball because of the incoming runner. This is particularly true in the case of a right-hand batter.

THROWING TO CATCH RUNNERS

The ability to throw quickly to the various bases from a set pitching position is a factor in catching base runners. In some instances it forces runners to shorten their leads, and thereby reduces the chance of advancement.

THE MOVE TO FIRST BASE

The quickest and most deceptive throw of a pitcher to first base from a set stance is called the "move" of a pitcher. A right-hand pitcher makes the throw by pivoting quickly to the left on his right foot and stepping toward the base with his left foot. The speed of this action may be increased by hopping on the pivot foot as it is turned toward the base, first coming down on it, then on the other foot. A left-hand pitcher has a more natural move to first since he is partially facing the base. He merely turns slightly to the left on his left foot and steps toward the base with his right foot. In both moves a moderate step is combined with shortarm action.

The rules specify that once a pitcher moves any part of his body toward the plate the ball must be thrown in that direction or a balk is committed. The rules also state that once a pitcher moves any part of his body, other than his head, toward first base, the ball must be thrown to first and a step toward the bag must accompany the throw. If these rules were strictly followed, the move to first base might be less significant. There are slight infractions, however, which are rarely observed. These involve the head, shoulder, arm, hip, and knee. A slight movement toward the plate of any of these members and a quick throw to first base are often all that are needed to catch aggressive base runners. Not every pitcher can develop a balk move, therefore some pitchers are more renowned for their moves than others. This particularly concerns a right-hand pitcher. A left-hand pitcher, as has been previously explained, is in better position to make a quick throw to first base, and his move is more deceptive because the start of his throw is almost the same as when he pitches to the plate. Even so, some left-hand pitchers develop more body deception than others; therefore base runners are less apt to take substantial leads when they are pitching. Whitey Ford and Warren Spahn were left handers who had tricky moves. Many left handers throw to first when they are looking toward the plate. A lazy swing of the right leg toward the rubber is another tactic. However, if the foot passes over the front edge of the rubber the pitcher must throw to second base or to the plate. (This rule also applies to the left foot of right-hand pitchers with third base occupied.)

Left handers also pitch (or throw to first) with a fast, jerky straight-up-front leg motion while staring toward first. This frequently makes the runner retreat and, of course, prevents steals.

The speed and manner of throwing to first base are varied. Most pitchers follow a medium-speed throw with a quick throw. (Never lob the ball to first base with third base occupied; otherwise the runner may attempt to steal home.) This works as a change of pace in deceiving the runner. The ball may be pitched after some medium-speed throws because the runner frequently expects a quick throw to follow. The ball is often thrown as the pitcher takes his position on the rubber. An advantageous time for a right-hand pitcher to throw is either as the hands are being raised overhead or as they start down to the chest position, because the runner is then taking his lead (Fig. 2–14). A quick return throw is also used after an unsuccessful attempt to catch the runner. In this case the pitcher turns and throws as he steps back to the pitching mound after receiving the ball from the first baseman. A number of consecutive throws is another means to combat the base runner. This tires the runner, and may force a shorter lead.

THE THROW TO SECOND AND THIRD BASES

A step is also required in the direction of second or third base if a throw is made to these bases. A throw to third base is seldom attempted, but throws to second are common. The throw to second is usually made by pivoting on the back foot and making a half-turn and step in the direction of the base with the front foot. A right-hand pitcher usually pivots to the left, and a left-hand pitcher to the right. The speed of this action is aided by hopping on the foot against the rubber as the pivot is made. A few pitchers pivot the opposite way. This seems a better way for a sidearm or under-

Fig. 2–14. Pickoff at first base.

hand pitcher, since the body action conforms in part with that used to deliver the ball to the plate.

In some instances, the pitcher's turn depends on the type of pickoff play he employs with his shortstop. The shortstop generally teams with the pitcher because he plays behind the runner. A play may develop after a fake pickoff or after a foul, a double, or a time out. Two methods are commonly employed.

a, b. The throw starts as the hands are being brought to the set position (also as the runner takes his lead).

c, d. The body pivot and step toward first. A hop on the right foot in (a) helps to make a quick turn. Note shortarm action is used.

e, f. The arm and shoulder follow-through toward first.

Fig. 2–14. *(Continued)*

Method 1.   The pitcher transfers the ball to his glove hand after the fake, and gives a signal to the shortstop such as rubbing his shirt with the pitching hand. The shortstop answers with a similar signal. The shortstop may also initiate the play with a signal or by placing daylight between himself and the runner. (Diag. 9–1, p. 166, illustrates this daylight method.)   In the former method the pitcher takes his pitching position while looking toward the runner,

knowing that when he turns his head toward the plate the shortstop will immediately break for the bag. He thus looks momentarily
toward the batter, then turns and makes his throw. Another way
to execute the play is for the pitcher to count three before throwing,
in which case the shortstop starts on the count of two. A turn
toward the glove hand is more effective in this method. The pitcher
throws when the shortstop breaks in the daylight method, usually
turning the opposite way.

Method 2. The shortstop breaks for the bag when he thinks the
runner is off guard. (The player designated to cover may drive the
runner back to set up a pickoff play for the other member of the
double play combination. This is explained in Chapter 7.) The
shortstop also may break for the bag after first retreating toward
the runner's left. He backs up slowly. This retreat acts as a signal
to the pitcher, and although it apparently takes the shortstop back
to his original position it actually keeps him about the same distance
from the bag. In either case the pitcher watches the shortstop so
that he can turn and throw as soon as the break is made for the
bag. Consequently, a turn to the left or right can be made with this
method. (See the "Fade Method," Diag. 9–2, p. 166.)

A successful pickoff play requires perfect timing, since the throw
is usually made before the shortstop actually gets to the bag. Therefore it is not employed unless the pitcher has proved himself especially adept at making the play. Even then, it is only attempted
when the run, if scored, might have a final bearing on the game. A
good time to work the pickoff play is when the count is three balls
and one strike or three balls and two strikes, because the runner
is frequently given the go signal in these situations (also at first
base). This is particularly true with a left-hand batter at the plate,
since the shortstop then plays nearer second base.

In some cases a fake to throw is executed to keep the runner
close to the bag. A throw or fake to throw with the base unoccupied
cannot be used as a ruse to catch a runner at another base because
it constitutes a balk. This also applies to throws or fakes to throw
to other unoccupied bases.

FIELDING THE POSITION

Many games hinge on the ability of the pitcher to field his position. He can be rightfully called another infielder because his
duties, aside from pitching the ball, include the fielding of ground
and fly balls, making throws to the various bases, covering first

base and home, and backing up these bases as well as second and third bases. In addition he handles the ball when runners are caught between bases and, in specific cases, acts as the cutoff man.

FIELDING FLY BALLS

The pitcher permits the catcher and infielders to catch fly balls near the pitching box because they are better qualified to do so and are more adept in handling the ball once it is caught. This, however, does not exclude a pitcher from catching such balls, because occasionally there will be one that cannot be caught by the catcher or one of the infielders, and unless the pitcher accepts the responsibility the ball may fall safely. The outcome of a game may rest on the judgment of the pitcher in such a situation.

The pitcher may start a double play with first base occupied and none out by trapping a bunted ball and then throwing to first base. This is only done when the runner on first base retreats to the bag and the batter fails to run from the plate. A similar situation may occur with first and second bases occupied, in which case the throw may go to second if both base runners retreat.

FIELDING GROUND BALLS

Because the pitching position is a target for many hard-hit balls, the pitcher is content to knock many of them down with his glove hand, thus avoiding finger injuries on the throwing hand. However, many bunted balls and easy-hit balls that are topped by the batter roll lazily in front of the plate. These are fielded cautiously because there is usually a great amount of spin on the ball. The catcher and first and third basemen are permitted to field these balls if they call for them. If the first baseman is the likely fielder, the pitcher covers first.

Because the catcher is in the best position to judge the rightful fielder of balls hit near the plate, the pitcher listens for his voice, especially when it is not clear who can field the ball most advantageously. If the pitcher's name is called, he concentrates on fielding the ball and listens for the catcher's instructions as to where to make the throw. If the ball rolls along the foul line and it is unlikely that the batter can be retired, the pitcher permits the ball to roll in the hope that it will go foul. If this occurs, he immediately picks up the ball or brushes it into foul territory with the glove or bare hand. The pitcher also picks up a ball rolling in foul territory when there is a possibility that it might roll fair and that the runner might reach first base safely. The ball is permitted to roll if the batter fails to run with the bases unoccupied.

The pitcher checks his speed when running directly to the foul line for balls by sliding on the inside of the foot nearest the ball. This is particularly effective when a right-hand pitcher goes to the third-base side of the pitching mound, or when a left-hand pitcher goes to the first-base side. In this case the ball is caught with the feet in a spread position.

MAKING THROWS TO BASES

If a ground ball is fielded and the proper play is to second base for a force-out and possible double play, the throw is made slightly to the third-base side of the bag if the shortstop covers late, to permit him to catch the ball just before he reaches the bag. Similarly, if the second baseman covers late, the throw is to the first-base side of the bag. If the player is able to cover quickly, the throw is direct to the bag. The throw to first base when a ball is fielded near the plate or along the first-base line is also to the side of the base. In this case it is always two or three feet to the second-base side of the bag to prevent hitting the runner with the ball.

When there is ample time to make throws, the pitcher uses his most natural way of throwing, which generally conforms with his normal delivery to the plate. In all of these situations it is better to delay the throw, and then put something on the ball, rather than to make a quick, easy, or lob throw. If there is little time to make the throw, the pitcher uses the quickest means of getting the ball to the receiver, which may result in the ball being flipped with the arm close to the ground, or, as is often the case on short throws, tossed underhand. In all situations where the pitcher fields the ball with his back to the base where the intended throw is to go, he pivots toward his glove hand on the foot from which he throws, and steps in the direction of the base with his opposite foot. A right-hand pitcher pivots to the left, and a left-hand pitcher to the right.

Although an alert catcher tells the pitcher where to throw the ball when it is hit to him, this is not always a reliable procedure. For this reason the pitcher must use good judgment in making decisions as to where to throw the ball and in making the throw itself. If the ball is hit directly back to the mound and the stage is set for a double play by way of second base, the pitcher pivots quickly toward the base and makes a deliberate throw. (The ball is thrown home when all bases are occupied.) The ball is thrown at about three-quarter speed so that it can be handled easily by the player receiving it. When an attempted sacrifice is played to second base, a quicker and harder throw is made, because in most cases the covering shortstop anticipates the bunt and is waiting at the bag. The throw to third base on an attempted sacrifice is also a quick throw. These throws are made hurriedly because the loss of a fraction of a second may mean that the runner will reach the bag safely. If the sacrifice is part of a successful running squeeze play with second and third bases occupied, the catcher yells "check third" to indicate that the runner on second might attempt to score, thus enabling the pitcher to check the runner before making a throw to first.

If a runner is caught between bases, the pitcher breaks toward the player until an attempt is made to advance or retreat, then stops and makes his throw.

As a rule, an attempt to catch a runner at third base on a sacrifice is generally a preplanned play. In other words, there must be an understanding between the players involved; otherwise the pitcher may pick up the ball and throw to an unoccupied bag. The detailed assignments and technique for this play are described in Chapter 17, Drill 11.

COVERING FIRST BASE

One of the most important duties of the pitcher is to cover first base. He starts for the base on every ball to the right-field side of the pitcher's mound unless a high fly is hit. If a hard-hit ball goes along the base line with the first baseman playing deep, the pitcher takes the throw while moving over the bag. For this reason he circles into the bag and keeps to the inside of the base line to avoid a collision with the runner (Diag. 2-1). Such a run permits the pitcher to face the first baseman, thus providing a better target for the putout. This method of making the putout may have to be used for all fast runners regardless of where or how the ball is hit. If the ball is fumbled by the first baseman, it may be necessary to stop at the bag.

When a similar ball is hit away from the base line, the run is usually direct to the bag (Diag. 2-2). In such an approach the base is watched and not the player fielding the ball. The bag is reached in this case before the first baseman makes his throw; therefore the pitcher checks his speed and steps on the bag with his right foot, then reaches for the ball. A left-hand pitcher may hit the

bag with his right foot, then simultaneously hop and replace his
right foot with his left as he reaches for the ball. Covering the bag
in this manner makes possible a double play, if the first baseman
throws to second base, then is unable to cover the bag. However,
when the first baseman holds a runner on the bag the curved approach is best since a grounder is usually fielded close to the base.
If other bases are occupied, the pitcher turns into the diamond after
the curved approach and is alert for another play. (A left-hand
pitcher may stop on his left foot and turn to the right.)

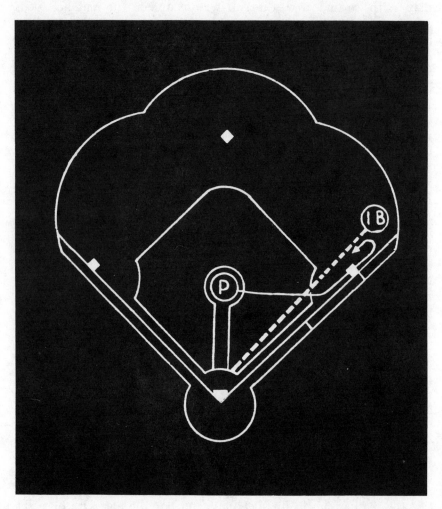

Diag. 2–1.   Covering first base: the run parallel to the base line.

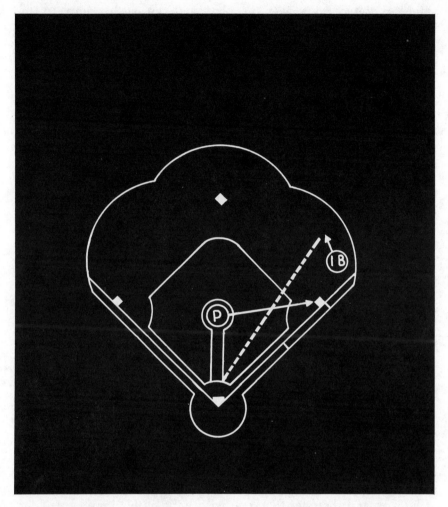

Diag. 2–2. Covering first base: the run direct to the bag.

COVERING HOME

The pitcher also covers home on short flies near the plate with third base occupied and less than two out, and on all balls that elude the catcher if any base is occupied, because the ball continues in play. This also involves third strikes or fourth balls that evade the catcher. The pitcher runs to a point in front of the plate on such occasions and stands in a crouched position facing the catcher if there is to be a play. By being in this position, he can catch accurate throws over the plate and can easily complete the tag.

BACKING UP BASES

There is a potential back-up play on every ball that goes to the outfield regardless of the number of runners on base. The pitcher considers the stage of the game, the speed with which the ball travels to the outfield, the territory to which it is hit, the speed of base runners, and the strength of the arm of the outfielder in deciding which base to back up. Ordinarily third base and home are more often backed up, but it is not uncommon for overthrows to occur at first or second base. Once the pitcher has decided to which base the throw is likely to be made, he runs to a point fifty to sixty feet behind that base and in line with the player making the throw. From this position he can easily retrieve all balls that may rebound past or carom from the intended receiver. If the pitcher is in doubt whether to back up third base or home, he runs into foul territory between these bases, and then backs up the base to which the throw is made. The pitcher also covers a base that is unguarded because the catcher or an infielder has left his position. (For additional information on backing up bases, see "Defensive Assignments on Throws from the Outfield," Chapter 11.)

THE WARM-UP

The warm-up varies according to the physical characteristics of a pitcher and the temperature of the day. For example, a heavily muscled pitcher usually requires more time to loosen the muscles of his arm and shoulder than one with light supple muscles. Older pitchers are also likely to need more time than younger ones. The temperature plays some part because it takes longer for the muscles to respond to throwing when the day is cold. The pitcher is the sole judge in this matter. It is well to remember that failure to survive the first or second inning is often due to the lack of a sufficient warm-up. On the other hand, some pitchers expend part of their pitching energies during the warm-up period; consequently they falter in the late innings.

As a general rule the warm-up varies from ten to fifteen minutes. It is timed so that the pitcher is ready to pitch at game time. Easy throws are made at first from a distance of thirty or forty feet from the catcher, and the speed of the ball is increased gradually. Some pitchers spin the ball in the early warm-up stage, since the arm is more relaxed when pitching a short distance. However, the majority of pitchers employ a curve or other breaking ball only after four or five minutes of throwing. Progress is gradual, the ball being spun until pitches show a decided break. The pitcher is then ready to throw his entire assortment of pitches. In doing so, he follows four or five fast balls with a like number of curves (or the breaking ball used) and slow balls, always informing the catcher when he decides to throw a different pitch. An attempt is made to hit the corners of the plate with both high and low pitches as is done in the game.

Once fully warmed, the pitcher throws five or six good fast balls and retires to the bench. He then removes the perspiration from his hands and face and covers his arm and shoulders, meanwhile taking a seat on the bench protected from the wind. This is especially important when the pitcher is a member of the visiting team, because if scoring occurs in the first half of the first inning it may be ten or more minutes before he is required to pitch. A similar procedure is practiced after each inning.

When the pitcher goes to the mound for his turn to pitch he makes the allotted warm-up pitches to the catcher. These may be medium-speed pitches, or several medium-speed pitches may be followed with a good fast ball and a curve. If the previous inning has been long, the pitcher attempts to get to the mound immediately after the third out, and make as many warm-up tosses as the umpire will permit. This, of course, rewarms the muscles. When there is a delay in the game the pitcher tosses the ball to the catcher or an infielder for the same reason. In taking return throws from the catcher it is advisable to catch the ball in the glove hand to avoid injury to the pitching hand.

The actual warm-up for the game is made from both the wind-up and set positions, preferably with a batter at the plate, and is always the pitching distance; otherwise the pitcher's control may be affected. The ball is also thrown approximately the same direction in which it will be thrown in the game, because if there is a strong wind blowing from the plate toward the pitching mound or across the path of the ball, various pitches may react differently than when the wind is blowing toward the plate or when there is no wind. This is particularly true of breaking balls, since they depend on air resistance to some extent for their break.

The warm-up in preseason practice conforms closely to the previous description. Approximately two weeks are devoted to throwing and general conditioning in the form of pepper games and running. The pitcher then goes on an every-other-day throwing routine and starts to work up to his normal capacity, always continuing his running to help condition his arm and build up endurance.

Some pitchers (and other players) use a series of exercises to loosen the muscles prior to throwing. If exercises or a weight-training program is employed it is advisable to stress stretching and strengthening muscles to develop muscle tone—not to build muscles. Weight training may be beneficial for all players but it must be properly supervised.

SUMMARY

1. Place the foot from which the ball is pitched across the rubber for a windup; across or against the rubber when taking a set position. Watch the runner on third in delivering the ball with a windup to prevent a steal of home (concentrate on the batter in a bases filled, 3–2, 2-out situation)—pitch low inside if a steal is attempted (low outside to a left-hand batter). Hold the hands stationary before pitching from a set position. Keep the shoulders level, chin up, eyes on batter.

2. Start some pitches from a set position with the eyes toward the runner on first base if left handed; always toward the batter if right handed. Vary the procedure with a runner on second base; right-hand pitcher can look toward third base, a left-hand pitcher toward first base. Concentrate on the batter if the runner is slow.

3. Step back with the foot which is in contact with the rubber (without breaking the hands), if a runner on first breaks for second with third base occupied, as this is a preplanned play to score a run. Fake a throw to the second baseman, then spin toward third (back to second if the runner does not attempt to score).

4. Decline the catcher's sign occasionally even though you want to deliver the particular pitch signaled. This prevents the batter from correctly guessing the signal patterns of certain catchers.

5. Check the positions of defensive players before stepping on the rubber. You must have possession of the ball to step on or straddle the rubber; otherwise, a balk is committed. Stand in back of the rubber for a hidden ball trick.

6. Develop an assortment of pitches which includes a fast ball, curve, and slow ball.

7. Break the wrist down for a fast ball and roll the pitch from the ends of the middle and index fingers. Pitch high inside or low outside.

8. Snap the wrist a half-turn outward and down to throw a curve, releasing the ball from the middle finger. Keep the wrist relaxed

and do not attempt to throw the ball too hard. Pitch a curve low outside. It can also be broken in toward the batter's knee.

9. Throw a medium-speed fast ball or curve for a slow ball. Increase the stride and drag the back foot. Keep the pitch low outside.

10. Keep relaxed on the mound so that pitches can be delivered with a controlled effort rather than a wild explosion of energy. Whip the arm forward to an extended position, driving the shoulder down.

11. Push from the rubber and step slightly to the left of a direct line to the plate, if right handed; to the right, if left handed.

12. Study each batter carefully and give special attention to the third-, fourth-, and fifth-place hitters who are normally the best hitters.

13. Pitch high inside if you anticipate a sacrifice or a squeeze play (high outside to a left-hand batter). If the ball is bunted with second and third bases occupied, check third before throwing to first to prevent a double squeeze play. The catcher should yell, "Check third."

14. Attempt to get ahead of each batter. Try to pitch a strike if the previous batter was retired on a first pitch, because the following batter is usually instructed to take.

15. Move to the left or right on the rubber if pitches are too wide. Release ball sooner if pitches are too low; later if pitches are too high.

16. Throw a fast ball on a pitchout sign and keep the ball high and away from the batter unless the catcher gives an indicator for high inside.

17. Attempt to catch a runner off first base by swinging your right leg lazily back toward the rubber, then step toward the bag, if you are left handed. Throw as you take your pitching position, if you are right handed. Hop on the right foot and turn left as your hands are being brought down and step toward the bag with the left foot.

18. Plan a pickoff play with your shortstop. It is effective with a left-hand batter at the plate, since the shortstop plays near the bag. If the shortstop (or second baseman) breaks for the bag and a throw is not made, permit him to resume his regular position before pitching. Always step toward the base when attempting a pickoff.

19. Permit infielders to catch pop flies but make the catch if necessary.

20. Watch the ball in fielding bunts and spin toward the glove hand to throw to all bases. Make a three-quarter speed guided throw.

21. Throw to second base after fielding a ground ball directly to the mound when first base is occupied with less than two out and to the plate with all of the bases occupied. (Spin toward the glove hand and make a three-quarter speed guided throw—always know which player will cover second before stepping on the rubber).

22. Make the throw after fielding sacrifices according to the bunt. Make the safe play early in the game or when in doubt where to throw.

23. Break toward first to cover on every ground ball between the pitcher's

mound and the bag. (The proper way to cover is shown in Diags. 2–1, 2, and in Chapter 17, Drill 9.)

24. Back up the plate and third base from a point at least 50 feet in back of the intended receiver. If in doubt which base to back up, take a position between the bases until the outfielder makes his throw. Cover the plate if the catcher leaves his position (or any other base which is left unguarded).

25. Warm up so that you are ready to pitch when the game starts.

DISCUSSION QUESTIONS

1. When does the pitcher deliver the ball from a set position? (State bases occupied.) When is a windup used? State an exception to this procedure.

2. What combination of pitches do most pitchers employ, and where is each pitch most effective?

3. How does a screwball differ from a curve? Explain in relation to speed, break, and release.

4. Describe the two grips for knuckle balls. How is each pitch released?

5. Where is a pitchout made if a right-hand hitter is batting and the catcher wants to throw to third base?

6. Suggest pitching tactics which might be used to catch a runner off first base.

7. Why do pitchers differ as to the proper way to turn to catch a runner off second base?

8. What is the proper way to step from the rubber once a pitching position is taken? Why is this important?

9. When does the pitcher make a direct run from the mound in covering first base? When does he circle into the bag?

10. Why do most overhand pitchers grip the ball with the fingers across the widest separation of seams, and sidearm pitchers along the narrow seams?

11. Classify batters and give the weaknesses of each. Explain your answer in relation to fast balls, breaking balls, and slow balls.

12. When is an intentional pass considered good baseball? How does the tactic of pitching carefully to the batter fit into the intentional pass situation?

13. Why is it important for the pitcher to watch the entire sign series of the catcher? (This assumes that the catcher gives several finger signals for each pitch.)

14. What is meant by general and specific control? Suggest the strategy of a right-hand pitcher who is facing a right-hand batter for the first time.

15. Discuss the warm-up of a starting pitcher. Explain in detail from the moment the first toss is made until the pitcher resumes his seat on the bench.

TRUE–FALSE QUESTIONS AND ANSWERS

T F 1. Both feet do not necessarily have to touch the rubber during the pitcher's windup.

T F 2. The pitcher commits a balk if he steps on the rubber without possession of the ball.

T F 3. A sinking fast ball can be thrown from an overhand, sidearm, or underhand delivery.

T F 4. The majority of pitches are made with a three-quarter over-hand delivery.

T F 5. Pitchers who can consistently hit the extremities of the strike area with pitches are bound to be successful.

T F 6. It is difficult for a right-hand batter to hit an inside fast ball behind the runner.

T F 7. A point about 30 feet in back of the intended receiver is a good back-up position for the pitcher.

T F 8. The pitcher always runs to a point 8 or 10 feet up in the base line and then to the bag in covering first base.

T F 9. Leading pitchers combine overhand, sidearm, and underhand pitches to fool the batter.

T F 10. It is good strategy for the pitcher to throw a first strike to a good hitter, if the previous batter was retired on a first pitch.

T F 11. If a slow runner is on first base, there is no threat of a break for second on the pitch.

T F 12. When second and third bases are occupied, the pitcher starts his windup, then glances toward third to make sure the runner is not stealing home.

T F 13. It is usually advisable for the pitcher to refrain from throw-ing slow balls when the batter has two strikes charged against him.

T F 14. An attempted sacrifice is usually thrown to second base by the pitcher with less hesitation than a batted ball.

T F 15. The rules state that if a pitcher is on the rubber, a step toward the base must accompany the throw to catch a runner.

ANSWERS

T	T	T	F	F	T	F	F	F	T	F	T	T	T	T
15	14	13	12	11	10	9	8	7	6	5	4	3	2	1

3

The Catcher

A team's greatest need is a skilled and clever catcher. From this focal point stems the confidence of all players, and a pitching staff can rise above mediocrity when it believes in the judgment of the catcher. An effective catcher is able to handle pitched balls cleanly, make quick accurate throws, and direct the defense.

TECHNIQUE

GIVING THE SIGN

In giving signals the catcher stoops with the feet close together and pointing straight ahead, and the knees apart, and the trunk bent slightly forward. Since all catchers are right-hand throwers, the left arm rests on the left thigh and the glove hand extends palm inward beyond the knee. The signs are given with the right hand flat against the inside of the right thigh. This is called the inside method of giving signals, and is preferred because it prohibits the coaches and all members of the opposing team, with the exception of a runner on second base, from seeing the sign (Fig. 3–1a-c). It also applies to the first and third basemen, and so an outside signal, such as rubbing the hand over the uniform or touching or handling the catching equipment a certain way, is usually given for a pitchout when runners are on first or third. An outside pitchout signal is also given when second base is occupied. (See Chapter 19, for complete catching signs.)

STANCE AND TARGET

The catcher moves forward after giving the sign, and crouches as close to the plate as possible without interfering with the batter's swing. (Interference entitles the batter or base runners to advance one base, depending on whether or not the runners were stealing.) Injuries on foul tips and low pitches that might overwise hit the ground are thus minimized, and pitches that pass over the plate knee-high are more likely to be called strikes. A comfortable and relaxed catching position is important so that shifts to either side of the plate can be quickly made. Some catchers prefer to keep their feet parallel and in the same plane, whereas others plant their left foot slightly ahead of the right. This is an individual matter, although the former method seems a better position for shifting either to left or right.

The hands are held according to the particular kind of target with which the pitcher works best. If the pitcher is more effective pitching fast balls high, the glove is held above the belt with the thumbs together and the fingers up (Fig. 3–1d, e). If the pitcher is more effective pitching fast balls low, the hands are held close together between the knees and the belt with the thumbs out and the fingers down. Many catchers give a low target from more of a squat position with the thumbs together and the fingers up as shown in the illustrations. In either case the pitcher usually aims for the hands. Some pitchers prefer to aim their pitches toward a certain part of the catcher's body. In this case the catcher spreads his hands with the thumbs out and fingers down (Fig. 3–1f). The thumb of the bare hand rests against the index finger on the inside of the hand regardless of the type of target.

If the batter is able to hit a high or low ball exceptionally well, the target may be given to the batter's weakness instead of the pitcher's strength. This works in some instances, but in others the pitcher may be more effective pitching over the plate where it is natural for him to pitch. It is therefore necessary for the pitcher and catcher to have an understanding of how to pitch to each hitter. The infielders and outfielders also share this information in order to defend the batter properly.

One thing that must be guarded against is tipping off the pitch. Young catchers often hold the fingers down when a breaking ball is to be pitched and the fingers up if a fast ball is expected. They also tip off the pitch by taking a position closer to the plate when a breaking ball is to be pitched. Some member of the opposing team is likely to detect such habits, so it is better to stand in one

a, b, c. Signal position.

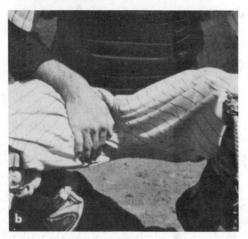

Fig. 3–1. Signal position and targets.

position and hold the glove where the pitcher delivers the ball most of the time.

CATCHING PITCHED BALLS

The positions of the hands and body are factors in catching pitched balls. They may also decide the ruling of the pitch and determine the effectiveness of a throw once the ball is caught.

Position of the Hands and Body. Low balls are caught with the fingers down and high ones with the fingers up (Fig. 3–2a, b).

d. Hand target (side view).
e. Hand target (front view).
f. Body target.

Fig. 3–1. *(Continued)*

The hands are retracted gradually up and in on low pitches, and
down and in on high ones. Similarly, all pitches that are slightly
wide of the plate are brought in. Questionable pitches are often
called strikes if caught in this manner. Some catchers develop a
habit of jerking the ball up or down or over the plate. This, however, is an admission that the pitch passed outside the strike area,
and in most such cases the pitch will be ruled a ball by the umpire.
An exception to the above rule of retracting the hands is the pitch
just off the corner of the plate. In this case the pitch is sometimes

a. Catching a low pitch.   **b.** Catching a high pitch.

c, d. Catching a wide pitch to the first-base side of the plate.

e, f. Catching a wide pitch to the third-base side of the plate.

Fig. 3–2. Handling pitched balls.

g. Blocking a low pitch.
h. Position of hand for catching ball.

Fig. 3–2. *(Continued)*

ruled a strike if the catcher holds his hands where the ball is caught, since the glove covers a portion of the plate.

The body is kept in front of the ball as much as possible. This requires shifting the feet for many pitches. Pitches that pass over the plate in the strike area, and many others just removed from the strike area, are caught without any change in the normal catching stance. Pitches that are wide, however, are usually caught by stepping to the side to which the ball is thrown. The step may be slightly forward if the pitch is away from the batter. When the pitch is to the first-base side of the plate, the step is sideward right with the right foot (Fig. 3–2c, d). A similar step is made to the left with the left foot for pitches to the third-base side of the plate (Fig. 3–2e, f).

Handling Pitched Balls. The distinction between a catcher and a great receiver is determined by the manner in which very wide pitches and low pitches are handled. Wide pitches are often stopped by throwing the body toward the ball. The low ones are blocked by dropping down to the ground on one or both knees (Fig.

3–2g). The catcher can practice blocking balls on the sidelines by having a coach or player throw him short bounces. Some catchers extend their glove hand to block low pitches. If a pitcher is exceptionally wild or very fast, it may be difficult to catch wide pitches with a shift. In this case a wider stance may help to solve the problem.

The catcher ordinarily knows where the pitcher will attempt to pitch by familiarity with the pitcher's style, by the type of pitch signaled, or, as is often the case, by a pitch indicator (described below) and its subsequent target. The pitch really gives the information. For instance, because curves are only effective low, the catcher knows the pitcher will attempt to make all such pitches low. The same holds true for other breaking balls and slow balls. Fast balls, on the other hand, follow almost a straight path once they leave the pitcher's hand, but they may be effective high inside or outside and low inside or outside. For this reason some catchers indicate to the pitcher where to aim some fast balls. This is done by holding the four fingers of the right hand close together and manipulating the fingers up or down and to either side. An indicator is usually only given when a hit is likely to prove damaging and when the catcher thinks the batter will be unable to hit a specific pitch. The catcher also gives an indicator for a pitchout in situations wherein the ball might be pitched inside.

It is important to keep the muscles of the arms and fingers relaxed in catching the ball. The trunk and knees must also be flexible to permit lowering the body for low pitches and raising it for high ones. The ball is caught with the arms slightly extended. It is advisable to extend the bare hand so that, as the ball nears the glove, the hand follows the pitch and simultaneously covers the ball as it hits the glove. The back of the hand is thus exposed to the flight of the ball, and the fingers will give if hit by the ball. To further minimize finger injuries it is advisable to keep the hand slightly cupped and hold the thumb against the inside of the index finger (Fig. 3–2h).

There are times when it works to advantage to permit the ball to fall to the ground. For example, if a runner has a good break on an attempted steal and the batter tips the pitch with less than two strikes charged against him, no effort is made to recover the ball because the runner will probably complete the steal. Another example is the pitch slightly below the knees with the bases unoccupied. If the ball is caught, the pitch will probably be ruled a ball; but if the glove is held slightly above the line of the pitch and the ball is permitted to hit on the end of the glove, it is possible that the umpire may rule it a strike, thinking the ball hit in the pocket of the glove before falling to the ground.

FIELDING FLY BALLS

One of the most important responsibilities of the catcher is to catch high fly balls near the plate. The quickest possible start must be made for these balls. Usually inside pitches to the batter are lifted toward the batter's side of the plate and outside pitches to the opposite side. In starting for the ball most catchers employ conventional footwork, using a crossover step for starts forward and to the side, and a step back with the foot nearest the ball for starts to the rear. However, a few catchers pivot on the foot nearest the ball and take a crossover step in starting back, believing this particular footwork helps to avoid contact with the umpire. It is best to make the catch about eye level, preferably with the palms of the hands up (Fig. 3–3a, b).

Playing the Sun. The position of the ball with respect to the sun is another important factor in catching the ball. Most fields are laid out so that the late afternoon sun usually only bothers the catcher on fly balls in back of the plate. The infielders, on the other hand, are required to look into the sun on fly balls most of the time. For this reason the catcher attempts to catch balls in front of the plate unless they are called for by an infielder. On a very high fly near the plate, it often helps if the catcher glances toward the ground to clear his vision, then back toward the ball. This is particularly true if there is a high sky. The same maneuver may be applied for lights in night baseball.

Playing the Wind. The wind, sun, and direction the ball is hit are all factors in catching the ball. With very little wind, the ball, if raised in foul territory, has a tendency to rotate toward the playing field. This means the catcher can keep approximately arm's length from an easy catch in foul territory. However, he must remain almost underneath the same type of fly in fair territory. A strong wind may, of course, equalize the spin of the ball toward the field and even force the ball to move toward foul territory. On the other hand, a strong wind toward the outfield will always drive the ball toward the playing field since the spin of the ball is in that direction. Balls that rotate or blow away from the catcher are much more difficult to catch than those that come toward him. Therefore the ball is pursued with these factors in mind. When the ball is hit a considerable distance from the plate, it is not always possible for the catcher to utilize such factors to his advantage; but on high flies almost directly overhead, the catcher can usually align his body so that the ball will be drifting toward him. After a fly is caught in foul territory the catcher runs toward the diamond

a. Palms of the hands up to receive a high fly near the plate.

b. Making the catch —at eye level.

c. Flinging the mask away from the approach.

d. Permitting the mask to fall backward on a bunt.

Fig. 3–3. Discarding the mask.

with the ball or throws ahead of a runner. This is also important when a passed ball or wild pitch is recovered behind the plate.

Discarding the Mask. If the ball is hit high and near the plate, the catcher slides the mask over his head, definitely locates the ball, and then flings the mask away from the plate to prevent the possibility of stepping on it while attempting to make the catch (Fig. 3–3c). If the ball is some distance from the plate, the catcher slides the mask over his head as he starts for the ball, permitting the mask to fall backward (Fig. 3–3d). Because it is unlikely that the mask will interfere on such a ball, the mask need not be thrown. In either case it is usually removed by catching the thumb in the lower part of the mask as the arm is brought up.

The catcher also slides the mask over his head prior to receiving thrown balls and when it is necessary to leave the plate to field hit balls, retrieve pitched balls, cover first and third bases, or back up first base. The mask is dropped to the rear in such situations. When there is to be a play at the plate, the mask is thrown away from the path of the runner to prevent injuries. The bat may also be removed from the base line, if the catcher has time.

FIELDING GROUND BALLS

The catcher is required to field many bunts and balls that are topped and roll slowly a short distance from the plate. A ball to either side of the pitching mound is usually fielded with the body to the third-base side of the ball regardless of where the throw is to be made, because doing so keeps the play in front of the catcher. The legs are comfortably spread in the direction the ball is rolling, and the feet are at right angles to its path. Most catchers jump into this position and pick up the ball by bringing the hands together with a sweeping movement through the same plane the ball is moving (Fig. 3–4a, b). As soon as the ball is fielded, the weight is transferred to the right foot and a step is made with the left foot in the direction of the throw. A hop may precede the throw —on the right foot in the direction of the throw (Fig. 3–4c-f).

The pitcher and first or third baseman can often field the ball more easily than the catcher. The catcher calls the throw in these situations because the player coming in has his back to the play. If no runner can be retired, he calls "No play." When the ball rolls along either foul line and the batter cannot be thrown out at first base, the catcher permits the ball to roll in the hope that it may go foul. If this happens, he immediately picks up the ball or

a, b. Picking up the ball (by bringing the hands together).

c, d. Throwing to first base: hopping forward to the right foot and stepping in the direction of the throw with the left foot.

e, f. Releasing the ball overhand and following through.

Fig. 3–4. Fielding a bunt and throwing to first base.

brushes it into foul territory. This is also true of a ball rolling in foul territory, because in this case the ball might roll fair and the batter reach first base. (The ball is permitted to roll if the batter fails to run with the bases unoccupied.) If another player is closer to the ball, the catcher calls "Let it roll" in the former case, and "Pick it up" in the latter.

A double squeeze play is sometimes attempted by the opposing team to score runners from second and third. In this case the runner on second breaks for third as the pitcher starts his windup. If this occurs, the catcher yells "Check third" if the ball is bunted, to warn the pitcher that the runner on second might attempt to score.

THROWING

The throwing success of a catcher depends on his ability to get the ball away quickly. A strong arm is an important asset, but if there is an accompanying inability to throw without hesitation, its value is reduced. Thus it may be that a catcher with only a moderately strong arm will be responsible for more put-outs than one with a much stronger arm. The ability to make quick and effective throws requires balance; therefore a catcher must first perfect weight control. To learn this properly he should wear equipment to practice throwing, first concentrating on footwork and the technique of throwing, then speed of getaway.

Throwing Position. Since the ability to get the ball away quickly is such an important factor in throwing, the catcher considers every base runner a potential stealer, provided the base ahead is unoccupied. To get into position to throw, he swings both hands back toward the right shoulder, then extends the left hand and cocks the right wrist (palm up) to the side of the ear (Fig. 3—5). The readiness to throw also involves dropped pitches on which a base runner might attempt to advance. In this case the mask is discarded in the act of picking up the ball. Infielders and a coach on the bench may give assistance by calling "Second base," "Third base," or "No play."

When the catcher does not have to shift for the pitch, he is in position to throw and merely shifts his weight to the right foot after catching the ball and steps in the direction of the throw with his left foot. He is also in position to throw when a shift is necessary to the first-base side of the plate for a pitch, since this transfers his weight to the right foot. However, if the pitch is to the third-base side of the plate it is often necessary to make a complete shift after catching the ball. This is done with a hop, the left foot

Fig. 3–5.   The throwing position.

being replaced with the right foot (Fig. 3–6). Most catchers use a
similar transfer of weight when a shift is made to the first-base side
of the plate and a left-hand batter obstructs the catcher's view of a
runner on first, the catcher first taking a short step toward his original position with his left foot. A hop in place also accompanies
the throw in some instances when no shift or a shift to the first-base
side of the plate is made.

   In cases where the batter obstructs the view of the runner's start,
it is important for the catcher to jump forward after the ball is
caught and come to a throwing position. This is particularly true
if first base is occupied with a left-hand batter at the plate or when
second base is occupied with a right-hand player in the batting box.
Some catchers take a short step with the right foot in the latter case
regardless of whether a throw goes to first, second, or third base.
This is done in the act of throwing the ball. However, as a general
rule, it is advisable to throw from behind the plate. The catcher
must remember that when a left hander is pitching, or the ground
is wet or soft, he will have an extra split second to make his
throw.

   Types of Throws. In the majority of cases an overhand throw
is made because it is the most accurate way to throw and the ball
is more easily handled by the receiver. The throw is made from

a. Catching a wide pitch to the third-base side of the plate.
b. Shifting weight, replacing left with right foot.
c, d. Cocking arm and stepping to throw.

Fig. 3–6.   Alignment for a throw.

the shoulder, and it is not a complete sweep of the arm. A good self-drill is to stand with your feet in the regular catching position with the arm cocked, then step to throw. Keep the knees slightly bent so that you can comfortably swing the hips to the right to coordinate the stride and arm swing.

A modified overhand or sidearm throw to first base is often necessary, particularly if a left-hand batter is at the plate. This type of throw is also used when runners are caught between bases. The ball is tossed in these situations with a forearm snap. It is important for both the catcher and the infielder, who participates in the play, to keep in fair territory to avoid the danger of hitting the runner with the ball. (The run-down is described and illustrated in Chapter 5.)

Bunts or topped balls that are fielded near the plate are thrown in a number of ways. If there is ample time to make the throw, the catcher straightens his body after fielding the ball and throws overhand. A hop toward the bag on the right foot frequently accompanies the throw. When there is little time, the ball is thrown underhand or sidearm from a low body position. In some cases a snap throw is made without a step.

In returning the ball to the pitcher, an overhand throw is employed, and an attempt is made to make the ball travel on a level with the pitcher's eyes. The catcher puts snap into his throw to keep the pitcher and other players on their toes. (Never lob the ball; otherwise a runner on first base may attempt to steal second.) With a little added effort, the return to the pitcher becomes a perfect throw to second base. It is also advisable to make your throw from behind the plate—walking into the diamond delays the game.

CATCHING THROWN BALLS

The position of the catcher depends upon whether he is to make a force play or tag a runner.

For a Force-Out. In the case of force-outs, the catcher frequently plants his feet on the front of the plate or straddles the plate so that he can shift according to the throw. He may also stand behind the plate and move toward the throw. On accurate throws he reaches toward the player making the throw. He keeps his left or right foot on the plate and steps in the direction of first base with his opposite foot to relay the ball to the first basemen if there is a possibility of a double play. If the reach is with the right foot, an additional step must, of course, be taken with the left foot to throw. Throws that are received wide of the plate are caught by stepping to the side on which the ball is thrown. For example if the throw is to the third-base side of the plate the step is to the left with the left foot. A similar step is made to the right with the right foot on throws to the first-base side of the plate.

Since the infielders are usually playing in when a force play is made, a fairly accurate throw can be expected. For this reason some catchers place their left foot on the plate and give a target in foul territory for throws from the first and second basemen and the pitcher (Fig. 3–7); and in fair territory for throws from the shortstop and third baseman.

For a Tag. When a runner must be tagged, the catcher stands to the side of the plate. (Some catchers straddle the base in the same way that an infielder does.) If the throw is from the right-field side of second base, he stands in foul territory on the third-base side of the plate. The feet are comfortably spread and approximately at right angles to the foul line, with the right foot opposite the third-base side of the plate (Fig. 3–8a, b). If the throw is from the left-field side of second base, he stands similarly on the first-base side of the plate, in fair territory, with the left foot opposite the first-base side of the plate. These positions permit the catcher to catch accurate throws over or just removed from the plate. After catching the ball, the catcher drops down in front of the plate on one or both knees to complete the tag (Fig. 3–8c-f). The put-out is normally made with two hands, with the back of the glove toward the runner to avoid injury to the throwing hand. However, it may be necessary to execute the tag with the ball in the bare hand. Fig. 3–8 illustrates the tag with the throw from the right-field side of second base.

When the catcher waits for the throw in the above manner, the base runner has a clear view of the plate, and ordinarily he thinks that he can avoid being tagged out by making a hook slide to the

Fig. 3–7. Catcher's position on a force play.

a, b. Taking the throw in foul territory on the third-base side of the plate.

c, d. Dropping to the ground to block the plate.

e, f. Tagging the runner (the runner slides into the ball).

Fig. 3–8.   Catcher's position for tagging a runner: throw made from the right-field side of second base.

unguarded side of the plate. This is exactly what the catcher wants him to think, since he can block this type of slide very easily, and without fear of injury. In addition, the slider reaches the plate a fraction of a second later when a hook slide is used.

Blocking the plate as previously described, although premeditated, is not a deliberate intention of preventing the player from reaching the base. In fact, if the ball does not arrive soon enough there is no contact whatsoever. A deliberate block consists of standing in the base line while waiting for the throw, thereby making it impossible for the runner to reach home unless he either knocks the catcher from in front of the plate or runs wide of the base line. This constitutes interference.

Wide Throw. On throws that are wide of the plate, the catcher leaves the plate to catch or block the ball instead of trying to reach for it. This is especially true if there are additional runners on base, because an overthrow under these conditions may permit advancement. If there is still a chance to retire the runner after catching a wide throw, the catcher dives with his arms outstretched and tries to lay his hands on the third-base side of the plate so that the runner will be forced to slide into the ball.

Ball on Bounce. Many throws, although accurate, are difficult to handle because they bounce either too close to the plate or too far from it. When the game warrants a definite attempt to prevent a runner from crossing the plate regardless of whether or not other runners may advance (if the winning run is approaching the plate late in the game), the catcher attempts to catch the ball over the plate. The same holds true when any potential run is approaching the plate with no other runner advancing to a scoring position, regardless of the stage of the game. On the other hand, it is sometimes more important to keep a runner or runners from advancing than to make what might be a futile attempt to retire a player at the plate. If in such a situation the catcher sees that the ball is going to be difficult to handle and the put-out consequently doubtful, he goes into the diamond for the ball and tries to prevent other runners from advancing.

Call for Cutoff. When the catcher is waiting for a throw to tag the runner and the ball is wide of the plate or arrives too late for the put-out, he calls "Cut" to the cutoff man. The cutoff man then intercepts the ball and tries to catch the batter or another player rounding a base, or attempting to advance. "Cut, second," "Cut, third," or "Cut, home" in this case means cut the ball off and throw to second, third, or home respectively. The catcher also calls for the ball to be intercepted if the batter who hit the ball represents the tying or winning run, when he thinks the player might not be caught at the plate. This prevents the batter from advancing to second. No call is made if he thinks the runner can be retired at the plate.

COVERING AND BACKING UP

The first baseman frequently goes a great distance from the bag to field ground balls and is then unable to return quickly if the ball continues to the outfield. Base runners often take advantage of this situation, and round the bag at full speed. The catcher follows behind the batter on such balls, if the bases are unoccupied, and runs to the bag when he is sure the ball will not be fielded. A similar procedure is followed when the first baseman attempts to field short fly balls. First base may be occupied in this case. The catcher also covers third base when a bunt or slow-hit ball is fielded by the third baseman with only first base occupied. (Refer to Chapter 5, p. 110, for the technique of a run-down.)

The catcher backs up first base with the bases unoccupied on all batted balls which might result in overthrows. He also backs up first base when a ball is hit that might result in a double play with only first occupied. However, he returns to the plate if a force-out is not completed at second base, because in this situation a mishandling of the ball frequently results in a scoring opportunity.

STRATEGY

The catcher is the control point of many different and changing game situations. He must combat a variety of steals, see that the defense is properly placed, be alert for weaknesses and omissions of the opposing team, and perform numerous other duties which are related to strategy.

DOUBLE STEAL: FIRST AND THIRD BASES OCCUPIED

With runners on first and third bases, the opposing team may attempt a double steal (described in Chapter 14). Actually, there are two ways for a catcher to combat this play: (1) glance toward third (Fig. 3–9a) and throw to second (Fig. 3–9b–e), and (2) glance

a. Glance toward third to check runner.
b, c. Arm cocked and start of overhand throw to second.
d, e. Release of ball and follow-through.

Fig. 3–9.   Combatting the double steal, first and third bases occupied.

toward third and fake a throw to second by bringing the arm forward past the ear, then attempt to catch the runner off third. (A similar fake may encourage a runner on second base to break for third.) The first method is generally employed if the defensive player covering second base has a strong arm, or when the runner advancing from first base is the tying or winning run; the second method, if the winning run is already on third. In making the fake throw, the catcher continues forward to his right foot after completing his arm swing. This brings him to a good throwing position even though a right-hand batter is usually in the batter's box on such occasions. In some cases a throw to the pitcher is used to trap the runner off third base. This requires a signal with the pitcher. The catcher must be especially alert for the double steal when the pitcher is in-the-hole (also when there is a full count) because the runner on first base is usually breaking on the pitch.

A double steal with first and third bases occupied often originates with a delayed steal from first. It is important to keep alert for this play, since the runner breaks for second when the catcher brings his arm back to return the ball to the pitcher. (A single steal may also originate as a delayed steal.)

In a variation of this double steal the runner breaks for second as the pitcher takes his set position. The batter may also break for second after receiving a walk. If the runner on third base attempts to score in either case, the catcher yells "Home."

DOUBLE STEAL: FIRST AND SECOND BASES OCCUPIED

A double steal may also be attempted with first and second bases occupied. The catcher considers the speed of the runners, and makes his play accordingly. Invariably the throw goes to third base, but a throw to second base is more likely to result in a put-out since the runner advancing from first base gets a late start because he must wait for the runner on second to break for third. Furthermore, this double steal is often attempted with a slow runner on first simply because most catchers try to catch the more advanced of the runners. A smart catcher can take advantage of this fact.

WATCHING BASE RUNNERS

The catcher watches the action of opposing players from the signal position, particularly base runners and the batter. Base runners who take long leads are occasionally caught by a snap throw. In some instances the mannerism of a base runner may indicate that an attempt will be made to steal or use the hit-and-run play. (A longer lead may be taken, or only the pitcher may be watched, thereby revealing that a sign has already been received from the batter or coach.) A fast-ball pitchout is employed in this situation unless another ball will result in a walk for the batter. There are exceptions to this, however. In the 1935 World Series Gabby Hartnett worked a pitchout to catch a runner off third base with two out, first and third bases occupied, and the count three and two on the batter. This was good strategy because it occurred late in the game with the winning run on third base. It would have been sound strategy even though the runner had not been caught, since the following batter was a less capable hitter. In addition, the batter who walked was left handed, with a greater chance to drive the ball through the hole at first.

Additional strategy involves the runner when the batter swings through a pitch or fails to bunt the ball when attempting to sacrifice. In these situations the catcher comes up throwing because he may catch the runner off balance.

WATCHING BATTERS

The batter may similarly tip off a hit-and-run play or an intention to bunt or hit behind the runner. A hit-and-run play is combatted by a fast-ball pitchout and the intended bunt by a curve-ball pitchout. A curve-ball pitchout is only used when a right-hand pitcher is pitching to a right-hand batter with first or second base occupied, or when a left-hand pitcher is pitching to a left-hand batter with second base occupied. The curve-ball pitchout often results in the runner being picked off base because the bunter usually follows the pitch with the bat until the pitch is outside the strike area. In so doing he encourages the runner to venture farther from base, thinking the ball will surely be bunted. If a curve-ball pitchout is not called, a fast ball is signaled and a target given high, because high fast balls are difficult to bunt. If an attempt is made to hit behind the runner, a target is given outside to a left-hand batter and inside to a right-hand batter. However, when a right-hand batter steps back from the plate to be able to hit inside pitches to right field, a low outside pitch is frequently effective because it is difficult to reach. In this situation the catcher rarely signals for a slow ball or slow breaking ball with a left-hand batter at the plate, because these pitches are likely to be pulled.

In some instances the stance of the player in the batting box, the manner in which the bat is gripped and held prior to the pitch, and the leg, arm, and body actions in the swing at the ball may reveal batting weaknesses. These points are discussed with the pitcher before and during the game, because what may prove an effective means of retiring the batter at one time may result in a safe hit at another. This is often the result of the batter changing his tactics against the pitcher; for that reason the catcher tries to remember what each player did the previous times at bat, and then gives the pitcher a signal accordingly. This may mean the same pitch if the batter was retired on an easy chance, but if the ball was hit hard another pitch is usually signaled. This depends, of course, on the control of the pitcher, because he may pitch the same ball to a batter's strength at one time and to his weakness at another.

WATCHING COACHES

Infrequently a sign to bunt, steal, or hit and run may be picked up from one of the opposing coaches. In some instances players on the bench discover signs and then inform the catcher. On rare occasions a steal sign is observed by an infielder, who in turn relays it to the catcher by means of a prearranged sign or the sign commonly used to answer the catcher's pitchout sign. The catcher then gives a pitchout sign both to the infielder and to the pitcher.

USE OF THE PITCHOUT

The catcher refrains from making needless throws and calling for pitchouts unless catching the runner may win or decide the game. As a general rule good base runners are seldom caught and the wasted pitch becomes a handicap for the pitcher. Of course, if a runner takes a long advance and can be easily caught a pitchout is in order. It may also follow a close play on an attempted pickoff by the pitcher, since this often tips off an attempted steal. However, if your team has a substantial lead the signal may be omitted to set up the runner for a pickoff in a future game.

DROPPED THIRD STRIKE

The batter can run on a dropped third strike with first base occupied and two outs or with first base unoccupied regardless of the number of outs. Under these conditions, the catcher attempts to tag the batter after recovering the ball or throws to first base. He tags the plate if all the bases are occupied. This also holds true for third strikes that are caught after they have first hit the ground. These are not considered legally held balls by the rules and therefore must be played as dropped third strikes. Balls that lodge in the catcher's clothing or equipment are likewise not considered legal catches.

INTENTIONAL PASS

If the manager wants the batter intentionally passed, he informs the catcher. The catcher relays the message to the pitcher by pointing toward first, then steps away from the batter as the ball is released, or stands to the rear and side of his normal catching position, depending on the rules in effect. In the former case a crossover step is made, and the free foot is brought to a position so that the feet are as they were before the pitch. If the stationary position is employed, the catcher must stand within the boundaries of the catcher's box. In a variation of this method, the catcher stands close to the batter with his feet together near the outside edge of the box, then steps wide as the ball is pitched. The catcher should tell the pitcher to put something on the ball in an intentional pass situation — not to lob the ball.

When an intentional pass signal is flashed by the manager or coach with third base occupied and less than two out, it is advisable for the catcher to signal to the pitcher from the regular squat position, then take his normal catching stance. This frequently thwarts a squeeze play on the first pitch. If no play is attempted, the catcher takes his usual erect position for the next three pitches. It is important for the pitcher to know this strategy so that his first pitch will be delivered high and away from the batter.

WORKING WITH THE PITCHER

A pitcher usually accepts the first sign of an experienced catcher. For this reason the catcher studies his pitcher, and has an understanding with him as to how he intends to pitch to each batter. Some pitchers prefer to throw fast balls when a hit is likely to produce scoring opportunities, whereas others favor a breaking ball or slow ball. If the catcher can consistently signal for the pitch desired at such stages of the game, battery confidence is established that may mean the difference between a winning and losing pitcher.

As part of battery strategy, the pitcher and catcher consider the fact that the majority of players usually anticipate breaking balls and slow balls when the pitcher is ahead of the batter, and fast balls if the advantage lies with the batter. This, of course, requires a pitcher with good control. The pitcher also declines some signals as part of battery strategy. This is done to prevent batters from correctly guessing signal patterns. In this case the catcher repeats his original signal.

When the bases are unoccupied or the opposing team is behind several runs, it is advisable for the catcher to signal the pitch which is easiest to control. This is normally a fast ball. There is no point in pitching carefully at this stage of the game unless, of course, the batter represents the tying or winning run. In fact most catchers call for approximately four fast balls to three of other pitches. This seems a proper ratio for the average pitcher. Fast balls are also effective late in the day or when the game is played on a dark day.

The prevention of steals also requires cooperation between the pitcher and catcher. Most steals are completed because there is lost motion in the pitcher's delivery. The catcher keeps alert for such flaws so that he can improve his chances of catching the runner. Fast pitches are also recommended in steal situations.

WILDNESS OF THE PITCHER

If pitches just miss the strike area to either side of the plate, the catcher tells the pitcher to move to the left or right on the rubber. The pitcher who is wild low is told to release the ball sooner; the one who is wild high is told to hold onto the ball longer and follow through. In some instances the stance of the catcher and target affect the control of pitches to either side of the plate. The catcher remedies this by changing his position. Wildness may also be the result of the pitcher working too fast. In this event the catcher delays giving the sign, or asks the umpire to call time, and walks to the mound to talk to the pitcher. Excessive conferences, however, are avoided because they consume time and often upset the pitcher. An imperfect or damaged ball is another factor that may affect control although normally it is best to keep a used ball in play. Wildness may also be a problem during the pitcher's pregame warm-up. In this case the catcher wears shin guards to protect his legs.

INFRACTIONS OF THE RULES

The catcher calls the umpire's attention to any infraction of the rules, such as the batter not having both feet in the batter's box when the pitch is made or stepping across the plate while attempting to hit or bunt. An infraction also occurs if the batter interferes with a player fielding or throwing the ball. The latter includes interference by the batter running to first. (The batter is required to run the last half of the distance from the plate to first base in the 3-foot lane along the first-base line when a throw is made from near the plate.) On the other hand, the catcher has to be careful not to interfere with the bat of the hitter. If the catcher interferes, the batter is entitled to first base. He must also refrain from blocking the third-base line when not having possession of the ball. If he should do so, the runner is permitted to score. In the former case the pitcher is charged with a balk if the interference occurs during an attempted steal of home or during a squeeze play.

SUMMARY

1. In signaling, rest the hand flat against the inside of the thigh so that the opposing team cannot steal signals. (Regular battery signals are discussed in Chapter 19.)
2. Give a good target and do not move unnecessarily behind the plate.
3. Step to the side to catch wide pitches and retract the hands gradually toward the center of the strike zone.
4. Flash an indicator signal to the pitcher if you think the batter may be fooled by an inside or outside fast ball.
5. Catch fly balls with the thumbs out and fingers up. Throw the mask away from an intended approach on high flies over the plate.
6. Stay to the left side of swinging bunts and sacrifices. Make the pickup by bringing the hands together through the same plane the ball is rolling, then straighten the body to throw to first, if the ball is fielded near the plate. Keep the ball to the inside of the base line to avoid hitting the runner.
7. Call throws for the pitcher and first and third basemen, as these players frequently field balls with their backs to the play. Yell "Let it roll" if a slow-rolling ball along the foul line might go foul.
8. Yell "Check third" if the ball is bunted on what may be a double running squeeze play.
9. Assume that every base runner is a potential stealer and jump forward after catching each pitch if a batter obstructs your view. Use an extra split second to make your throw when a left hander is pitching, or the ground is soft or wet.
10. Return the ball to the pitcher shoulder-high and at about three-quarter speed and throw from behind the plate, because walking into the diamond delays the game.

11. Give a target to the first-base side of the plate on force plays, keeping the left foot on the plate.
12. Make the runner slide in front of you on tag plays. Take throws from right field on the third-base side of the plate and throws from left field on the right-field side.
13. Call "Cut" to the cutoff man if a throw to the plate is wide or if the runner cannot be retired. No call means not to intercept the ball.
14. Cover third base on bunts with only first base occupied; also first base on some occasions when the first baseman goes away from the bag to field a ground ball (bases unoccupied) or a fly ball (first base may be occupied).
15. Back up throws to the first baseman with the bases unoccupied or with first base occupied, but return to the plate if the ball is mishandled, because this may set up a potential score.
16. Always glance toward third base before throwing to second in a double steal situation (first base and third base occupied).
17. Plan definite throwing strategy in a double steal situation (first base and third base occupied): (1) Throw to second; (2) Fake throw to second; (3) Throw to pitcher (this must be done by signal).
18. Yell "Home" when the pitcher is taking his position on the rubber, if a runner attempts to score on a preplanned first and third maneuver. Yell "Cover first" if a grounder is hit to the right of the pitcher.
19. Use a pitchout if you think a runner can be caught off base. The catcher gives the pitchout signal to an infielder, then after the infielder signals acknowledgment, he gives the pitchout to the pitcher. Also use a pitchout if you think a runner might be caught stealing.
20. Remember that a batter can run on a dropped third strike any time first base is unoccupied, as well as when the bag is occupied with two out. The plate may be tagged if all of the bases are occupied with two out.
21. When intentionally walking a batter with third base occupied and less than two out, first give a signal from the regular squat position to guard against a squeeze play (point toward first) then take an erect position for the final three pitches. This may thwart a squeeze play on the first pitch.
22. Signal a slow ball or curve when good hitters have the pitcher in the hole (if the pitcher has control), because most players look for a fast ball in this situation.
23. Call for a fast ball when good hitters are behind the pitcher since the tendency in this case is to look for a slow ball or curve; also when the bases are unoccupied or the opposing team is behind several runs.
24. If the pitcher declines the signal, repeat the same signal. (Pitchers frequently decline the signal to prevent batters from correctly guessing signal patterns.)

25. If the pitcher is wild to either side of the plate, change your catching position or have the pitcher move to the left or to the right on the rubber.

DISCUSSION QUESTIONS

1. Describe the position of the feet, knees, trunk, and hands in a good catching stance.
2. Why is it inadvisable for the catcher to jerk pitches over the plate? When is it an advantage to hold the hands where the ball is caught?
3. How does the catcher shift to the right of the plate for a wide pitch and execute his throw? How does the action differ to the left?
4. What is the accepted catching technique for fielding bunts? Why is it favored?
5. Why is the speed with which a throw travels through the air not necessarily the most important factor in catching a runner attempting to steal?
6. What alternatives does the catcher have if the runner on first base breaks for second, with first and third bases occupied? How are these applied in the following situations:
   a) Third inning, score tied, and one out?
   b) Fifth inning, opposing team ahead four to three, and two out?
   c) Seventh inning, opposing team behind two to one, and none out?
   d) Ninth inning, score tied, and one out?
7. Why do catchers stand to the side of the plate when waiting for a throw to tag a runner?
8. Under what circumstances does the catcher back up first base? When does he cover first base?
9. How may the catcher help the pitcher to overcome a streak of wildness: (a) high; (b) low; (c) to either side of the plate?
10. State two infractions of the rules by the catcher; two by the batter; one by the base runner.

TRUE–FALSE QUESTIONS AND ANSWERS

T F 1. Pitches that pass over the plate knee-high are more likely to be called strikes if the catcher stands close to the batter.

T F 2. The sign or signal which the catcher gives for the ensuing pitch is called a pitch indicator.

T F 3. On high fly balls directly overhead, the catcher lets the mask fall to the rear of the plate so that it will not interfere with his approach to the ball.

T F   4. A throw is never made to second base on an attempted double steal, with first and second bases occupied, because the catcher is more than 35 feet nearer third base.

T F   5. The catcher may throw to second on an attempted double steal, with first and third bases occupied, without bluffing the runner on third base back to the bag.

T F   6. On force-outs the catcher keeps his right foot on the plate so that a quick throw can be made to first base to complete a double play.

T F   7. "Let it go" is called to the cutoff man on throws from the outfield if the catcher thinks the runner attempting to score can be retired.

T F   8. The catcher covers third if the third baseman fields a bunt which is intended to sacrifice a runner from first to second base.

T F   9. Dropped third strikes are always thrown to first base by the catcher with two out and all the bases occupied.

T F 10. When an intentional pass is given, the catcher is not permitted to leave the catcher's box until the pitcher releases the ball.

ANSWERS

T F T F F T F F F T
1 2 3 4 5 6 7 8 9 10

4

Factors Determining
Defensive Positions

Defensive players must have and use a comprehensive knowledge of a variety of baseball situations, of the capabilities of the offensive players, and of the condition of the field and other elements affecting the game to guide them in adopting an appropriate defensive pattern.

GENERAL DEFENSE

The defensive positions of the infielders and outfielders usually conform to the stage of the game and the ability of the batter. Thus if the stage of the game warrants playing back with a left- or right-hand straightaway hitter at bat, the defense plays deep, and is concentrated toward the middle of the diamond. In defending a right-hand pull hitter or a left-hand opposite-field hitter, the defense swings toward the left-field line, and the left-field side of the defense plays deeper than the right. The defense is swung similarly toward the right-field line for a left-hand pull hitter or a right-hand opposite-field hitter. When the stage of the game warrants playing in for the purpose of making a play at the plate, the defense moves forward from these positions, infielders playing about in the base line. (The entire movement of the defense is discussed in Chapter 20.)

The defense normally plays nearer the left-field line than is shown in Diag. 4–1 when a right-hand hitter is at bat, and nearer the right-field line when a left-hand batter is at the plate. Playing the defense in this manner concedes the strength of right-hand batters in left field and left-hand batters in right field. Because the majority

93

of batters come under this classification, when a team is being met for the first time, and no advance information is available concerning the various players, each player is considered a pull hitter. Definite decisions are often reached in this matter by watching the pregame practice. In fact, the practice is watched, even though the team has been played previously or scouting tactics have been employed, because there is always the possibility that some batter may reveal a flagrant weakness that heretofore has been unknown; a recheck can then be made as to where the various players hit the ball and how hard they hit it. This involves all players, as well as the manager and coaches.

The forward and backward movement of the defense is controlled by the manager because if players were allowed to shift for themselves some might play in and others back under the same conditions. For the same reason the manager also decides where the defense is to be concentrated. This is done prior to the start of the game so that the infielders and outfielders will know where to play as soon as the batter steps to the plate. The manager often alters the position of various players during the course of the game, but because of his many duties and the fact that the defense covers a wide area it is impossible for him to do so throughout the game. For this reason it is important for the defensive players to know where each batter is likely to hit the ball, and to move accordingly. This must be done as a unit to give the defense balance.

DEFENSIVE POSITIONS

Each defensive player must adapt his defensive position to a variety of game situations. Any adaptation involves all players.

FIRST BASEMAN

The first baseman plays on the bag with first base or first and third bases occupied, except when a runner is not likely to attempt a steal. In this case the first baseman stands two or three steps behind the runner.

INFIELDERS

The third baseman plays in the short position, when there are less than two outs, until two strikes are charged against the batter

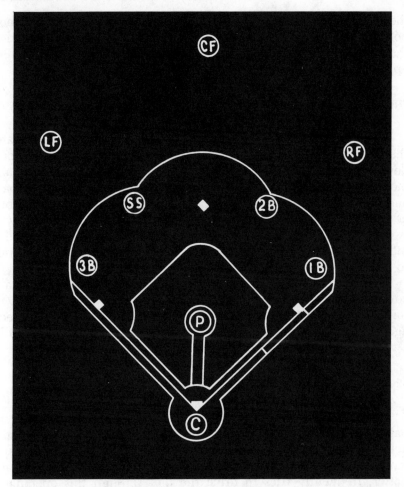

**Diag. 4–1. Positions of infielders and outfielders when the pitcher is
ready to deliver the ball.**

who might bunt. He also plays in this position when weak-hitting
pitchers have two strikes charged against them and the base situation warrants a bunt. The first and second basemen often move two
or three steps toward the batter from the deep position for the same
reason. When a sacrifice bunt is likely, the third baseman plays a
step or two in from the short position, and the second baseman
moves in and toward first base to be able to reach the bag before
the bunter. If the bunt is an attempt to sacrifice a runner to third
base, the first baseman plays a step or two in from the short position, and the shortstop usually plays close to second base to shorten

the lead of the runner. The first baseman also plays in the short position with third base occupied, first base unoccupied, and less than two out, to guard against a squeeze play. Diags. 13–1 to 13–4 (pp. 234–35) illustrate the defensive positions mentioned above.

SHORTSTOP AND SECOND BASEMAN

The shortstop and second baseman move a step or two nearer the plate when first base is occupied to increase the chances for a double play. The player covering second on attempted steals also moves in two or three steps when the count becomes three balls and one strike, or three balls and two strikes with less than two out, as well as when the count becomes three balls and one strike with two out. This permits delaying the start to cover until the ball is hit or passes the batter. In addition it places the player in position to cover quickly on a delayed steal.

If an intentional pass is being issued, the player who normally covers second base takes a deep position, and the other player who forms the double play combination plays on the bag. This protects against a careless pitch, in which case the ball is more likely to be hit to the opposite field.

SECOND BASEMAN AND RIGHT FIELDER

When first base is occupied and the first baseman plays on the bag, the second baseman and right fielder move toward the right-field line to protect the opening between first and second bases. In most systems of baseball a right-hand batter, as well as a left-hand batter, frequently tries to drive the ball through this opening in order to advance the runner to third base. This is especially true with less than two outs in the latter part of a close game, until at least one and sometimes two strikes are charged against the batter. In this case the right fielder moves three or four steps toward the infield, because the batter usually hits the ball low and only moderately hard.

INFIELDERS AND OUTFIELDERS

When the pitcher is in the hole (two balls and no strikes, or three balls and one strike charged against the batter), the defense shifts toward the batter's strength and plays deep because a harder-hit ball is more likely under these conditions. The outfielders shift several steps and the infielders about a step. An exception to the above tactics is made for the batter whose hitting power is to the opposite field. He is defended best by having the defense play to his strength in a set manner. The same is true in defending a "straightaway hitter."

OUTFIELDERS AND FIRST AND THIRD BASEMEN

The outfielders of a team in the lead play deep to keep balls from going for extra bases. By holding batters to singles, a force-play is always possible at second base, thereby often preventing scoring opportunities. This is done with two out and the bases unoccupied, regardless of the score, since the prevention of an extra base hit may require at least two additional batters to face the pitcher to score. For a similar reason the first and third basemen play nearer the foul lines.

ELEMENTS AFFECTING POSITIONS

The ground-covering ability of the defensive player, the ability of the batter both as a hitter and as a runner, the ability of the pitcher, the construction of the ball, the velocity and direction of the wind, the resistance of the air, and even the condition of the field are additional factors in defense.

ABILITY OF THE FIELDERS

Each infielder takes a defensive position according to his own fielding ability. For example, an infielder who cannot go to the right as well as to the left, or vice versa, or who cannot come in fast for a ball, attempts to guard against these weaknesses. For a similar reason a slow outfielder plays deeper than one having speed. The inability to go back for balls is another outfield weakness to be protected.

ABILITY OF THE BATTER

The driving power and speed of the batter are also taken into consideration. When known hard hitters, big men, or those who swing the bat from the end are batting, the defense plays deep; and if known weak hitters, small men, or those who choke the bat are at the plate it moves closer to the infield. This particularly concerns outfielders because of the large area that must be covered. The infielder, on the other hand, considers the speed with which the batter is able to get away from the plate and reach first base. Fast, quick-breaking players, of course, are not defended so deeply as those who are slow to reach the bag. Most left-hand batters come under the former group because they bat from a position closer to first base. In addition, the follow-through of their swing is in the direction of first base, whereas that of a right-hand batter is normally toward third base.

ABILITY OF THE PITCHER

In some cases the defensive positions are influenced by the pitcher's control and assortment of pitches, because smart pitchers waste their least effective pitches and make the batters hit their best pitch. A pitcher who depends on fast balls for his success usually causes batters to hit late. Fast-breaking knuckle balls and fork balls are also hit late. On the other hand, the pitcher who relies on curves and slow balls finds the batter pulling the ball most of the time.

CONSTRUCTION OF THE BALL

Since the construction of balls varies—in the type of center, the winding of the yarn, the thickness of the cover, and the sewing of the seams—it becomes a factor in defensive play. Some balls speed through the infield faster and have greater carrying power than others. This type of ball, of course, requires a deeper defensive position than one less lively.

DIRECTION AND VELOCITY OF THE WIND

The wind is an element to be considered because it either obstructs or aids the flight of fly balls. This only concerns the outfielder in respect to defensive position, but it is a point to be considered by other players because it is often an aid in starting for the ball as well as in getting into position to make the catch. For example, if a high fly is hit directly over a player's head, the first step is back with the right foot if the wind is blowing from center to left field, and with the left foot when the wind is blowing from center to right field. The character of the wind is determined by observing trees, smokestacks, or flags, or by tossing bits of grass or some loose dirt in the air. Something high is preferred because if the field is enclosed by high stands and fences the wind near the ground may not be the same as that at the height where high fly balls travel. This is very important, for the ball hit high in the air is the only one the wind affects to any great extent.

DENSITY OF THE AIR

Damp or heavy air hinders the progress of long fly balls, and dry or light air provides little resistance. The latter is particularly noticeable in high altitudes. These factors likewise only involve outfield positions. Outfielders note the carry of balls in fielding practice with respect both to the wind and to air resistance, and make repeated observations regarding these factors because they may change during the course of the game. The possibility of wind change is also watched by the infielders.

Pitched balls are likewise affected by the air. For example, curve balls have less of a break in high altitudes. This also applies to other breaking pitches.

CONDITION OF THE FIELD

The defensive position of the infielders is also affected by the condition of the field. Some infields are harder and faster than others, and require a deeper defensive position. If the field has been slowed by recent rains, players avoid quick starts, and run at modified speed to prevent slipping. Because it is more difficult to throw a ball when it becomes wet, all such throws are more carefully made. It is also important to smooth rough places on the ground and remove obstacles such as rocks and bits of paper. These may all affect the fielding of ground balls.

SUMMARY

1. Assume that the strength of right-hand batters is in left field and left-hand batters in right field.
2. Watch the pregame batting practice of the opposing team because this may reveal specific batting weaknesses.
3. Analyze every situation, since a ball or strike may change your responsibility on defense.
4. Move in a step or two (infielders) for left-hand batters and players who might attempt to beat out bunts.

5. Shift toward a pull hitter's strength when the pitcher is in the hole (infielders one step and outfielders several steps).
6. Consider your ability to move left and right and to come in and go back in taking your defensive position.
7. Determine the direction and velocity of the wind as soon as you arrive on the field.
8. Avoid fast starts and handle the ball carefully if the field is wet.

DISCUSSION QUESTIONS

1. Where is the ball most likely to be hit with the following players at the plate?
   a) a right-hand pull hitter
   b) a left-hand opposite-field hitter
   c) a left-hand straightaway hitter
2. What is the best way to determine the batting ability of opposing players?
3. Describe each infielder's position under the following conditions: eighth inning, score tied, first and second bases occupied, and no outs.
4. Why does the shortstop move two or three steps nearer the plate when the count reaches three balls and one strike, or three balls and two strikes on a left-hand pull hitter with first base occupied and less than two out?
5. In addition to the ability of the batter and stage of the game, name other factors that affect defense.
6. State a situation wherein the third baseman might play in with two out and two strikes on the batter.
7. Suggest an occasion when it might be good strategy for outfielders to play deeper. How might the same situation affect the positions of the first and third basemen?
8. When is it important for the double play combination to reverse their normal procedure relative to driving a runner on second base back to the bag? Why is this done?
9. Explain the action of pitched balls and high fly balls in damp, heavy air and in dry, light air. What must defensive players keep in mind if the field is wet?

TRUE–FALSE QUESTIONS AND ANSWERS

T F 1. Left-hand pull hitters are defended about the same as right-hand opposite field hitters.
T F 2. When an intentional pass is being given to a left-hand batter,

the shortstop plays deep and the second baseman plays on the bag.

T F 3. The entire defense shifts several steps toward the hitter's strength when the pitcher is in the hole.

T F 4. Pitchers who depend on knuckle balls or fork balls for their effectiveness require a slightly different defense than pitchers who rely on curves and slow balls.

T F 5. The direction and velocity of the wind are best determined by tossing loose dirt into the air.

T F 6. A fly ball which is hit in a high altitude is more likely to travel farther than one which is hit in a low altitude.

T F 7. The second baseman never covers second base on sacrifice bunts if a normal defense is employed.

T F 8. When the wind is blowing from center to right field, an outfielder steps back with his left foot to start for a fly ball which is hit directly over his head.

T F 9. The majority of players are considered straightaway hitter: because they hit most pitches between the shortstop and sec ond baseman.

ANSWERS

F T T T F T F T T
9 8 7 6 5 4 3 2 1

5

Defensive Tactics
for Infielders

The main test of an infield is whether it functions as a unit. To make it really efficient as a group, each infielder must react quickly to every situation, whether the responsibility is fielding, throwing, or performing some other defensive action. In this way the infield develops the timing and rhythm which are necessary for good infield play.

Each infielder has specific duties to perform, but some defensive points are related and must be coordinated for a good infield defense.

TECHNIQUE

FIELDING FLY BALLS

A routine function of the four infielders is to catch fly balls in their territory and attempt to catch fly balls over the pitching mound. In the latter case, it is important to keep after the ball unless another player calls for the ball or unless the catch cannot be made. All of these balls rotate away from the catcher, if there is little wind, because the batter cuts under the ball. Thus infielders know that a ball over the infield will rotate toward them, and that the one in outfield territory will rotate away from them. The first and third basemen are especially alert on balls toward the plate because the catcher is sometimes late in starting for the ball. The first and third basemen, on the other hand, are often playing short, and as a result cannot reach many balls in back of the infield. These are usually easy chances for the second baseman and shortstop. In fact, the shortstop and second baseman are the logical fielders of most short fly balls in outfield territory unless the fly is near enough to an outfielder for him to make the catch. Outfielders can usually catch these balls in better position to throw. On many such balls it is better for an infielder to keep out of the outfield so that collisions will not occur. This particularly concerns what appears to be difficult chances. Such a practice increases the efficiency of outfielders, and eliminates the likelihood of fly balls falling between two or three players. When two players go after the same ball, some base is, of course, left uncovered. The player not calling for the ball returns to the bag. If the fly ball is in foul or outfield territory, an infielder runs into the diamond with the ball after making the catch if there are runners on base, unless an immediate throw is necessary.

FIELDING GROUND BALLS

An infielder normally catches ground balls as described and illustrated in Chapter 1. The maneuver into the fielding position is the main factor in catching most ground balls as well as in making a subsequent throw. It generally requires an advance, or a break to the side then an advance (Fig. 5–1). This enables the infielder to move in and play the ball (not wait and let the ball play him) and be in position to complete his throw (Fig. 5–2A).

Hard-hit balls and slow-rolling balls also require special handling. Hard-hit balls are frequently blocked because the batter can usually be retired even though the ball may not be fielded cleanly. Blocking is described and illustrated in Chapter 10.

Most slow-hit balls are fielded with two hands, in the same manner as the average grounder, but it is necessary to field some of them in motion; otherwise the runner will be safe. The throw is made simultaneously with the picking up of the ball, and the body continues in the direction of the approach to the ball (Fig. 5–2B). In some cases the bare hand is used to field the ball. This technique is described and illustrated in Chapter 10. Two hands are usually employed when ordinary slow-rolling balls are fielded because there is less likelihood of the ball being fumbled. On the other hand, the one-hand method is favored when the element of missing the ball must be discounted.

Another variation in footwork occurs when it is necessary to go directly to the side to stop the ball. In this case the catch is made

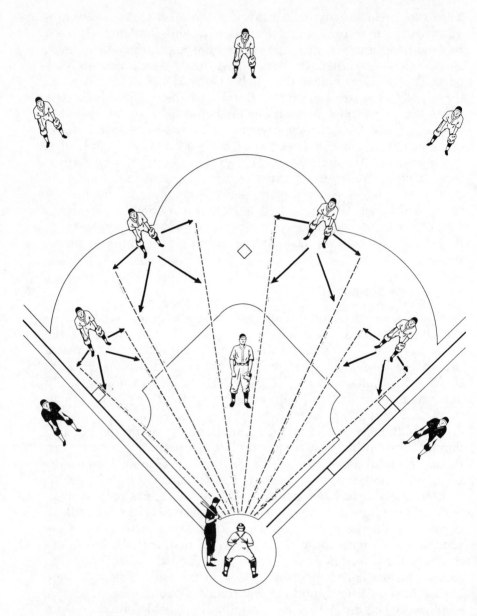

Break to the side for hard-hit balls; come in for routine grounders and slow-hit balls.

Fig. 5–1.   Correct approach on ground balls.

with the feet in a straddle position, and the ball is often flipped to the receiver without the aid of a step. The speed of a player is frequently checked in fielding such a ball by sliding on the inside of the foot nearest the ball. This is especially effective when a right-hand thrower goes to the right, or a left-hand thrower to the left. In some instances the slide on the inside of the foot follows the catching of the ball. This occasionally happens on high bounding balls.

If a ball is fielded close to a bag, and a force-out and possible double play can be made, an infielder generally steps on the bag with his right foot and then in the direction of the throw with his left foot. A first baseman who throws left-hand, of course, uses reverse foot action, and a right-hand first baseman may step on the bag with his left foot prior to stepping in the direction of the throw with the same foot. When making only a force-out under similar circumstances, an infielder steps on the bag and either continues in the direction of his approach or steps back from the bag just as if a thrown ball had been received.

THROWING

Throws by the infielders are made overhand, sidearm, or under-hand, depending on the speed with which the ball is received and the speed with which the throw must be made. In some instances the throw is governed by the height of the hands in making the catch. If the ball is caught in a stationary position, or if a stop can be made after catching the ball, an overhand throw is usually made. However, the demand for a quick throw frequently neces-sitates a sidearm or underhand throw even though the ball is fielded in a position to throw overhand. This is particularly true on short throws because the possibility of an erratic throw is lessened. Many of these throws are mere flips of the arm in front of the body, and not long arm sweeps.

The sure play is always made when there is doubt where to throw. This is particularly true when your team is ahead or when there are two out. In this case first base is usually the logical play. A careful throw is also made on the first half of a double play, and then a hurried throw for the second runner. This guarantees one put-out and makes possible a second, whereas a hurried attempt for the first put-out often means that both runners will be safe. If the infield plays in, the logical place for the throw is, of course, to

a, b, c, d. Break is wide, then in to get in front of ball. Note excellent fielding position—elbows, knees, and trunk are bent, eyes are on ball.
e, f, g. A hop forward occurs after ball is caught and a step is made in direction of first for long overhand throw.

A. Ground ball.

Fig. 5–2. Fielding and throwing to first.

a, b, c. The ball is caught as the left foot comes down on the ground. The snap sidearm throw is made as the weight continues forward to the right foot.

d, e. The arm swings across the chest as the weight returns to the left foot.

B.   Slow-hit ball.

Fig. 5–2.   *(Continued)*

the plate. However, once again judgment is involved, because on a slow-hit ball the proper throw might be to first base.

It is normal practice to hold a recovered free or fumbled ball unless there is a definite chance to retire a player. A fake throw under these conditions frequently makes it possible to catch a run-

a, b. An infielder straddles the base to take the throw.

c, d, e. The put-out is executed by dropping the glove to the ground in front of the bag.

Fig. 5–3. Tagging a runner.

ner off base. A fake throw works similarly after some thrown balls are caught. A variation of this throw occurs when hard-hit balls are fielded with the infield in. In this case the fake is used to drive the runner on third base back to the bag, unless an attempt is made to score.

TAGGING RUNNERS

An infielder straddles the bag to take the throw when it is necessary to tag a runner. This position permits catching accurate throws over the base and the tag is executed by dropping the glove hand to the ground in front of the bag. The runner then slides into the

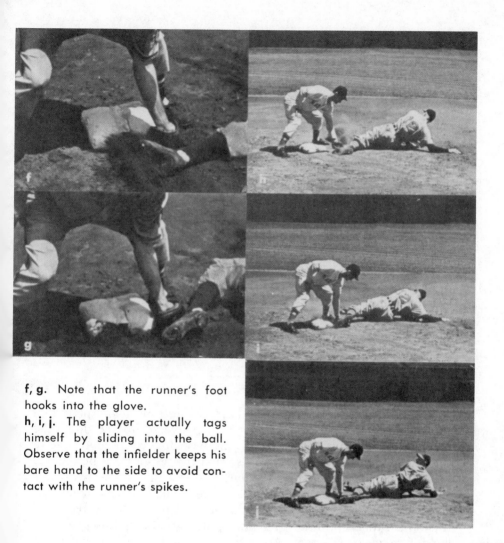

f, g. Note that the runner's foot hooks into the glove.

h, i, j. The player actually tags himself by sliding into the ball. Observe that the infielder keeps his bare hand to the side to avoid contact with the runner's spikes.

Fig. 5–3. *(Continued)*

ball (Fig. 5–3). Some coaches insist that the back of the hand be exposed to the slider to avoid the danger of having the ball kicked out of the glove. However, it seems just as likely that the ball will be kicked into the glove when it is held facing the slider as out of the glove when the back of the hand is exposed. The chances are the technique is not too important since most tags are sweeps of the glove and the defensive player moves into the diamond to be ready for another play. It is also doubtful if a fumble can develop if the defensive player is really intent on holding on to the ball. A good trick to fool base runners is to act as if the ball is not coming. This often encourages a player to slacken his speed or decide not to slide.

If the runner stops and concedes the put-out, the ball is transferred to the throwing hand and two or three steps are taken toward the runner to complete the tag. This is done to prevent a final effort by the runner to slide wide of the bag. For this reason the defensive player always remains between the bag and runner.

A base runner must, of course, be tagged unless he is required to leave the base from which he is advancing by a force-out situation. It is necessary for the defensive player to keep this in mind, because frequently the stage is set for a force play, then changed before the ball is thrown. Players may help each other on such occasions by yelling "Tag him."

Many wide throws may be comfortably caught with little change in the position of the feet at the bag. However, if a throw is exceptionally wide the player leaves the bag to make the catch. In some instances he can return to the bag and complete the tag. In others it may be necessary to dive back with the tagging hand extended.

THE RUN-DOWN

A runner is chased toward the base farther from home plate in a run-up or run-down. (The runner is maneuvered up and down the base line.) The player guarding this base follows behind and to the side of the runner for a throw so that the put-out can be quickly made (Fig. 5–4a-d). This frequently retires the runner with one throw in the run-down, as illustrated, thus making it less likely that other runners will advance. A fake or bluff to catch the ball may trick the runner into slowing down, thus enabling the player in pursuit to make the tag. After the put-out is made, a defensive player is always alert for another play (unless the out retired the side), because the run-down usually occurs after a batted ball has been fielded (Fig. 5–4e, f). This means that even though the player caught was the only player on base at the time, the player who hit the ball is now a base runner and may try to advance.

In the run-down other players have definite back-up duties to guard against the runner getting by players handling the ball. The pitcher in this case usually backs up the first baseman when a runner is caught between first and second bases and backs up the third baseman if the run-down is between second and third. In these situations the shortstop and second baseman work as a team, one handling the ball and one backing up. This depends, of course, on

who becomes involved in the run-down first. On run-downs between third base and the plate, the pitcher generally backs up the
catcher, and the shortstop backs up the third baseman (Fig. 5–4).

An alert infield plus a good catcher usually retires a runner
caught between bases in no more than two throws. However, smart
base runners may require more. In such situations the player making a second or third throw follows past the runner and protects
the next continuation of the run-down. This frequently happens
when the two defensive players handling the ball get very close together.

A modified overhand or sidearm throw is used in run-downs because the runner often obstructs the vision of the thrower. The ball
is not thrown, but tossed with a forearm snap. It is important to
maneuver to the side of the runner prior to making this type of
throw unless a position to the side of the runner has already been
established. This eliminates the danger of hitting the runner with
the ball. A fake throw with an emphasis on forearm action is also
effective in run-downs.

It is important to avoid blocking the runner when not in possession of the ball. Blocking constitutes interference and permits the
runner to advance one base. Other runners can also advance. In
fact, some smart base runners deliberately attempt to run into a
player without the ball when they know further advancement is
unlikely, hoping that interference will be called. Infielders must
guard against these tactics.

Other players, of course, usually try to advance during a run-
down. This often results in a runner arriving at the base involved
in the run-down. In this case an alert infielder or the catcher
drives the player who is caught in the run-down back to the bag.
He then tags the intruding player because the runner who originally
occupied the base is entitled to the bag.

ACTING AS THE CUTOFF MAN

When an infielder is required to act as the cutoff man on throws
from the outfield, he takes a position about 50 or 60 feet in front
of the base to which the play is likely to be made, and in line with
the throw. He waves his arms to give the outfielder a good target.
The ball is frequently intercepted from this position, to catch a runner attempting to advance. (A right-hand thrower turns to the left,
and a left-hand thrower to the right, if the ball is cut off and a throw
is made to the base for which the original throw was intended.)
The cutoff man listens for the player covering the bag to call "Cut."

Fig. 5–4. The run-down: runner caught between third and home.

a, b, c. The third baseman moves in and to the side of the runner to take the catcher's throw. The shortstop and pitcher back up the play.

d, e, f. The third baseman makes the tag and is alert for another play.

Fig. 5–4. *(Continued)*

113

"Cut, second" or "Cut, third" in this case means cut the ball off and throw to second or third respectively. No call means "Let it go." When there is no call the cutoff man bluffs catching the ball, to check base runners. If the throw is definitely too late to catch the runner, the cutoff man advances toward the ball so that he can intercept the throw sooner. Additional information on cutoffs may be found in Chapter 11.

STRATEGY

TRAPPING A FLY BALL

As a general rule all fly balls are caught. There are, however, exceptions. For example, when a runner retreats toward a base with less than two outs, some fly balls may be purposely trapped and two players retired. This can be done with first base, first and second bases, and even all the bases occupied, provided the subsequent double play is likely to be an important factor in deciding the game. The ball must be bunted or hit on the line with first and second bases or all the bases occupied because the infield-fly rule is in effect under these conditions.

The trapped ball is thrown to first base with only first base occupied. The first baseman or second baseman who takes the throw has two alternatives: (1) if the runner returns to the bag he catches the ball with his feet off the bag, then tags the runner and the bag; (2) if the runner attempts to advance he catches the ball on the bag, then throws to second base. To make this play with only first base occupied, the batted ball must reach the defensive player before the batter starts from the plate, otherwise there is not enough time to retire two players.

A similar procedure is followed with first and second bases occupied. In this case the throw is made either to first or to second base, depending on where the play can be more conveniently made. As a general rule the throw goes to second base because most batters run after hitting the ball and are thus nearer their objective than the runner advancing toward second; besides, the batter is running, whereas a base runner usually stops when he sees the ball hit into the air. For this reason an outfielder can trap a short fly ball in back of second base and start a similar play; therefore it is important for both the shortstop and second baseman to keep this in mind.

Although rarely executed with all the bases occupied, there is an opportunity for such a play in the eighth or ninth inning of a game when your team has a two-run lead. Of course, with none out a run will score, and a run may frequently score with one out, but most managers are willing to concede a run at this stage of the game for the chance to retire two players and reduce the scoring opportunity.

Another exception to the rule of catching fly balls occurs when foul flies are hit with the winning run on third base and less than two out in the first or last half of the last inning. These are frequently permitted to drop unless, of course, the runner can be thrown out at the plate. This is particularly true in the last half of the last inning; otherwise the game will be over.

If an infield fly is dropped, base runners can advance at their own peril (unless the fly hits a runner). Infielders must guard against this situation because even though an umpire declares infield fly, automatically retiring the batter, the fly is occasionally dropped.

WORKING PITCHOUT WITH THE CATCHER

The catcher has a pitchout sign with each infielder so that plays may be worked at all bases. A pitchout play usually originates with a sign from the catcher, and the infielder responds with a signal, such as touching the peak of the cap, to inform the catcher he has received the sign and will cover. When an attempt is made to catch a runner with a pitchout, the infielder breaks for the base after the ball is pitched. The catcher may attempt to catch an aggressive runner without a pitchout (particularly after the batter swings through the ball or fails to bunt). An infielder must break for the bag in these situations when the ball passes the batter. Alertness in covering also involves throws by the pitcher and other infielders.

YELLING INFORMATION

Infielders continually yell words of encouragement and points of importance about the defensive situation to keep the pitcher and catcher, as well as the entire infield, alert and ready to meet every emergency. "Heads up for a bunt," "He might steal," and so on, are phrases involving the pitcher and catcher, and "Let's get two," "Look out for a hit-and-run," and so on, involve the infielders.

"There he goes" also proves an aid to the pitcher and catcher when a runner breaks on a steal or hit-and-run play. Calling the throw or "No play," gives similar assistance to infielders handling the ball.

WATCHING BASE RUNNERS FOR INFRACTIONS

Defensive players should note whether or not base runners tag the bases. The infielders also note whether or not a runner attempting to advance on a fly ball leaves the base too soon. The nearest infielder to the base makes the check. If a base is missed, or a runner is thought to have left a base too soon on a fly, the infielder calls for the ball and tags the base or calls to another defensive player to tag the runner, meanwhile calling the umpire's attention to the fact. A similar procedure is followed if a runner on first base advances past second base on a long fly ball to the outfield and then fails to touch the bag on his retreat to first base after the ball is caught. If "Time" has been called after any of the above situations it is necessary for the pitcher to take a legal position on the rubber (to put the ball in play), then back off to make the proper play. The appeal play must be executed in 20 seconds.

ALIGNING BASES

The alignment of bases which are improperly anchored may also prove an advantage. The third baseman kicks third base toward second base, and the shortstop and second baseman kick second base toward left field. In the former case the moving of the base may mean the difference between a fair and foul ball, whereas in the latter situation the distance between first and second bases is increased and may result in a put-out instead of the runner reaching the bag safely. The first baseman can also kick the first base toward second base for the same reason that the third baseman kicks third base in the same direction. However, since the first baseman often gets to the bag at about the same time as the ball, it is important for the bag not to move toward foul territory. Therefore it is advisable for him to kick the bag toward first base occasionally to ensure solid footing.

SUMMARY

1. Attempt to catch all fly balls in the vicinity of the pitcher's mound. Do not permit the pitcher to make the catch.

2. Break in for pop flies near the plate because the catcher may get a late start for the ball.

3. Refrain from pursuing short flies in back of the infield if it appears the ball will be difficult to catch. These are usually easy chances for the outfielders, and collisions are avoided.

4. Run toward the diamond after catching a fly ball in foul or outfield territory, unless an immediate throw is necessary.

5. Do not catch foul flies with the winning run on third base and less than two out in the first or last half of the final inning, unless you can throw the runner out at the plate.

6. Make the put-out unassisted and throw to first for a possible double play, if a ground ball is fielded near second or third.

7. Throw overhand on long throws. Use short arm action when near the intended receiver.

8. Pounce on a fumbled ball, then fake a throw and attempt to catch a runner off base, if the batter cannot be retired at first.

9. Straddle the bag to take the throw if a runner must be tagged. Drop the glove hand in front of the base and let the runner slide into the ball.

10. Chase a runner toward the base farther from the plate in a run-down (follow behind and to the side of the runner).

11. Avoid interfering with players who are rounding bases.

12. Act as the cutoff man on throws from the outfield from a point about 50 or 60 feet in front of a base. Intercept the ball if the throw is wide, if you think the runner cannot be retired, or if the player at the bag calls "cut."

13. Be alert if an infield fly is dropped, because baserunners may advance. (The infield fly is discussed in Chapters 5 and 14.)

14. Talk it up on the infield and help each other by yelling information such as, "Home," "There he goes," or "No play."

15. Watch runners for the following:
    a) Leaving base too soon on a fly ball
    b) Failing to touch bases
    c) Failing to touch second base on a retreat to first after advancing past the bag on a fly ball. (In above cases get the ball, then call attention of the umpire and tag the runner or the bag.)
    d) Passing another runner (passer is automatically out)

DISCUSSION QUESTIONS

1. Why is it important for an infielder to stay out of the base line when not in possession of the ball? When does he have the right of way?

2. Suggest the strategy of a smart second baseman if the first baseman traps a sacrifice bunt with first base occupied.
3. Give the basic principle of the infield-fly rule. State three infractions of the rules by base runners. How does an infielder obtain the correct ruling from the umpire for any of these infractions?
4. When is the one-hand method of fielding slow-hit balls recommended for infielders? Describe the footwork in fielding and throwing when a slow-hit ball is fielded with two hands and the throw is made in motion.
5. What factors determine an infielder's method of throwing? Which is the most effective type of throw if the intended receiver is more than 90 feet away?
6. How does a good double play combination start a double play? Explain your answer in relation to the success of any double play.
7. Recommend several ways in which infielders can help each other by the use of words.
8. Where is it logical to make a play if there is any doubt about the throw? How can a fake or bluff throw be used to advantage?
9. Describe the proper way to execute a run-down between third base and the plate. Which player is safe if two runners are tagged while standing on third base?

TRUE–FALSE QUESTIONS AND ANSWERS

T   F   1. The batter is declared out if an infielder purposely drops a high fly ball which is descending in fair territory.
T   F   2. Infielders usually take the catcher's throw from a position in front of the bag to tag a runner attempting to steal second or third.
T   F   3. A good cutoff position for infielders is a point about 30 feet in front of the base to which the throw is made.
T   F   4. An infielder breaks to cover on a pitchout as the pitcher starts his delivery.
T   F   5. Runners who advance beyond second base on long fly balls, and who then fail to touch the bag on their retreat to first base after the ball is caught, must be tagged out.
T   F   6. An alert infielder and a good catcher can retire most runners who are caught between bases with one or two throws.
T   F   7. A smart cutoff man intercepts some throws from the outfield several steps in front of the conventional cutoff position.
T   F   8. Failure of a base runner to touch third base in scoring from second on a single does not constitute an automatic out.

T F 9. It is advisable for infielders to attempt to catch all fly balls in foul territory regardless of the score.

T F 10. An infielder moves in on all hard-hit grounders because if the ball is fumbled there may still be time to make a play.

T F 11. When there is little or no wind, fly balls near the plate will drift toward the infielders and fly balls behind the infield will drift toward the outfielders.

T F 12. Infielders normally have the right of way when a fly or grounder is hit but only if they are pursuing the ball or moving to a base to carry out a defensive assignment.

ANSWERS

1	2	3	4	5	6	7	8	9	10	11	12
T	F	F	F	F	T	T	T	F	F	T	T

6

The First Baseman

The first baseman has many duties to perform, but if he can catch a variety of thrown balls with regularity he has accomplished the greatest need at first base. This qualification of a first baseman enables the infielders to make their throws with confidence; consequently it becomes a big factor in over-all infield play. Skill in shifting to catch thrown balls and the ability to field ground balls cleanly are important factors in first-base play.

TECHNIQUE

CATCHING THROWN BALLS

When there is to be a play at first base, the first baseman tries to get to the bag and face the player making the throw. From this position a shift to the left or right, a stretch into the diamond, or a reach into the air is easily made. If the ball is thrown to the right-field side of the bag, the shift is to the right, and the bag is touched with the toe of the left foot. A similar shift to the left is made on the throw to the plate side of the bag, and the base is touched with the right foot. This often results in crossing in front of the runner and making the catch in foul territory. In either case the step on the bag usually precedes the shift or step to the side.

A left-hand first baseman who has trouble shifting in the above manner can plant his left foot on the bag and a right-hand first baseman, his right foot. This permits shifts to the right and left respectively, the same as was previously described, but for a shift to the opposite side a cross-over step must be made. If the throw is directly to the bag, a stretch is made into the diamond, usually with the same foot as the glove hand. This is especially

a. Position in front of the bag ready to shift for a throw.

c. Shifting to the left of the bag to catch a throw.

b. Shifting to the right of the bag to catch a throw.

d. Stretching into the diamond to catch a low throw.
e. Reaching into the air to catch a high throw.

Fig. 6–1.   Catching thrown balls.

important on low throws. On throws that are accurate but high, a reach is made into the air. In rare cases the first baseman backs over the bag into foul territory to catch a throw. Footwork for catching various types of throws is illustrated by Fig. 6–1.

When the ball is fielded near the plate by the catcher, pitcher, or third baseman, the first baseman makes a target to prevent the possibility of the runner being hit by the ball. The left foot remains on the bag in this case, and the right one is planted about 3 feet toward second base. The hands are cupped to the side of the face (Fig. 6–2). A similar target is given in foul territory if a third strike rolls behind the catcher, and the batter is permitted to run.

The first baseman generally uses two hands in catching the ball, but adeptness with the glove hand is important on wide throws because a greater reach is possible. This particularly concerns throws near the runner. On extremely wide throws, the first baseman leaves the bag to catch or stop the ball instead of making a futile

Fig. 6–2.   Giving a target at first base for a throw from near the plate.

effort to retire the runner. This is especially important with a runner or runners on base, because if the ball is not blocked, runners may advance. The same holds true on many throws that hit the ground wide of the bag, even though the ball may be reached with one hand. Some wide throws cannot be stopped when the body is not in front of the ball; therefore, unless the game is likely to be decided on the failure to make the catch, the bag is frequently left to make sure the ball is blocked. On all such throws the first baseman hurries back to the bag after retrieving the ball, and attempts to tag the bag, or to tag the runner if the catch is made up the base line.

It is also important for the first baseman to be alert for another play after receiving a throw. Frequently a runner on second base rounds third and scores on a routine out. This normally happens because the first baseman fails to anticipate the play. In some cases it occurs because a safe call by the umpire is questioned.

FIELDING GROUND BALLS

The first baseman considers his ground-covering ability as well as that of his second baseman in fielding ground balls. This, plus the knowledge of where the second baseman is playing for various hitters, enables him to know how far he need venture from the bag. For example, if a right-hand pull hitter is batting, the second baseman will be nearer second base than if a left-hand pull hitter is at the plate. Thus what may be a difficult chance for him when defending the former may be an easy one when defending the latter. This particularly concerns hard-hit balls, since there is little time to move; therefore the first baseman attempts to field such balls when his judgment tells him they may be reached. The second baseman can field many slow-hit balls in the same territory because his approach to field the ball takes him nearer first base.

Making the Unassisted Put-Out. When a ball is fielded near the foul line and the runner can be beaten to the bag, the first baseman transfers the ball to his throwing hand and runs along the line in fair territory. He tags the bag with his left foot, if possible, thus avoiding contact with the runner. If the ball is fielded away from the line under similar conditions, he runs directly to the bag and continues into foul territory after making the put-out (Fig. 6–3). A slide into the bag is made if such a play is likely to be close; otherwise there might be a collision with the runner. In some of these

a. Running along the foul line

b. Running across the foul line

Fig. 6–3. Making an unassisted put-out.

cases it is advisable for the first baseman to call, "I have it," or "I'll take it," or indicate with his glove hand that he will make the play.

Teaming with the Pitcher. If the first baseman fields a hard-hit ball deep and near the foul line, he steps toward the pitcher and tosses the ball underhand (more than one step, if there is time). A right-hand first baseman steps with the left foot, and a left-hand first base-man with the right foot. The ball is released so that it reaches the pitcher shoulder-high when he is a step or two from the bag (Fig. 6–4). The play is made in a similar manner when the ball is fielded near the bag. If the ball is fielded from a deep position and wide of the bag, the ball is thrown directly to the bag.

a. First baseman tossing ball.   **b.** Pitcher making put-out.

Fig. 6–4. Teaming with the pitcher to retire the batter.

The former method may have to be used with an overhand toss or throw for extra-fast runners, regardless of where or how the ball is hit.

THROWING TO SECOND BASE

The throw to second base for a force play is usually made to the third-base side of the bag, if the runner is approaching from the right (when the first baseman plays in), and directly to the bag or to the right-field side of the bag, if the runner's approach is from the left (when the first baseman plays back—Diag. 6-1). A left-hand first baseman merely catches the ball and steps toward second base with his right foot to make the throw. The right-hand first baseman, however, must pivot to the right on his right foot, and make a quarter- or half-turn of the body and step toward second for the throw. The one exception occurs when he is moving toward the left and back, and is unable to get his body in front of the ball. He then pivots to the left on his right foot, and makes a half-turn to the left (Fig. 6–5). The first baseman hurries back to the bag after completing his throw because it may be necessary to take a return throw from second. A quick glance toward first base after throwing to second helps to complete this maneuver.

Similar footwork is used when the ball is fielded near the bag and the put-out is made prior to throwing to second. Then a left-hand first baseman touches the bag with his left foot, and a right-hand

a, b. The ball is fielded with the weight on the left foot.

c, d, e. A pivot to the left is made by transferring the weight to the right foot, or doing a jump spin, replacing the left foot with the right.

f, g, h. The step is toward second with the left foot. Note that the arm swings down, since an overhand throw is more accurate.

Fig. 6—5. A right-hand first baseman fields a ground ball to his left and turns left to throw to second base.

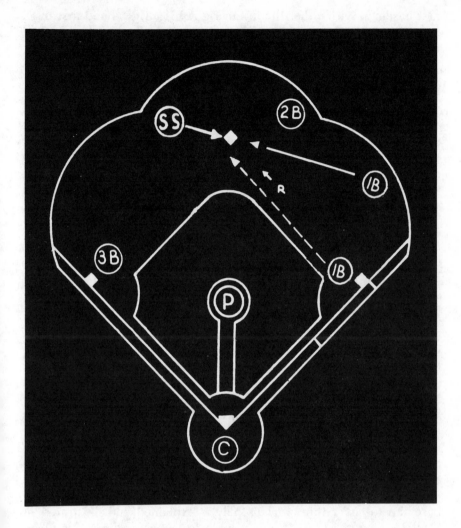

Dotted line. The throw from a position near
the bag—to the third-base side
of second.
Solid line. The throw from a deep position—direct to the bag.

Diagram. 6—1. The throw to second base from a position near the bag and
from a deep position

first baseman with either the left or right. If a right-hand first baseman completes the tag with his left foot he may make a left or right
turn and when the right foot is used, he turns left.

HOLDING A RUNNER ON BASE

With first or first and third bases occupied, the first baseman
stands in front of the bag and faces the pitcher with his left foot
near the foul line and his right foot opposite the corner of the bag
nearest the pitcher (Fig. 6–6a). This position enables the first baseman to catch throws from the pitcher just in front of the base and
sweep the glove to the ground to complete a tag.

Moving from the Bag. As soon as the pitcher starts to pitch, two
steps from the bag are taken toward second base (unless a bunt is
expected), and the regular defensive stance is assumed facing the
batter. The first baseman jumps into this position, first taking a
step with the left foot (Fig. 6–6b, d). The length of the two steps
is governed by the batter.

Handling Bunts. If a bunt is likely, the first baseman runs toward the batter as the ball is pitched. The approach is several feet
from the base line. Good judgment is required in making throws
after fielding such balls. Hard-bunted balls are often played to
retire a runner attempting to advance (unless, of course, the runner
started with the pitch), whereas slow-bunted balls are always
thrown to first base. This also concerns other ground balls. The
attempt to advance a runner to third base with a sacrifice is often
combatted with preplanned defensive assignments. In this case
the first baseman covers the area to the pitcher's mound and the
pitcher covers the area to the third-base line. This enables the third
baseman to cover third. (This play is explained and illustrated in
Drill 11, Chapter 17.) It is advisable to listen for directions when
in doubt where to throw, because the catcher usually calls the play.
If a bunted or hit ball rolls along the foul line and the batter is
likely to reach first base safely, the first baseman permits the ball
to roll in the hope that it might go foul. If this occurs, he picks up
the ball or brushes it into foul territory. A ball rolling in foul territory is also picked up because in this case the ball might roll fair
and the batter reach first base. The ball is permitted to roll if the
batter fails to run (with the bases unoccupied). If another player
fields the bunt, the first baseman permits the second baseman to
take the throw at first. He also lets a throw go through on a second
baseman–catcher pickoff play.

a. The position to hold a runner on the bag.

b, c. The crossover step into the diamond with the left foot.

d. The fielding position. The first baseman can jump into this position after his left foot hits the ground in (c).

Fig. 6–6. The position for holding a runner on base and the fielding position after the pitcher releases the ball.

ACTING AS THE CUTOFF MAN

In most systems of baseball, the first baseman acts as the cutoff man on all throws to the plate with the exception of those made after hard-hit singles toward the left fielder. There are other systems but this method seems to give the best protection for all bases

129

and strategic areas. This is described in detail under "Defensive Assignments on Throws from the Outfield" (see Chapter 11).

BACKING UP

The first baseman backs up second base on all throws from the left-field side of second base when the bases are unoccupied. If the hitter stops at first base, the first baseman does not venture from the bag unless it is necessary to retrieve an overthrow. He also covers second base and the plate when these bases are left uncovered (the latter when a runner is caught between third and the plate, in which case the ball may have to be handled in the run-down). The first baseman has priority in the run-down situation and the pitcher backs up.

STRATEGY

TAGGING THE BATTER

When a first baseman fields a ball near the base line and toward the plate, it may be necessary to tag the batter. In this case it is advisable to run toward the player, if he stops, to make a quick put-out. This assumes that third base is unoccupied. When third base is occupied, the first baseman, of course, immediately throws to the plate if the runner tries to score, and pursues the former tactic if the runner remains on third.

SETTING UP THE RUN-DOWN PLAY

In the event a runner is caught off first and breaks for second, it is advisable for the first baseman to throw the ball to the second baseman as soon as possible unless there is a runner on third (he pursues a runner who does not break). This, of course, sets up defensive players for the fastest and most effective run-down. If the pickoff occurs with third base occupied, the first baseman must guard against an attempt by the runner to score. This is often a preplanned play. The first baseman may combat the maneuver with a fake or bluff throw to second. In some cases it can be prevented even though a throw is made, if the second baseman is only a short distance away. An alert first baseman also advances toward second base after the ball passes the batter in a double steal situation (first and third bases occupied) so that the runner advancing from first base can be quickly retired, if he stops in the base line.

DRIVING THE RUNNER BACK TO THE BAG

On some teams the first baseman breaks in from his deep position and drives the runner back (first and second bases occupied) when the pitcher is in the hole on a right-hand pull hitter. This is based on two factors: (1) the batter is more likely to hit toward the shortstop or third baseman when he is ahead of the pitcher and (2) by driving the runner back it increases the chances of making a force play at second base on a routine grounder, and the runner may be prevented from advancing past second on a hit. In some cases the first baseman plays on the bag to get the same results but the drive-back method is best because the runner is usually going back to first when the pitcher is delivering.

PLAYING THE RUNNER

The first baseman frequently moves off the bag to a position slightly in back of a base runner who is not likely to steal to provide a better defense (also count of 3 and 2 with 2 out). He may back up a step or two from this position when the pitcher starts to deliver the ball. He informs the pitcher before making such a change; otherwise an attempt might be made to catch the runner, thereby causing a balk or wild throw. This is done by crossing the hands. When an attempt to sacrifice a runner to third base is the logical play, the first baseman plays off the bag. He stands in front of the runner in this case, if first base is occupied. The first baseman also moves in from his deep position when third base is occupied with less than two out, to guard against a squeeze play (except with known hard hitters at the plate).

WORKING A PITCHOUT

The pitchout is used when the first baseman holds a runner on base or plays in a deep position. In the former case the play is usually made when a bunt is likely. The first baseman fakes going in as the ball is pitched, then breaks back to the bag. In the play from a deep position, which is used more often, the first baseman tries to maneuver to a position closer to the runner, then breaks for the base as the ball is pitched. The maneuver usually comes in the form of a drive-back before the pitchout signal is given. He then takes the shorter position to set up the play. A similar maneuver with first and second bases occupied can set up a pickoff play with the pitcher. This requires special timing so signals are required the same as for a pickoff at second base.

SUMMARY

1. Get to the bag as quickly as possible so that you can shift left or right to receive throws. Shift from a position in front of the bag or place your right foot on the bag if you are right handed; your left foot, if left handed.

2. Stretch into the diamond for throws directly to the bag, particularly low throws.

3. Give a target to the inside of the bag when the catcher, pitcher, or third baseman makes a throw to first base from near the plate.

4. Leave the base to catch extra wide throws. Block the ball if necessary to prevent advancement.

5. Make the put-out unassisted if you field a ball fairly close to the bag. Team with the pitcher if necessary. Toss the ball to the pitcher when near or in back of the bag; throw the ball from out in the diamond.

6. Step toward second base in making a throw for a force play. A right-hand thrower pivots either to the left or right on his right foot.

7. Throw to the third-base side of second base for a force play when the runner is approaching from the right, and directly to the bag or to the right-field side of the bag when the runner's approach is from the left.

8. Play on the bag when a steal is possible (with first or first and third occupied). Take a crossover step into the diamond as soon as the pitcher starts his delivery.

9. Catch a throw by the pitcher at the bag on an attempted pickoff and swing the glove hand to the ground in front of the bag, forcing the runner to slide into the ball.

10. Run in from your position as the pitcher starts his delivery in sacrifice situations so that you are ready to field a bunt toward first base. Permit slow-hit balls along the foul line to roll when the batter cannot be retired at first. Pick up the ball if it rolls foul.

11. Cover the area to the pitcher's mound if an attempt is made to advance a runner from second to third base by a sacrifice.

12. Permit the second baseman to take the throw at first base on throws by the catcher in sacrifice situations (unless you are working a pickoff play with the catcher).

13. Take the cutoff position for throws to the plate after singles to center and right fields and after all extra base hits and fly balls, as well as on throws and errors that roll to the outfield.
14. Back up second base on doubles to left field; also be ready to retrieve overthrows to second base after singles to left field.
15. Cover the plate in run-downs and handle the ball if necessary.
16. Throw the ball to second as soon as possible if a runner is caught off first base unless a runner on third base attempts to score.
17. Advance toward second base after the ball passes the batter in a double steal situation (first and third occupied), so the runner advancing from first can be quickly retired if he stops in the base line.
18. Stand slightly in back of a player who is not likely to steal (slow runners and pitchers) when a left-hand hitter is at the plate. Inform the pitcher before making the change.
19. Move in from your deep position when third base is occupied with less than two out to guard against a squeeze play.
20. Give way to the second baseman on fly balls in back of first base. (See Chapter 5.) Be alert for fly balls toward the plate because the catcher frequently gets a late start for these balls.

DISCUSSION QUESTIONS

1. Describe the position of the first baseman's feet and hands in catching (a) a high throw from the shortstop which is wide to the right-field side of the bag; (b) a low throw from the second baseman which is direct to the bag.
2. What factors determine the distance a first baseman goes toward second base for ground balls?
3. State three ways a first baseman makes a put-out unassisted, and give reasons for each.
4. Why is it necessary for the first baseman to toss the ball to the pitcher covering first base in some situations, and to throw it in others? When are these generally employed?
5. Where does the first baseman usually play with two out and the following bases occupied: (a) first and second bases; (b) second and third bases; (c) first and third bases? What footwork is used in moving from the bag?

TRUE–FALSE QUESTIONS AND ANSWERS

T F 1. It is necessary for the first baseman to shift into foul territory to catch some throws.

T   F   2. A right-hand first baseman always pivots to the right in throw-
           ing to second base after fielding a ground ball.
T   F   3. The position of the feet, knees, trunk, and hands remain about
           the same regardless of where the first baseman plays.
T   F   4. Bunts that roll along the first-base line in foul territory are
           immediately picked up by the first baseman.
T   F   5. The first baseman acts as a cutoff man on all extra base hits.

ANSWERS

T   F   T   F   T
5   4   3   2   1

7

Double-Play Combination

Efficient second-base play depends on the ability of the short-stop and second baseman to work as a unit. Teamwork by the double play combination is very important since each player covers the bag under different circumstances and when a player is not covering he has to perform some related duty. This means that the shortstop and second baseman must have an understanding with each other and move with precision as a unit as soon as a ball is hit or a base runner attempts to steal or tries to advance.

TECHNIQUE

COVERING SECOND BASE

There are some definite rules for covering second base. For example, the shortstop covers the bag on attempted steals when the batter is likely to hit to the right-field side of second base, and the second baseman covers if the batter is more apt to hit to the left-field side of the bag.

Signals for Covering. In some instances the player selected to cover is governed by the type of ball pitched, because some batters bring their bats around a fraction of a second sooner when slow balls and breaking balls are pitched (fast-breaking knuckle balls and fork balls excepted). This is particularly true when straight-away hitters are defended, since both the shortstop and second baseman play approximately the same distance from the bag. The short-stop and second baseman employ mouth signals to convey information. An open mouth means that the player giving the sign will cover, whereas a closed mouth means that the other player covers (Fig. 7–1). The more experienced player usually gives the sign as the pitcher takes his position on the rubber, thus preventing the opposing team from knowing who is covering and what will be pitched. This guarantees that the base will always be covered. It is, of course, not necessary to cover if the catcher throws back to the pitcher or to third base in a first and third double steal situation. This is usually done by signal so the double play combination can remain in its normal defensive position.

If a slow ball is to be pitched, the second baseman and shortstop relay the information to the first and third basemen respectively, with a verbal sign ending with the player's name. "Heads up" and "Be alive" are phrases that are commonly employed. This enables them to be alert for a ball to be pulled along the foul lines. For a similar reason on some teams the shortstop or second baseman flash battery signals to the outfielders. In this case a closed fist indicates a fast ball and an open hand a breaking ball (Fig. 7–2). The fingers are wiggled if a slow ball is to be pitched. These signals, when employed, are given as the pitcher is ready to deliver the ball, so that the opposing team cannot steal the sign and transmit the information to the various batters.

The Force-Out. The approach for a force-out is usually a controlled stutter step in line with the throw. This widens the base

a. "I'll cover."   b. "You cover."

Fig. 7–1. Signals to insure that second base will be covered on steals when a straightaway hitter is at the plate.

a. Fast ball.   b. Breaking ball.

Fig. 7–2. Battery signals for the outfielders.

for a quick pivot on a double play. When only a force-out is necessary, or a double play cannot be completed, footwork may corre-
spond to that used in pivoting; or a reach toward the ball can be
made with one foot on the bag (to the side for a wide throw). In
either case the defensive player makes sure of the force-out and then
moves off the bag to avoid contact with the slider. After some
force-outs a runner may be caught rounding third. This throw can
be perfected during routine double play practice.

Taking Throws.   The shortstop usually takes the throw from the
pitcher, catcher, or first baseman after batted balls are fielded because he is in better position to throw to first. The second baseman takes the throw from the third baseman for the same reason,
and he may take the throw from the pitcher or catcher when the
shortstop plays far from the bag. On a sacrifice the shortstop covers
the bag. The second baseman covers first base in this situation.
The double play combination must also be alert to retrieve errant
throws by the catcher.

THROWING TO SECOND BASE

The method of throwing or feeding the ball to second base for
a force-out or possible double play depends on the distance the
grounder is fielded from the bag. For example, when the catch
is made at a considerable distance from the bag, it is usually necessary to employ arm, leg, and body action in making the throw. On
the other hand, if the ball is caught near the bag, arm action may

suffice. This may be accompanied by a step. In this case the step is taken toward the receiver with either the left or right foot, depending on the position of the feet when the ball is caught, and the ball is tossed underhand. The palm of the hand is kept up, if possible, so that the ball can be easily seen (Fig. 7–3). A backhand toss without leg action is often necessary by the shortstop from behind the bag. This technique is also used by the second baseman on some throws from near the bag. Very short throws from close to the bag may be tossed underhand with both hands, again with the omission of a step. In some of these situations the player fielding the ball, of course, tags the bag. It is advisable for the player fielding the ball to yell "I have it" in this case so that the other player forming the double play combination will not attempt to take the throw at the bag.

It is an advantage in some plays if the pivoter can receive the ball slightly to the side of the bag. However, if the ball is purposely thrown to the side of the bag, some throws will obviously arrive wide of the bag. In such cases it may be impossible to throw for a double play. In fact, even the force-out may be missed; therefore, it is a good general rule to aim all throws for the bag.

Fig. 7–3. Underhand toss near the bag for a force-out at second base.

ACTING AS CUTOFF MAN

The shortstop or second baseman acts as the cutoff man when an outfielder makes a throw to second base. The shortstop acts as the cutoff man on throws from left and left-center fields, and the second baseman acts as the cutoff man on throws from right and right-center fields. In this case the player covering the base calls "Cut" if the throw is wide of the bag or if the runner cannot be retired. No call is made if he thinks the runner might be caught. The shortstop also acts as the cutoff man on throws to third base provided he does not have to cover third base or act as a relay man (see Diag. 11–1, p. 193).

ACTING AS THE RELAY MAN

The shortstop and second baseman act as relay men on long hits and balls that elude the outfielders. The shortstop performs this duty on balls to the left-field side of second base, and the second baseman on those to the right-field side. It is done from a point between 100 and 150 feet from the outfielder catching or retrieving the ball and in line with the base to which the throw is to be made. The arms are waved to give the outfielder a good target. (See Diags. 11–4, 11–5, p. 195.) A throw is always intercepted from the relay position unless the ball arrives on a short bounce. A bouncing ball is difficult to handle on a relay, so it is best to let the throw continue to the infield.

In relaying the ball, a pivot is always executed toward the glove hand after the ball is caught. An overhand arm swing is used on all relays, and the throw is kept low so that the ball can be intercepted by the cutoff man if necessary. The throw is made so that the ball will reach the receiving catcher or infielder on the first bounce except on some short throws. In this case the throw is made on the fly.

STRATEGY

COMBATTING THE DOUBLE STEAL

The batter usually determines whether the shortstop or second baseman will cover on a double steal with first and third bases occupied, the same as on a single steal. Normally it is the second baseman, because the majority of players are right-handed and hit more often to left field. Actually, the second baseman is the logical player to cover, since his approach to the bag enables him to watch the action of the runner on third base. When covering the bag in this situation, an attempt is made to reach the front of the bag, because the position is an advantageous one from which to run in to meet the ball if the runner on third starts for the plate. (The double steal with first and third bases occupied is described in Chapter 14.) If the runner gives no intention of leaving third, an attempt is made to tag the player coming from first. However, the runner approaching second base often stops. This, of course, necessitates a run-down, in which case the runner on third base is watched to thwart an attempt to score.

Some managers prefer to combat this play by having one player cover and the other player stand 15 or 20 feet in front of the bag in line with the throw. This permits the player in the short position to intercept the throw if the runner on third base attempts to score or allows him to let the ball go through to the player covering second if the runner remains at third. This is a questionable practice because it requires either the shortstop or second baseman to play out of position in order to reach this station in time for the throw unless a straightaway hitter is defended in a halfway position or the infield plays in. However, it is a good tactic if a pitchout is employed. If the double team method is used, the player who normally covers takes the short position.

If the tying run is on third base and the winning run is on first base, the tying run is frequently disregarded when the team has an even chance to win because if an attempt to retire the runner on third fails, the winning run goes to second base and may eventually mean the decisive run in the game. The runner on third is also disregarded when the team has a commanding lead. On the other hand, if the winning run is on third base, the put-out at second base is sacrificed at the expense of preventing this run from scoring.

The above strategy may be altered in cases where players have proved they can consistently break up the double steal. In fact, clever catchers and infielders with good arms almost always prevent scoring under these circumstances. An alert defense also considers the fact that a runner on third must be fast; otherwise a double steal is not likely to be attempted.

FAKING A CATCH

If a fly ball is hit while a runner is attempting to steal second base, the shortstop or second baseman frequently fakes catching a ground ball with less than two out. This often encourages the runner to continue his advance. The player not covering fakes the catch in this case because the player covering can then continue on to the bag and make it appear that he is expecting a throw.

COVERING ON A DELAYED STEAL

A variation in the duty of covering second base is needed when the opposing team uses a delayed steal. (The delayed steal is described in Chapter 14.) The player covering moves several steps toward second base after the ball passes the batter, thus insuring that the bag will be covered if the runner employs a delayed start.

DRIVING THE RUNNER BACK

The player designated to cover also drives a runner on second base back to the bag to prevent a long lead, thus permitting the other member of the double play combination to protect adequately the area where the batter is likely to hit the ball. The latter can frequently break for the bag after the first maneuver and catch the runner. This may be a preplanned play, in which case the shortstop passes in front of the runner after the drive-back. (See Chapter 9, p. 167.) The drive-back in some cases prevents the runner from stealing the catcher's signals.

A variation of this tactic is used by some teams to prevent a run from scoring on a single. In this case the player who is not designated to cover does the drive-back. This is occasionally done with pull hitters when the pitcher is in the hole, because then the ball is more likely to be hit to the opposite side of the bag.

SUMMARY

1. Use mouth signals to decide who will cover second base on some straightaway hitters. (A closed mouth means, "I'll cover," an open mouth, "You cover.") The pitch usually determines who covers.
2. Employ a verbal sign to inform the first and third basemen when a slow ball will be pitched. Use the player's name preceded by "Heads up" or "Be alive."
3. Use a closed fist for a fast ball, an open hand for a curve, and wiggle the fingers for a slow ball, if pitches are signaled to the outfielders.
4. Stretch for a throw to complete the force-out at second base if a double play is not likely to be made, as well as when there are two out.
5. Be alert to retrieve an errant return to the pitcher by the catcher.

6. Toss the ball underhand to second base for a force-out if you are fairly close to the bag. Throw the ball when you are far from the bag.

7. Step on the bag (usually with the right foot) to complete a force play unassisted when you field the ball very near the bag; then throw to first if there is a possibility of a double play.

8. Call "I have it" if you can make the force-out at second base unassisted, so that the other member of the double play combination will not attempt to take the throw at the bag.

9. Call "Cut" to the cutoff man if a throw to second base is wide or if the runner cannot be retired. No call means not to intercept the ball.

10. Take a position approximately 100 to 150 feet from an outfielder when acting as a relay man. Spin toward the glove hand to throw and attempt to make the ball reach the intended receiver on the first bounce.

11. Stand just in front of the bag when handling a throw at second base on a double steal with first and third bases occupied. Break in to take the throw if the runner on third attempts to score, unless it is more important to catch the runner advancing from first.

12. Fake the catching of a ground ball if a fly ball is hit while a runner is attempting to steal second base with less than two out. This often encourages the runner to continue his advance.

13. Practice the double team pickoff play. The player designated to cover fakes a pickoff; then the other player breaks for the bag.

14. Move in a step or two with first base occupied to increase the chances for a double play. (See Chapter 4.)

15. Take your normal defensive position when designated to cover second base in an intentional pass situation, to guard against an errant pitch. The other member of the double play combination holds the runner on the bag. (See Chapter 4.)

DISCUSSION QUESTIONS

1. Why is it necessary for the shortstop and second baseman to use signs? What method of signaling is employed and when is the sign given?

2. How do the shortstop and second baseman trick some base runners on hit-and-run plays?

3. Who takes the catcher's throw at second base if a runner on first attempts to steal with a left-hand pull hitter at the plate? What are the player's duties in the above situation if third base is occupied with the score tied in the ninth inning?

4. Describe three ways the shortstop and second baseman feed the ball to second base for a force play.

5. When does the cutoff position become the responsibility of the short-stop and second baseman on throws to second base from the outfield?

TRUE–FALSE QUESTIONS AND ANSWERS

T F 1. Battery signals never determine whether the shortstop or second baseman covers second base on attempted steals.

T F 2. Second base is covered by the shortstop on all sacrifice bunts if a normal defense is used.

T F 3. The second baseman acts as the cutoff man on throws to second base from right field.

T F 4. A throw to second base to catch a runner attempting to steal is always returned to the plate if a runner on third attempts to score.

T F 5. The shortstop acts as the relay man on long hits to left field.

ANSWERS

F T T F T
1 2 3 4 5

8

The Second Baseman

An effective second baseman is able to cover ground, field hit balls cleanly, and make quick short throws. Quickness is a second baseman's greatest asset. This is important because the second baseman handles a variety of slow-bounding balls which require quick snap throws to first. A snap or flip type of throw is also effective when making the pivot on a double play, since the second baseman's approach for the force-out does not generally permit a full arm throw to first.

TECHNIQUE

FIELDING GROUND BALLS

The second baseman is the logical fielder of most ground balls toward first base because he is moving in the direction of the bag. He calls loudly "I have it" or "I'll take it." This, of course, enables the first baseman to take the throw at first base, and eliminates the possibility that the pitcher will fail to cover. In addition it is more likely that the put-out will be made in this manner than if the first baseman teams with the pitcher.

Fielding the Ball in the Base Line. If a ground ball is fielded near the base line with less than two out and a runner is advancing from first, the second baseman attempts to tag the player, then throws to first. The player may have to be pursued. In this case the second baseman must remember that if the runner is not tagged a run may score from third with one out. In the pursuit situation the runner must not be pursued at the expense of the batter. It is best to throw early to retire the batter. The first baseman can then pursue the runner, or throw to the shortstop for the second out. The runner often runs out of the base line to avoid being tagged. When the second baseman thinks the runner has run out of line (running three feet out of line to prevent being tagged automatically retires the runner) he throws to first (Fig. 8–1A). If the runner does not run out of line and avoids being tagged, the throw is often made to second provided, of course, he can still be retired.

Throwing to Second Base. When the ball is fielded a considerable distance from the bag and the proper play is to second base for a force-out or possible double play, the second baseman pivots to the right on the right foot and steps toward the bag with his left foot to make the throw (Fig. 8–1B). However, if the second baseman is moving toward the left and back and is unable to get in front of the ball, he pivots to the left and makes a half turn of the body to throw. The ball is usually caught with the weight on the left foot. There are two ways to make the pivot: (1) Transfer the weight to the right foot; and (2) hop on the left foot and replace the left foot with the right (illustrated in Chapter 6, page 126). A hop may also accompany the conventional right turn. On the right turn and for throws from near the bag the ball is generally released from a low body position with a forearm snap.

MAKING THE DOUBLE PLAY

The second baseman's footwork in making the throw to first base to complete a double play depends on the accurateness of the throw to second base, the speed with which the second baseman is able to cover the bag, and the distance of the runner from second base when the ball is caught. Some players time their approach so that the ball is caught in motion, whereas others attempt to get to the bag as soon as possible so that they can wait for the throw. The footwork often depends on the speed with which the bag is reached. For example, when the second baseman arrives late, he must catch the ball in motion and continue over the bag to throw. In this case the put-out is made by stepping over the bag with the left foot and dragging the right foot against the bag, or by stepping on the bag with the left foot and then into the diamond with the right foot (Fig. 8–2A and B). A hop may accompany either of these pivots.

If the second baseman approaches the bag with his speed controlled, or he can get set at the bag, he may step to the inside or outside of the base line to throw. He can execute the force-out with his right foot and throw directly from the bag, stepping either to the outside (Fig. 8–3), or inside (Fig. 8–4A), or he may make the

a, b, c. The runner goes in front of the second baseman thinking he can avoid the tag (if he runs more than three feet out of the base line he is automatically out).

d, e. The second baseman knows the runner has violated a base-running rule so he stops his pursuit and throws to first.

A. Handling a ground ball in the base line with a runner advancing from first.

Fig. 8–1. The second baseman.

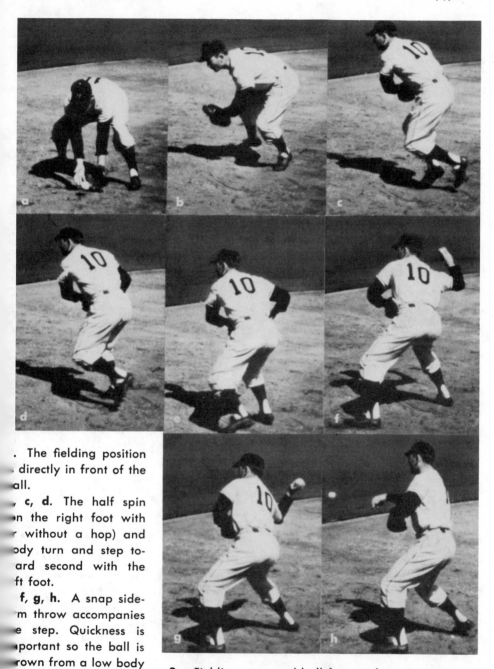

. The fielding position
directly in front of the
all.

, c, d. The half spin
n the right foot with
r without a hop) and
ody turn and step to-
ard second with the
ft foot.

f, g, h. A snap side-
m throw accompanies
e step. Quickness is
portant so the ball is
rown from a low body
sition.

B.   Fielding a ground ball from a deep position
and throwing to second base.

Fig. 8–1.   *(Continued)*

a. The step over the bag with the left foot.   d. The step with the left foot to throw.

b, c. The drag of the right foot over the bag   e, f. The arm swings down for an overhand
and transfer of the weight to the right foot.   throw.

A.   Stepping over the bag with the left foot and dragging the right foot
over the bag to throw.

Double play pivot by the second baseman.

a. The step on the bag with the left foot.   c, d. The step with the left foot to throw.
b. The step over the bag, transferring the   e, f. The arm swings across the chest for the
   weight to the right foot.   throw.

B. Stepping on the bag with the left foot and into the diamond to throw.

Fig. 8-2.   (Continued)

Fig. 8–3. Double play pivot by the second baseman: stepping on the bag with the right foot and to the outside of the base line with the left foot to throw.

putout with the left foot and push back to throw (Fig. 8–4B). The throw from the inside may originate with a hop from right to right foot. The pivots over the bag in Fig. 8–2 can also be executed from a controlled or timed approach.

There are, of course, other types of footwork. Some players prefer to wait for the throw with their feet opposite the sides of the bag. On accurate throws they catch the ball in a stationary posi-

a, b, c. The shortstop's throw is caught as the right foot comes down on the bag. (Note the shortstop's hips face the bag, enabling the second baseman to easily follow the ball.)

d, e, f. The step to the outside of the base line with the left foot and the snap throw.

Fig. 8–3. *(Continued)*

tion and drag the left foot back to the bag before stepping to throw. They then step toward first base or to the inside or outside of the base line. Most players favor the step inside because it prevents bodily contact with the runner and permits seeing the first baseman even though the runner fails to slide.

In a second method involving a stationary position, the player covers the right-field half of the bag with the balls of his feet. The ball is caught with a shift. If the throw is received slightly to the left-field side of the bag, the second baseman simultaneously steps

a. The approach is in line with the throw from the third baseman.
b. The ball is caught as the right foot comes down on the bag.
c, d. The step is to the inside of the base line with the left foot to throw.
e, f, g. The overhand throw. Note that the body follows through and swings out of the path of the slider.

A. Stepping on the bag with the right foot and to the inside of the base line with the left foot to throw.

Fig. 8–4. Double play pivot by the second baseman.

a. The ball is caught as the left foot comes down on the bag.

b. The weight is pushed back from the bag to the right foot to throw and to avoid contact with the slider.

c. The step with the left foot to throw (slightly to the outside of the base line).

d, e, f. The across-the-chest snap throw and complete weight transfer to the left foot.

B. Stepping on the bag with the left foot and pushing back to the right foot to throw.

Fig. 8–4. *(Continued)*

to that side of the base with the right foot and drags his left toe against the corner of the bag nearest first base. He then steps directly toward first base with the left foot to throw. If the throw is received over or slightly to the first-base side of the bag, he shifts similarly to the first-base side of the bag and drags his right toe against the corner of the bag nearest left field. The throw in this case is made by stepping directly toward first base or to the inside or outside of the base line.

COVERING AND BACKING UP

The second baseman covers second on all ground balls and most fly balls that are hit to the left-field side of the bag. He also covers second on singles that go through or over the right-field side of the infield unless an attempt to catch the ball takes him away from the bag. If a runner on first breaks toward second before the pitcher gets set, or if the runner is caught off first, the second baseman moves to the base line to be ready to handle the ball.

In addition the second baseman covers first base when the first baseman leaves the bag to catch a fly ball, unless it is possible for him to make the catch; takes the throw at first base on sacrifice bunts; and also covers first base if the first baseman takes the cutoff position on a single, provided, of course, the shortstop can cover second base. It is, of course, impossible to cover first base if the hit goes to the second baseman's right. However, an alert second baseman can at least prevent the runner from taking undue liberties.

Many of the approaches in covering first and second are straight to the bag because time is the main factor. However, if possible, the approach is made in line with the throw. When a pitchout is worked at first, the second baseman circles into the bag. This places him in a good position for the catcher's throw.

The second baseman backs up first base on throws from the catcher and pitcher and on those made by the third baseman from near the plate. He also backs up second base when the shortstop covers on throws from the pitcher and catcher and on those made by the outfielders from the left-field side of second base.

SUMMARY

1. Call "I have it" or "I'll take it" if you can field a slow-hit ball toward first base so that the first baseman will cover the bag.
2. Tag a runner coming from first base if you field a ground ball in the

base line. (The runner is out if he runs more than three feet out of the base line to avoid being tagged.)

3. Get to second base quickly but under control for force plays and use the footwork which is natural for you in pivoting on double plays.

4. Cover second base on all ground balls and most fly balls that are hit to the left-field side of second base.

5. Cover first base on all sacrifice bunts. Move in and toward first before the pitch.

6. Cover first base if possible when the first baseman takes the cutoff position on a throw to the plate after a single to center or right field.

7. Back up throws to first and second bases unless you are performing some other duty on defense.

8. Cover second base on attempted steals with a right-hand batter at the plate. (See Chapter 7.)

9. Move in two or three steps when covering second base on steals, if the pitcher gets in the hole (with count of 3–1 or 3–2), so that the bag can be covered after the pitch passes the batter. (See Chapter 4.)

10. Take fly balls behind first base because you are in a much better position to make the catch than the first baseman. (See Chapter 5.)

11. Take the cutoff position at second on a potential double to right field; also on singles which permit a runner to advance easily from first to third. (See Chapter 7.)

12. Watch for a pitchout signal from the catcher, particularly when an attempt might be made to advance a runner from first to second base with a sacrifice. (See Chapter 5.)

13. Move several steps toward second base after the ball passes the hitter when covering the bag with first and third bases occupied to guard against a delayed steal. (See Chapter 7.)

14. Drive a runner on second base back to the bag with a right-hand batter at the plate. (See Chapter 7.)

15. Go to the outfield for the relay on a long hit to right or right-center field. Let the ball continue to the infield if the outfielder's throw arrives on a short hop. (See Chapter 7.)

DISCUSSION QUESTIONS

1. Explain the second baseman's tactics if a ground ball is fielded in the base line with a runner advancing from first base.

2. What factors determine the footwork of the second baseman in making a force play and throw to first base for a possible double play?

3. How do most second basemen prevent the base runner from interfering with their throw to first base after making a force play at second?

4. When does the second baseman cover (*a*) first base? (*b*) second base?
5. Describe the approach of the second baseman for both easy- and hard-hit balls toward the right-field line.
6. Where does the second baseman make his throw with first base occupied if he fields:
   a) A hard-hit ball to his right with one out?
   b) A slow-hit ball directly toward him with none out?
   c) A hard-hit ball to his left with two out?

TRUE–FALSE QUESTIONS AND ANSWERS

T   F   1. A step toward second base usually accompanies a throw to the shortstop when the second baseman fields a ground ball fifty or sixty feet from the bag.
T   F   2. The second baseman covers second base when the batter hits a line drive down the left-field line.
T   F   3. It is an automatic out if in the umpire's judgment a player runs more than three feet out of the base line to avoid being tagged.
T   F   4. The first baseman has priority in the fielding of all ground balls which are hit between the first and second basemen.
T   F   5. On a sure triple down the right-field line, the second baseman runs to the outfield and takes the relay position in line with the plate.

ANSWERS

T   F   T   T   T
5   4   3   2   1

9

The Shortstop

Good shortstop play requires the ability to cover ground, field hit balls cleanly, and make long, accurate throws. The shortstop is the key player on the infield. This develops from the fact that the shortstop plays farther from the first baseman than the other two infielders; consequently he must have the strongest arm. In addition he must possess sure hands, because if he fumbles a ground ball, it usually means the batter cannot be retired at first.

TECHNIQUE

FIELDING GROUND BALLS

The shortstop can often catch a runner advancing to third base when the ball is hit directly toward him or to his right. This, however, is not attempted with two out unless a play cannot be made to either first or second base; nor is it attempted with one out when the defensive team has a substantial lead late in the game. If the ball is fumbled and a play cannot be made to first, second, or third base, a similar throw sometimes catches the runner after he has made his turn. A third baseman frequently cuts in front of the shortstop to field slow-hit balls. If the shortstop can field these balls more advantageously, he calls "I have it." This is especially important with first base occupied because only a short throw is necessary to complete a force play.

MAKING THE DOUBLE PLAY

Footwork in making the force-out at second base and the throw to first base to complete a double play depends on the accurateness of the throw to second base and the distance of the runner from second base when the ball is caught. The shortstop, unlike the second baseman, generally catches the ball while moving toward the base to which he intends to throw. If possible, he times his approach so that the ball is caught just as he reaches the bag. Some players prefer to catch the ball and step on the bag at approximately the same time (step-on-the-bag method—Figs. 9–1 and 9–3), whereas others prefer to make the catch with the foot off the bag and drag the toe against the bag (drag-the-toe method—Figs. 9–2 and 9–4).

Players who favor the step-on-the-bag method and hit the bag with their right foot step either toward first or slightly to the outside of the base line to make the throw. This, of course, depends on the angle at which the ball is received. In another variation the step is completed to the outside of the base line, and the body is simultaneously shifted with a hop to throw, the left foot being replaced with the right (Fig. 9–1). (Some players prefer to hop into this position without the aid of a step with the left foot, hopping immediately from right to right foot after the ball is caught.) This carries the body out of the path of the runner. It is not the quickest method of throwing, but it is particularly effective when the runner approaching second base is near the bag and the batter is far from first. Two other variations of the step-on-the-bag method: In the first, the ball is caught as the left foot hits the bag and a direct hop to the right foot is executed to the outside of the base line (Fig. 9–3A). In the second, the ball is caught as the right foot comes down about a stride from the bag. In this case the throw is completed with a natural step to the bag, and the weight is transferred back to the right foot with a hop to the side of the bag.

A player who employs the step-on-the-bag method to the outside of the base line normally uses similar footwork on a throw from the first baseman to the inside of the base line. The ball is caught as the left foot comes down on the bag, or from a target position with the left foot on the bag. In the former case the weight is usually transferred to the right foot with a hop after the catch, and a step is made toward first with the left foot (Fig. 9–3B).

Players who use the drag-the-toe method normally catch the ball just before they reach the bag or as they step over it. In either case the ball is caught with the weight on the right foot, and the throw is completed by simultaneously hopping to the outside of the base line and dragging the right toe against the bag (Fig. 9–2).

The drag-the-toe method is also an effective means to complete the play from the inside of the base line. In this case the ball is caught in back of the bag, or as a step is made over the bag, just as

a. The ball is caught as the right foot comes down on the bag.
b. The step with the left foot to the outside of the base line. (A hop to the right foot accompanied by a body swing toward first is made from this position.)
c. The hop returns the weight to the right foot.
d, e, f. The step with the left foot and throw.

Fig. 9—1.   Double play pivot by the shortstop: stepping on the bag with the right foot, then to the outside of the base line with the left foot to throw.

a. The approach is timed so that the ball can be caught as the right foot comes down near the bag.

b. The step past the base with the left foot. (A hop to the right foot accompanied by a body swing toward first is made from this position.)

c. The right foot drags over the bag during the hop forward.

Fig. 9–2. Double play pivot by the shortstop: stepping near the bag with the right foot, then over the bag with the left foot to throw.

d, e, f. The hop returns the weight to the right foot and the step is made toward first with the left foot to throw.

Fig. 9–2. *(Continued)*

a. The ball is caught from the second baseman as the left foot comes down on the bag. (A hop and body swing toward first base is made from this position.)

b, c. The hop transfers the weight to the right foot for the throw.

d, e, f. The step with the left foot and throw.

A.   Stepping on the bag with the left foot, then hopping to the outside of the base line to the right foot to throw.

Fig. 9–3.   Double play pivot by the shortstop.

a. The ball is caught from the first baseman as the left foot comes down on the bag. (A hop toward first base to the right foot is made from this position.)

b. The hop transfers the weight to the right foot for the throw.

c, d, e. The step with the left foot and throw.

B. Stepping on the bag with the left foot, then hopping to the inside of the base line to the right foot to throw.

Fig. 9–3. *(Continued)*

when the throw is made from the outside of the base line. However, the left toe is dragged against the bag (Fig. 9–4). The throw in this case can be made with or without a hop.

COVERING AND BACKING UP

The shortstop covers second base on sacrifices and all ground balls and most fly balls that are hit to the right-field side of second base. He also covers the bag on hits that go through or over the right-field side of the infield because the second baseman's attempt to catch the ball usually takes him away from the bag.

A phase of covering second base involves the position of the shortstop when an attempt is made to prevent the advance of a runner from second to third base by a sacrifice. In this situation a position is usually taken over or near the bag to shorten the lead of the runner (Diags. 13–2 and 13–3, pp. 234, 235). Another method requires teamwork with the pitcher. In this case the shortstop plays just behind the runner and tries to drive him back to the bag when the pitcher is ready to deliver the ball (see Drill 11, Chapter 17).

The shortstop also covers third base when the third baseman leaves his position to field fly or ground balls, unless it is possible for him to make the catch. He performs this same duty when sharp singles are made to left field with second base occupied and a throw is made to the plate, because the third baseman acts as the cutoff man. The shortstop also takes the throw at third base in some systems of baseball if a runner on second base attempts to advance on a fly ball to the outfield with first base unoccupied.

The shortstop backs up second base when the second baseman covers the bag on throws from the catcher or pitcher and on those made by the outfielders from the right-field side of second base. He also backs up third base on throws from the catcher.

STRATEGY

PICKOFF PLAY

The shortstop is the logical player to attempt a pickoff at second base because he plays behind the runner. A fake pickoff usually sets up the play. This permits the shortstop to move nearer the runner. Two basic methods are used in the pickoff.

Either the shortstop or pitcher gives the pickoff signal and the other player answers with a similar signal. The shortstop then

a, b. The ball is caught as the left foot comes down near the bag.

c, d. The step over the bag with the right foot. (A hop in place accompanied by a body swing toward first base is made from this position and the left foot is dragged over the bag.)

e, f, g. The step toward first with the left foot and the throw.

Fig. 9–4. Double play pivot by the shortstop: stepping near the bag with the left foot, then over the bag with the right foot to throw.

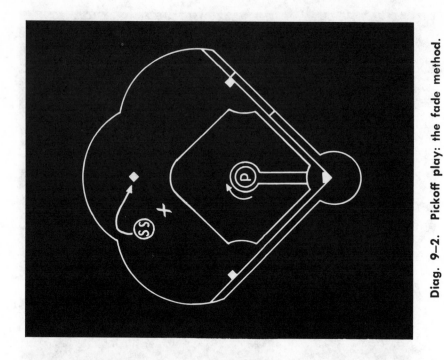

Diag. 9–2. Pickoff play: the fade method.

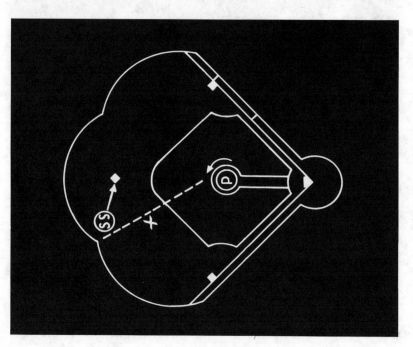

Diag. 9–1. Pickoff play: the daylight method.

breaks for the bag when the pitcher looks momentarily toward the batter (or on a specific count). In a variation of this play, the shortstop gives an automatic signal to the pitcher by placing daylight between himself and the runner. A long lead by the runner may also establish the daylight. The daylight method is illustrated in Diag. 9–1.

In a second basic method the shortstop indicates to the pitcher that he will cover by retreating slowly to the runner's left, then breaks for the bag at an opportune time (Diag. 9–2). The retreat is two or three steps to bait the coach into yelling for the runner to resume his lead. The pitcher must continually watch the shortstop when the play is made in this manner. This play, as well as the one with a definite signal described in the first method, can be executed from the third-base side of the runner, if the shortstop is in the proper depth position. This often leads both the coach and runner into false security.

In a variation of the fade method the shortstop drives the runner back, then passes in front of him (to block the runner's vision) to set up a pickoff play for the second baseman. A quick break can be made anytime by the shortstop after daylight has been established in the first method.

Either of the two basic pickoff plays is more likely to be successful with a left-hand batter at the plate because the shortstop is then playing nearer the bag. The count on the batter is another factor, since the runner is more anxious when the pitcher is in the hole. This particularly applies with the count three balls and one strike or three balls and two strikes, because the runner may be breaking on the pitch.

Very few pitchers are successful in catching a runner off second base. For this reason the shortstop tries to work the play only with capable pitchers. Even then it is only attempted during a stage of the game when the put-out, if made, is likely to be an important factor in deciding the game.

SUMMARY

1. Attempt to catch some runners advancing to third base with less than two out on hard-hit ground balls directly toward you or to your right.
2. Get to the bag quickly but under control for force plays and use the footwork which is natural for you in pivoting on double plays.
3. Drive a runner on second base back to the bag with a left-hand batter at the plate. (See Chapter 7.)

4. Cover second base on sacrifice bunts and all ground balls and most fly balls that are hit to the right-field side of the bag.
5. Cover third base on singles to left field with second base occupied, because the third baseman leaves his position to act as the cutoff man in line with the plate.
6. Back up throws to second and third bases unless you are performing some other duty on defense.
7. Cover second base on attempted steals with a left-hand batter at the plate. (See Chapter 7.)
8. Move in two or three steps when covering second base on steals, if the pitcher gets in the hole (with count of 3–1 or 3–2), so that the start to cover can be delayed until the ball is hit or passes the batter. (See Chapter 4.)
9. Take fly balls behind third base because you are in much better position to make the catch than the third baseman. (See Chapter 5.)
10. Watch for a pitchout signal from the catcher, particularly when an attempt might be made to advance a runner from second to third base with a sacrifice. (See Chapter 5.)
11. Move several steps toward second base after the ball passes the batter when covering the bag with first and third bases occupied, to guard against a delayed steal. (See Chapter 7.)
12. Take the cutoff position in front of second base on a potential double to left field; also on singles with first and second bases unoccupied. (See Chapter 7.)
13. Take the cutoff position in front of third base when a single is hit with first base occupied. (See Chapter 7.)
14. Go to the outfield for the relay on a long hit to left or left-center field. Let the ball continue to the infield if the outfielder's throw arrives on a short hop. (See Chapter 7.)
15. Plan a pickoff play with your pitcher to catch a runner off second base. This is particularly effective with a left-hand batter at the plate.

DISCUSSION QUESTIONS

1. Where does the shortstop make his throw after fielding a hard-hit ground ball that comes directly toward him if only second base is occupied and the runner attempts to advance to third in the following situations:
    a) Seventh inning, opposing team ahead seven to one, and one out?
    b) Fourth inning, score tied, and two out?
    c) Ninth inning, opposing team behind six to three, and none out?

2. What footwork is employed by the shortstop in making a force-out at second base and throw to first base to complete a possible double play?
3. When does the shortstop cover second base? third base?
4. Describe two ways the shortstop teams with the pitcher to catch a runner off second base.
5. State three characteristics of a good shortstop. Why are these important?
6. What are the back-up duties of the shortstop with respect to second and third bases?

TRUE–FALSE QUESTIONS AND ANSWERS

T F 1. If a hard-hit grounder goes directly toward the shortstop with only second base occupied and one out, there should be no hesitation about throwing to third if the runner tries to advance in a close game.

T F 2. The shortstop can work a pickoff play more effectively with the pitcher when a left-hand pull hitter is at the plate.

T F 3. On a single to center field with first base occupied, the shortstop covers third.

T F 4. A unique method which some shortstops use to make a double play is to catch the ball as the right foot comes down near the bag, then take a natural step to the bag to throw to first.

T F 5. When second base is occupied in a sacrifice situation the shortstop always plays on the bag to keep the runner from getting a big lead.

ANSWERS

F T F T T
5 4 3 2 1

10

The Third Baseman

A successful third baseman must be able to field slow-rolling bunts, block hard-hit balls, and make long accurate throws. The third baseman has a unique problem since he must be adept in handling both easy- and hard-hit balls. He can, of course, combat bunts by shortening his position, but in so doing he lessens his chances of fielding a hard-hit ball cleanly. His only recourse in this case is fearlessly to block the path of the ball. This is a characteristic of a good third baseman.

TECHNIQUE

FIELDING GROUND BALLS

Since it is good defensive strategy for the third baseman to play in to guard against a bunt (until two strikes), hard-hit balls frequently arrive before the batter gets started from the plate. For this reason the ball can often be knocked down or blocked, then recovered in time to make the play at first. The ball is usually blocked with the feet together. The hands are also held close so that the ball cannot go through (Fig. 10–1a and b).

The third baseman generally has ample time to make his play to first after fielding a ground ball in the vicinity of his normal position. Therefore he can hop forward to make his throw, or he can straighten his body and throw directly from the fielding position (Fig. 10–1c-h). It is important not to hurry the throw from third base but rather, first, to get into a good throwing position. The object in throwing is to make an accurate, on-balance throw, not the fastest and hardest throw.

When a grounder is hit to the second-base side of the third baseman, it is often necessary to cut in front of the shortstop and field the ball with the glove hand. This particularly concerns slow-hit balls, because in this case it is almost impossible for the shortstop to retire the batter. However, if the grounder is hit fairly hard and cannot be reached in a balanced position, the third baseman permits the ball to go through to the shortstop. This is especially true if the shortstop calls for the ball. Danger of deflecting the ball is thus avoided, and the shortstop can usually field the grounder and complete the put-out. This is very important with first base occupied, because only a short throw is necessary to complete a force play at second base. The third baseman usually makes his throw to second base with first base occupied, provided the put-out can be easily made and a play at the plate is not in order. This not only saves a long throw to first base, but frequently makes it possible for the second baseman to complete a double play. A rule which can be generally followed in this case is to throw to second when a right-hand batter is defended, and to first when a left-hand batter is at the plate. In the latter case it is often difficult for the second baseman to reach the bag in time to make the put-out because of a deeper defensive position.

The third baseman fields all slow-hit balls on the third-base side of the pitching mound and toward the plate, if, of course, he can field the ball in position to throw. He listens for the catcher's voice after fielding such balls when in doubt where to make the play. When a slow-hit ball or bunt rolls along the foul line and the batter cannot be retired, the third baseman permits the ball to roll in the hope that it might go foul. If this occurs, he immediately picks up the ball because the batter is then forced to return to the plate. A ball rolling in foul territory is also picked up because the ball might roll fair and the batter reach first base. An exception occurs if the batter fails to run from the plate with the bases unoccupied.

Since most bunts are made toward the third-base side of the pitcher, the third baseman studies each batter carefully, and moves in or back accordingly. Frequently a batter indicates his intention to bunt before the ball leaves the pitcher's hand. The third baseman is alert for any such mannerisms and breaks toward the plate once they are observed.

Most bunts are fielded with two hands because there is less likelihood that the ball will be fumbled. This conforms to the normal method of fielding ground balls, described and illustrated in

a, b. The ball is blocked with the feet together.

c, d, e. The weight on the throwing (right) foot and stride with the stepping (left) foot.

f, g, h. The arm swings down for an overhand throw to first.

Fig. 10–1.   Blocking a hard-hit ball and throwing to first.

Chapters 1 and 5.   However, on some well-placed bunts and slow-hit balls that result from hard swings, the bare hand is occasionally used.   The hand in this case is extended palm upward so that the ball will roll into the fingers.   The ball is usually fielded with the weight on the left foot, and the throw is made by stepping in the direction of the approach to the ball (Fig. 10–2).   This corresponds to the throw which is made after fielding a slow-hit ball with two hands (Fig. 5–2, p. 107).

COVERING AND BACKING UP

The third baseman covers third base under almost all circumstances. However, on a hard-hit single to left field with second base occupied he acts as the cutoff man for the throw to the plate. It is, of course, necessary to leave the bag to field some fly balls and ground balls. In this case the third baseman returns to the bag as soon as possible after making the play. The third baseman assists the cutoff man (shortstop) on throws to third from the outfield. He calls "Cut" if the throw is wide, or if the runner cannot be retired. No call is made if he thinks the runner can be caught.

The third baseman backs up second base on throws from right and right-center fields unless there is a possible play at third base. He backs up third base when the shortstop takes the throw on attempts by a runner on second base to advance after a fly ball to the outfield with first base unoccupied. He also backs up the pitcher on throws from the first baseman.

ACTING AS CUTOFF MAN

It was previously stated that the third baseman acts as the cutoff man when throws are made to the plate after hard-hit singles toward the left fielder. This conforms to the normal procedure on cutoffs and is described in detail under "Defensive Assignments on Throws from the Outfield" in Chapter 11.

STRATEGY

FAKE THROW OR BLUFF

When only second base is occupied with less than two out, the third baseman frequently fakes or bluffs a throw to second base after fielding a hard-hit ball prior to making his play to first. This usually prevents the runner from advancing. A runner on third base is bluffed back in a similar manner with a fake throw home, if first is unoccupied. The third baseman can also fake a pickoff at third to prevent the runner from taking a long lead.

THROW WITH FIRST AND THIRD BASES OCCUPIED

If there are runners on first and third bases, the throw is immediately made to the plate to retire the player attemping to score,

Fig. 10–2. **Fielding a bunt and throwing to first.**

or to second base for a double play from second to first. In this case the throw frequently goes to the plate with none out, and to second base with one out, depending, of course, on the position of the infield with respect to the score of the game. This strategy primarily concerns the first and third basemen when they are playing in and when the shortstop and second baseman are playing back. In such a situation a throw is usually made to second base for a possible double play with none out, if the opposing team is

a, b, c. The ball rolls into the palm of the hand as the left foot comes down on the ground.

d, e, f. The weight continues forward to the right foot—in the direction of the approach.

g, h, i. The arm swings up and across the chest for an underhand throw as the weight returns to the left foot.

Fig. 10–2. *(Continued)*

behind several runs, to lessen the chances of a big inning. Naturally, if the double play combination plays in, the throw usually goes to the plate.

The way the ball is hit and the reaction of the runner on third may influence the final decision because the third baseman may sense that a double play cannot be made. In this case he might throw home if the runner attempts to score. However, if the opposing team is far behind, this runner is generally disregarded.

SACRIFICE PLAY

When an attempt is likely to be made to sacrifice a runner from second base, the third baseman tells the pitcher whether he intends to field the ball or cover the bag. This, of course, may depend on the type of bunt. Frequently detailed assignments can be pre-planned to prevent the runner from advancing (see Drill 11 in Chapter 17). This is especially important when a successful sacrifice might win the game. If first base is occupied, the third baseman charges a hard-bunted ball and tries to force the runner at second base in the hope that a double play can be made. If a fake or bluff bunt is made with second base occupied it may be an effort to draw the third baseman in so that the runner can steal third. The third baseman must be alert for this play and return to the bag once the ball passes the batter. For a similar reason it is important to return to the bag after fielding a bunt with first base occupied, since the runner may try to advance to third as part of a bunt-and-run play. The third baseman must also guard against a squeeze play with third base occupied and less than two out.

SUMMARY

1. Block hard-hit balls because the batter can very often be thrown out at first base even though the ball may not be fielded cleanly.
2. Attempt to field slow-hit balls to your left because these are usually difficult chances for the shortstop.
3. Listen for the catcher's voice if in doubt where to make a throw.
4. Permit slow-hit balls along the foul line to roll when the batter cannot be retired at first. Pick up the ball if it rolls foul.
5. Field bunts with two hands if possible. Hold the palm of the hand toward the ball when it is necessary to field a bunt with one hand, permitting the ball to roll into the open hand.
6. Cover third base unless you are required to perform some other duty on defense.
7. Call "Cut" to the cutoff man (the shortstop) if a throw to third base is wide or if the runner cannot be retired. No call means, "Do not intercept the ball."
8. Back up a return throw to the pitcher by the first baseman. Back up a throw to second base from right field if necessary.
9. Take the cutoff position for throws to the plate after singles to left field.
10. Play in the base line between second and third bases until there are two strikes on the batter (with two strikes on some pitchers in sacri-

fice situations) to guard against a bunt.

11. Be alert for a squeeze play with third occupied and less than two out.
12. Play nearer the foul line with two out to prevent a ball from being hit over the bag for a potential extra base hit. Also play nearer the foul line when your team has a substantial lead, regardless of the number of outs. (See Chapter 4.)
13. Give way to the shortstop on fly balls in back of third base. (See Chapter 5.) Be alert for fly balls toward the plate because the catcher frequently gets a late start for these balls.
14. Fake or bluff a throw to second base before throwing to first after fielding a hard-hit ball with less than two out and first base unoccupied. Check a runner on third base for the same reason.
15. Be alert for a fake or bluff bunt with second base occupied. This may be specific strategy to help the runner steal third.

DISCUSSION QUESTIONS

1. What are the third baseman's tactics if a hard-hit ground ball is fielded with only second base occupied in the following situations:
   a) Third inning, opposing team ahead three to one, and none out?
   b) Sixth inning, score tied, and two outs?
   c) Ninth inning, opposing team behind seven to four, and one out?
2. Where does the third baseman make his throw if he fields (a) a slow-rolling sacrifice bunt with first and second bases occupied and none out? (b) a fast-rolling sacrifice bunt with first and second bases occupied and none out? (c) a fast-rolling swinging bunt with first and second bases occupied and none out?
3. Why is it possible for the third baseman to fumble a ball and still retire the batter at first?
4. Describe a game situation in which the third baseman permits a slow-rolling foul ball to roll.
5. When does the third baseman back up (a) second base? (b) third base? (c) the pitcher?
6. How can the third baseman use a bluff or fake throw to advantage? When is it advisable to use this type of throw?
7. What batting strategy must the third baseman guard against with a fast runner on second base?
8. Where does the third baseman normally make his throw with first and third bases occupied, if a right-hand batter drives a hard-hit grounder toward him in the following situations:
   a) second inning, opposing team behind four to two, and one out?
   b) fifth inning, opposing team ahead six to three, and none out?
   c) eighth inning, opposing team behind two to one, and two outs?

TRUE–FALSE QUESTIONS AND ANSWERS

T   F   1. A quick-thinking third baseman permits some ground balls to roll to the shortstop.

T   F   2. The third baseman steps in the direction of his approach to the ball in throwing to first base after picking up a bunt with the bare hand.

T   F   3. It is good strategy for the third baseman to throw some hard bunted balls to second base with first and second bases occupied and none out.

T   F   4. The third baseman covers third when a hard-hit single goes directly toward the left fielder with second base occupied.

T   F   5. Most third basemen place their feet together to block hard-hit balls.

T   F   6. The cutoff position is taken by the third baseman if a runner on first base attempts to score on a two-base hit to left field.

T   F   7. An alert third baseman always drives the runner back to second base with a fake throw before making his play to first if only this base is occupied.

T   F   8. The three most desirable qualifications of a third baseman are the ability to (*a*) field slow-rolling bunts; (*b*) block hard-hit balls; (*c*) make long throws.

ANSWERS

T   F   F   T   F   T   T   T
8   7   6   5   4   3   2   1

11

Outfielders

The qualifications of the three outfielders are normally evaluated on the basis of the duties to be performed. A center fielder, of course, needs to be the best outfielder because he has the most territory to cover. In this respect the left fielder comes next in importance since the majority of players are right-hand batters who hit fairly consistently to the left side of second base. A strong arm, on the other hand, is more of a requirement in right field because of the long throw to third base. Some coaches and managers also feel it is necessary to have a right-hand thrower in left field and a left-hand thrower in right field. These are all general guides which may be difficult to follow.

TECHNIQUE

FIELDING FLY BALLS

The majority of outfielders attempt to reach fly balls as soon as possible. This is especially true with the bases unoccupied, since a quick throw is not necessary after making the catch. This does not mean that an outfielder stands motionless and waits in the exact spot where he thinks the ball will fall. He does, however, try to keep the ball in front of him (Figs. 11–1 and 11–2). This prepares him for any peculiar action of the ball that may be caused by the wind, the weight of the air, or the manner in which the bat made contact. Balls that carry near the sun are exceptions. Many of these have to be kept in sight at all times, thus making it necessary for a player to regulate his speed in order to arrive at the exact moment when the ball comes down. It is also necessary to turn the head once or twice

179

A.   **a, b, c, d.** The ball is caught with the weight on the left foot. The weight continues forward to the right foot to throw, with a hop to get maximum power behind the arm swing.

e, f, g. The throw and follow-through. An excellent body position for this throw with the arm extended in the direction of the throw and the right leg in the opposite direction.

B. a, b, c, d. There is reverse foot action in this sequence, the ball being caught with the weight on the right foot. The hop is again used, going from right to right foot.

e, f, g, h. The step and throw. The arm and shoulder continue forward for a good follow-through.

Fig. 11–1. *(Continued)*

A.   **a, b, c, d.** The catch is made as the weight comes down on the right foot. Note the excellent fielding position—arms extended with the elbows bent (this technique may be observed in all of the sequences). The body pivot and step begins from the fielding position. **e, f, g, h.** The step and overhand throw. A hop from right to right foot could have been made from the (c) position to place more power behind the throw.

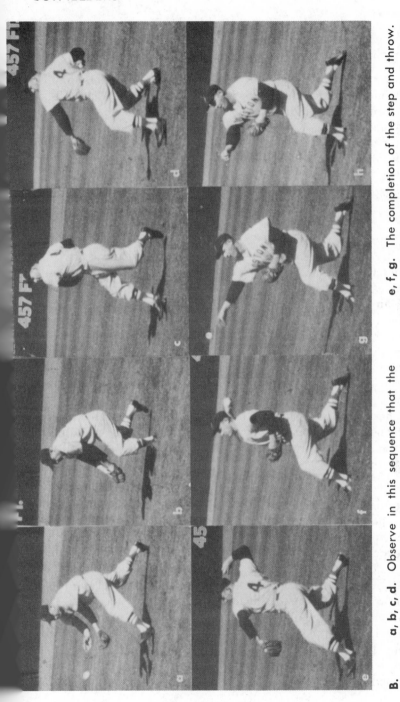

B. **a, b, c, d.** Observe in this sequence that the ball is caught as the weight comes down on the left foot; also the fingers are down because the catch is below the belt. The weight continues forward with a hop to throw.

e, f, g. The completion of the step and throw. The combination of a hop and the forward motion of the body places power behind the arm swing.

Fig. 11-2. *(Continued)*

to locate a long fly ball when running back. The fly over an out-fielder's head is the most difficult to catch so it is important to per-fect the technique of starting and going back in practice.

Calling for the Ball. Frequently either of two outfielders may be able to catch the same ball. The first player calling "I have it" is given preference, although at times the second player might make the catch more easily. The direction of the wind and the conditions of the game govern this decision. For example, if the wind is toward right field and the ball is hit midway between the center and right fielders, the latter usually makes the catch. If an important throw must be made, the player with the stronger arm attempts to catch the ball, provided, of course, a good throwing position can be at-tained. In cases of doubt, the center fielder is given the right of way.

There are times when two outfielders and an infielder or two in-fielders and an outfielder will reach a short high fly at about the same time. Under normal conditions the outfielder catches the ball be-cause he can usually do so with greater ease and because he is facing the diamond in position to throw. This is especially true when there is little wind or if the wind is blowing toward the outfield. As long as baseball is played, balls will occasionally fall safely in such situ-ations because it is difficult for three players running at full speed and meeting at approximately the same time and place to determine which one should bear the responsibility of making the catch. Each player is hesitant about saying "I have it" for fear another player can catch the ball more easily. One way to avoid such situations is for infielders to keep out of the outfield if they know a fly ball will be difficult to catch.

Playing the Sun Field. Experience in playing the sun field is nec-essary for all outfielders. Most fields are laid out with the sun facing the right and center fielders, but occasionally the left fielder finds the sun facing him—an unfortunate situation if the left fielder has had no experience catching balls near the sun. There are times when outfielders are not dependable even though they have prac-ticed in the sun field. This necessitates a switching of positions which might have a noticeable bearing on the game, since each out-field position has its peculiarities.

Outfielders are supplied with sun glasses to increase their chances of catching balls near the sun. Three types of glasses have been employed, but two of these are now more or less obsolete. One of the discarded models resembled the usual pair of glasses in that they

Fig. 11–3. Flipping the sun glasses down in starting for a fly ball near the sun.

were kept on the eyes while the player was in the field. The other discarded model was screwed permanently on the peak of the cap, and operation was necessary only when a fly ball passed near the sun. In this case the glasses were pulled down with the finger. The former proved dangerous because of badly bouncing balls, whereas the latter were impractical because they frequently became impaired owing to mishandling. The glasses in current use fit around the head with an elastic band. They are operated by tapping the peak of the cap as the outfielder starts for the ball (Fig. 11–3). Playing a ball in the sun is also described and illustrated in Chapter 1 (Fig. 1–4).

Playing Rebounds. It is necessary for outfielders to know how balls rebound from walls or fences. The quality of a wall or fence which may affect the rebound of a ball is usually determined by having the fungo batter hit several balls against it in practice. This also includes balls which may carom from obstructions in foul territory. If a ball is over an outfielder's head and near a wall or fence, it is advisable to run to this boundary then along it, if necessary, or retreat and be ready to play the rebound. In the latter case a pivot toward the glove hand is made to throw.

An outfielder who is not retrieving the ball or backing up the play tries to line up approximately halfway between the relay man and the player picking up the ball. (He avoids standing directly between the outfielder and the relay man.) He watches the runners from this position and calls the play (for the relay man). If two outfielders are chasing the same ball, the one that ultimately does not pick up the ball aids the other outfielder in a similar manner.

FIELDING GROUND BALLS

When a close play can be made on a runner, the ball is fielded with the feet in approximately the normal walking position (Fig. 11–4). This is especially true if the winning run is advancing to a scoring position, or the tying run, if the winning run is not on base. In this case the approach is timed so that a bounding ball can be caught at the highest point of a bounce if possible. An outfielder is then in a good position to stride ahead or hop forward to throw.

There are times when the status of the game warrants hurrying the ball even though it is doubtful whether or not the runner in question can be put out. This makes possible the trapping of a runner on the cutoff play. However, if the put-out is unlikely, or if there is a possibility that the ball might be missed if fielded in a conventional manner, it is best to block the ball. This is done with the feet together or with one knee on the ground (described and illustrated in Chapter 1). The feet together method (described and illustrated in Chapter 10) is preferred by infielders, whereas the one knee on the ground method is more popular in outfield play (Fig. 11–5a and b). Blocking the ball is particularly effective when a slow runner drives a hard single to the outfield with the bases unoccupied. Because there is little chance that the runner will advance beyond first base, it is best to make sure of stopping the ball. It is also advisable to block hard-hit balls when your team has a commanding lead.

THROWING

The best way to catch a fly ball to throw quickly is to make the catch in a natural way (Figs. 11–1 and 11–2). Two different types of footwork are shown in the illustrations. Footwork also varies for catches that are made while running. A hop-step or step and hop usually accompanies all throws to place power behind the arm

a, b. The ball is caught at the maximum height of the bounce.
c, d. The weight is transferred to the right foot with a hop.
e, f, g, h. The hop brings the body to a position for the step and throw.
i, j, k. The overhand throw and follow-through with the arm and body.

Fig. 11–4. Fielding a ground ball for a quick throw.

a, b. The ball is blocked with the right knee on the ground.
c, d. As the body is raised, a hop forward is made to the right foot.
e, f, g. The hop brings the body to a good throwing position.
h, i, j. The step and the overhand throw.

Fig. 11–5. Blocking a ground ball with one knee on the ground.

swing. It is important to return the ball to the infield immediately, even when a runner is not advancing. Any hesitation is the same as a dare, and base runners frequently accept the challenge and successfully advance.

An outfielder makes all throws overhand. The ball is thrown low so that it will reach the receiving catcher or infielder on the first bounce, except on short throws and relays. When the throw is kept low, the infielder acting as the cutoff man may intercept the ball and keep runners from advancing. Short throws and relays are thrown on the fly to the receiver. In the latter case the throw is made so that the ball will reach the relay man shoulder-high.

The direction and velocity of the wind are also factors in throwing. Outfielders with weak arms give this special consideration because they are frequently forced to throw the ball higher in the air to get distance. As part of over-all throwing strategy it is advisable for outfielders to throw between innings or during delays in the game; otherwise it may be difficult for the arm to respond efficiently to every throwing responsibility.

BACKING UP

It is very important for the outfielders to back up thrown balls to the bases and balls hit to the infielders and other outfielders. If possible, they run to a point behind and in line with the fielder and the player hitting or throwing the ball.

The *left fielder* backs up third base on all throws by the pitcher, catcher, and first baseman, and on throws from the right and center fielders in the territory from right-center field to the right-field line. The latter throws involve only potential three-base hits. He also backs up second base on throws from the first and second basemen, and those made by the right fielder from near the right-field foul line.

The *center fielder* backs up second base on all throws from the pitcher, catcher, and first and third basemen.

The *right fielder* backs up first base on throws from the pitcher, catcher, and third baseman, and those made by the shortstop from near third base. He also backs up second base on throws from the shortstop and third baseman and on those made by the left fielder from near the left-field foul line.

When outfielders see a runner break on a *steal* or *hit-and-run* play, they do not leave their positions until the ball has passed the batter, because a hit may be made to the place vacated. The same is true even though the catcher signals a pitchout, for on the hit-and-run play a batter will often be able to hit the ball unless the pitch is exceptionally wide.

Outfielders assist infielders on a *run-down*. They hurry to the infield when a runner is caught between bases and handle the ball if necessary.

An outfielder frequently misses a *rebound* from a wall or fence. It is the duty of the nearest outfielder to recover it.

STRATEGY

GETTING THE SIGNAL FOR THE PITCH

Since most hitters swing their bats a fraction of a second sooner when slow balls or medium-speed balls are pitched, some managers have their outfielders take a sign from the shortstop or second baseman for the ensuing pitch in the hope that a quicker start can be made when the ball is hit. In this case a closed fist means fast ball, and an open hand a breaking ball (illustrated in Chapter 7). If a slow ball is to be pitched, the fingers are wiggled. The fact that the control of pitchers is not always consistent makes this practice questionable. If a signal system is employed, the outfielders do not immediately move in the direction they expect the ball to be hit, but make ready to move. A change in position may inform the opposing team what type of ball is to be pitched.

DOUBTFUL CATCH

Many times it is questionable whether an outfielder can catch a ball in front of him. When one or more runners are in scoring position, on second or third, he attempts to catch the ball unless his team is far behind or has such a commanding lead that the run or runs if scored will not result in a close score. The ball is then played to make sure it is stopped. With no runners in scoring position, the ball is played similarly. An attempt to catch the ball may make it necessary to leave one's feet. If so, there must be little muscle tension; otherwise serious injury might result. Some outfielders hit the ground in a flat position with the arms extended, whereas others double up and roll. In some instances a slide is made before making the catch. If so, a bent-leg slide is used which is similar to the one used in sliding into bases (see Chapter 15). When an outfielder decides at the last moment that he will be unable to make such a catch, he drops to the ground and blocks the path of the ball with his body. This often prevents extra base hits. In this situation, with less than two out, smart outfielders frequently fake a catch to hinder advancement.

CATCHING FLY BALLS

Hard-hit balls that carry low and on a line near the foul lines always curve toward foul territory. The left and right fielders give this point special consideration with the winning run on third base and less than two outs in the first or last half of the last inning. In this case long fly balls that are too deep to be thrown to the plate and short fly balls or line drives that curve into foul territory and result in the outfielder being out of position to throw are often allowed to drop. This is particularly true in the last half of the last inning, because if the runner scores the game is over.

TRAPPING A FLY BALL

An outfielder infrequently traps a fly ball in short center field with first and second bases or all the bases occupied and less than two out and then throws to second base and starts a double play. This corresponds to an infielder trapping a line drive or a bunted ball as described in Chapter 5.

THROWING AFTER CATCHING A SHORT FLY BALL

If a short fly ball is caught, it is thrown to the plate regardless of whether first and third bases, second and third bases, or all of the bases are occupied. The chances are that a player will not try to advance on such a ball. Even if he does, and the throw is wide of the plate, the first baseman can intercept the ball from the cutoff position and make a play on the runner for whom the throw was intended or on another player who might try to advance.

THROWING AFTER CATCHING A LONG FLY BALL

When all of the bases are occupied, long fly balls are thrown to second base if the runner on first base is tagged up. If the runner on first base is not tagged up and the one on second base is, the ball is generally thrown to third base. This principle is followed with runners on first and second bases, first and third bases, or second and third bases. The nearest outfielder calls where to throw.

THROWING AFTER FIELDING A SINGLE

When a long single is made to the side of an outfielder, the ball is thrown to second base if only this base is occupied. The throw is to third base if first base is occupied, provided there is a chance to retire the runner, or if by means of a cutoff play the batter can be prevented from reaching second base. Sharp singles directly toward an outfielder are thrown home with only second base occupied, and to third base with only first base occupied. The throw with first and second bases or with all of the bases occupied is either to the plate or to third base, depending on the speed of the runner and the stage of the game. In some cases a throw to second base might be the logical play, particularly when your team has a substantial lead; or it may be used to prevent the tying or winning run from advancing to a scoring position.

If a hit is made on a hit-and-run play, the ball is thrown to second base on almost all occasions. The exception occurs when a weak hitter who is played close to the infield hits sharply and directly to the outfielder. The ball is then played to third base when only first base is occupied. If first and second bases are occupied, the ball is thrown either to third base or to home. The stage of the game and the speed of the base runner determine this decision.

THROWING AFTER FIELDING A TWO-BASE HIT

Two-base hits are thrown to third base when hit into the territory between the left-field foul line and the center fielder, and to second base if hit between the right-field foul line and the center fielder, unless there is a runner on first base. If first base is occupied, the throw goes to the relay man, who lines up with home because the runner may attempt to score.

DEFENSIVE ASSIGNMENTS ON THROWS
FROM THE OUTFIELD

As part of over-all team strategy, every player must execute assignments of covering and backing up bases and acting as relay or cutoff man when a ball is hit to the outfield. Then if the outfielder

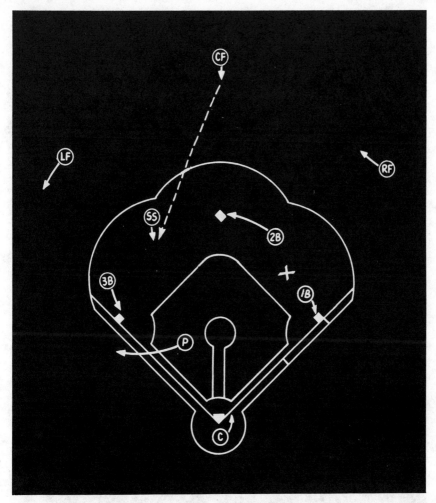

Diag. 11–1. Single to left, center, or right field with first base occupied.

makes the proper throw, there is a chance that a base runner might be caught attempting to advance or might be prevented from advancing.

Diags. 11–1 to 11–5 show how the assignments may vary. (The dash-line indicates a thrown ball; the X, a runner.) The assignments may differ further, depending on what cutoff system a manager or coach employs. Most teams use one of two systems:

Method 1: The third baseman acts as the cutoff man on singles, and the first baseman acts as the cutoff man on extra base hits, fly balls, and overthrows to the outfield.

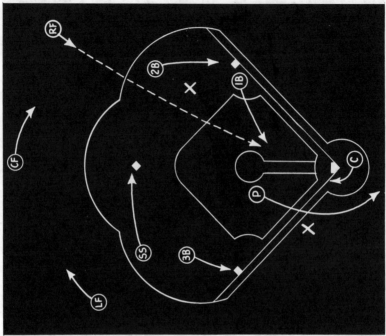

Diag. 11–3. Single to center or right field with second base occupied.

Diag. 11–2. Single to left field with second base occupied.

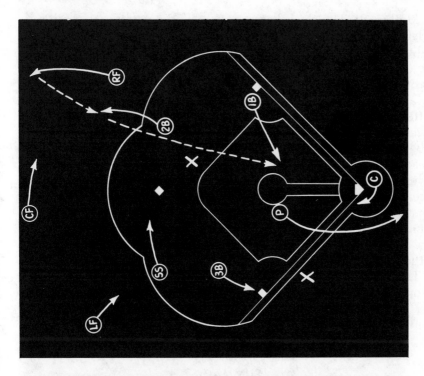

Diag. 11—5.   Extra base hit to right or right-center field with first base occupied.

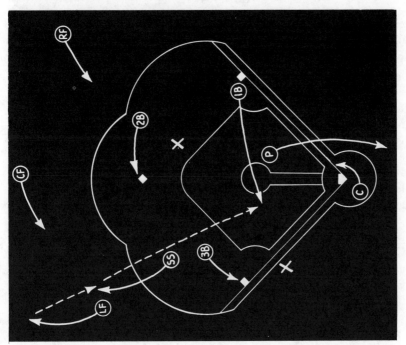

Diag. 11—4.   Extra base hit to left or left-center field with first base occupied.

Method 2: The third baseman acts as the cutoff man on singles to left field, and the first baseman acts as the cutoff man on singles to right and center fields, extra base hits, fly balls, and overthrows to the outfield.

Both systems have advantages: Method 1 because first base is always covered on a single, thus making possible the trapping of the batter rounding first; and Method 2 because third base is always covered, thereby eliminating the danger of a runner advancing to a better scoring position. The second of these seems to give the greater advantage, although this method makes it impossible to cover first base on some singles to right and center fields; that is, when the second baseman, the player designated to cover, has to pursue the ball and cannot get to the bag. On the other hand, the main objective of the cutoff play is to prevent runners from advancing, and the first baseman can usually do so from the cutoff position if the outfielder keeps his throw low.

The Method 2 system for cutoffs is followed in the description throughout this text. (Some high-school and college teams have the first baseman act as the cutoff man on all throws to the plate to simplify assignments.)

SUMMARY

1. Shift the weight forward when the pitcher is ready to deliver so that you are ready to start forward or to go back. (See Chapter 1.)
2. Play nearer the left-field foul line for a right-hand batter than for a left-hand batter unless you have specific information that a batter hits to the opposite field. Outfielders shift as a unit. (See Chapter 4.)
3. Move several steps toward a pull hitter's strength when the pitcher is in the hole—a count of two balls and no strikes or three balls and one strike. (See Chapter 4.)
4. Play deep for big men and players who take a hard swing; move in for small men and players who choke their bats. Play deep when ahead. (See Chapter 4.)
5. Consider the direction and velocity of the wind both in taking your position and in pursuing the ball. (See Chapter 4.)
6. Call decisively for fly balls, "I have it" or "I'll take it." Give the center fielder the right of way. (See Chapter 1.)
7. Practice going back after flies because these are the most difficult balls to catch. Practice catching fly balls in the sun. Use sun glasses so that you will be accustomed to their operation in the game.

8. Attempt to catch short flies toward the diamond because you are in better position to field and throw the ball than infielders. Fake or bluff a catch if you cannot reach the ball. This may fool runners with less than two out.

9. Guard against hard-hit balls that carry on a line near the foul lines because they always curve toward the foul lines—usually by a left-hand batter toward left field, and by a right-hand batter toward right field.

10. Trap a fly ball in short center field with first and second bases occupied and less than two out, if you think you can start a double play via second base.

11. Spin toward the glove hand after recovering a long hit or after taking the rebound from a fence or wall and make your throw reach the relay man shoulder-high.

12. Time your approach on ground balls when a quick throw is necessary so that you can make the catch at the maximum height of a bounce.

13. Block hard-hit balls with the feet together or place one knee on the ground (knee of the leg from which you throw) unless a quick throw is necessary.

14. Use a hop-step or step and hop to place power behind your arm swing on long throws. Time your approach to catch the ball if possible so that you can execute the proper footwork.

15. Return the ball to the infield as quickly as possible; otherwise, base runners may be able to advance. If you field a ball just behind the infield run in with the ball, unless a quick throw is necessary.

16. On a hit-and-run play make your throw to second base because the runner at first gets a running start; therefore he is not likely to be caught advancing to third base.

17. Make throws to the bases on the first bounce so that the cutoff play can be worked. A two-bounce throw is more effective than an attempted one-bounce throw which goes too far.

18. Back up bases:

   a) Left fielder back up third base on throws by the pitcher, catcher, and those made from first base and right field; back up second base on throws by the first and second basemen and throws from right field.

   b) Center fielder back up second base on throws by the pitcher and catcher.

   c) Right fielder back up first base on throws by the pitcher, catcher, and third baseman; also the first baseman (on sacrifices); back up second base on throws by the shortstop, third baseman, and left fielder.

19. Back up outfielders who are attempting to make catches or who are playing rebounds from walls or fences.
20. Cover bases and take part in run-downs, if necessary.
21. Yell to a player where to throw the ball if you are not making the catch. The proper call may depend on whether or not runners are tagged up.
22. Never let the tying run move to second or third base at the expense of a futile attempt to throw a runner out at the plate (the winning run if the tying run is approaching the plate).
23. Throw to the plate when an obvious two-base hit is made with first base occupied because the runner may attempt to score.
24. Make your throw to second base when a single is made in a run-and-hit situation (or on a hit-and-run play) so that the batter cannot advance past first; also on long singles (to the side of an outfielder) when a player is not breaking on the pitch.
25. Permit foul flies to fall with the score tied and less than two out if third base is occupied in the last half of the final inning, unless the runner can be thrown out.

DISCUSSION QUESTIONS

1. What are the general qualifications for the three outfield positions? Give the reasons for your answers.
2. Suggest a solution to prevent short fly balls from dropping safely between infielders and outfielders.
3. When can an outfielder employ a fake catch to fool a runner? Give the exact time the fake should be executed.
4. Describe the arm action of an outfielder in making a throw to the infield. What does the outfielder keep in mind if the throw is made to (a) the plate? (b) the relay man?
5. Where does an outfielder make his throw if he fields (a) a long ground-ball single with second base occupied? (b) a two-base hit with first base occupied? (c) a short line-drive single with second and third bases occupied?
6. Who is given the right of way in outfield play? When is there an exception to this rule?
7. Discuss the two methods of blocking ground balls in the outfield. When is it advisable to block the ball?
8. Why does an outfielder devote the majority of his practice time to going back for fly balls? Give two reasons for your answer.
9. When might it be good strategy for an outfielder to trap a ball? Explain your answer in relation to the location of the fly ball and the subsequent throw.

10. What is the proper stance for an outfielder? Describe the position of the trunk, knees, and hands; also explain the distribution of the weight as the ball is pitched.
11. Discuss the strategy of throwing in outfield play in the following situations: (a) the opposing team is ahead in the seventh inning 2 to 1 with second and third bases occupied and one out. A long fly ball is hit to center field; (b) Your team is ahead 10 to 1 in the fifth inning with second base occupied and two out. A single is lined over the third baseman's head; (c) The score is tied in the eighth inning with first and second bases occupied and two out. A pop fly single is hit into right field.
12. Why is it inadvisable for an outfielder to break from his position when he sees a runner start on a steal? What type of steal is an exception?
13. In catching a ground ball for a quick throw what is the first rule for an outfielder to keep in mind relative to the actual catching of the ball? What is a second rule to follow if the basic rule cannot be executed?
14. Where should the outfielder make his throw in the following situation: On a hit-and-run play with first and third bases occupied, the batter hits a ground ball single into right field? What is the reason for your answer?
15. State the back-up duties of the left, right, and center fielders relative to both thrown and batted balls.

TRUE–FALSE QUESTIONS AND ANSWERS

T   F   1. An attempt to catch a short fly ball which is difficult to reach may be poor outfield strategy.
T   F   2. The left and right fielders never attempt to catch foul fly balls in the ninth inning if third base is occupied with one out and the score tied.
T   F   3. Permanent sun glasses are less effective for outfield play than adjustable ones.
T   F   4. A line-drive single is blocked by an outfielder if first and second bases are occupied.
T   F   5. The center fielder seldom throws to third base if he catches a long fly ball with all the bases occupied and one out.
T   F   6. An outfielder usually makes his throw to second base when a single is made on a hit-and-run play.
T   F   7. Long throws from the outfield are frequently accompanied by a hop.

T   F   8. A throw to the plate which carries on the fly may not necessarily be poor outfield strategy.

T   F   9. The direction of the wind may determine which of the two outfielders should catch the ball.

T   F   10. An open hand means a fast ball and a closed fist a breaking ball when an infielder signals pitches to the outfielders.

T   F   11. In starting forward and to the left for a fly ball, an outfielder steps first with his left foot.

T   F   12. The left and right fielders never try to catch long foul flies with the score tied and less than two out, if third base is occupied in the last half of the final inning.

T   F   13. When a single is hit to the outfield on the count of 3 and 2 with the bases filled and two out an outfielder usually makes his throw to second base.

T   F   14. The climax of a run-down may find an alert outfielder on the infield handling the ball or covering a base.

ANSWERS

1	2	3	4	5	6	7	8	9	10	11	12	13	14
T	F	T	F	T	T	T	T	T	F	F	T	T	T

II

OFFENSIVE
BASEBALL

12

Batting

It is obvious that some players are more gifted with defensive ability than others, and the same holds true in batting. Although there are some opinions that batters can be made, most authorities believe that individuals are or are not potentially good batters and that, regardless of teaching, only a limited amount of improvement can be expected. This is proved in part by the fact that in major-league baseball many players compile their highest batting average in their first year. In other cases the first-year record may not be so high as that of some other year or years, but it is often higher than the final lifetime average.

Further proof occurs in the minor leagues, where a player either moves up to the big leagues quickly or remains exclusively a minor-league player. The same pattern is followed in the various classifications of minor leagues. A few players, of course, move forward gradually from one league to another, and even go to the major leagues. However, most of these players showed natural ability early, and a step-by-step advancement was necessary because experience was needed.

In the college field there is little difference. Either a player shows adeptness or a lack of it when he is screened. Since coaching time is limited, a workable squad must be selected quickly. Mistakes on personnel in this event are negligible; if there are any, they are confined to the final few men of the squad, who are not likely to make the varsity anyway.

Drop a step further to the high-school level, and the same situation prevails. The talent is there or it is not there, and baseball scouts usually have appraised the material long before the day of graduation. In addition various baseball schools that are conducted by major-league teams for this particular age group seldom uncover any appreciable talent not previously known. The logical conclusion, then, is that most batters are born, not made.

It is possible that the selection of an improper bat or a wrong position in the batter's box may have a detrimental effect on the batting of a player, but it is impossible to insist that a certain bat should be used or that the hands must be placed at a specific position on the bat. Nor can a player be told to stand near or far from the plate, in the front or back of the batting box, or with the feet close together or spread. Such things must be determined by individual players in their execution of batting, because everyone differs physically. In other words, each player must select a bat that feels good in his hands, then find the grip and stance that fit his natural ability.

TECHNIQUE

There are, of course, a number of common factors in batting, such as picking good balls to hit and watching the entire flight of the ball from the time it leaves the pitcher's hand. Courage and determination are other important factors because without these qualifications no player can become a successful batter. Some points relative to technique are also basic for most players.

BATTING FUNDAMENTALS

1. Stance: A fairly erect stance is taken facing the plate with the hips, shoulders, and eyes level, the knees slightly bent, and the weight equally distributed on the balls of the feet.
2. Hitting Position: The weight is shifted to the rear foot, the front of the body is turned toward the plate, and the bat is brought back with the arms slightly away from the body as the ball is being pitched. Each of the five batting fundamentals is dealt with separately. Before reading the breakdown first study Figs. 12–1 and 12–2, which illustrate the batting fundamentals in action sequence.
3. Step: A moderate low step is taken toward the pitcher with the front foot during the approach of the ball.
4. Swing and wrist action: The arms lag as the step is being made, then whip the bat into the ball in front of the plate as the weight is transferred to the front foot. The wrists break in line with the swing as the ball is hit, and the arms roll to an extended position.
5. Follow-through: A pivot is made away from the pitcher, and the bat is permitted to continue, by its own momentum, to the rear of the body.

The Stance. A comfortable stance is employed, one that makes the batter feel at ease regardless of the pitcher or the batting pres-

a, b. Stance and hitting position—note hips are turned in (b), bringing right shoulder nearer plate.

c, d. Step and start of swing.

e, f, g. Swing: Arms and wrists roll—body pivots to complete swing.

h, i, j, k. Hips move with bat—front leg is straight as bat makes contact.

Fig. 12—1.   Batting fundamentals: left-hand batter.

a. Stance and hitting position (note hips are turned in so left shoulder is nearer plate).

b, c, d. Step and start of swing.

e, f, g. Continuation of swing with accompanying wrist action.

h, i, j. Roll of arms and wrists, and body pivot to complete follow-through.

Fig. 12–2. Batting fundamentals: right-hand batter.

a, b, c, d. The square stance (feet about the same distance from the plate) with short stride.

e, f, g. Completion of swing and follow-through.

Fig. 12—3. Swing: from a square stance with a short stride.

sure. It should be close enough to the plate so that the bat can properly meet outside pitches. A number of players stand with their feet approximately parallel and at right angles to the sides of the batter's box (Fig. 12—3a). This is often referred to as a square stance. Most players turn the front foot slightly toward the pitcher, but too much of a turn may prohibit the free inward swing of the body which normally precedes the step (tension can be felt in the front knee). Some players face the pitcher with their front foot farther from the plate than the back foot. This is called an open stance (Fig. 12—4a). Others stand with their bodies turned away from the pitcher. In this case the front foot is nearer the plate.

a, b, c. The open stance (back foot nearer the plate) and low carriage of the bat.

d, e, f. Completion of swing and follow-through.

Fig. 12–4. Swing: from an open stance with a low carriage of the bat.

This is called a closed stance (Fig. 12–5a). It is more conducive to straightaway hitting whereas the open stance is best for pull hitting. Experiments with these stances or variations of them may help players who get into batting slumps or have trouble hitting specific pitches. For example, players who find it difficult to hit outside pitches may be more successful if they move closer to the plate and use an open stance. There is also a theory that an open stance is an aid to vision when left- and right-hand batters face left- and right-hand pitchers respectively.

The stance with regard to the front and back of the box is also considered, a position toward the front of the box being favored for batting against pitchers who throw a great many sinking fast balls

a, b, c. The closed stance (front foot nearer the plate) with high carriage of the bat.

d, e, f. Completion of swing and follow-through.

Fig. 12–5. Swing: from a closed stance with a high carriage of the bat.

and slow-breaking balls, and one toward the back of the box for batting against pitchers who rely chiefly on overhand fast pitches.

Although, as previously stated, it is impossible to tell a player to stand a certain way at the plate, a wide spread of the feet may prove helpful in the elementary stage of batting. This eliminates an early step and long stride, and helps to prevent pulling the body away from the plate. These are faults which must be overcome before even moderate success in batting can be expected.

Hitting Position. The bat is brought back with the arms slightly away from the body when the ball is being delivered. Both the hips and shoulders accompany this movement. The hands are held comfortably in front of the rear shoulder and the bat forms approximately a forty-five-degree angle with the shoulder line. Most batters hold the forward arm parallel to the ground. Some coaches consider this the guiding arm, feeling the rear arm gives power, but other coaches believe just the opposite. Actually power is provided by both arms. The majority of players hold the elbow of the rear arm slightly below the shoulder. This is a comfortable position and helps to keep the muscles relaxed.

Most players hold the hands about shoulder high because this seems the best control position for hitting both high and low pitches. Many players dip their hands as the ball is being delivered but resume the higher position prior to starting the bat forward. When this is improperly timed with the pitcher's delivery it becomes a hitch. Other faults include wiggling the bat and permitting the barrel end of the bat to hang below the shoulders. A smart battery takes advantage of these faults by pitching fast balls, usually high and inside. For a similar reason, it is advisable for a batter only to turn his head laterally with the natural movement of the shoulders and hips and to refrain from lifting the back foot.

Step. The actual planting of the front foot is delayed until the location of the pitch is anticipated. This permits stepping toward or away from the plate for some pitches, thereby increasing the likelihood of perfect timing and making it possible for some players to hit the ball where it is pitched. A slight inward body turn as the pitcher starts his arm forward helps to control the weight so that the step can be delayed and timed with the pitch. This also brings the wrists and body to the desired hitting position. The majority of players do not withhold their step in this manner but step early and as a result pull most pitches. These players are almost all good fastball hitters, because an early step offers the best means of hitting a fast pitch. On the other hand, they usually have a decided weakness against a curve or slow ball, since at least part of their weight is transferred from the back foot too soon. The player who delays his step has no such weakness, and because he can normally hit to all fields, a less effective defense can be formed.

In a well-coordinated swing the weight is transferred from the ball of the back foot to the ball of the front foot. This permits free movement of the hips, which is necessary for perfect timing. In order to feel the hip action, bend your arms at right angles to the sides of your hips and place a bat behind your back and through the angle formed by the elbows. Now swing the hips back then forward without moving the feet. The forward action of the hips actually starts the rotation of the body and weight toward the pitch.

A general rule to follow in batting is to aim through the pitcher's box. Then if the pitch is inside a quick stride and swing can be made to pull the ball; and if the pitch is outside the action can be delayed to drive the ball to the opposite field.

Swing and Wrist Action. The swing usually varies according to the grip. For example, players who use an end grip generally make a complete sweep with the arms, whereas those who employ a choke grip move the arms a shorter distance. The bat is whipped into the ball with loose arm action regardless of the type of grip. Some coaches emphasize this fundamental of batting by saying, "Throw the club end of the bat at the ball." This is especially true when an inside pitch is pulled (Figs. 12–1, 12–2).

The bat is swung parallel to the ground on pitches above the belt, but on low pitches the barrel end of the bat is lowered. Some players always use an uppercut swing even though they are not long hitters. A downswing is better, particularly on high pitches, because it increases the chances of line drives and consequently makes possible more hits. Attempt to hit the upper part of the ball with the lower part of the bat. A preliminary forward swing of the bat enables some players to keep relaxed in the batter's box, thus helping them to bring the bat into a pitch in the proper manner. This, of course, must be completed before the pitcher releases the ball.

Maximum driving power results from quick action by the arms and hips. To get the best results, keep the rear arm bent and close to the body. Both arms are extended as the wrists snap into the ball. The wrists roll after the ball is hit as a continuation of the swing.

The speed with which the bat is brought forward is a big factor in batting. Many players favor a very hard swing, which frequently results in poor timing. It is better to use a moderately hard swing and emphasize strong hands and wrists. The effort may be characterized as follows: maximum effort with the wrists and hands and about four-fifths effort with the arms. This permits the bat to do the work. The speed of the swing is particulary important when hitting a slow ball. In this case, it is better to stress meeting the ball rather than taking a hard swing. An effective tactic is to hit such pitches to the opposite field. This principle also applies to breaking balls. Of course, if the pitcher fails to hit his objective of low outside and throws the ball over the middle of the plate or over the inside corner, the pitch should be hit straightaway or pulled.

a, b, c. The high leg action and long stride.
d, e, f. The swing and follow-through.

Fig. 12–6. Swing: with a high leg action and a long stride.

In a well-timed swing, the bat normally contacts the ball in front of the plate as the weight is transferred to the stepping foot. This corresponds to the step and arm action in pitching or throwing, except that the front foot is more firm in batting. The striding foot hits the ground first in both cases, and the bat or arm swing comes as an explosion of energy with the complete transfer of weight. Actually it means the bat is swung against the stride. It must not be construed as step then hit, but rather step to hit.

The swing in relation to the action of the wrists is particularly important if the batter is attempting to hit to the opposite field, or, as often happens, when a right-handed batter tries to hit an outside pitch behind the runner. In this event the hands move ahead of the hitting end of the bat, and a short snap of the wrist is employed instead of the conventional swing because the ball is hit late. The elbow of the rear arm passes along the belt line, and there is fast but short hip action. (Fig. 12–8.)

The main objective of the batter is, of course, to advance base runners. This is very important when a runner (or runners) is breaking on the pitch, particularly on the count of 3—1 and 3—2 with less than two out because the break is then based on strategy and not the ability of the runner to steal. In this case the batter should attempt to hit the ball on the ground (unless the pitch is outside the strike zone.)

The swing actually originates with a pulling action by the front arm. This delays the uncocking of the wrists and makes for live hands, which are necessary for successful batting.

Follow-Through. Perfect balance, with the body leaning toward the direction of the batted ball, is characteristic of a good follow-through. The front foot is solidly planted, but only the back toe rests on the ground. This places the entire weight behind the swing and makes possible maximum driving power. The actual body turn varies according to where the ball is hit, a complete turn being executed when inside pitches are pulled (quick and full pivot of the hips), and less of a turn on drives to the opposite field. Both hands are usually kept on the bat through the entire swing. However, a few players drive the ball for distance even though they remove the top hand shortly after contact, thus proving that power is attained in the first half of the swing.

SELECTING A BAT

Length, weight, and balance are considered in selecting a bat. Requirements vary, of course, according to the physical characteristics of the player. The majority of major-league players favor a 34½-inch, 32-ounce bat. Because these measurements seem to give the greatest balance and swinging effectiveness, it is logical to assume that most players should use these lengths and weights, or shorter and lighter bats, not longer and heavier bats. A point which should be considered in this connection is the fact that about four out of every seven pitches are usually fast balls. This makes it doubly important to select a light bat. A properly weighted bat is also considered throughout the season because illness or loss of weight may make it advisable to switch to a lighter bat.

THE GRIP

The bat is usually gripped at the end or about an inch or an inch and a half from the end, with the hand of the forward arm rest-

a, b, c. The crouched stance and dip of the front shoulder.
d, e. The delayed action of the arms—behind the pivot of the body.
f, g. The swing and wrist action.
h. The follow-through of the arms and body.

Fig. 12–7. Swing: from a slight crouch with a front shoulder dip.

ing nearer the handle end of the bat. The former is commonly called an end grip and the latter a modified choke grip. A position of the hands several inches from the end is considered a choke grip. Both hands are normally on the bat and rest against each other (Fig. 12-9). A few players have employed unique grips to advantage.

a, b, c. The hands move ahead of the bat—the elbow of the rear arm passes along the belt line.

d, e. The ball is hit late with short hip and wrist action.

f, g, h. Completion of swing—roll of wrists and follow through of arms and body.

Fig. 12—8. Swing: at an outside pitch.

However, the grips shown are basic for most players. In gripping the bat the middle knuckles of the top hand should never be lined up beyond the base knuckles of the bottom hand. The bat should also rest lightly in the fingers toward the front of the hands regardless of the type grip, thus keeping the muscles relaxed for an effective swing. It is also important to keep the trademark up when the bat is swung (if a wooden bat is used), to avoid breakage.

Variations in batting technique can best be determined by analyzing a series of batters (Figs. 12–1 to 12–8). The stance, hitting position, step and swing, and even the follow-through differ to some degree for all of these players. This would be true for any group of players, and some might have unusual batting characteristics. For example, Heine Groh used a bottle-shaped bat and faced the pitcher; Mel Ott lifted his front foot high and lowered the arms in the early stage of batting; Earl Averill swept at the ball with stiff arm action; and both Joe Medwick and Al Simmons pulled away from the plate. Perhaps these players would have been better batters if they had used more conventional standards, but in view of their major-league records it would seem that their styles, whatever they might have been, were satisfactory. The point is that these players developed methods of batting which conformed to their natural ability, and an attempt to alter them would probably have meant unnaturalness and less effectiveness in batting.

STRATEGY

ANTICIPATION OF PITCH

Most players always look for a fast ball. It is better to anticipate an outside pitch and concentrate on a delayed step and swing. If you follow this suggestion it may be difficult to get the bat around on inside fast balls but these are seldom strikes anyway because they are thrown primarily to bait the batter into swinging. A late swing, of course, enables a player to hit outside pitches to the opposite field. It also keeps the hands and hips in the ready position to hit breaking balls and off-speed pitches. If you employ this batting theory, no pitcher can throw the ball by you outside, and the late action of the wrists and hips will enable you to hit most pitches which are over the plate, including some inside fast balls.

Confidence. A player who believes he can hit, of course, has the best chance to become a good batter; therefore, it is important to feel that you can get a hit, regardless of who is on the mound. After-all, every pitcher has to throw the ball into the strike zone and in each time at bat a player usually gets at least one pitch to his liking. You can improve as a batter by learning to time the stride and swing to hit inside and outside strikes. These fundamentals of batting can be practiced with a tee (Fig. A–8 and Fig. A–9, pages 396 and 397).

Modified-choke grip

End grip   Choke grip

Fig. 12—9. Batting Grips

HITTING THE FIRST STRIKE

As a general rule the batter attempts to hit the first good strike with a runner or runners in scoring position except when the count is three balls and no strikes, provided the run or runs, if scored, will increase a lead, break a tie score, or reduce the margin of the opposing team to a point where the score will be close. This includes a sacrifice situation if a bunt signal is not given, because the defense is usually out of position on the first pitch. Of course, this eliminates the possibility of getting in the hole, and increases the chances of hitting the ball safely. The batter is careful, however, not to swing at a questionable pitch when first base is open—first base is open if only second base or second and third bases are occupied—and the batter is not the potential tying or winning run, because the pitcher frequently attempts to pitch every ball to the batter's weakness in these situations, since a walk is not likely to prove damaging. This is particularly true when the defensive team is behind, or if the following player in the lineup is a less capable hitter.

TAKING THE FIRST STRIKE

The batter usually takes a first strike when the opposing team is more than three runs ahead, when the previous batter hits the first ball for an out, or when the pitcher has trouble controlling the ball. This forces the pitcher to make additional pitches and may cause him to tire late in the game. A fake to hit or bunt is made in such situations so that the pitcher will not deliberately ease the ball over for a strike, the batter meanwhile remaining fairly erect, to give the umpire an adequate strike zone, and watching the ball into the catcher's glove. A similar procedure is practiced, or a position taken toward the back of the batter's box, when the batter knows a runner is attempting to steal, because this may affect the handling of the ball by the catcher. In this case a fake bunt often draws the defensive player out of position and aids in the completion of the steal. If a player is stealing home, the fake bunt prevents the catcher from moving forward to catch the ball. It is important not to block the catcher in these situations because interference might be called.

When there are less than two out, and the batter senses that a steal to second is not likely to be completed, he attempts to hit the ball on the ground unless the pitch is outside the strike area for a fourth ball. This protects the runner and makes possible an improved scoring opportunity. On the other hand, if the runner gets a running start as a result of the pitcher winding up, the batter takes the pitch, unless two strikes are charged against him.

SWING AT THE BALL

The swing at the ball is frequently altered to meet the game situation. For example, when the infield plays in, emphasis is placed on meeting the ball rather than on taking a hard swing. The advantage in this case lies in the ability to hit the ball past the infielders but not over an outfielder's head. On the other hand, a definite attempt is made to hit for distance when the bases are unoccupied with two out, because if the batter only reaches first base it may be necessary for two additional batters to make hits to score the run unless the batter is a good base runner and can steal second base or the following player in the lineup hits a long ball. For a similar reason an attempt is made to drive a runner home from first base when there are two outs and only this base is occupied. It is also good judgment in some instances to swing for an extra base hit with first and second bases occupied and the opposing team three or more runs ahead. A long hit under these conditions makes it possible to score both runs, and eliminates a force play at second base, whereas a single will only score one and sets the stage for a double play with less than two out.

STEPPING OUT OF THE BATTER'S BOX

If the pitcher takes excessive time it is advisable to step out of the batter's box. In this case, it is necessary first to ask the umpire to call time. Such a request must be made before the pitcher starts his windup or gets set to deliver the ball; otherwise the pitch will be ruled a ball or strike in relation to the strike zone (unless the umpire declares an emergency, as a result of a gust of wind, for example). In college the pitch is ruled a strike.

WAITING IN THE BATTER'S CIRCLE

A player occasionally helps himself as well as his teammates by observing defensive weaknesses while awaiting his turn at bat. For example, the movement of an infielder or mannerism of a pitcher may tip off a certain pitch, and an exceptionally deep position of the first or third baseman, or a poor follow-through position of the pitcher, makes possible successful bunts. Likewise, definite points involving the pitcher's method of working on the batter and throwing to first base can be noted.

Encouraging the batter and offering advice in the form of "You can do it," or "Not too hard," and guiding the runner into the plate are other important points. In the latter case the body and hands are used to inform the runner whether or not to slide, an erect position with the palms toward the runner meaning "Stay up," and a crouched position with the hands down, "Slide."

Seeing that the mask and bat are removed from the path of the runner, urging the runner to hurry across the plate when the third out may be made at another base, and yelling to the batter to run after a ball has been hit or after the catcher misses a third strike are other factors which are considered. In addition, assistance is given to base runners on balls that evade the catcher. Arm action is used in this case, the arm raised with the palm of the hand toward the runner meaning "Remain on the base held," and short arm action in the direction of the next base, "Advance."

APPROACHING THE PLATE

The batter delays his approach to the plate until the coach is free to give a signal. The sign may then be given early, thus permitting the coach to fake giving a signal when the batter nears the plate. This frequently confuses any attempt by the opposing team to steal signs. The batter aids in this matter by repeatedly glancing toward the coach to make it appear that he is looking for a signal. This is practiced regardless of the count, the score, or stage of the game, because it makes it more difficult for the opposing team to know when an actual sign is given.

Most players take two bats to the plate and swing these several times prior to taking their position in the batter's box. This makes the bat to be used seem lighter, and the swinging bat can be used to remove any dirt imbedded between the spikes on their shoes. In the latter case it is advisable to employ the hitting end of the bat for this purpose because use of the handle may mar the gripping surface. (Most teams carry a knife or sharp piece of metal to remove the mud on rainy days.) Some use a weighted bat for warm-up swings. A removable metal donut weight for the regular bat is also popular.

It is important to step out of the batter's box or refrain from getting into the box when there is a delay in the game. This is particularly important in the former case after a foul ball, because it is necessary for runners to return to their bases.

HITTING BEHIND THE RUNNER

Hitting behind the runner is an offensive tactic involving the batter that is usually attempted only when first base is occupied and there are less than two out. The object of the play is to advance the runner on first base to second by hitting the ball on the ground toward the opening between the first and second basemen. There is a definite weakness in this direction because the first baseman is playing on the bag. Therefore, if the ball is properly placed, the second baseman will have to field the ball; and since this means that he must move to the left it lessens his chances of making a force play at second base. When hit hard, many of these balls roll to the outfield for hits because of the weakness at first base. This is a decided advantage because the runner can usually continue on to third.

Hitting behind the runner is also good strategy with first and second bases occupied (or with only second base occupied) and preferably none out. There is more chance that a force play will be made at second base in this situation because the first baseman plays off the bag and is able to field many ground balls which otherwise might roll to the outfield. However, because it is unlikely that a double play will be completed at first, even though a force play is made at second base, an improved scoring opportunity is provided, since first and third bases are then occupied, with one out. This gives the batter the same advantage as with only first base occupied, because the first baseman must resume his position at the bag.

In hitting behind the runner, an attempt is made to meet the ball, rather than to swing hard. The arms are also brought down to hit the ball on the ground, the rear arm of a right-hand batter being kept close to the body in order to bring the bat into the pitch late. Some pitchers anticipate this tactic and try to pitch inside to a right-hand batter and outside to a left-hand batter. A right-hand batter often backs up from the plate slightly to counteract such strategy. This enables him to hit an inside strike in the direction of right field. The left-hand batter has an advantage in hitting behind the runner because he normally hits the ball to the right-field side of second base. Because most right-hand batters do not drive the ball to right field naturally, they must pick an outside pitch to hit in this direction. This is usually done until one strike is charged (or the count becomes two balls and no strikes), when the strategy is changed to straightaway hitting. When the first two pitches are outside of the strike area straightaway hitting is better since the pitcher is then in the hole. The runner on first base frequently breaks for second as part of this offensive maneuver.

THE HIT-AND-RUN PLAY

The hit-and-run play is an offensive tactic involving both the batter and base runner, and is usually attempted with only first base occupied and less than two out. Because it is strictly a gamble play, it is generally tried when your team is ahead, when the score is tied, or when the opposing team is ahead no more than one or two runs. In addition the batter is usually ahead of the pitcher, or at least does not have fewer balls charged against him than strikes, because the pitcher then normally tries to throw the ball over the plate.

The object of the hit-and-run play is to prevent the defense from making a double play on a ground ball to the infield. For this reason the runner on first base breaks for second as the pitcher starts to deliver the ball. The batter normally attempts to advance the runner to third base by means of driving the ball on the ground through an opening in the defense. The batter originates the play by giving the runner a hit-and-run signal, such as covering the belt buckle with the hand. The runner then starts for second as the pitcher begins his delivery. This makes it necessary for either the shortstop or second baseman to cover second base; otherwise the runner might complete a steal. It is through this opening that the batter tries to hit the ball.

The batter considers whether the shortstop or second baseman will cover second base, so that he will know where to attempt to hit the ball. This usually depends on the ability of the batter. As a general rule the shortstop covers when a left-hand batter is hitting, and the second baseman covers when a right-hand batter is at the plate. Therefore, under ordinary conditions, a left-hand batter attempts to hit the ball through the shortstop position and a right-hand batter through the second-base position.

The best time to attempt the hit-and-run play is with one out. In some instances it is good strategy to use it with none out. However, in the latter case the manager frequently has the batter sacrifice or hit behind the runner if normal straightaway hitting is not employed. Of course, this depends on the score, the stage of the game, and the ability of the batter. These are safety-first methods of advancing the runner. If they fail and the batter is retired, or if the batter reaches first base at the expense of the runner being forced out at second base, the following batter is sometimes given the opportunity to use the hit-and-run unless he hits a long ball or is a left-hand "pull hitter." The former may, of course, score the runner from first and the latter may be able to drive the ball past the first baseman, since the runner has to be held on the bag. The hit-and-run play is really more adapted to right-hand batters. There is no weakness on the left-field side of the diamond where most right-hand batters normally hit the ball; and besides, more double plays are started from this side of the diamond.

The hit-and-run play is also attempted with first and third bases occupied. However, in the majority of these cases the runner is started in natural run-and-hit situations, that is, with three balls and one strike or three balls and two strikes charged against the batter. The batter, of course, does not swing at a wide pitch with such a count because a ball results in a walk. On the hit-and-run, the batter attempts to hit the ball even though the pitch is outside the strike area. This is, of course, done to protect the runner. On such pitches the batter usually tries to hit the ball on the ground and disregards any intention of hitting toward a certain position on the field. In fact, he may even throw his bat at a very wide pitch to help the runner.

Infrequently the hit-and-run play is used with only second base or first and second bases occupied, thereby making it necessary for the third baseman to cover third. The defense is thus weakened in this direction, and the batter attempts to hit the ball accordingly. This is a decided advantage to the right-hand batter, since he normally hits toward the left-field side of the diamond. There is an added weakness in the same direction for a left-hand batter, with first and second bases occupied, because the shortstop is required to cover second base on an attempted double steal. However, since a player is in scoring position when he arrives at second, it is generally considered better judgment to let a left-hand batter hit straightaway in this situation rather than have him attempt to hit the ball toward a certain part of the field. In addition, the defense has no chance to make a double play on a ground ball with only second base occupied, and less chance to make one with first and second bases occupied than with only first base or first and third bases occupied, because the first baseman usually plays deep, thus permitting the runner on first base to take a longer lead.

With only first base occupied and the runner very fast, a batter sometimes bunts the ball toward the third baseman on the hit-and-run play. A well-placed bunt in this case often makes it possible for the runner to reach third base. This is a particularly effective play with a left-hand batter at the plate, since the shortstop must break for second to guard against the apparent steal; therefore it is difficult for him to cover third. Occasionally a runner scores from second on a similar play. A fake or bluff bunt in the latter situation may draw the third baseman in and permit the runner to steal third. It is better for a right-hand batter to work this play because he obstructs the catcher's view. A fake bunt followed by a swing is another tactic which may catch the defense out of position. In this case an attempt should be made to slap the ball by a charging first or third baseman—not try to drive it over his head.

SUBSTITUTE BATTER

It is important for a substitute batter, as well as other players entering the game, to report to the umpire unless the captain or manager (or coach) has reported for him. Failure to do so does not cause a game penalty, but the player's team becomes subject to a fine (professional rule). A substitute batter usually hits the first good strike regardless of the score, unless the count becomes three balls and no strikes. Because he has been sitting on the bench, it is a greater disadvantage for him to take a strike than a regular player.

SUMMARY

1. Employ a fairly erect stance with the hips, shoulders, and eyes level, the knees slightly bent, and the weight equally distributed on the balls of the feet.
2. Shift the weight to the rear foot and turn the body slightly inward toward the catcher as the ball is being pitched, keeping the hands approximately shoulder high and away from the body.
3. Take a moderate low step toward the pitcher with the front foot during the approach of the ball. Use a wider stance if you overstride. Most batters are pull hitters because they step too soon.
4. Allow the arms to lag as the step is being made, then whip the bat into the ball as the weight is transferred to the front foot. Swing down at high pitches, up at low ones and bring the arms and hips around faster to hit inside pitches.
5. Break the wrists in line with the swing as the ball is hit and let the arms roll to an extended position.
6. Follow through by pivoting away from the pitcher and permitting the bat to continue, by its own momentum, to the rear of the body.
7. Select a bat that you can handle, bearing in mind that about four out of seven pitches are usually fast balls. Most major league players favor a 34½-inch, 32-ounce bat.
8. Keep relaxed and feel and act confident in the batter's box. Courage and determination are important qualifications of a successful batter.
9. Permit the bat to rest lightly in the hands so that the wrists can be snapped as the arms whip into the ball.
10. Do not wiggle the bat or let the barrel end of the bat hang below the level of the shoulders and keep the back foot stationary. A smart battery may take advantage of these faults by pitching fast balls.
11. Study every pitcher because each has some weakness which can be exploited.
12. Swing at the first good strike when runners are in scoring position because you may get only one good pitch to hit.
13. Hit the first pitch if it is over when given the privilege to hit in a sacrifice situation. On the first pitch the defense is out of position.
14. If the previous batter was retired on the first pitch, take a strike to make the pitcher use energy, unless a decisive run or runs are on the bases.
15. Wait out a pitcher if he is wild or if your team is four or five runs behind.

16. Employ your normal stride or fake a bunt if you intend to take a pitch, but provide a reasonable strike area for the umpire. Move close to the plate and stay fairly erect.
17. Remain in the batter's box and fake a bunt if a runner attempts to steal home so that the catcher cannot move forward to catch the ball.
18. Consider the position of the defense because if the infield is in, there is a percentage in your favor to punch the ball past an infielder.
19. Call "time" to the umpire and step out of the batter's box if you have a legitimate reason for getting out of the box.
20. While waiting in the batter's circle, yell to the batter to run after a missed third strike or when a high fly ball is hit near the plate.
21. Assist a runner trying to score and remove the bat or mask from the base line if the catcher fails to do so.
22. Analyze each game situation and be alert for signals as you approach the plate.
23. When hitting behind the runner, select an inside or outside pitch (inside for a left-hand batter and outside for a right-hand batter) and try to drive the ball on the ground past first base.
24. Always attempt to hit the ensuing pitch on a hit-and-run play and preferably on the ground to prevent a possible double play.
25. If you enter the game as a substitute batter, hit the first strike to your liking unless the count becomes three balls and no strikes.

DISCUSSION QUESTIONS

1. Discuss the relationship between stride, swing, and weight control in batting. Which of these is most important?
2. What are the main factors to consider in the selection of a bat? Suggest three ways to grip a bat. Explain the advantage of each.
3. Is it possible for a batter to hit successfully if a high step and long stride are used? Give the reason for your answer.
4. Why are most players able to hit fast pitches better than slow balls and curves? How is this sometimes overcome?
5. When is it logical for the batter to attempt to hit the ball for extra bases?
6. What defensive weaknesses encourage an attempt to hit the ball behind the runner? Why is this often good strategy even though the batter is retired at first?
7. Explain the action of a batter who is taking a pitch. In what respect is the umpire involved?

8. When is it advisable to hit the first pitch? take the first pitch? Do you recommend any exceptions to this procedure?

9. Describe the hit-and-run as it relates to left- and right-hand batters. What is the main objective of the play?

10. How can a succeeding batter be helpful to his team? Explain your answer in relation to the preceding batter and runners on base.

TRUE–FALSE QUESTIONS AND ANSWERS

T F   1. Expert coaching is not likely to produce a great amount of improvement in an individual's batting.

T F   2. Players who stand with their feet widely spread are seldom good batters.

T F   3. Long hitters generally hold the bat on the end because a choke grip does not permit a free arm swing.

T F   4. A high carriage of the bat is recommended even though low balls are more difficult to hit than high ones.

T F   5. Maximum driving power can only be obtained if the batter grips the bat tightly throughout the entire swing.

T F   6. The batter usually refrains from swinging at a pitch outside the strike area on the hit-and-run play.

T F   7. A player who is considered a good curve-ball hitter is more likely to be a better batter than one who is known as a good fast-ball hitter.

T F   8. On pitches above the belt a downswing is more effective than an upswing.

T F   9. It may be good strategy for three consecutive batters to hit first pitches even though an out occurs each time at bat.

T F 10. The terms "hit-and-run" and "run-and-hit" are interchangeable.

ANSWERS

F T T T F F T T F T
10 9 8 7 6 5 4 3 2 1

13

Bunting

There are two types of bunts: the sacrifice or team bunt, so characterized because it is executed to advance a base runner or runners at the expense of the bunter; and the individual offensive bunt, an offensive means for individual players to reach first base by surprising the defense. The former is ordinarily a very easy-hit ball, and is not necessarily perfectly disguised because it is usually anticipated. The latter is either a short bunt similar to a sacrifice, or a harder-hit drag or push bunt, and is concealed as much as possible to increase the runner's chances of reaching first base safely.

TECHNIQUE

SACRIFICE BUNT

The sacrifice bunt is made by pivoting toward the pitcher from the normal hitting position, or by shifting the feet and facing the pitcher. In both methods the trunk, knees, and elbows are slightly bent and the arms are extended. The legs are comfortably spread with the weight on the balls of the feet. It is important to hold the bat parallel to the ground in front of the plate and angled according to the direction of the bunt. The hand nearest the handle controls the bat. This hand remains stationary, and the other hand is moved up the hitting surface to about the trademark. The bat rests lightly on the fore and middle fingers with the thumb on top (Fig. 13–1a, b). Another method is to let the bat rest on the tips of the fingers. In the former method the fingers are angled to the side, whereas in the latter method the fingers and thumb point in the direction in which the ball is to be bunted.

The bat is held stationary in making the sacrifice; in other words, a player makes the ball come to the bat, and does not attempt to start from the plate until the ball is bunted (Fig. 13–1c, d). This is frequently described as catching the ball on the bat. Young players often place too much emphasis on concealing their intention when sacrificing. As a consequence the body is frequently brought into the bunting position late. This means that the bat is moving forward as the bunt is made, thus making it less likely that a runner or runners will be advanced, because the ball travels faster toward the defense. As has been previously mentioned, the defense usually anticipates a sacrifice; therefore coming to an effective bunting position and making a good bunt is of greater importance than fooling the opposition.

The method of taking the bunting position facing the pitcher varies for players because batting stances differ. Normally players who stand close to the plate merely pivot on the back foot and turn toward the pitcher. Players who stand away from the plate, on the other hand, usually pivot on the front foot, making sure not to step beyond the batter's box with the inside foot as the bunting position is taken. This often requires a supplementary step left with the pivot foot to give the proper distribution of weight. In either case the position is toward the front of the box. This increases the chances for a well-placed bunt and gives the defense less time to make a play.

INDIVIDUAL OFFENSIVE BUNTS

In all individual offensive bunts it is important to make the body action the same as that employed for hitting until the pitcher is about to release the ball. (The same thing applies to the running squeeze play bunt.) The position of the body and method of holding the bat are practically the same as for a sacrifice, but the batter is moving toward first base as the ball is bunted. Some players take a step which is almost identical with the normal batting stride in making the bunt, whereas others take a short step away from the plate, then stride in the direction of first base with the back foot. In both methods the ball is bunted with the weight on the front foot. As a general rule, individual offensive bunts are confined to fast runners. However, they are used occasionally by all players, or a fake to bunt is made to draw the first and third basemen closer to the plate, thereby increasing the chances of hits in these directions. A bunt is also faked if the runner on third base attempts to steal home, because to do so forces the catcher to remain behind the plate. In this event it is important not to interfere with the catcher; otherwise the runner will be declared out.

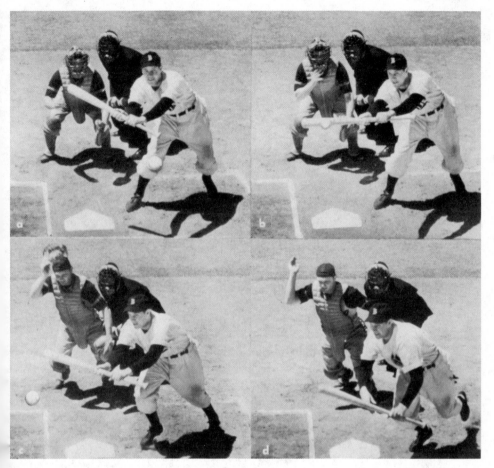

a, b. The ball is bunted in front of the plate with the body facing the pitcher (the weight is on the balls of the feet).
c, d. The start from the plate is made after the ball is bunted—with the foot farthest from first base.

Fig. 13–1. Sacrifice bunt.

The *short bunt* corresponds to the sacrifice except that the batter starts for first base as the ball is bunted (Fig. 13–2b). It is usually made along the third-base line, and is particularly effective against pitchers and third basemen who are not adept in fielding slow-hit balls (Diag. 13–4). This type of bunt is also a means to reach first base when a good fielding third baseman plays deep.

Fig. 13–2.   Short bunt for a hit.

The *push bunt* is an offensive tactic of right-hand batters, and is only made when the first baseman plays deep. The ball is pushed just hard enough between the pitcher and first baseman to prevent the pitcher from fielding the ball (Diag. 13–4). Unlike the sacrifice and individual offensive short bunts, the push bunt requires more tenseness of the muscles of the fingers, wrists, and arms. The push effect is obtained by extending the arms in the direction in which the ball is bunted. At same time the batter leans forward, and a step is made in the direction of the bunt (Fig. 13–3b).

The *drag bunt* is an offensive tactic of left-hand batters that is also made when the first baseman plays deep. Placed similarly to the push bunt, it is slightly different in execution because the batting box of a left-hand batter is nearer first base. This permits a quicker start, but necessitates bunting the ball with the bat in back of the weight. The arms lag as the stride is made, and the bat is carried at right angles to the side of the body (Fig. 13–4b).

Some players attempt to push or drag the ball between the pitcher and third baseman, a maneuver that sometimes works when the third baseman charges very fast. However, if either the pitcher or third baseman fields such a bunt, it is likely that the bunter will be retired because the first baseman is waiting for the throw at first base. On the other hand, the bunt to the right of the pitcher often makes it necessary for the first baseman to field the ball and then throw to the pitcher covering first base. This, of course, requires perfect timing and frequently results in the runner being safe.

The ball is bunted in front of the plate from the normal batting stride with the weight on the forward foot, permitting a step with the back foot for a fast start.

Fig. 13–2. *(Continued)*

STRATEGY

There are specific points which a player must consider in order to be a successful bunter.

SACRIFICING

A sacrifice bunt is usually attempted with only first base, or second base, or first and second bases occupied, none out, and less than two strikes charged against the batter. (A batter may sacrifice with none or one out and two strikes against him, but if the pitch is fouled he is automatically out.) This involves situations wherein the advancement of the runner or runners will make it possible to tie the score, break a tie score, or increase a lead with a single or a long fly ball. Since the defensive team anticipates a bunt under these conditions, the batter considers the number of runners on base and notes the position of the first and third basemen, then makes his bunt accordingly. The placement of bunts in varying situations is illustrated by Diags. 13–1 to 13–3. If the bunt is to advance a runner from first to second base, the ball is normally placed midway between the pitching mound and the base lines. In this event, a bunt toward the first-base side is usually effective, since the first baseman is required to stay on the bag until the pitcher starts his delivery. On the other hand, if the bunt is to advance runners from

The arms extend to bunt, the
weight is on the front foot, permitting a step with the back foot for
a fast start.

Fig. 13–3.   Push bunt for a hit.

Fig. 13–4.   Drag bunt for a hit.

first and second bases, the bunt is made approximately three or four
feet from the third-base line. When first base is unoccupied, the
ball is placed along the line or bunted moderately hard toward the
third baseman. In the latter case it is necessary for the third baseman to field the ball, which, of course, leaves third base uncovered.
The third baseman may throw a hard-bunted ball to second base
with first base occupied and complete a double play. A bunt along
the first-base line may prove just as adequate in the above situation,
since the runner advancing from second base must be tagged.

Aside from the fact that a defensive team usually anticipates a
sacrifice bunt and moves its defense accordingly, the pitcher is in-

Fig. 13–3. *(Continued)*

The arms drag behind the body to bunt, the weight is on the front foot, permitting a step with the back foot for a fast start.

Fig. 13–4. *(Continued)*

structed to pitch high inside fast balls to the batter because they are difficult to bunt on the ground. Therefore the batter looks for such a pitch under these conditions and stays fairly erect so that the bat can be lowered to bunt the ball. This means bunting over the ball rather than under it, as frequently happens when a lower body position is used, and may often mean the difference between a successful sacrifice and an out with no advancement. As a general rule it is much easier for a left-hand batter to bunt such pitches to the third-base side of the diamond and a right-hand batter to the first-base side. Consequently, these pitches are bunted with this in mind, unless, of course, the defensive player plays very close. This

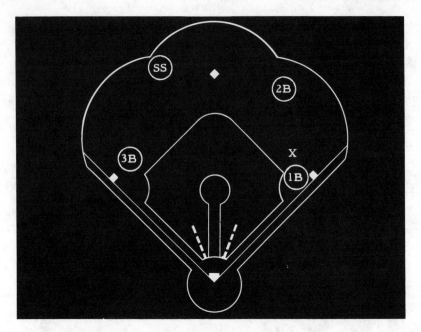

Diag. 13–1.   Sacrifice with first base occupied.

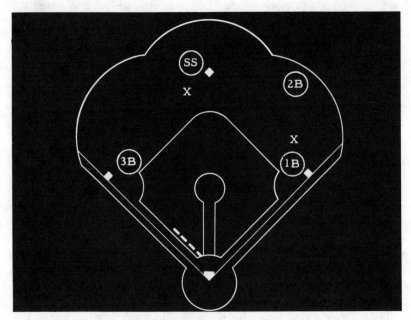

Diag. 13–2.   Sacrifice with first and second bases occupied.

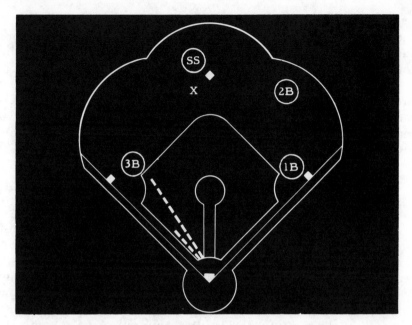

Diag. 13—3. Sacrifice with second base occupied.

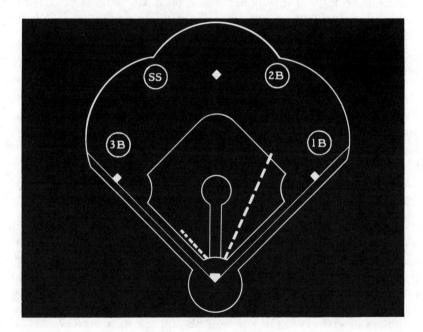

Diag. 13—4. Placement for Hits.

particularly concerns the first baseman when the advancement of the runner to third base is likely to tie the score or win the game. In such cases the right-hand batter attempts to make the bunt to the third-base side of the pitcher.

The previous explanation also involves the squeeze play. However, the squeeze play is not anticipated as often as the ordinary sacrifice because it is usually attempted when a long fly ball will score the run from third base. Therefore pitchers frequently throw low curve balls in this situation in the hope that a ground ball will be hit to an infielder and thereby prevent the run from scoring.

BEATING OUT A BUNT

In addition to the placement of the ball with respect to the position and ability of the defense, the pitcher's ability and the stage of the game are taken into account when the bunt is used as a means to reach first base. For example, a pitcher who relies on a great many curve balls and slow balls is more favorable for bunting than one that depends on fast balls. Such pitches, aside from being aimed low and usually away from the batter, approach the plate with less speed, and therefore increase the chances of a well-placed bunt. This is especially true when a short bunt is made. On the other hand, a fast ball can be satisfactorily pushed or dragged if it is outside to the right-hand batter and inside to the left-hand batter.

It is also important to use good judgment in making this type of bunt because no signal is given for its execution. For example, it is never attempted with two strikes charged against the batter, nor with two out, unless your team is no more than one run behind and the following conditions prevail: (1) the bases are unoccupied and you are a potential base stealer, or a long-distance hitter follows you in the lineup; and (2) third base is occupied and the defensive first or third baseman is in an exceptionally deep position.

SQUEEZE PLAY

The squeeze play is an offensive tactic involving both the runner and the batter, and it is worked with third base occupied and generally one out. The object of the play is to score the runner on third base by means of a bunt. Strictly a gamble play, it is usually only attempted in situations wherein the run, if scored, will tie the score, break a tie score, or increase a small lead.

There are two types of squeeze plays, the safety squeeze and the running squeeze. The former is employed when either the first or third baseman plays back, and it necessitates a well-placed bunt. The latter, on the other hand, is usually attempted when either or both of these players is in a short position and almost any kind of bunt will score the run because the player on third breaks for the plate as the pitcher releases the ball.

In the *safety squeeze* the batter attempts to bunt the ball so that the runner on third base can beat the throw to the plate with his normal advance. Therefore it is not necessary to bunt a certain pitch, but one to the batter's liking. For this reason a prearranged signal is not given to inform the runner that a bunt will be made. The runner merely keeps alert for such a play under the conditions previously described. This is particularly true if the runner is fast and the batter is only a fair hitter, although it is possible to score a slow runner with a well-placed bunt.

This type of play is often attempted when a weak-hitting pitcher is at bat with none or one out and first base occupied. Then the runner on third does not try to score unless the bunt is well placed or an attempt is made to make a double play by way of second base.

In the *running squeeze* play the batter gives the runner a running squeeze signal, such as pulling up the belt with both hands. The runner then starts for the plate as the pitcher is about to release the ball, and the batter attempts to bunt the pitch. If the ball is bunted, the runner usually scores because he is in motion toward the plate. This play, unlike the safety squeeze, can be used with a very slow runner, but it is much more difficult to execute because the pitch may be difficult to bunt. The running type of play is also used as a double squeeze play with second and third bases occupied. In this case the runner on second base breaks for third as the pitcher starts his delivery, and attempts to score on the throw to first.

Since the batter must bunt a specific pitch in the running squeeze play, a manager uses this tactic only when he thinks the pitcher will come over the plate with the ball; in other words, when the batter is ahead of the pitcher. It is very important for the runner to refrain from starting for the plate until the ball is about to be released; otherwise the pitcher will anticipate the play and deliver a pitch that cannot be bunted.

SUMMARY

TO SACRIFICE

1. Stand fairly erect because pitchers usually throw high fast balls in sacrifice situations.

2. Pivot from your normal hitting stride or shift your feet and face the pitcher. Bend the trunk and knees slightly so that the weight rests on the balls of the feet.
3. Keep the hand nearest the handle of the bat stationary and move the other hand to about the trademark. Permit the bat to rest lightly in this hand.
4. Let the ball come to the bat and refrain from starting for first until the bunt has been made. Making a good bunt is the main objective.
5. Bunt the ball slowly between the pitcher's mound and either foul line to advance a runner to second base.
6. Bunt the ball slowly along the third-base line to advance runners to second and third bases.
7. Bunt the ball slowly along the third-base line or moderately hard toward the third baseman to advance a runner to third base.
8. Always attempt to bunt the ball on a running squeeze play; otherwise the runner will be an easy out at the plate. The best time to execute the play is when the pitcher is behind because then an attempt is usually made to throw a strike.

TO BEAT OUT A BUNT

1. Lean the weight forward and break from the plate as the bunt is made. Some players use their normal stride, or move the rear foot back from the plate, whereas others step back with the front foot and take a crossover step. Hold the bat lightly, the same as for a sacrifice, to make a short bunt.
2. Bunt the ball slowly along the third-base line to beat out a short bunt. A curve is easier to bunt. Anticipate it when the pitcher is ahead.
3. Push (right-hand batter) or drag (left-hand batter) the ball hard toward the first baseman to beat out a long bunt.
4. Employ a fake or bluff bunt occasionally to draw the defense in.

DISCUSSION QUESTIONS

1. Describe the proper bunting technique for (a) a sacrifice; (b) a short bunt for a hit.
2. When is it generally advisable to use the sacrifice? Give your answer in relation to the number of outs, bases occupied, and the stage of the game.
3. Where are sacrifice bunts placed to advance runners from the fol-

lowing bases: (a) first base? (b) second base? (c) first and second bases?

4. Suggest two occasions when it might be good strategy to try and beat out a bunt with two out.

5. Why is it dangerous to bunt the third strike? When is this recommended?

6. Can a batter sacrifice successfully if the pitcher keeps the ball high over the inside corner of the plate? Explain your answer with regard to the position of the batter and the direction of the bunt.

7. What are the two types of squeeze play? State the strategy behind each.

8. Toward which base is it more natural to bunt the ball for a sacrifice: (a) left-hand batter? (b) right-hand batter? When must this procedure be altered?

TRUE–FALSE QUESTIONS AND ANSWERS

T F 1. It is good strategy to bunt the ball moderately hard toward the third baseman to sacrifice a runner from second to third base.

T F 2. A ball which rolls foul along the base line from the moment it is bunted is a foul ball even though it may eventually roll fair.

T F 3. Short bunts for hits are placed midway between the pitching mound and the third-base line.

T F 4. The most important factor in the sacrifice is that the batter conceal his intention to bunt.

T F 5. A low outside curve ball is easy for a right-hand batter to bunt along the third-base line.

T F 6. An attempt to beat out a bunt is not generally recommended with two out.

T F 7. Two right-hand batters who face the pitcher to sacrifice may use different footwork to attain the proper bunting position.

T F 8. In a successful sacrifice the bat is usually stationary when the ball is bunted.

ANSWERS

T T T T F F F T
8 7 6 5 4 3 2 1

14

Base Running

The fastest player is not necessarily the best base runner. In many situations speed is the sole factor, but in the majority of cases judgment in relation to speed determines the value of a base runner.

TECHNIQUE

RUNNING TO FIRST BASE

A batter, of course, becomes a base runner in various ways, but he is only required to run to first base when he hits the ball or when the catcher misses a fourth ball or drops or misses a third strike. (The batter is permitted to run on a dropped or missed third strike unless first base is occupied with less than two out.) The ability to start quickly and get into running stride often makes the difference between reaching the bag safely and being retired. In other instances it permits advancement which otherwise would be impossible. The key to a quick start after hitting the ball is a good follow-through. This transfers the weight to the front foot, thus permitting a first step with the rear foot (see Chapter 12).

The start on a bunt for a hit is slightly different since the main objective is a fast getaway. In addition, players vary as to their methods of bunting. All players, however, have their weight forward when they make the bunt, and hence the principle of starting is similar to that for batting (see Chapter 13).

There are only two things to remember when leaving the plate: to run directly to first base or to round the bag. (The batter runs directly to the bag if the catcher drops a third strike, but if a third strike or fourth ball rolls a considerable distance from the plate he is alert for a possible chance to continue on to second base.) Because the batter knows by the way he hits the ball which of the two

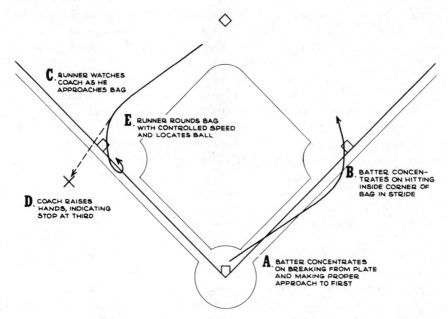

Fig. 14–1. Rounding first and third bases on a single to the outfield.

things to do, it is not necessary to watch the ball continually. This is important, since greater speed is possible when the eyes are focused in the direction of the run (Fig. 14–1,A). It also insures touching the bag. Thus, if the batter hits a ground ball that is likely to be fielded by the pitcher, catcher, or an infielder, he runs straight to the bag without so much as a glance at the ball. The run may be either to the inside or to the outside of the base line, provided the ball is fielded in the diamond. However, if the ball is fielded near the plate or along the first-base line and the throw is made from in back of the runner, it is necessary to run in the three-foot lane as prescribed by the rules. This is not a hardship to the left-hand batter because his start for first base is in foul territory. Because the right-hand batter, on the other hand, starts in fair territory, he must remember to run out of the path of the throw. On a straight run into the bag the runner normally continues outside the base line. (Fig. 14–3). However, he does not necessarily have to turn into foul territory after he passes the bag. He may remain in fair territory if his path is a natural continuation of his run and if he makes no intent to advance to second.

If it is possible to advance past first base, the runner bears slightly to the right and away from the base line until a distance from the bag is reached wherein he can coveniently turn and approach the bag in good position to continue on to second base (Fig. 14–1,A and B, and Fig. 18–1, p. 327). The execution of the turn is aided by leaning the body toward the base line.

In rounding first base it is advisable to run without watching the ball until the bag is reached. The ball can then be located to determine whether or not it is possible to advance, unless, of course, the batter knows that at least two bases can be made on the hit, or unless the coach points with both hands toward second base. This also involves high fly balls in back of the infield, because second base can usually be reached if the ball falls safely. In this case the batter is careful not to run past a runner already on first base. (A runner is declared out if he passes another runner.) A similar precaution is taken on long fly balls to the outfield because the player on base sometimes attempts to advance by tagging-up. The batter listens for aid from the coach on such plays. "Go for two" indicates to continue on to second base, "No, no" to remain on first base, and "Watch the runner ahead" to round the bag cautiously. In some instances the nature of the play makes it impossible for the coach to give any definite word information other than "Round the bag." The coach points with the right hand toward second base in this case. The runner uses his own judgment in these situations, making his turn and proceeding according to his ability as a runner, the throwing ability of the defensive player, the score, the number of outs, and the stage of the game. In some instances the ability of the following batter is considered.

RUNNING TO SECOND AND THIRD BASES

The path to second base on an uninterrupted run from the plate is a continuation of the curve when rounding first base, as are advances to third base and home. A similar path is followed if it is possible to advance more than one base when starting from first or second base. In this case the runner starts directly toward the next base, just as he does when running to first base from the plate, then swings wide to the right of the base line. The run is straight to the bag if an advance of only one base can be made.

A runner must use his own judgment when rounding second base. This is particularly true if the ball is hit or rolls into the territory to the left-field side of second base, because the ball can be seen during the approach to the bag. In other words, the ball is in front of the runner. However, when the ball goes in the territory to the right-

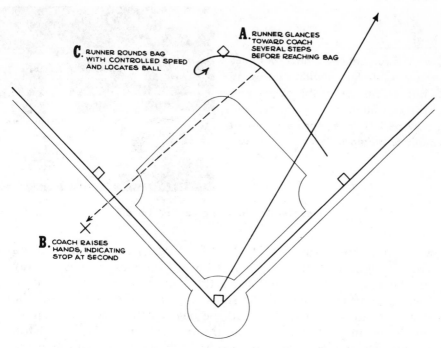

Fig. 14–2. Rounding second base on a single to right field.

field side of second base it is often impossible to know definitely whether or not to continue on to third base. If this cannot be determined by a flash glance at the ball, the runner looks toward the third-base coach for information, whose waving of the right arm means "Continue on to third base," and whose hands raised mean "Stop at second base" (Fig. 14–2,A and B). The runner continues past the bag under controlled speed if he sees this signal, meanwhile turning left and locating the ball (Fig. 14–2,C). When the coach points to the bag, it means "Stay on the bag." The runner also locates the ball in this case but he knows the signal indicates the ball is near the bag or a throw is coming toward the bag.

The runner approaching third base is completely guided by the coach because it is impossible for him to watch the ball during his run to the bag. (See Chapter 18.) Thus, if the coach crouches to either side of the bag and holds his hands down, the runner slides to that side of the bag. An erect position near the bag with the palms of the hands facing the runner means "Stop at the bag" (Fig. 14–1,C and D). The runner continues past the bag under controlled speed and turns left and finds the ball, as is done at second

a, b. The run between the 3-foot lines —to avoid interfering with a throw by the pitcher, catcher, or third baseman. **c.** The continuation of a straight run. (It may be in fair territory if no intent is made to advance beyond first base.)

Fig. 14–3.   Running to first base.

base on a similar signal (Fig. 14–1,E). When the coach, from an erect position near the bag, points toward the base, it means "Stay on the bag." The runner locates the ball the same as is done at second base, even though the signal indicates the ball is near the bag or a throw is coming toward the bag. If the coach is a considerable distance up the base line, the runner rounds the bag at full speed. This position indicates a scoring opportunity. In this event the arms again reveal the judgment of the coach, the waving of the left arm meaning "Continue on to the plate," and raised hands "Stop and retreat to third base." The runner also listens for the coach's voice, since advice may be given in this manner. For example, in some cases it is necessary for the coach to encourage the player to run as fast as possible even though the throw goes to another base; otherwise, the third out might be made before the run scores.

In running the bases, and also in long runs on the defense, greater speed can be attained, of course, if the proper running technique is used. This normally corresponds to the running technique of a sprinter. It may be described as follows: let the heel ride up in back, relaxing the upper part of the leg, and throw the leg forward from the hips and attempt to land on the back part of the ball of the foot. Meanwhile, swing the arms freely near the body, the elbows forming approximately a right angle, with the hands loosely folded and the thumbs up, swinging the hands alternately backward and forward past the hips and to a point in front of the nose. A controlled stride is best on wet days, in order to avoid the danger of slipping.

Fig. 14–3. *(Continued)*

RUNNER ON FIRST BASE

Once first base is reached, and there is no subsequent play, the runner remains on the bag until the pitcher straddles or steps on the rubber (Fig. 14–4a). This prevents a hidden-ball trick and applies to all bases because the pitcher must have the ball when he straddles or steps on the pitching rubber; otherwise a balk is committed. A position on the bag is also the logical place to take signals for the same reason. In this case the runner continually watches the coach for steal signals. This is important, even though runners may not have base-stealing ability, because players are frequently started as part of a run-and-hit type of offense. With first and third bases occupied, and a fast runner on third base, the runner is alert for a double-steal sign. If no sign is given, the runner looks toward the batter for a hit-and-run sign if such a play is used. The coach may also give this signal. The hit-and-run is also advisable with the game close, and preferably with less than two out and fewer strikes than balls charged against the batter. It applies to all players because speed is not a factor. The runner repeats the procedure of looking several times regardless of whether or not a sign has been given, meanwhile recalling how many are out, the score, the stage of the game, and the throwing ability of the outfielders. He must also observe how deep the defense is playing; if the base ahead is occupied; and listen to instructions from the coach. The habit of looking alternately at the coach and batter is a good one to acquire and is always practiced because it prevents the opposing team from

a. The runner on first.
b. The lead off first.
c, d, e. The walking advance as the pitcher starts his delivery—eyes follow the ball.

Fig. 14—4.   The runner on first—lead and advance.

knowing a sign has been given. The failure of a player to do so often indicates to the opposing catcher that a sign has been received and may be combatted with a pitchout. If there is doubt whether or not a hit-and-run sign has been given, the runner motions to the batter to step from the batting box, since this automatically cancels any previous sign. In the event that the runner cannot attract the batter's attention, he requests the umpire to call time, then fakes tying his shoe to accomplish his purpose.

It is important for runners both on first and on second bases to be alert for the pitcher taking a windup when a set pitching position is logical. This occasionally permits an easy stolen base.

In the last half of the final inning, a runner on first base should advance to second when the winning run is scoring on a hit with two out; otherwise the run may be nullified. This rule also applies to a runner on second with first and second bases occupied and runners on second and third bases with all of the bases occupied.

RUNNER ON SECOND BASE

The procedure followed when the runner has reached second base is similar to that at first base. However, in this case an attempted steal of third base is not advisable with two out because the runner is already in scoring position; therefore the advantage gained by reaching third base is not worth the risk of being thrown out. An attempted steal with none or one out and a left-hand batter at the plate is also considered poor judgment because the catcher has a clear vision of the left side of the diamond, and consequently is more likely to throw the runner out than if a right-hand batter

Fig. 14–4. *(Continued)*

were at the plate. Nor is a hit-and-run play attempted with second base occupied except under rare circumstances. A few right-hand pull hitters employ this means to force the third baseman to the bag so that a big opening is provided between the shortstop and the base line through which to hit. However, there is more chance that the batter will drive the run home by picking a good ball to hit rather than by trying to hit a specific pitch.

RUNNER ON THIRD BASE

When a runner reaches third base, he also follows a routine like that practiced at first base. However, he does not have to look for a steal sign because a steal of home is rarely attempted except as the second part of a double steal with first and third bases occupied. In this case the third-base coach tells the runner to try to score if the catcher indicates he will throw to second base. If the runner on first base is exceptionally fast and the score is tied or the opposing team is behind, the coach often instructs the runner to remain on third base because a throw to second base may not be made. Similar strategy may be used in some situations even though a throw to second is anticipated. In this case the coach reminds the runner to fake a break for the plate, just after the ball leaves the catcher's hand, to make the defense think that a double steal is being attempted. The runner does this from a short lead in the base line.

It is not necessary for the runner on third base to look for a hit-and-run sign unless the running squeeze play is used. A hit-and-run sign may be used for this play, but a separate sign is preferred because with first and third bases occupied the batter might be giving a sign to the runner on first base, yet the runner on third base would be involved.

With the count of three balls and two strikes on the batter, with first and second or all of the bases occupied and two out, all runners start as the pitcher begins his windup. The runner on third base runs wide into foul territory so that he will not confuse the batter. A quick break down the base line affects the control of some pitchers in this situation because they think the runner is attempting to steal home. The effectiveness of such a tactic is often increased by making the break just before the pitcher raises his arms.

THE LEAD

The runner takes his lead when the pitcher begins to assume his pitching position. This usually is taken in the base line, except when the runner is on third base, because it shortens the distance to the next base. However, some base runners prefer a lead in back of the base line at second to be able to approach third at the best possible angle to round the bag and score. The lead of the runner from third base is in foul territory to prevent the possibility of being retired by a batted ball. (A runner is declared out if he is hit by a fair ball before it touches an infielder, except when he is hit by an infield fly while standing on a base.) If the first baseman or shortstop take their defensive position in the base line the lead must be taken behind the infielder.

A runner moves gradually away from the base when taking a lead. The first step may be a crossover (front or rear) or backoff step. However, a slide step is advisable when increasing the lead. The pattern is: step sideward with the right foot, bring the left foot to the right, then step sideward again with the right foot to provide the proper base for the stance (Fig. 14–4b). Two things must be avoided: (1) A crossover step more than a step from the bag; and (2) a jump lead. These invite pickoffs.

A safe lead varies according to the quickness and speed of a player and the score of the game. A long lead unquestionably worries a pitcher but, unless a steal is to be attempted, it is not an advantage. A moderate lead is more practical because it permits a moving advance as the ball reaches the plate (Fig. 14–4c, d, e). A similar advance from a long lead requires stopping or retreating; otherwise the catcher may be able to pick the runner off base.

It is always important to watch the pitcher when taking a lead. If the defense plays back, the runner is guided by the coach. "All right" designates no danger, and "Look out" or "Get back" means to retreat to the bag. The runner on second base listens to the third-base coach. The lead at second base, except when stealing, should be such that the runner does not have to retreat until the pitcher indicates he may attempt a pickoff. This prevents the defense from specifically driving the runner back to prevent both a successful sacrifice and a potential score on a hit. The shortstop, of course, does this in the former situation and the player designated to cover in the latter situation, usually on the count of three–one and three–two.

The lead at third base should be a step greater, if the pitcher delivers the ball from a set position. This may provide the difference between safe and out in many base-running situations.

BASE-RUNNING STANCE

The base-running stance, whether the lead is taken from first, second, or third base, is a crouched position with the legs comfortably spread (feet approximately eighteen inches apart), the feet parallel and in the same plane and at right angles to the base line, the hands on the knees, and the weight on the balls of the feet (Fig.

The weight is forward, permitting a fast start or retreat.

Fig. 14–5. The base-running stance.

14—5a). Many players prefer to stand in a similar manner with the hands removed from the knees (Fig. 14—5b). To facilitate a break on a steal (or a retreat), a position may be taken slightly in back of the base line. This has the effect of opening up the stance, since the first step is not directly toward second but toward the base line which is in line with the bag.

Some managers advocate a short lead and a lean toward the next base for stealing and a long lead and a lean away from the next base if no steal is to be attempted. The reasoning is that the runner can get a better start if he is not afraid of getting caught off base and that a runner with a long lead will bother the pitcher. These are called "one way" leads.

START ON A STEAL

The start on a steal is made by pivoting on the right foot and making the first step with the left foot (Fig. 14—6). This foot action is reversed for a retreat, the runner attempting to swing back to the bag with the left foot. On an attempted steal, the runner takes short steps at first and increases them until maximum speed is reached. In the meantime the body is gradually raised from the crouched position. The eyes are focused on the base ahead throughout the start and run unless the ball is hit. Swinging the left arm forward and the right arm to the rear helps to make a fast getaway. A runner must have courage to steal. It is better to risk a quick start—a conservative break may result in an easy out.

If the runner is not starting on the pitch, he takes a walking advance as the pitcher starts his delivery, meanwhile watching the flight of the pitch. The basic footwork involves four quick, short steps, beginning with a cross-over step. This gradual movement means that the body is moving toward the next base as the pitch reaches the plate, thus permitting a quick start if it is possible or necessary to advance. It also enables a runner to return safely to the bag if the ball is not hit. If you take a slightly longer lead, a walk of three steps may be adequate. In this case the first step is made with the right foot.

Some pitchers are bothered when a runner on third base fakes a steal of home. However, a short lead accompanied by a walking advance is more practical since it frequenly permits scoring on short passed balls and routine ground balls to the infielders. If a fake steal of home is used, it is important for the runner to look over his shoulder as he retreats to third after the pitch. This will enable him to break for the plate if the ball is hit or evades the catcher.

a. The pivot on the right foot and lean of the body toward second base.

b, c. The weight continues forward, permitting a crossover step with the left foot for a fast start.

Fig. 14–6.   The start on a steal.

TOUCHING THE BASES

In rounding bases it is, of course, an advantage if the foot comes down on the bag in natural running stride. This cannot always be done in running straight to first base, nor to the plate if there is a possible force play; so it is often necessary either to break the stride, making the last step a short one, or to increase the stride of the last step. The latter method is frequently criticized because the body remains off the ground momentarily. On the other hand, a delay is involved when a short step is used. Undoubtedly both of these methods may be employed, an increased stride being advisable when the foot is likely to come down a moderate distance from the bag, and a short stride if it comes down a considerable distance away.

In running directly to the base, an attempt is made to touch the middle of the bag. There is less chance of an ankle injury if the bag is touched in this manner because the middle of the bag is generally a flat surface. This is particularly true when touching first base, since the bag rests above the ground. In rounding the bases, the corner of the bag nearer the pitching mound is touched with either foot, depending, of course, on which foot reaches the bag. It was formerly thought that it was necessary to touch the bag with the

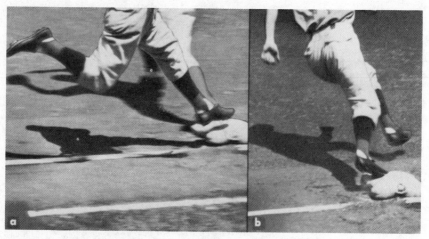

a. The middle of the base is tagged on a straight run to avoid an ankle injury.

b. The inside corner of the base is tagged when an advance is possible.

Fig. 14–7. Touching the bases.

left foot. This may be the most effective method of rounding the bag, but the fact that the regular stride of a player often finds the right foot coming down on the base makes it an impossible rule to follow. (See Fig. 14–7.)

STRATEGY

ADVANCING ON THE BASES

As a general rule the number of outs controls aggressiveness in base running. For instance, with none out, base runners usually play it safe, and only attempt to advance when they are sure the next base can be reached safely. Many rallies are thus started or continued, whereas the desire to take a chance often results in a put-out and subsequent curbing of the attack. Because the element of chance is increased with one and two out, even though the runner anticipates a close play, an attempt to advance may be good strategy. This is especially true with two out, but such a situation excludes advances to third base because the runner is in scoring position when he reaches second base. A similar situation exists when the runner reaches second base with one out, but the additional scoring opportunity at third base with one out often makes an attempted advance worth the chance. However, if a base runner is forced to stop or slow down to permit a batted ball to pass in front of him, or is delayed in any other way, an advance of only one base is usually advisable.

When it is impossible to advance after rounding first base, the runner stops and retreats, if necessary, to a position that will permit returning safely. This depends, of course, on where the ball is hit and the base to which the throw is made. For instance, when the ball is hit to left or center field, first base can be rounded farther than if the ball goes to right field. Similarly, when the throw goes to third base or the plate from left or center field, more of a turn can be made than when the ball is thrown to second base. This also involves throws to the various bases from right field. The runner fakes running to the next base in some of these situations to draw a hurried throw. This frequently results in a mishandling of the ball, thus permitting advancement.

When the throw goes to third base or the plate, the runner knows that a defensive player may intercept the ball and make a play for him. Because this is impossible on high throws, the runner advances if the next base is unoccupied or if the player who occupied this base is advancing. An advance is also possible on low throws if an infielder fails to take the cutoff position.

Ground Balls.   A runner must, of course, advance from first base on ground balls. The runner on second base advances similarly except in the case of a hard-hit ball toward or to the third-base side of the shortstop (or toward the pitcher), with first base unoccupied and less than two outs. This prevents being thrown out at third base, and keeps the run in scoring position. Another exception occurs with second and third bases occupied, none or one out, and the infield in. In this case the runner on second base must know what the runner on third intends to do. The third-base coach usually informs the runners not to advance with none out until the ball goes through the infield, and to advance with one out because there is a good chance the run will score. The runner on third base always advances on ground balls when first base is occupied with less than two outs, because a double play is often made or attempted by way of second base in such a situation. An advance is also made on ground balls to the shortstop and second baseman with first base unoccupied, if the double play combination plays back.

When advancing on ground balls, it is important not to interfere with a defensive player fielding the ball, for this constitutes a violation. If this occurs, the runner and possibly the batter will be declared out. Thus, when the ball is fielded in the base line and it is impossible to continue to the next base without interfering with the catch, it is necessary to stop and either force the defensive player to chase you or wait until the ball has been thrown and then attempt to advance (Fig. 14–8A, a and b). This often happens in running from first to second base. If the runner can continue his advance in the above situation, he must run behind the defensive player; otherwise he may be declared out (Fig. 14–8A, c and d).

The success of any bunt, with the exception of the running squeeze bunt, depends on the placement of the ball with respect to the defense. It is therefore not necessary for the runner to have an exceptional lead. The runner takes a short lead and normal advance and then starts for the next base if the ball is bunted. This prevents being caught in case the batter fails to bunt the ball. When the running squeeze play is attempted, the runner on third base also takes his normal walking advance with the start of the delivery and breaks for the plate in foul territory as the pitcher is about to release the ball.

Short Fly Balls.   On short and moderately deep fly balls with less than two out, the runner, whether on first, second, or third base, advances to a point between the bases from which he can return safely to the base he previously occupied if the ball is caught. (A runner on third base tags-up if an infielder is likely to make the catch running toward the outfield.) The runner stands in a position which is almost the same as the usual base-running stance and faces the player or players attempting to make the catch (Fig. 14–8B). This permits a quick retreat if the ball is caught, as well as an advance to the next base if the ball falls safely. If the catch is complete, the runner returns to the bag as quickly as possible, and gets ready to advance if the defense mishandles the ball.

The base runners know they are not forced to run even though fair fly balls are dropped, bunts and line drives excepted, with first and second bases or all the bases occupied and less than two outs, if an infielder is able to face the diamond in fielding the ball (infield-fly rule). On the other hand, because runners may advance at their own risk, it is advisable to be ready to run if the ball rolls away from the defense. An exception occurs if the fly hits a player standing on a base before it is touched by a fielder. In this case the ball is dead.

Occasionally the pitcher or an infielder may purposely trap a bunt or line drive in the above situation and attempt to make a double play. An outfielder may trap a short fly ball in back of second base for a similar reason. The runners are then forced to advance because the infield-fly rule is not in effect. In this connection it must be remembered that fly balls and line drives cannot be dropped purposely to force out fast base runners. The batter is automatically out if the umpire so judges, and runners are not required to advance.

Long Fly Balls. On long fly balls the runners on second and third bases tag-up. This also includes first base if the runner is fast and the fielder is likely to make an easy catch. An exception occurs if there is one out, because if the ball is caught and the runner on first is thrown out at second before the player crosses the plate, the run is nullified. This rule also applies to a runner advancing to third.

When it is doubtful that the ball will be caught, the runner usually advances as far as possible. When second base is unoccupied, the advance may be beyond second. In this case the bag must be touched on a retreat if the ball is caught; otherwise the appeal play may be used.

In tagging-up, the runner faces the side of the field on which the ball is hit, resting the toe of one foot on the inside edge of the bag. The body is slightly crouched, and the legs are comfortably spread with the feet pointing in the direction of the intended run. As the ball nears the fielder, the weight is transferred to the front foot so

a, b, c, d. The runner must stop—(a) and (b)—or run behind the defensive player—(c) and (d)—if a ball is fielded in the base line.

A.   A ground ball in the base line.

Fig. 14–8. Base running.

that the first step can be made with the back foot (Fig. 14–8C). This saves a full step as against pushing from the bag. It is advisable to break from the tag-up position even though it may be impossible to advance. This often forces an erratic throw.

SINGLE STEAL

The single steal involves one runner and may be executed from first, second, or third base.

Ready position between bases—
to advance or retreat if fly ball
drops or is caught.

The weight is on the forward
(or advanced) foot for a tag-up,
permitting a first step with the
back foot.

B. A fly ball in back of infield.   **C.** A fly ball requiring a tag-up.

Fig. 14–8. *(Continued)*

Stealing Second Base. A steal of second or third base depends on
the ability of a runner to start quickly with the pitcher's first intention of delivering the ball. Bases, as a general rule, are stolen at the
expense of the pitcher, not of the catcher. For this reason, base runners study the action of each pitcher when taking a lead. This is
particularly true at first base because the first baseman plays on the
bag and prevents a long lead. Aside from the fact that most pitchers
have very poor moves to first base, some pitchers lean their bodies
at the start of the pitch, some use high or excessive leg action, and
others turn their trunks toward the base in watching the runner, then
start the pitch with the front shoulder pointing in the direction of the
base instead of toward the plate. These are flagrant weaknesses that
aid a runner in his start. This applies to right-hand pitchers. Left-
hand pitchers are in a better position to make a quick throw to first
base, and the move of a left-hand pitcher is more deceptive, since
the start of the throw is the same as when a pitch is made to the
plate. On the other hand, a few right-hand pitchers have perfected
balk moves to first base and successfully prevented steals by this

means. They move some part of the body, such as the head, shoulder, arm, hip, or knee, toward the plate prior to throwing to first base. The object is to trick the runner into thinking the ball will be thrown to the plate and then throw to first base. This constitutes a balk, but often it is so cleverly disguised that it is not observed by the umpire. However, if the runner makes the pitcher throw to first base, he knows it is not likely that a pitchout has been signaled, and this is an advantage in stealing.

Stealing Third Base and Home. Stealing third base is usually only attempted with a right-hand batter at the plate. Third base is much easier to steal than second; a longer lead is possible from second base than from first because an infielder does not play on the bag, and the catcher is forced to throw over or from the side of the batter. There is also much less chance of a runner being caught off second base by the pitcher, since perfect timing with a moving shortstop or second baseman is required. The fact that an alert coach continually warns the runner when a defensive player comes near reduces this danger still further.

Stealing home is not advised primarily because it is almost an impossibility if the pitcher is alert. However, such a steal may be completed if the pitcher carelessly takes a long windup. As a preliminary to his break for home, the runner usually fakes a steal once or twice. This often leads the pitcher to believe the runner is only attempting to attract attention to affect his control.

When To Steal. All single steals are gamble plays, and therefore are only attempted by fast runners and under certain conditions. For example, a steal of second base is usually advisable with two out, your team in the lead, the score tied, or the opposing team ahead no more than one run. Or the opposing team may be ahead two runs with third base occupied. It is best to make the attempt with a regular batter at the plate; otherwise, the pitcher may have to lead off the next inning, and preferably with a left-hand batter, because he is more of a hindrance to the catcher. These are also general requirements for an attempted steal of home, except that a right-hand batter is more likely to prove a handicap to the catcher. (A steal of home is not usually employed when a team has more than a one-run lead, nor with a good hitter at the plate.) Similar points are also considered before attempts are made to steal third base. In this case the same conditions with regard to the score usually apply with two out. These are, of course, general rules and they do not apply to players with unusual speed and base-running ability. A pitcher with a very slow delivery or a catcher who throws poorly are other factors which alter conventional base-running rules.

The steal is used in fake form occasionally to worry the defense. This is done by taking two or three quick steps as the pitcher starts his delivery. The fake is also used as a means to draw infielders out of position. In this case the movement of either the shortstop or second baseman on a fake from first base shows the batter which player is covering second base, and may prove an important point should a hit-and-run play be attempted on a later pitch.

Delayed Steal. The single steal from first base is occasionally executed as a delayed steal. A casual fake toward first precedes the start, to make the catcher think a return will be made to the bag. This is done with a short step back toward first with the left foot (at the end of the four-step walk). Since second base is uncovered when the runner starts, the catcher is forced either to throw immediately, with the possibility that the ball may continue on into center field, or to delay his throw to make sure that the shortstop or second baseman will be on the bag. This is a particularly effective maneuver with both the shortstop and second baseman far from the bag because it makes the element of timing more difficult for the catcher.

DOUBLE STEAL

The double steal involves two runners and may be executed with first and second bases, first and third bases, or second and third bases occupied. With first and second bases or second and third bases occupied, it amounts to the more advanced runner executing a single steal and the less advanced runner following. For this reason it is especially important for the less advanced runner to watch the runner ahead of him. This is rarely attempted with second and third base occupied because it involves a steal of home.

With First and Third Bases Occupied. When the double steal is executed with first and third bases occupied, the runner on first base starts with the pitch. Meanwhile the runner on third base jumps about two steps toward the plate and stands on the third-base line so that it is impossible for the catcher to see the bag. This position corresponds to the regular base-running stance except that the body is slightly raised and the hands may be removed from the knees (Fig. 14–9b). If a player stands in this manner, the catcher cannot determine by a quick glance the extent of the runner's lead. The

a. The normal lead off third base.

b. The position taken during the pitcher's delivery.

Fig. 14–9. The double steal with first and third bases occupied.

fact that the runner is stationary also makes it impossible for the catcher to know whether or not an attempt will be made to score should he throw to second base. If the catcher's actions indicate that he intends to throw to second base, the runner on third base breaks for the plate as the ball is about to be released. (On some high-school and college teams the runner may leave after the catcher throws if the opposing shortstop and second baseman have weak arms.) The runner approaching second base, on the other hand, stops and, if necessary, permits himself to be caught in a run-down so that the runner on third base may score. Very often the defensive player covering second base cuts into the diamond for the throw and attempts to make a play for the runner at the plate. This permits the runner coming from first base to continue on to the bag and complete the double steal, provided, of course, the runner on third base scores (also see Note under Drill 8, page 300).

The double steal with first and third bases occupied may also originate as a delayed steal. Another variation begins by having the runner on first base start for second base as the pitcher takes his position on the rubber. (The runner may purposely get caught off base, then attempt to go to second base.) In this case the runner on third base breaks for the plate as the pitcher's attention is attracted to first. This play may also originate after a base on balls, the batter breaking for second as soon as he reaches first.

In some situations a single steal is attempted from first base with third base occupied. The runner on third base in this case takes a short lead in the base line, then fakes going home after the ball leaves the catcher's hand, meanwhile yelling "Home." Such a maneuver frequently causes the player covering second base to cut into the diamond for the throw, thinking an attempt is being made to score. This makes it possible for the runner coming from first base to complete his steal easily. Because a similar procedure works when the batter fails to hit the ball on a hit-and-run play, it is necessary for the runner on third base to be informed of such a play. If the catcher attempts a pickoff at third in this situation, the runner should retreat in the base line to force a high throw.

Some teams attempt to pick a runner off third base with a specific play when first base is occupied. In this case the pitcher backs off the rubber, fakes a play to first base, and then throws to third. The runner must maintain his short lead in such a situation, and not attempt to advance up the base line unless the pitcher throws to first.

With First and Second Bases Occupied. The double steal with first and second bases occupied is usually attempted with one out, and requires two fast runners, because a smart catcher may throw to second. It is strictly a gamble play and is generally used only when a team is ahead, the score is tied, or when the opposing team is ahead by no more than two runs. The double steal with first and third bases occupied, on the other hand, requires only that the runner on third base be fast, and is usually attempted with two outs. It is also a gamble play that is generally used only when a team is ahead, the score is tied, or when the opposing team is ahead by no more than one run. Since the former steal usually involves a throw to third base and the latter a possible throw, these plays can be worked to greater advantage with a right-hand batter at the plate.

TRIPLE STEAL

A triple steal involves three runners and thus requires all the bases to be occupied. It corresponds to a double steal with first and second bases occupied, since the most advanced runner executes a single steal and the other runners follow. This means that the runner on third base must steal home, and inasmuch as such a steal is difficult to execute, the triple steal is usually omitted as a specific offensive tactic.

HIT-AND-RUN PLAY

If a runner on first or second base is given a hit-and-run sign by the batter, he takes a moderate lead and then starts for the next base with the pitcher's first intention of pitching the ball. In making the start, the runner glances toward the plate, after taking two or three steps, to make sure that the ball has not been hit in the air. Some managers insist that the runner take a stealing lead on this play because they feel that if the ball is missed a steal may be completed. However, the success of the hit-and-run play depends on the batter hitting the ball and not on the runner starting quickly. For this reason, only a moderate lead is advised rather than one that may make it possible for the pitcher to catch the runner off base. This **also applies to natural run-and-hit situations. In these cases it is advisable for the runner to break the same as on a hit-and-run so that** the location of the ball is always known.

RUN-DOWN

When caught between bases, a player runs as fast as possible toward the more advanced base until a safe distance from the defensive player receiving the ball is reached, and then retreats similarly in the opposite direction. (If the defensive player covering the more advanced base has the ball, the run is toward the less advanced base.) A continuation of this procedure consumes time, and makes it possible for another runner or runners to advance. Running out of the base line just prior to being tagged is also an offensive trick that often works. In this case a defensive player may chase the runner and consume valuable time.

It is, of course, important for other runners on base to advance during the run-down if possible. This often ends with two players on the same base. The defensive player usually tags both runners in this case, but the player who originally occupied the base is entitled to the bag. Since such a play can get involved, a player does not leave the base until the umpire declares him out. This is practiced on all plays, whether running or sliding into the bag, since the defensive player may juggle the ball or remove his foot from the bag too soon. The same rule applies when it is doubtful whether or not a batted ball is fair or foul, because a defensive player may attempt to fool the runner.

STEALING THE CATCHER'S SIGNALS

If a runner attempts to steal the catcher's signals from second base, it is best to do this on the bag. This, of course, prevents being caught by the hidden-ball trick. In relaying signals it is inadvisable to manipulate the hand in front of the body to indicate a fast ball and curve because the catcher will then switch signs. Most players use a prearranged signal such as pulling up the belt or rubbing the uniform in a certain way to denote a curve. No signal is given for other pitches because the majority of pitches are fast balls, and a slow ball is frequently thrown on a curve-ball sign. In other words, the batter is always looking for a fast ball unless the runner gives the designated signal. In some cases the runner first gives a signal to inform the batter that he has discovered the catcher's method of giving signals. This is a good practice since it permits the runner to relay signals immediately.

SUBSTITUTE BASE RUNNER

In the event a substitute base runner is sent into the game, it is advisable for the player who is being replaced to stay on the bag until the substitute arrives. Play is usually suspended in this case, but it is best to remain on the base to guard against the failure of the manager or coach to request the umpire to call time.

SUMMARY

1. Break fast from the plate even though the batted ball may appear to be a potential out. Watch the base—not the ball. Run in the 3-foot lane the last half of the distance to first base if the ball is fielded near the plate; otherwise, interference may be called. You may run past first base in fair territory if you do not make an intent to advance to second.
2. Run on a dropped third strike with first base unoccupied; also when first base is occupied with two out.
3. Swing to the right of the base line in rounding bases and lean the body toward the infield.
4. Watch the runner ahead of you because his action will determine whether you should attempt to advance or retreat; also note if the cutoff position is occupied.
5. Consider the throwing ability of the outfielders and note their positions for the various batters.

6. Look toward the third base coach for assistance when rounding second base if a ball is hit to the right-field side of the diamond.

7. Follow the instructions of the third base coach when approaching third base: (a) Round third if the coach is up the base line. (b) Check your speed and find the ball if the coach is near the bag. (c) Stop on the bag if the coach points toward the base.

8. Run hard past the bag on a straight approach to first to arrive at maximum speed. Run hard over the plate with two out because the third out may be made before you score nullifying the run.

9. Remain on the bag until the pitcher places his foot on the rubber or straddles the rubber. He must then have the ball.

10. Advance to second base from first in the last half of the final inning when the winning run is scoring on a hit with two out; otherwise the run may be nullified.

11. Start as the pitcher begins his delivery when first, first and second, or all of the bases are occupied when the count is three balls and two strikes with two out. A runner on third runs in foul territory so that the batter can swing if the pitch is over.

12. Take your lead off third base outside the base line because if a runner is hit by a batted ball in fair territory he is automatically out. Stand behind an infielder who takes his position in the base line.

13. Make sure the ball is going to be pitched before starting when given the steal signal on the count of three balls and two strikes, or on three balls and one strike, as this is a natural run-and-hit situation.

14. Employ a short lead and walking advance unless you are stealing. In taking a lead avoid crossing the legs when a step from the bag; otherwise, the pitcher may pick you off base.

15. Crouch with the weight forward and the hands on the knees so that you can advance or retreat. Pivot on the right foot and employ a crossover step with the left foot for a fast getaway on a steal.

16. Stay on second base if a hard-hit ball goes toward or to the third base side of the shortstop (or toward the pitcher) when first base is unoccupied with less than two out, unless the ball is fumbled or goes through the infield.

17. Score from third base on a ground ball to the shortstop or second baseman when first base is unoccupied with less than two out and the shortstop and second baseman are playing back. The runner on second base advances if the ball is hit to the shortstop's left.

18. Hit the bag in stride. Step on the inside corner of the base in rounding a bag and on top of the base when running straight to the bag. Use a controlled stride on wet days to avoid the danger of slipping.

19. Play it safe with none out. Take a chance with one out. With two

out, try to score from second on a single—to stretch a single into a double but not a double into a triple. Refrain from trying to reach third from first on a single unless you are sure you can advance.

20. Be content to advance one base if you are forced to stop or slow down to permit a batted ball to pass in front of you.

21. Make the ball roll to the outfield to advance from second and third bases if the infield plays in with none out and first unoccupied.

22. Start for the plate from third base on a ground ball with one out regardless of the position of the infield.

23. Break for the plate from third base on all ground balls when first base is occupied with less than two out because the defense usually attempts to make a double play, second to first.

24. Do not start until the ball is bunted on a sacrifice. Start on a running squeeze play when the pitcher is about to release the ball.

25. Stop or run behind a player who is fielding a ball in the base line, as the defense has the right of way.

26. Take a halfway position on short flies but tag-up at third base if a player runs away from the infield to make a catch.

27. Return to the bag on an infield fly because the batter is automatically out. Base runners can run at their own peril if an infield fly is dropped. The ball is dead if the fly hits a runner on a base.

28. Tag-up on long fly balls except when on first base and the catch is doubtful. Then advance as far as possible. If past second base touch the bag on a retreat to first base when the ball is caught.

29. Be careful at first base when left-hand pitchers are on the mound as these players usually have good "moves" to the bag.

30. On a double steal with first and third bases occupied, stop in the base line in running to second base. Take a crossover step toward the plate and hop to a position on the base line at third base; then break for the plate as the catcher's arm comes forward to throw.

31. Step directly forward to the base line at third base when a single steal of second is attempted with first and third bases occupied; then fake going home after the ball leaves the catcher's hand.

32. Break for the next base on a hit-and-run play the same as for a steal, but glance toward the plate after taking two or three steps to make sure the ball is not hit in the air.

33. Maneuver back and forth in run-downs to consume time and permit other players to advance.

34. Stay on the bag until the umpire declares you out or informs you a ball was foul. Do not take advice from opposing players.

35. In the event that you are to be replaced by a substitute runner, remain on the bag until the runner reaches the bag.

DISCUSSION QUESTIONS

1. Give the basic principles of the hit-and-run play. In what way does the start of the runner differ from that of a player who is attempting to steal?
2. Where is the 3-foot lane? When must the batter run within its limits?
3. On what part of the bag does a batter step if he tries to beat out a bunt? Why is this done?
4. How does a runner on third base try to fool the defense if (a) a double steal is attempted with first and third bases occuped? (b) a single steal of second is attempted with the same bases occupied?
5. Discuss the strategy of the runner on second base on hard-hit balls toward or to the third-base side of the shortstop (or toward the pitcher) with first base unoccupied and less than two out.
6. What is the recommended position for the base runner on short fly balls? Describe the action of the runner after such a ball is caught. When does the runner tag-up on a short fly ball?
7. How does a base runner move off the bag to take his lead? Describe a good base-running stance.
8. Why is it important for a base runner to maintain speed in running over the plate? Suggest two situations wherein failure to run fast may prove a disadvantage.
9. Does the base give the runner protection on batted balls? When is there an exception to this rule?
10. Discuss general base-running strategy with none out, one out, and two out.

TRUE–FALSE QUESTIONS AND ANSWERS

T F 1. In the last half of the final inning, it is important for a base runner advancing from first base to touch second on a single which scores the winning run; otherwise, the run may be nullified.

T F 2. With first and third bases occupied, the runner on third always breaks for home if the batter hits the ball on the ground.

T F 3. If the batter p .sses a base runner, the runner and not the batter is automatically out.

T F 4. Base runners can run at their peril if an infield fly is dropped.

T F 5. The runner who was originally on the bag is out if two players are tagged on the same base.

T F 6. On a dropped third strike the batter can never run to first base if the bag is occupied.

T F 7. When a defensive player is waiting for a batted ball in the base line, it is usually advisable for the runner to stop or run behind the fielder.

T F 8. In sacrifice situations base runners break for the next base as soon as the batter indicates that he intends to bunt.

T F 9. A base runner must take his lead in back of an infielder if the player's defensive position is in the base line.

T F 10. In rounding bases the runner steps on the inside corner of the bag with either the left or right foot.

ANSWERS

T T F T F F T F T T
10 9 8 7 6 5 4 3 2 1

15

Sliding

The ability to slide both directly toward and to the side of a base is an important factor in good base running. Sliding is primarily a means of checking the speed so that the body may be stopped at the bag. It is also an aid in avoiding the defensive player attempting to make the tag. In some instances a clever use of the feet at the end of a slide into second base prevents a defensive player from making an accurate throw to first base to complete the second half of a double play.

Sliding is really controlled falling. Eight or ten feet from the bag, a player drops to the ground with the body aligned according to the type of slide involved. The momentum of the run does the rest. Since there is a terrific impact as the body hits the ground, the muscles are kept relaxed at the time of contact. This lessens the danger of ankle injuries or body bruises, and makes possible a more effective slide. Because of the danger of injury, players practice sliding in a pit filled with sand, tanbark, or some similar material that will give when a slide is made.

TECHNIQUE

There are four types of slides: the bent-leg slide, the conventional hook slide, the feet-first slide, and the head-first slide. The hook slide is an evasive slide to either side of the bag, whereas the other slides are usually made directly to the bag. However, the bent-leg slide may be an evasive slide similar to the hook slide, and the feet-first and head-first slides may be evasive to the extent that the slide may be made to the side of the bag so that an extended foot or hand touches only the inside or outside corner of the bag.

a. The take-off is made with either foot (usually the right foot)—arms are spread for balance.
b, c. The take-off leg is bent under the extended leg.
d, e. The bent leg acts as a spring at the end of the slide to regain the feet for an advance.

Fig. 15–1. The bent-leg slide straight to the bag.

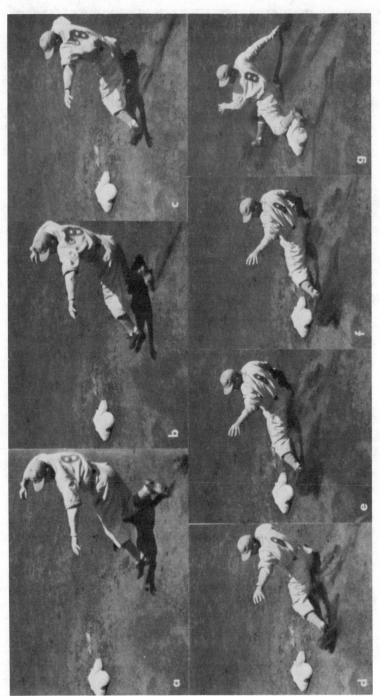

a, b. The take-off is from the right leg for a slide to the right of the bag.

c, d. The right leg is bent under the left leg.

e, f, g. The left leg trails, permitting the left foot to hook the right corner of the base.

Fig. 15–2. The bent-leg slide to the side of the bag.

BENT-LEG SLIDE

The bent-leg slide, as has been previously stated, may be exe-cuted directly toward the bag or to the side of the bag. In the former case the weight of the body is thrown toward the bag with one leg extended in a slightly bent position. The other leg is bent under it and receives the full impact of the slide. The take-off is usually made from the foot that ultimately receives the impact of the slide, but it may be made from either the left or right foot, ac-cording to the natural ability of the player (Fig. 15–1). The ex-tended foot remains in the air until the bag is reached. This pre-vents catching the spikes in the ground and, in the case of a slide to second base, makes it possible to use the foot in interfering with the step of the defensive player attempting to make a double play.

A bent-leg slide becomes an evasive slide by throwing the weight straight ahead but to the side of the bag. The extended leg is dragged into the base. The take-off is usually with the left foot if the slide is to the left and with the right foot if the slide is to the right (Fig. 15–2). This is sometimes called the parallel-leg slide because both legs drag into the base with the spikes pointing to the rear. (The bent leg may be extended to the rear.)

The bent-leg slide is the most effective slide because it permits two approaches to the bag. It is also less dangerous, since the spikes are not likely to be caught in the ground even though the slide is made directly to the bag. In addition the chance of a body burn is minimized, since the contact with the ground is made with the fore-leg and not, as in other slides, with the thigh (the head-first slide excepted). Another advantage is the ability to get up quickly after reaching the bag (Fig. 15–1d, e). This is very important when it is possible to advance because of an erratic throw or fumbled ball, and particularly concerns the slide directly to the bag. In this case the player, aided by the momentum of his slide, pushes the body from the ground with his hands and bent leg.

HOOK SLIDE

The conventional hook slide is made by throwing the weight of the body away from the line of momentum to the bag. If the slide is to the left of the bag, the weight of the body is thrown to the left of the momentum. The take-off is usually from the right foot, and the left foot is swung forward and away from the base with the foot turned up so that the spikes will not catch in the ground. The right leg drags in a bent position, and the hooking toe makes contact at about the middle of the front edge of the bag. There is a slight turn of the trunk to the left, and the arms are extended to the rear on that side of the body. The left hand usually drags along the ground with the palm down, whereas the right hand remains in the air to balance the body. The impact and slide are on the outer side of the left thigh and leg. If the slide is to the right of the bag, similar action is used to the right. In this case the take-off is usually from the left foot, and the right foot is swung forward and away from the base.

A hook or evasive slide, although ordinarily a deliberate attempt to hook the bag, is often used to slide past the bag when the defensive player is waiting with the ball. This is done by swinging the tagging foot forward just before it reaches the bag. As the player goes by the bag, he has two alternatives: either to reach for the bag with the hand closest to the bag, or make a quick body turn and reach for the bag with the other hand. A combination of the two often works to advantage. For example, the hand nearest the bag can be extended to bait the defensive player; then if an attempt is made to reach to make the put-out this arm can be withdrawn and the body turn and reach with the opposite hand executed.

FEET-FIRST SLIDE

The feet-first slide resembles the bent-leg slide in being executed directly to the bag except that both legs are extended toward the bag. Another difference is that the impact is on the side of the thigh instead of the foreleg. Since one leg must come in contact with the ground in making the slide, it is important to keep the foot turned up so that the spikes will not catch in the ground.

A feet-first slide, aside from being a quick means of getting to the bag, offers an advantage in breaking up double plays. In this case the left foot may be used to interfere with the step of the defensive player when the throw is made from the inside of the base line, and the right foot if the step is made to the outside of the base line. However, this type of slide is not encouraged because of the danger of catching the spikes in the ground, and it is only recommended in situations where the player is unable to master the bent-leg slide.

HEAD-FIRST SLIDE

The head-first slide is made by throwing the weight of the body toward the bag and extending the arms. The impact and slide are on the front part of the body with a slight pressure on the hands. This slide is not recommended primarily because the outstretched hands provide an easy target to the defensive player attempting to make the tag. As a consequence, the bag is frequently blocked, thereby making it impossible for the runner to reach the bag. This rarely happens when the feet are extended toward the bag.

The head-first slide, although not as practical as other slides, proves useful to players who have been injured sliding feet first, and who are afraid a similar injury may occur if they continue to slide in this manner. It is also useful when a player is caught off guard close to the bag. In this case a modified head-first slide is often used to dive back to the bag.

STRATEGY

If it is necessary for a defensive player to tag a runner, the slide is made to the opposite side of the bag on which the ball is received. If the throw is made from directly in back of the runner, the player runs toward the defensive player prior to making his slide. This makes it necessary for the throw to be made to the side of the bag to prevent hitting the runner and, of course, makes the tag more difficult.

SLIDE ON A FORCE-OUT

A slide direct to the bag is made on a force play. This is the quickest way to reach the bag, and on a slide to second, the foot can be used to interfere with the double play throw. A similar slide often works when the throw is accurate on a tag play.

A smart base runner slides in all cases wherein a decision whether or not to slide must be made just before the bag is reached. This prevents injuries, and always enables the runner to stop at the bag. A player who runs past the bag, on the other hand, can be frequently tagged out even though a force play was not completed. In this connection an overslide of first by the batter is ruled the same as a run past the bag, so the runner is not liable to be put out. A slide into first base is not used when running from the plate except to avoid a collision or when the first baseman fields the ball or catches a throw up the first-base line and attempts to tag the runner.

BREAKING UP A DOUBLE PLAY

If a runner slides into second base while a defensive player is in the act of making a throw to first base to complete a possible double

play, he attempts to make contact with the player, and thereby interfere with the throw. There are various ways to do this. Some base
runners attempt to roll into the defensive player, whereas others
slide into the bag with their spikes high. However, it is only necessary to unbalance the player to prevent an accurate throw. This
may be done by making contact with his stepping foot. It is important for a runner to remember that he may be charged with
interference if he slides more than three feet out of the base line
to hit the pivot man, or if he deliberately interferes with the throw.
When the umpire observes such an infraction, he declares the batter
out at first.

SUMMARY

1. Keep relaxed in hitting the ground, as this lessens the danger of injury and makes possible a more effective slide.
2. When using a conventional hook slide, take off with the right foot in
sliding to the left and with the left foot in sliding to the right.
3. Slide wide of the bag if the defensive player is waiting with the ball;
then attempt to reach the bag with either hand.
4. Perfect the bent-leg slide because it can be used either as an evasive
or straight-in slide. Take off with the leg which is to be bent under
for both approaches.
5. On tag plays slide to the opposite side of the bag on which the ball
is received. Go directly into the bag on force plays.
6. Always slide when a decision whether or not to slide must be made;
this lessens the danger of injury and enables you to stop at the bag.
7. Attempt to interfere with the pivot man's throw on a double play
by contacting his stepping foot with the instep of your nearer foot.
8. Avoid running or sliding more than 3 feet out of the base line to contact the pivot man, as this constitutes interference.

DISCUSSION QUESTIONS

1. How is a bent-leg slide executed? Why is it considered an all-purpose slide?
2. Give details regarding the take-off and final position of the feet, legs,
arms, and body if a runner hook-slides to the right of the bag. What
factor is important as the runner hits the ground? When is a hook
slide not recommended?
3. Why is a head-first slide less practical than other slides? What

players frequently use this type of slide to advantage?
4. Describe a base-running tactic before sliding if the ball is thrown from behind the runner. What dangers are involved when a runner makes a late decision not to slide?

TRUE–FALSE QUESTIONS AND ANSWERS

T F 1. The best way for a runner to break up a double play at second base is to contact the stepping foot of the player making the throw.

T F 2. A conventional hook slide is the most effective slide because it can be made to either side of the bag.

T F 3. It is advisable to slide into first base on some occasions even though a slide into this base is not generally recommended.

T F 4. The take-off is usually made from the foot which ultimately becomes extended when a player employs a bent-leg slide.

ANSWERS

F   T   F   T
4   3   2   1

III

PRACTICE TECHNIQUES

16

Batting and
Fielding Practice

A manager or coach must first screen or evaluate baseball candidates. This may be done inside, if an infield is available. The screening enables the manager or coach to: (1) Place players in their proper positions, and (2) Plan a training program which will familiarize players with these positions. The majority of action in baseball originates through the center of the diamond so it is important to give special attention to the battery (pitcher and catcher), the double play combination (shortstop and second baseman), and the center fielder.

The quickest way to determine the batting and running abilities of players is, of course, to let them hit and run down the base line. Generally speaking, if they do not have flexible wrists and a smooth swing the chances are they will not be good batters. This does not mean they cannot qualify for the team, because they may show exceptional speed or be outstanding defensive players.

Three factors are important in the evaluation of defensive ability: mobility or quickness to maneuver into a good fielding position; good hands, which implies the ability to catch all sorts of balls with regularity; and a strong arm. These qualifications can be determined during an infield practice.

When a great many players need to be screened, ground balls may be hit to a line of players at shortstop or third base. This is particularly helpful to learn which players have strong arms for the long throw to first base. The same effect may be obtained in infield practice. In this case the second baseman can be moved to shortstop or third base, and left-hand outfielders can work at first base and make some throws to third base. Normally, quickness and running speed are revealed by the movement of players to field ground balls. However, if more of a test is desired, short dashes can be run, either with groups in competition or against a stop watch.

If there are no inside facilities, the entire screening process can be conducted outside. This, of course, permits outfielders to be tested on their ability to catch and judge fly balls, to field ground balls, and to make long throws. However, outside screening encroaches on the time for teaching fundamentals unless the climate permits early spring practice.

It is advisable to have a standardized routine for both batting and fielding practice. Each player then knows what he must do and the practice sessions run smoothly. This is particularly valuable, because an organized practice at the games impresses spectators.

BATTING PRACTICE

It is important to have several rounds of batting practice each day, a round consisting of a complete cycle of the players batting. Pitchers, coaches, and players with good control usually pitch batting practice. However, before a game it is advisable to have the last round pitched by the same type of pitcher that will be faced in the game. The ball is thrown about three-quarter speed, with no attempt to fool batters. This increases their chances of hitting the ball and develops confidence.

Every team has a definite policy with regard to the number of balls hit, so that all players will have the same amount of practice. Many major-league teams bunt one and hit three to five fair balls the first round, then hit the same number of fair balls on succeeding rounds. (The pitcher usually bunts twice in each round.) Some teams favor a certain number of swings throughout the entire practice, counting each swing even though the ball is fouled or missed. This makes it more likely that batters will swing at good pitches and increases the number of rounds of practice. A popular trend is to have one round and give each player ten or twelve swings. This saves time going in and out of the batting cage. If additional time remains players then take one swing and for every hit they make they earn another swing. A good policy in high-school and college baseball is to allow each batter one bunt whether the ball rolls foul or fair to encourage better bunting. You can also take a swing away from the batter if he makes a poor bunt or steps across the plate and violates a rule of batting, and reward a good bunt with an extra swing.

To have a fast-moving batting practice, a feeder is placed about fifty feet back of the mound to supply balls to the pitcher. It is important that the feeder always be looking toward the plate when a pitch is being delivered to avoid being hit by a batted ball. As another precaution, players are instructed to make all returns to the feeder on the ground. It is also advisable for the pitcher to refrain from holding a second ball in his glove when he is delivering a pitch, to avoid the danger of injury by a batted ball.

It is a general practice to hit ground balls from near the plate to the infielders during batting practice. (Refrain from hitting the ball until a batter has hit the pitch, or the ball has passed the plate. This prevents infielders from getting injured.)

Many mechanical devices are available to facilitate batting practice. Chief among these are the batting tee, pitching machine, and protective screens for the pitcher and first baseman (see Appendix, pp. 395–97).

Most players can gain some benefit from the use of a *batting tee,* particularly in the angle of a swing in relation to the height of a pitch and the position of the ball over the plate. In the former case the emphasis is on the downswing and upswing for high and low pitches, whereas in the latter, stress is placed on fast arm and hip action, to pull inside pitches and delay action on outside pitches, to drive the ball to the opposite field. A tee can also help improve coordination of the stride and swing for both general purposes and during batting slumps. For any of these practices the ball may be hit off the tee either on the regular field or against a net or screen. In the latter case a soft ball can be used, if there is danger of injury. The tee should always be used with a thin rubber plate so that players will relate their swing to inside and outside pitches.

There is a variety of *pitching machines,* each of which has its merits, but none really simulates the actions of a pitcher. However, they fill a need where there is a scarcity of pitchers or where large groups of players must be screened. They have extreme value in teaching the mechanics of bunting, wherein the bunting practice can be divorced from batting. If a pitching machine is used for batting practice, it is advisable to climax the last round or two with live pitching.

Protective screens both for the first baseman and for the pitcher are, of course, beneficial. Some protection is advisable for the pitcher because he is less than sixty feet from the plate when the batter hits the ball. A four- or five-foot screen is advisable so that the pitcher can be fully protected after he delivers the pitch. This is placed in front of the pitching mound. Some managers prefer no protection, feeling that the pitcher will then learn to field his position better. However, in practice pitchers are frequently injured without a screen, and instinctively they will probably prove adequate fielders in the game.

Protective helmets come in the form of complete caps or fiber inserts for regular caps. These may be worn permanently throughout the game or worn for batting and removed upon reaching base.

FIELDING PRACTICE

A snappy fielding practice is an important part of baseball. In such a practice, the coach fungos the type of ball that is likely to be hit in the game. This applies to outfielders as well as infielders. Two or three ground balls are generally hit to each outfielder at the start of the practice so that throws may be made to second and third bases and to the plate. The infielders cover bases and take their various cutoff positions on such throws to remind them of the duties they are expected to perform in the game.

The coach hits to the infield from either side of the plate; he generally hits to the outfield from a point near the pitcher's mound for throws by the outfielders at the start of the practice. Fungos to outfielders for regular outfield practice are usually hit on the outfield side of the infield to avoid hitting the infielders.

A definite plan for fielding practice follows. Prior to any such practice, players warm up adequately, and when the regular practice begins pitchers hit fungos to the outfielders.

ROUTINE FOR OUTFIELD PRACTICE

The outfielders usually make throws to the various bases before the regular infield practice begins. This routine consists of three rounds in which case each outfielder makes a throw to complete a cycle for one round.

Round 1:
1. lf–2b (hit ball near left-field line)
2. cf–2b (hit ball to left- or right-center field)
3. rf–2b (hit ball near right-field line)

Round 2:
1. lf–3b (hit ball to left-center field or near left-field line)
2. cf–3b (hit ball to center field)
3. rf–3b (hit ball to right field)

Round 3:
1. lf–c (hit ball to left field)
2. cf–c (hit ball to center field)
3. rf–c (hit ball to right field)

ROUTINE FOR INFIELD PRACTICE

A common infield routine consists of approximately six rounds, in which case each infielder and the catcher field a ball to complete the cycle of players for one round. This may be increased to eight or ten rounds, depending on the amount of time required to complete six rounds. Prior to the first round, a good procedure is to hit the ball slowly to the third baseman, shortstop, and second baseman, and have these players throw to first; then, with the infield in, hit the ball slowly to each infielder, and have the throw go to the plate. This is often done at the end of the practice, but it is better done at first, since on a hot day it is advisable for some of the regular players to refrain from participating in the complete fielding practice. The catcher does not throw to the bases in this routine.

The following six rounds show a standard procedure for infield practice in which the ball is hit to the first player listed (in Round 1 under 1, the third baseman) and then the ball is thrown around the diamond as indicated. In getting one, the ball is thrown to first base; and in getting two, to second base. Exceptions occur for the first baseman in Round 5 and the catcher in Round 6.

Get one—Round 1 (hit ball toward infielder):
1. 3b—1b—c—3b—2b—1b—c
2. ss—1b—c—ss—3b—c
3. 2b—1b—c—2b—3b—c
4. 1b—ss—1b—c
5. c (along 1b line)—1b—ss—c

Get one—Round 2: Same as first round except hit ball to infielder's left.

Get two—Round 3 (hit ball to infielder's left):
1. 3b—2b—1b—c—3b—1b—c
2. ss—2b—1b—c—ss—3b—c
3. 2b—ss—1b—c—2b—3b—c
4. 1b—ss—1b—c
5. c (front of plate)—ss—1b—c

Get two—Round 4: Same as third round but hit ball to infielder's right.

Get one—Round 5: Same as Rounds 1 and 2 with ball hit to infielder's left, but roll ball along 3b line for catcher; also bring first baseman in and have him throw to third. (In all other rounds he throws to second.)

Get one—Round 6: Same as Round 5 with ball hit to infielder's right, but catcher throws to 3b. First baseman plays on bag and moves into diamond as ball is hit to him.

After the completion of the first baseman's turn in each round, the catcher lobs the ball to the coach. The coach then taps the ball into fair territory for the catcher's turn to complete the cycle for a round. In such cases the ball is sent around the diamond counter-clockwise if the throw is to first, clockwise after throws to second, and the third baseman makes his throw to first. In situations involv-ing infielders, the ball goes to the catcher from first and back to the player who originally fielded the ball. The throw in this case is taken on the bag. The ball then progresses around the bases coun-terclockwise and back to the plate. One exception involves the third baseman, who sends the ball clockwise around the diamond. Valuable time can be saved during the infield practice if the second baseman throws the ball home, at the end of the cycle involving the catcher, instead of to third. This enables the third baseman to get ready for the next ground ball. Time can also be saved if the catcher refrains from throwing to the first baseman in the first-base cycle.

If time remains, several pop flies are usually hit over the infield so that both the catcher and infielders can determine the drift of balls. This is always advisable during regular practice sessions be-cause flies directly over the infield are very difficult to catch.

In order to incorporate the above fielding routine into the ten minutes usually allotted for preliminary practice before a game, the coach uses three baseballs. This allows for poorly hit balls and omissions by the defense. An alert coach always keeps two balls in play, hitting a second ball just as soon as the ball previously hit reaches the catcher's glove to complete a cycle.

Infield Routine During a Game. A set infield procedure is also followed during a game after a put-out is made with the bases un-occupied. In this case the catcher and infielders advance several steps toward the mound and throw the ball quickly around the dia-mond either clockwise or counterclockwise, depending on which player makes the put-out, and the last throw goes to the third base-man, who feeds the ball back to the pitcher. If the out is made at first base, the original throw goes from the first baseman to the catcher in the back-up position behind first base.

PITCHING PRACTICE

Pitching is often considered responsible for 60 to 80 per cent of a team's success. For this reason the pitching position must be given a great deal of attention. Conditioning is particularly important since pitchers get less game activity than infielders and outfielders. Specific conditioning in the form of running can be accomplished with a fungo stick, since the catching of fly balls is interesting to players. On some teams the same objective is achieved by having the coach throw the ball to the pitchers from a point in the outfield. In this case the coach leads the pitchers with throws as they run back and forth across the field. The coach can throw two or three balls to each pitcher, throwing a ball after a short run, then another, and so on; or he can throw one ball after a long run. A similar procedure is followed for regular pitchers, in which case a player rests the day after he pitches, runs and throws lightly on the side lines or during batting practice the second day, rests the third day, then pitches the fourth day. This, of course, depends on the physical stamina of the pitcher and whether or not there has been a recent relief assignment. Pitchers who fail to throw on the second day as mentioned above usually take a light workout the day before they pitch. It is sometimes a good policy to have a player rest the day before he pitches, or terminate his practice early, if he desires a pre-game workout the day before he pitches.

PRACTICE GAMES

Practice games with members of the squad are beneficial for all teams in preseason practice, and in amateur baseball they are helpful during the regular schedule. This particularly concerns pitchers, who need two or three innings of game competition two days before they are expected to pitch (or three or four innings, three days before pitching). It is best to let each pitcher stay on the mound for six or nine outs, starting a new inning with the bases unoccupied after every three outs. The defensive team may remain in the field, or alternate on the offense and defense just as they do in a regular game. The former method saves time, but the latter method stimulates players and enlivens the practice. Some conditioning is also derived by players running to and from their positions. In such games it is advisable to reward players with another time at bat, if they walk or are hit with a pitched ball. In this case a substitute runner can be used. The action may be speeded up by making the count on each batter two balls and one strike.

It is usually advantageous to point out flagrant mistakes during intrasquad games. However, it is advisable not to stop the action repeatedly, because all mistakes can be brought to the attention of the squad after the game. It is also beneficial to point out mistakes during a regularly scheduled game. In this case it is important to make criticisms in a constructive manner.

If circumstances do not permit a practice game two days before a scheduled game, it is advisable to have pitchers throw some batting practice with a catcher behind the plate (or on the side lines if the field cannot be used). In this case it is practical to team the pitcher and catcher who are to start the ensuing game.

Specific plans for a given day and important announcements should always be listed on the clubhouse bulletin board. This can cover assignments and details relative to intrasquad games.

A modified form of an intrasquad game with easy pitching (Old Cat) is beneficial for small groups of players who report under informal conditions. In this case batting teams of two and three players can be used, only first base being employed with two batters and all of the bases with three batters. A base runner or batter who is put out (or a team after three outs) goes on the defense and players rotate from outfield to infield to pitcher to catcher.

SUMMARY

1. Select personnel carefully, with special emphasis on defensive strength through the middle of the diamond.
2. Adopt a definite policy relative to the number of swings in batting practice so that all players have equal batting opportunities.
3. Keep several batting tees available at all times so that players can practice the mechanics of batting.
4. Require all players to wear batting helmets, and provide a screen in front of the mound to protect the pitcher during batting practice.
5. Plan a definite routine for fielding practice so that players will have to execute the fundamentals which may have to be performed in the game.
6. Develop a training program which emphasizes conditioning and the individual and team performances as they are related to the game.
7. Give special attention to pitchers, and fungo fly balls to them periodically to develop pitching stamina.
8. Incorporate intrasquad games into practices, both during the preseason training and the regular schedule.

DISCUSSION QUESTIONS

1. Explain the words "a defense through the middle." Why is this important?
2. Suggest a way to screen baseball candidates to determine their offensive and defensive ability. What are the three important factors in evaluating defensive ability?

3. State several danger points which must be guarded against during batting practice. How can the danger be minimized?
4. Recommend two ways to use a tee to teach batting fundamentals.
5. What is the standard procedure for the first round of an infield practice? Trace the path of the ball from the time it is hit to the third baseman until it returns to the fungo hitter.
6. Where does the coach stand to hit fungos during regular outfield practice? Why is this done?
7. Give two important facts which must be considered in batting practice that relate to (a) the pitcher; (b) the feeder.
8. What is a complete cycle of players called in batting and fielding practice? Suggest a means by which the manager or coach can speed up infield practice before a game.

TRUE–FALSE QUESTIONS AND ANSWERS

T F 1. In selecting a defensive team the first five players should include the center fielder, pitcher, shortstop, catcher, and right fielder.

T F 2. A batting practice which stresses a certain number of swings is more practical than one which permits a specific number of fair balls.

T F 3. Two days is usually an adequate rest period before starting again, after a pitcher has completed a nine inning game.

T F 4. Throws around the bases in infield practice are the same for the first and second rounds, and the third and fourth rounds, respectively, after a ground ball has been fielded and thrown to first.

T F 5. The main objective in using the batting tee is to perfect the angle of the swing.

T F 6. In intrasquad games a good practice is to permit the pitcher to remain permanently on the mound for the number of innings he will pitch.

T F 7. Good hands, a strong arm, and mobility or quickness are the three basic qualifications for evaluating the defensive ability of a player.

T F 8. During batting practice it is advisable for infielders and outfielders to roll the ball to the feeder behind the pitching mound.

ANSWERS

F T F T T T T T
1 2 3 4 5 6 7 8

17

Practice Drills

In order to be successful, a baseball team must do a definite amount of running in early training. Conditioning should begin with simple jogging, then advance to sprinting with alternate walking.

Early in the season, it is wise for a pitcher not to throw to a catcher at all during the first week, and he should throw only every other day when the full training program gets under way. Most pitchers throw too much and run too little. Any player who is conditioned by a regular routine of running seldom suffers a sore arm.

Once a general conditioning program has been developed, the fundamentals of running, catching, throwing, and batting can be worked into drills to familiarize players with the offensive and defensive working of plays. (Refer to page 413 for a preseason conditioning and training schedule which incorporates these basic drills.)

GYMNASIUM DRILLS

Some drills can be planned for the gymnasium floor. Such drills can be performed with or without gloves. A simple beginning drill can be executed with two facing lines. Players roll the ball to the left and right of each other. After catching the ball a player returns to his position in line then rolls the ball and runs to the end of the opposite line. This type of drill can be performed by two players rolling the ball back and forth to each other. Another variation has one player rolling the ball. The other player takes a position on a starting mark and starts when the ball is rolled. In this case after the player fields the ball he returns it, then runs to the starting mark and resumes his defensive position for another start.

Another good drill is to have a single line of players throw against a wall (protected by a mat) and field the ball. After the ball is fielded each time, the player makes a throw, then moves in to field the next rebound. When the player gets near the wall, he permits the ball to go to the next player and runs to his place at the end of the line. This can be used as a one-man drill near the wall.

Similar drills can be performed with pitchers to practice fundamentals such as position on the rubber, throwing to catch runners off base, and fielding and throwing batted balls. In these cases one area may be designated as first, second, or third base. The pitcher can throw to the catcher or an infielder. Other players may act as base runners. The coach may roll or bounce the ball from near the catcher to simulate the game action of sacrifice bunts and balls which are hit toward the pitcher's mound.

DIAMOND DRILLS

When an infield is available, the fundamentals of running, catching, throwing, and batting are usually worked into game situations to familiarize players with the offensive and defensive working of plays. The drills which follow show how this is done. In the drills specific bases are occupied. certain defensive players are in their positions, and coaches can be stationed in the first- and third-base coaching boxes to give signals, if desired. Several players also line up on the first-base side of the plate to represent the batter, if one is needed. The coach sets up each play or situation. He originates the action in Drills 1–6 by fungoing the ball as indicated by the dotted lines. (Pitchers can be omitted in Drill 5.)

The pitcher initiates the action in Drills 7–11 by having the ball in his hand. In Drill 7, he pitches and in Drill 8 a base-running maneuver is begun while he is standing on the rubber. A pitch is made to the catcher in Drills 9–11 and the coach rolls a second ball into the diamond. In Drills 12–20 the pitcher delivers or throws the ball in relation to specific situations. For this reason it is usually advisable to work one pitcher at a time. Several pitchers may participate in Drill 9 in which case pitchers may toss the ball or fake a follow-through to start the action. The best day to do this is when the pitcher is scheduled for a regular workout. He can then warm up sufficiently to make the necessary throws.

In order to facilitate the action of some of the drills, it is advisable to break down each drill into its component parts, or at least first practice the basic fundamental involved in the drill. For example in Drill 9 the pitcher can stand two or three steps from the bag, then make the approach for the first baseman's toss or throw. The approach and toss can thus be perfected so that the proper timing can develop when the complete drill is executed. The same holds true for Drill 11. In this case the pitcher must know how to field a bunt and pivot and throw to third base. This can be done in two stages. First the pitcher can bend over with the ball in his hands, then spin toward his glove hand and throw to a player on the bag. In a second stage the coach can roll the ball to the pitcher, thereby establishing the situation that will prevail in the complete drill.

Drills 15–25 may be performed during batting practice. In this case the batter runs down the base line after his last swing, then takes his lead at first base. The coach can then perform the various drills according to the availability of players and his time schedule. In executing the hitting behind the runner phase of batting, the ball bag can be placed to the right-field side of the pitching mound in line with the batter and second baseman. Both left- and right-hand batters are then expected to pick a pitch and hit the ball to the first-base side of the ball bag.

In the hit-and-run play the batter is expected to hit the ensuing pitch on the ground. This play and the tactic of hitting behind the runner can be practiced on successive turns in the batter's box, in which case failure to complete the fundamental successfully can be penalized by subtracting a swing from a player's regular allotment of swings. This, of course, gives a premium for perfect execution. The sacrifice can be included in this procedure by placing the ball bag, or two gloves, midway between the pitcher's mound and the base lines and about thirty feet from home plate. Then the batter is expected to bunt the ball so that it will stop near the bag.

Many games are won because of the ability of players to execute properly the simple fundamentals of baseball. No special talent is required in many cases, but the know-how acquired through constant practice is essential. For example, the mere knowledge of when and how to start is important in the execution of such plays as the squeeze or double steal as well as in the defense against them. The twenty-five drills in this chapter include just about everything that a player needs to know on both the offense and the defense. Therefore, it is advisable for the coach or manager to incorporate them into early practice sessions and repeat them occasionally throughout the season. In this way players will become familiar with the strategy of plays, and they will perform the fundamentals better in competition. Improved performance, of course, may make it possible to win a few more games.

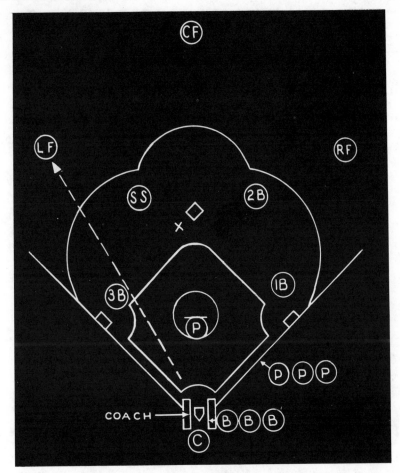

Runner attempts to score and batter tries to reach second, if the handling of the ball makes an advance possible. Infielders and pitcher take proper cutoff and back-up positions. (Defensive assignments for Drills 1, 2, and 3 are shown in Diags. 11–1 through 11–5, pp. 193–95.)

Start of drill. Coach hits ball to left fielder.

After drill. Runner joins line of batters (B), batter becomes next runner (X) at 2b, and pitcher joins line of pitchers (P).

Drill 1a. Base running and cutoff and back-up assignments on single to left field with 2b occupied.

Diag. 17–1a.

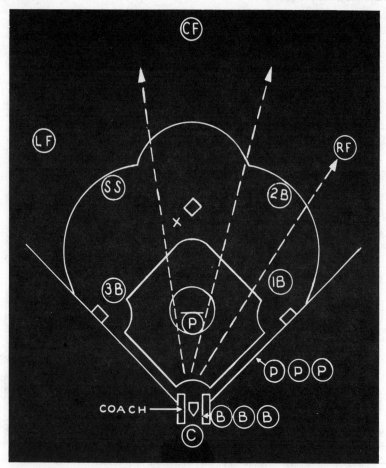

Runner attempts to score and batter tries to reach second, if the handling of the ball makes an advance possible. Infielders and pitcher take proper cutoff and back-up positions.

Start of drill. Coach hits ball to right and center fielders.

After drill. Runner joins line of batters (B), batter becomes next runner (X) at 2b, and pitcher joins line of pitchers (P).

Drill 1b. Base running and cutoff and back-up assignments on single to center or right field with 2b occupied.

Diag. 17—1b.

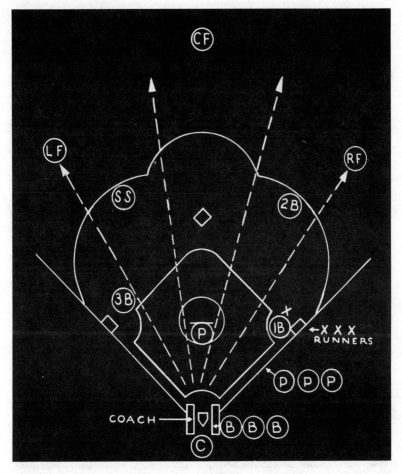

Runner attempts to advance to 3b and batter tries to reach 2b. Infielders and pitcher take proper cutoff and back-up positions.

Start of drill. Coach hits ball to left, right, or center fielders.

After drill. Runner joins line of batters (B), batter joins line of runners (X) at 1b, and pitcher joins line of pitchers (P).

Drill 2. Base running and cutoff and back-up assignments on singles with 1b occupied.

Diag. 17–2.

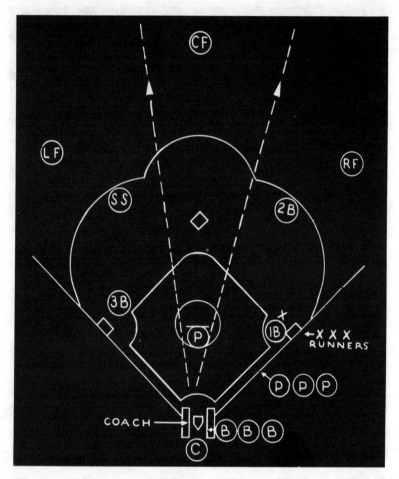

Runner attempts to score and batter tries to reach 3b. Infielders and pitcher take proper relay, cutoff, and back-up positions.

Start of drill. Coach hits ball between outfielders.

After drill. Runner joins line of batters (B), batter joins line of runners (X) at 1b, and pitcher joins line of pitchers (P).

Drill 3. Base running and relay, cutoff, and back-up assignments on extra base hits with 1b occupied.

Diag. 17–3.

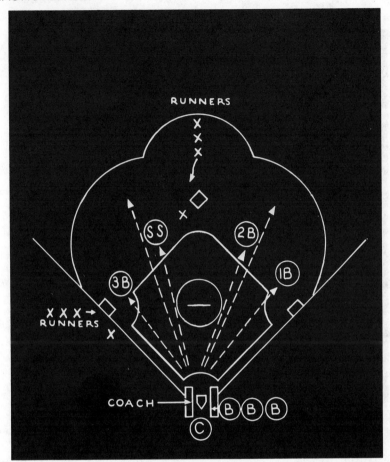

None out. Runners let ball go through infield before advancing.
One out. Runners usually advance immediately because there is pressure on infielders.
Start of drill.
   1. Coach calls none out and hits ball hard toward various infielders.
   2. Coach calls one out and hits ball slowly toward infielders.
   3. Coach calls none or one out and hits ball between infielders.
After drill. Runner on 3b joins line of batters (B), batter joins line of runners (X) at 2b, and runner on 2b joins line of runners (X) at 3b (he continues around to 3b or, if he scores on a hit, returns to 3b).

Drill 4a. Base running and defense, with 2b and 3b occupied, none and one out, infield in.

Diag. 17—4a.

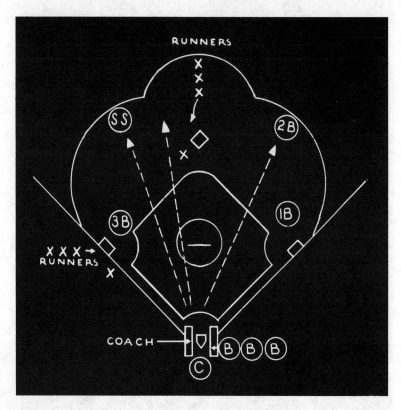

Runner on 3b always advances on ground ball to shortstop or second baseman. Runner on 2b only advances on ball to shortstop's left.

Start of drill.

1. Coach hits ball hard directly toward shortstop.

2. Coach hits ball hard to shortstop's left or toward second baseman. Balls can be hit to first or third baseman, in which case rule in Drill 4a applies with none out.

After drill. Runner on 3b joins line of batters (B), batter joins line of runners (X) at 2b, and runner on 2b joins line of runners (X) at 3b (he continues around to 3b or, if he scores on a hit, returns to 3b).

Drill 4b. Base running and defense with 2b and 3b occupied, none and one out, double play combination back.

Diag. 17–4b.

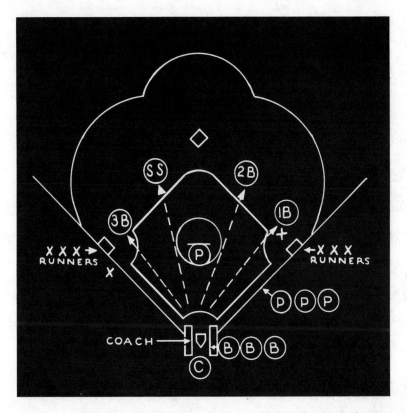

Runner on 3b always breaks for plate on ground ball when 1b is occupied with none or one out. Runner is trapped and batter and runner on
1b attempt to advance. Infielders and pitcher perform run-down duties.
Pitchers may be eliminated in this drill to save time.
Start of drill. Coach hits ball directly toward infielders.
After drill. Runner on 3b joins line of runners (X) at 1b, runner on 1b
joins line of batters (B), and batter joins line of runners (X) at 3b.

Drill 5. Base runners and defense—maneuvering in run-downs with 1b
and 3b occupied.

Diag. 17—5.

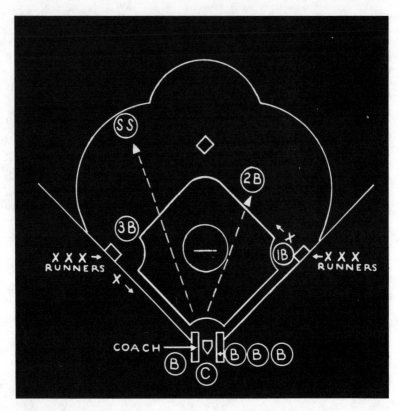

Runner advancing from 1b stops if second baseman is fielding ball in base line. He runs behind second baseman if he can avoid being tagged.

Start of drill.

    1. Coach hits ball hard directly toward shortstop.

    2. Coach hits ball moderately hard toward second baseman, who moves in and fields ball in base line.

Balls can also be hit toward first and third basemen, in which case throw can be made to 2b or plate.

After drill. Runner on 3b joins line of runners (X) at 1b, runner on 1b joins line of batters (B), and batter joins line of runners (X) at 3b.

Drill 6. Base runners and defense—strategy in double play situations with 1b and 3b occupied.

Diag. 17–6.

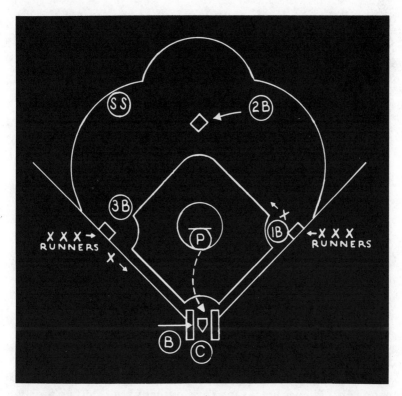

It is advisable to do separate base-running fundamentals (Drills 15 and 16) before doing complete double steal.

Runner on 1b. Runner breaks for 2b as pitcher starts delivery; he stops and gets caught in run-down if catcher throws to 2b (permitting runner on 3b to score); he continues on to 2b if catcher does not throw. This drill can be performed in two parts: 1. catcher makes all throws to second so that runners learn technique of play; 2. catcher tries to outmaneuver runners.

Runner on 3b. Runner jumps forward and toward plate (taking long lead in base line) as pitcher starts delivery, and breaks for plate as catcher's arm comes forward to throw to 2b. Runner can also break after catcher throws if player covering 2b has weak arm. Refer to Drill 16 for action of runner on 3b when player on 1b attempts single steal of 2b.

Start of drill. Drill begins when pitcher starts his delivery.

After drill. Runner on 3b joins line of runners (X) at 1b, and runner on 1b joins line of runners (X) at 3b.

Drill 7. Base runners and defense—double steal with 1b and 3b occupied as pitcher delivers ball.

Diag. 17–7.

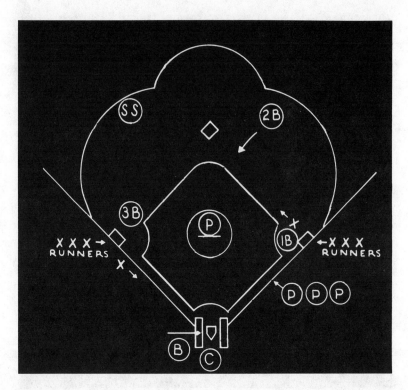

Runner on 1b. Runner breaks for 2b as pitcher's arms start up for stretch, or as pitcher looks toward 1b (runner may purposely get caught off base). He stops and gets caught in run-down as in Drill 7 if pitcher tries to catch him.

Runner on 3b. Runner walks up base line and breaks for plate as pitcher attempts to catch runner advancing to 2b.

Start of drill. Drill begins when pitcher is taking set pitching position. One pitcher can be used in this drill (on day he is taking a good workout).

After drill. Runner on 3b joins line of runners (X) at 1b and runner on 1b joins line of runners (X) at 3b.

Note: A similar type of play can originate by the runner purposely getting picked off first base by the catcher. The same type of play can also originate by a pickoff at second with second and third bases or all of the bases occupied. In these cases the batter takes and the first-base coach yells the proper base for the pickoff throw when the pitch is about halfway to the plate.

Drill 8.   Base runners and defense—double steal with 1b and 3b occupied before pitcher comes set.

Diag. 17–8.

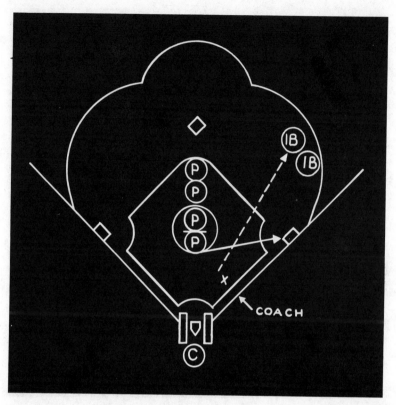

Pitcher takes straight approach, watching bag. He stops on bag and reaches for first baseman's throw. (First baseman throws overhand.) Pitcher turns left toward diamond after completing play to be ready for attempted advance of other runners.

Start of drill. Drill begins when pitcher delivers ball. When pitch reaches plate, coach rolls ball as indicated. Catcher may be omitted, in which case coach rolls ball after pitcher fakes delivery. Opposite first baseman keeps second ball in hand and teams with pitcher. This avoids delays caused by fumbles.

After drill. Pitcher returns to line of pitchers (P) on mound. First basemen alternate in two positions.

Drill 9a. Pitchers—covering 1b, straight approach to bag.

Diag. 17–9a.

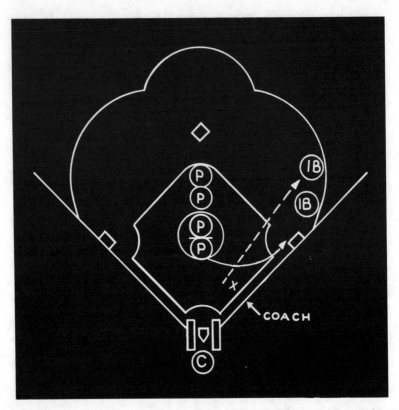

Pitcher makes curved approach, taking first baseman's toss while running over bag. (First baseman steps toward pitcher and tosses ball
underhand.) Pitcher turns left toward diamond after completing play to
be ready for attempted advance of other runners.

Start of drill. Drill begins when pitcher delivers ball. When pitch
reaches plate, coach rolls ball as indicated. Catcher may be omitted,
in which case coach rolls ball after pitcher fakes delivery. Opposite first
baseman keeps second ball in hand and teams with pitcher. This avoids
delays caused by fumbles.

After drill. Pitcher returns to line of pitchers (P) on mound. First basemen alternate in two positions.

Drill 9b. Pitchers—covering 1b, curved approach to bag.

Diag. 17–9b.

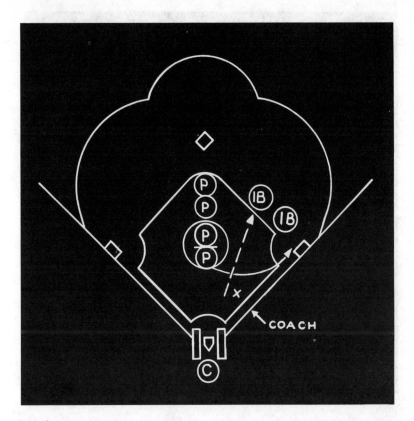

Pitcher fakes missing ground ball, then continues on to bag, making curved approach and taking first baseman's toss while running over bag. (First baseman steps toward pitcher and tosses ball underhand.) Pitcher turns left toward diamond after completing play to be ready for an attempted advance of other runners. This play is used when first baseman plays on or near bag.

Start of drill. Drill begins when pitcher delivers ball. When pitch reaches plate, coach rolls ball as indicated. Catcher may be omitted, in which case coach rolls ball after pitcher fakes delivery. Opposite first baseman keeps second ball in hand and teams with pitcher. This avoids delays caused by fumbles.

After drill. Pitcher returns to line of pitchers (P) on mound. First basemen alternate in two positions.

Drill 9c. Pitchers—covering 1b, curved approach to bag.

Diag. 17–9c.

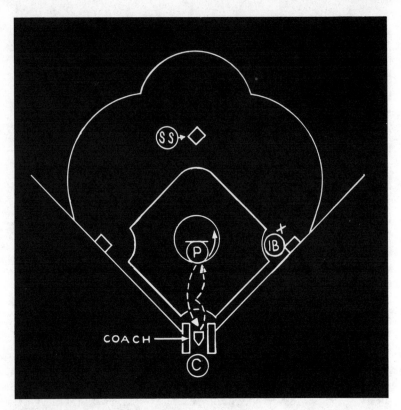

Force play at 2b. Pitcher delivers ball to catcher from set position and coach bounces second ball to pitcher who throws to shortstop covering 2b. He turns toward glove hand, throwing slightly to left-field side of bag, since shortstop usually covers late. Shortstop then throws to 1b for double play. (Runner may be omitted.)

Force play at plate. Pitcher throws to catcher after fielding ball to simulate force play at plate. Catcher then throws to 1b for double play. (Runner may be omitted.)

Pickoff play at 1b. By employing runner with first baseman, pitcher may attempt to pick runner off 1b. Row of runners can be used in this drill, in which case coach can give instructions in base running. (Runner returns to line after breaking for 2b.) See Drill 15.

Start of drill. Drill begins when pitcher delivers ball.

Drill 10. Pitchers—the turn and throw for force plays at 2b and home; for pickoff play at 1b.

Diag. 17–10.

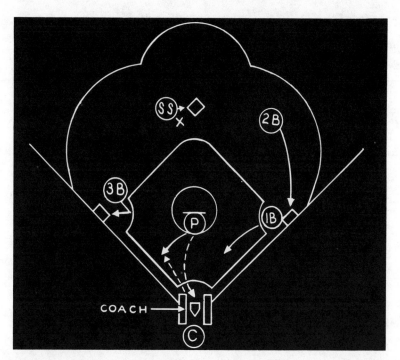

Put-out at 3b. This is a preplanned play, with pitcher covering area to 3b line and first baseman taking territory to mound. Two runners can alternate in this drill, acting as dupes and retreating when coach yells, "Get back." Pitcher comes set looking toward 2b. After pitcher's hands reach set position, shortstop breaks for bag. At first indication of retreat by runner, pitcher attempts to throw belt-high fast ball to batter, then breaks for 3b line, fielding ball rolled by coach and throwing to 3b. He spins toward glove hand to throw as in Drill 10. Coach can also roll ball slowly toward first baseman, or longer bunt toward third baseman. In latter case, third baseman fields ball and throws to 1b.

Pickoff play at 2b. By eliminating first, second, and third basemen, pick-off drill can be worked at 2b. This must be done with signals. Usually shortstop signals by rubbing across shirt and pitcher answers by touching peak of cap. Shortstop breaks for 2b on specific count, which he arranges with pitcher. Using a second baseman, the double team pickoff can be practiced. In this case, play works best by a fake pickoff by short-stop (he circles to bag, then in front of runner) followed by bona fide attempt by second baseman to catch runner.

Start of drill. Drill begins when pitcher takes position on rubber.

Drill 11. Catching base runner advancing to 3b on sacrifice; pickoff play at 2b.

Diag. 17–11.

Pitcher takes catcher's signal, then looks toward runner and starts windup, bringing arms directly up to overhead position. If runner breaks late as if running squeeze play is on, ball is pitched high outside to left-hand batter, high inside to right-hand batter. If runner breaks early as if to steal, ball is pitched low outside to left-hand batter, low inside to right-hand batter.

Pitch fast balls in this drill. Alternate left- and right-hand batters to simulate game conditions. Since this drill should not be performed until pitcher is thoroughly warmed up, it is a good time for coach to study pitcher's delivery and manner in which he throws various pitches from both windup and set pitching positions.

This drill may also be performed on the side lines, in which case pitcher dramatizes runner on base. Batter also dramatizes player stealing in this drill and maintains position at plate until runner is about to slide so that catcher cannot move up to make tag.

Start of drill. Drill begins when pitcher takes catcher's signal. Coach signals runner to steal home or break on a running squeeze play. In order to speed up drills it is best to omit actual batting. This prevents delays caused by fouled or missed balls.

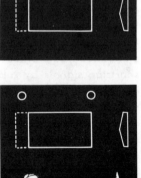

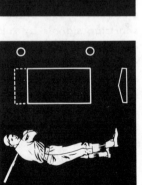

Drill 12. Pitchers—windup with runner on 3b.

Diag. 17–12.

306

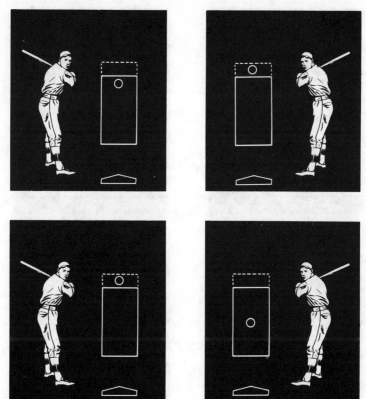

First pitch should be high in sacrifice situations. When first pitch is strike, second pitch should be above strike zone because batter may bunt this pitch in the air. If first pitch is ball, second pitch should be in middle of strike zone to prevent pitcher from getting in hole. This is particularly true early in game.

Pitch fast balls in this drill. Alternate left- and right-hand batters to simulate game conditions.

In order to speed up drills, it is best to omit actual batting. This prevents delays caused by fouled or missed balls and permits catcher to operate without equipment.

This drill may also be performed on the side lines, in which case pitcher dramatizes runner on base.

Start of drill. Drill begins when pitcher takes signal.

> **Drill 13.** Pitchers—the pitch in sacrifice situations.

Diag. 17—13.

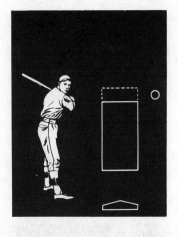 

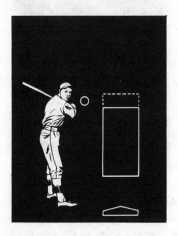 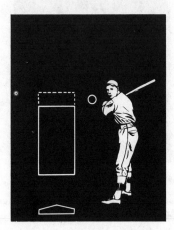

Pitch high outside when making conventional pitchout as well as when issuing intentional pass.

Pitch high inside if catcher gives indicator signal to drive batter from path of intended throw.

Pitch fast balls in this drill. Alternate left- and right-hand batters to simulate game conditions.

This drill may be performed on the side lines, in which case pitcher dramatizes runner on base.

In order to speed up drills, it is best to omit actual batting. This prevents delays caused by fouled or missed balls. The catcher should wear equipment in these drills to avoid the danger of injury.

Drill 14. Pitcher and catcher—making pitchout.

Diag. 17–14.

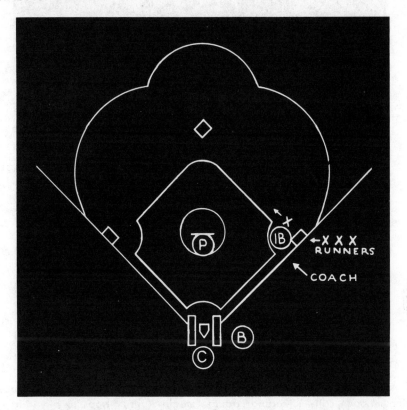

It is advisable to do separate base-running fundamentals (this drill and Drill 16) before going through complete double steal (Drill 7).

Players 1. take fast walk away from base while watching ball, in normal advance; 2. make crossover step for regular steal; 3. casually step back toward base after fast walk, then break, on delayed steal; and 4. start as for regular steal, then glance toward plate after taking two or three steps, on hit-and-run. Several players can break at same time by lining up behind regular base runner. Pitcher can make occasional throw to 1b, although this delays completing drills. Number 2 and 3 starts can be used as variations in double steal (Drill 7).

Start of drill. Runner takes lead with pitcher coming to set position. Coach calls 1. normal advance, 2. regular steal, 3. delayed steal, and 4. hit-and-run, and runner makes proper start as pitcher delivers.

After drill. Players return to end of line after running four or five steps.

Drill 15. Base running starts from 1b.

Diag. 17–15.

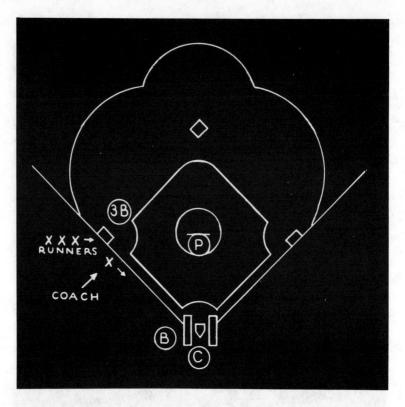

Double steal. Runner takes short lead with pitcher coming to set position. Coach calls 1. regular double steal. Runner hops to big lead on base line when pitcher starts delivery and breaks for plate as catcher returns ball to pitcher. Coach calls 2. delayed double steal. Runner's action is the same as for a regular double steal.

Fake to score. Coach calls single steal. Runner on 3b steps toward diamond to base line from short lead when pitcher starts delivery and fakes going home when ball leaves catcher's hand. In game this may force player covering to cut in for catcher's throw, thus making possible successful steal of second.

If coach stops action to instruct, he yells for pitcher to take windup so that all pitches are not delivered from set position.

Start of drill. Drill begins when pitcher starts delivery. Coach calls play.

After drill. Players return to end of line after running four or five steps. Drill can be continued by replacing pitcher, or line of runners can be dispersed and reassembled when next pitcher takes mound.

Drill 16. Base running starts from 3b on double steal with 1b and 3b occupied; proper fake to score when steal of 2b is attempted.

Diag. 17–16.

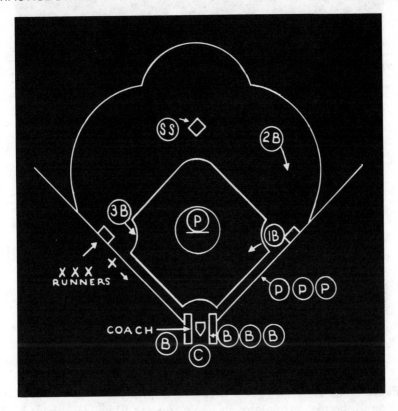

Runner on third makes normal advance during windup, then breaks for plate as pitcher is about to release ball. Batter bunts ball and starts for 1b, and runner scores.

Coach watches players to see that proper starting technique is used. It is usually advisable to work this drill with signals so that game conditions prevail and to have pitcher throw ball over plate so that batters and runners learn technique of play.

Start of drill. Drill begins when pitcher starts delivery.

After drill. Players alternate as batters and runners.

Drill 17. Running squeeze play.

Diag. 17–17.

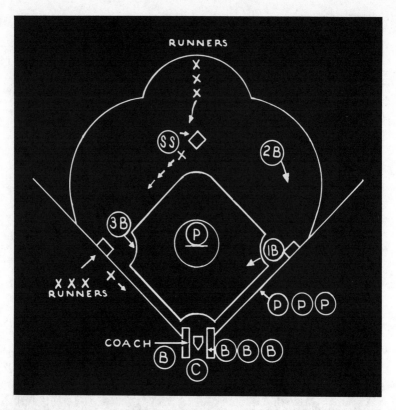

Offense. Runner on 2b breaks for 3b when pitcher starts windup. Runner on 3b breaks for plate as in single squeeze (Drill 17). Batter bunts ball and starts for 1b, and both runners score. Instead of the batter bunting, coach can roll ball, in which case signals can be used with runner on 2b to indicate stop at 3b or score. This variation is good training for pitcher.

Defense. Catcher yells, "Check third," when he anticipates play, thus informing pitcher to be alert for second runner's attempt to score. In this case pitcher fields ball, then glances over right shoulder to check player rounding 3b.

It is usually advisable to work this drill with signals so that game conditions will prevail and to have pitcher throw ball over plate so that batters and runners learn technique of play.

Start of drill. Drill begins when pitcher starts delivery.

After drill. Batter joins line of runners (X) at 3b, runner on 3b joins line of runners (X) at 2b, and runner on 2b joins line of batters (B).

Drill 18. Double running squeeze play.

Diag. 17–18.

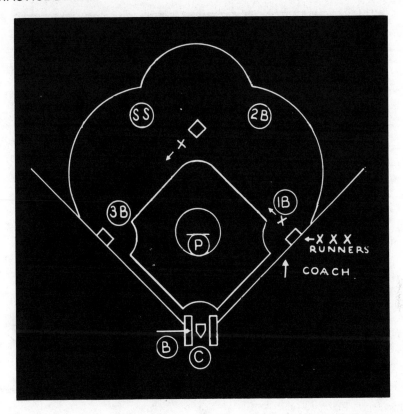

Runner on 2b breaks for 3b when pitcher starts delivery. Runner on 1b, watching 2b, follows his break.
Start of drill. Drill begins when pitcher starts delivery.
After drill. Players return to line of runners at first.

Drill 19. Double steal, 1b and 2b occupied.

Diag. 17–19.

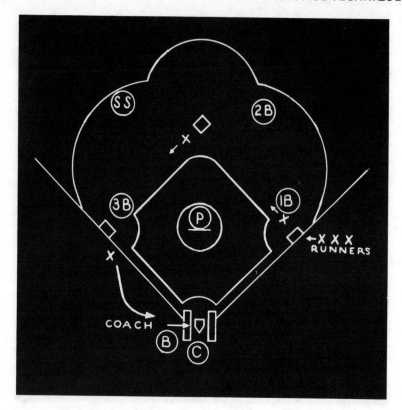

Coach makes sure runner on 3b runs wide of plate to permit batter to swing if pitch is over.

Start of drill.   Runners break as pitcher starts windup.

After drill.   Players return to line of runners at 1b.

Drill 20.   Break of runners with all bases occupied, two out, and 3 and 2 on hitter.

Diag. 17–20.

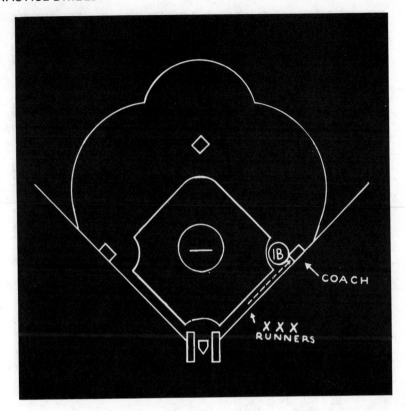

Runner breaks down base line and coach waves arm for straight run or points with right hand and waves left arm for curved approach. Coach makes sure player watches bag, not ball, keeps between 3-foot lines on straight run, or hits inside corner of bag when rounding bag.

After drill. Player returns to line of runners.

Drill 21. Base runners—approach to 1b.

Diag. 17–21.

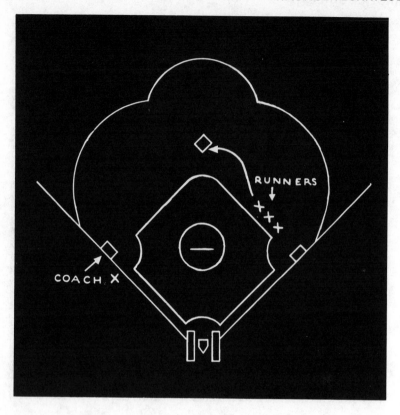

Runner approaches 2b and coach gives signal to stop or continue on to 3b (applies on ball hit to right field). Coach makes sure player turns and finds ball, if stop signal is given.

After drill. Player returns to line of runners.

Drill 22. Base runners—approach to 2b.

Diag. 17–22.

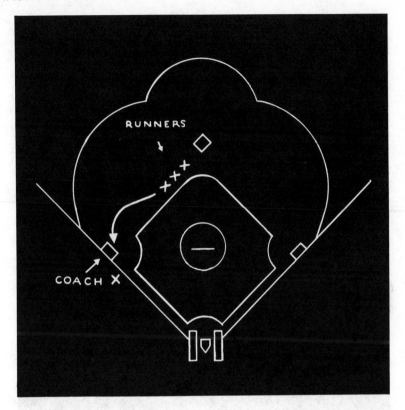

Runner approaches 3b and coach guides him into bag, giving stop signal (hands in air or finger pointed to bag) from near bag, and stop signal (hands in air) or go signal (arm waved) from up base line. Coach checks that runner finds ball when going past bag (on hands-up signal near bag), stops on bag (if finger is pointed at bag), or rounds bag at full speed when coach is up line.

After drill. Player returns to line of runners.

Drill 23. Base runners—approach to 3b.

Diag. 17–23.

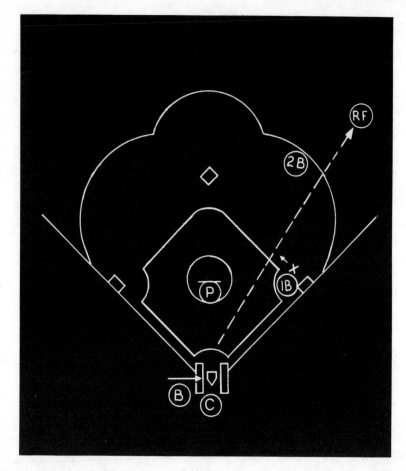

Coach calls, "Hit behind runner," and batter picks pitch and tries to hit ball on ground between first and second basemen. This usually advances runner to 2b (and to scoring position even though batter may be retired at first). It is advisable to call the strategy on an early swing so that player can be rewarded with an extra swing if successful or a swing can be deducted if unsuccessful.

This drill is performed during batting practice.

After drill. Batter runs to first after last swing and becomes runner.

Drill 24. Hitting behind runner.

Diag. 17–24.

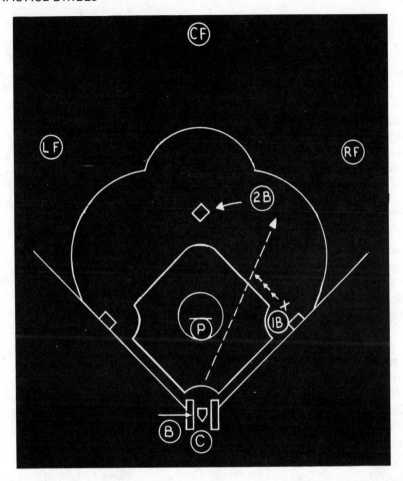

Coach calls, "Hit-and-run." Runner breaks on the pitch and right-hand batter tries to hit ensuing pitch on ground, preferably toward second baseman.
Second baseman leaves his position since he must cover on what appears to
be an attempted steal. Left-hand batter attempts to hit toward shortstop
for same reason. It is advisable to call the strategy on an early swing so that
player can be rewarded with an extra swing if successful or a swing can be deducted if unsuccessful.

This drill is performed during batting practice.

After drill. Batter runs to first after last swing and becomes runner.

Drill 25. Hit-and-run play.

Diag. 17–25.

CHECK SYSTEM

A smart manager or coach will use a check system, regardless of the number or type of drills employed, to check on the development of his players. One check system is shown in Fig. 17–1. Three forms are set up for checking base running and batting, pitching, and catching, and one for charting pitchers for control. For the first three, the name of the drill appears across the top and the players' names are written in on the left side. When a player performs the drill, a check is placed opposite his name. This kind of record is particularly valuable in high school and college, because players frequently miss important practice sessions.

To chart pitchers for control, the checking is usually done with alternate left- and right-hand batters at the plate, and fast balls, curves, and slow balls are recorded as balls and strikes. The pitching chart shown in Fig. 17–1 is based on 28 pitches of four similar sequences. Each sequence is delivered from alternate windup and set pitching positions with specific bases occupied. The charting may be recorded by drawing a line through the proper letter, B or S. It can become more detailed by considering the space on the chart as a strike zone. In this case, a dot in the middle of the space indicates a belt-high pitch over the middle of the plate and marks in the corners, pitches high inside, low outside, and others. In the final tabulations the number of balls is counted and subtracted from 28. The number of balls and strikes is then recorded in the second column ("Final Total"). This includes a breakdown of individual pitches as well as total balls and strikes. In conjunction with the pitching chart, a pitching target may also be used (see Appendix).

Most coaches do not have the time or facilities to employ such a procedure, in which case almost the same benefits can be obtained by working with one pitcher at a time on several occasions. In this case the coach can stand near the pitcher and call fast ball, curve, or slow ball. This is done loud enough so that the catcher knows what is being pitched. It is advisable to dramatize several "times at bat" in such a routine, meanwhile varying the calls in relation to the count on the batter. The coach can then judge the control of the pitcher and make corrections relative to technique.

This setup affords an excellent opportunity to stress the importance of variance in pitching from a set position to thwart base stealing. This can be done by giving commands such as "Come set; look toward first; look toward plate; pitch." On subsequent turns the coach can call, "Come set; back off rubber." "Come set; pitch." "Come set; look toward first; look toward plate; throw to first."

BASE RUNNING AND BATTING DRILLS

NAME OF PLAYER	Lead-Advance 1b, 2b & 3b				Fielder in Baseline		Double Steal 1b-2b, 1b-3b				Squeeze Play		Tag-Up	Infield In Back		Ball to ss	Run to Rounding			Sacrifice Bunt	Hit Behind Runner	Hit and Run
	N	S	DS	HR	Stop	Behind	All	Reg	D	OP	S	D	Up	3b	1b-3b	2b	1b	2b	3b			

PITCHING DRILLS

NAME OF PLAYER	Set to 1b	Force at Plate	DS (1b–3b)		Sacrifice		Pick-off 2b	Switch of Signals	Int. Pass	Pitch-out	Squeeze Play		Steal of Home	Fielding Grounder Throw to 2b	Cover 1b
			Back off	Back to Pitcher	Pitch Throw to 1b	Play to 3b					S	D			

KEY TO SYMBOLS:

OP—On pitcher
S—Single, slow ball, steal, or strike
b—Base

N—Normal
F—Fast ball
HR—Hit and run

B—Ball
C—Curve ball
D—Delayed or double

Fig. 17-1. Forms for checking technique and tactics.

NAME OF PLAYER	Double Steal		Pitchouts			Switch of Signals	Double Squeeze Play	Fielding Bunt	Fielding Fly Ball	Force Out	Tag Out	Back-up	
	1b-2b	1b-3b	Away	Toward	Int. Pass							1b	3b

PITCHING CONTROL DRILL

PITCHING CONTROL RECORD

NAME OF PLAYER	Final Total (28)	Breakdown Total				Windup (Unoccupied)					Set Position (1b)					Windup (3b)					Set Position (2b)				
		F	C	S	Pitch	F	C	B	B	B	F	C	B	B	B	F	C	B	B	B	F	C	F	C	S
					Call	S	S	S	S		S	S	S	S		S	S	S	S		S	S	S	B	S
					Pitch	F	C	B	B	B	F	C	B	B	B	F	C	B	B	B	F	C	F	B	S
					Call	S	S	S	S		S	S	S	S		S	S	S	S		S	S	S	B	S

KEY TO SYMBOLS:

B—Ball
C—Curve ball
D—Delayed or double

N—Normal
F—Fast ball
HR—Hit and run

OP—On pitcher
S—Single, slow ball, steal, or strike
b—Base

Fig. 17-1. *(Continued)*

322

GAME
STRATEGY

18

Duties of
Base Coaches

The judgment and alertness of coaches at first and third bases play an important part in the success or failure of a team. The primary duties of coaches are giving signals and assisting base runners. In addition they hit fly balls to the pitchers during the batting practice, and both ground balls and fly balls to the infielders and outfielders during the regular fielding practice. A good coach does more than this. He offers constructive criticism to the players and manager, pats players on the back for good work, and acts as a peacemaker in situations wherein the morale of the team might be affected. Another important duty involves the diagnosis of weaknesses in the opposition's offense and defense. The coach may also confuse the defense occasionally by calling the wrong base on throws, or by calling, "No play" to thwart a throw.

In amateur baseball, players are frequently required to act as first- and third-base coaches. Because this is normally covered by rule both for high schools and for colleges, it is advisable for such players to learn the routine duties of coaches.

FIRST-BASE COACH

The first-base coach, although not having to pass judgment like the third-base coach, nevertheless has important duties.

325

AIDING THE BATTER

Most batters make the mistake of watching the ball after it is hit. This retards their speed, and often means the difference between reaching first base safely and being retired. In many instances it results in an inability to advance. The first-base coach often prevents this by yelling, "Come on" and "Don't watch the ball," meanwhile waving his left forearm toward his chest. In the event that a throw is not made to first base, the coach holds his hands up and toward the runner, meanwhile yelling, "Find the ball," if there is any indication that an advance might be possible. When the ball in question is on the ground, and rolls away from, or through, an infielder's hands, he points and waves with the right and left hands respectively toward the diamond to inform the runner to round first, and also yells, "Make your turn." (Fig. 18–1.) The failure to run without looking at the ball is especially evident on fly balls that will apparently be caught. Since there is no guarantee that any ball will be fielded, the coach urges the batter to run to the best of his ability. This makes it possible to reach second or third base and even score if the ball is dropped or escapes the fielder. If there is a runner on first base when the ball is hit, the coach yells to the batter to watch the runner ahead of him as he approaches the bag. Infrequently a batter becomes absorbed in the flight of the ball and runs by a player already on base.

As a general rule, it is impossible to control the runner once he has passed first base. If, however, it is the coach's opinion that the batter cannot reach second base on what appears to be, at the crack of the bat, a potential two-base hit, he yells, "No, no" as the player rounds the bag. This is particularly important with none out. He calls similarly if he thinks the batter cannot reach second base on a fly ball over the infield even though the ball may be dropped. If he thinks the runner can advance he yells, "Go for two," and points toward second base with both hands.

AIDING THE RUNNER ON FIRST BASE

Once the batter reaches first base and cannot advance, the coach tells him to stay on the bag until the pitcher stands on or straddles the rubber to combat the hidden-ball trick. (The pitcher must have the ball if he straddles the rubber, or if his foot comes in contact with the rubber.) This is frequently done by merely saying, "Find the ball." He also reminds the runner of the number of outs, the throwing ability of the outfielders, and whether or not the outfielders

a, b, c. The arm is waved toward the body to encourage the batter to run. Both hands point toward second, indicating "Round the bag and continue your advance."

d, e, f. The runner circles into the bag from foul territory, leaning the body toward the diamond for a fast turn. The runner touches the bag, then locates the ball.

Fig. 18–1. Informing the batter to round first base.

are playing deep. With none out he tells the runner to play safe and not take chances. If there are less than two out, he advises the runner to avoid being tagged by the second baseman if a ground ball is fielded in the base line, and to break up a double play if possible by sliding into the pivot man.

When the pitcher is ready to pitch and the runner has taken his position off the bag, the coach sees that the lead is in the base line and is adequate according to the speed and starting ability of the player. He also refreshes the player's mind regarding the move of the pitcher to first base and whether or not the catcher has a good arm and likes to try to catch runners off base. Left-hand pitchers are extra tricky in throwing to first base so it is important to continually warn the runner. It is also advisable to yell, "Make sure he pitches" when the count is three balls and one strike or three balls and two strikes on the batter because the runner is usually breaking on the pitch. These are natural run-and-hit situations, since another ball will result in a walk; consequently, the tactic is different from an outright steal.

WATCHING THE FIRST BASEMAN

If first base is occupied and the first baseman plays on the bag, the coach may assume any position in the coaching box. (An exception occurs when the sacrifice bunt is likely.) The runner always

Fig. 18–2. First-base coach watching the first baseman for a pickoff play.

knows, in this case, that the first baseman will be near the bag, and can take his lead accordingly. However, because this is impossible when the first baseman plays back, the coach takes the responsibility of warning the runner. It is necessary to face the first baseman to do so (Fig. 18–2). The first baseman and catcher are thus prevented from working a pickoff successfully. The second baseman may also attempt to complete this play with the catcher when the first baseman goes in for a bunt (Diag. 18–1). A catcher may

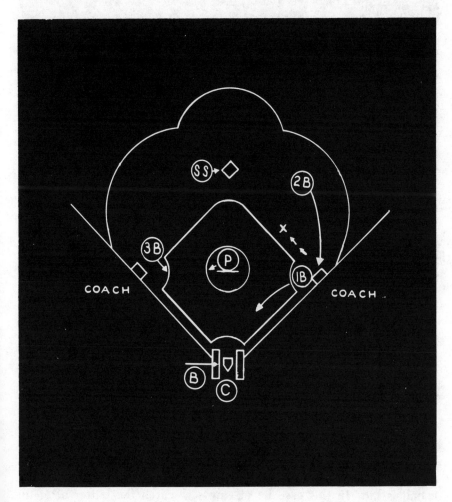

Diag. 18–1. Pickoff by second baseman when first baseman goes in for a bunt.

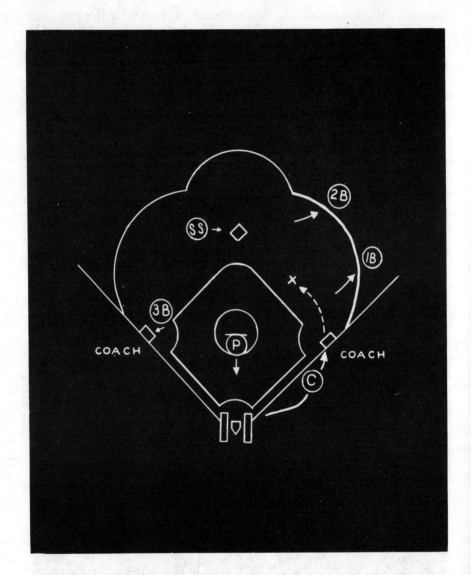

Diag. 18–2. Pickoff by catcher after trailing batter to first.

attempt to work a similar play by circling down the base line after a ball is hit. In this case he attempts to catch the batter after he has rounded the bag (Diag. 18–2). If any such play is attempted, or if the pitcher or catcher tries to catch the runner, the coach yells, "Look out" or "Get back."

CALLING ON FLY BALLS

If a short or moderately deep fly ball is hit with first base occupied, the coach calls, "Halfway" unless there are two out. He calls, "Tag-up" if the ball is hit deep, for the runner can frequently advance. This, of course, depends on the speed of the runner and the throwing ability of the outfielder catching the ball. If there is a runner on second or third base, or runners on second and third bases with first base occupied, and the runners tag-up, the runner on first is told to do likewise, for it is often possible to advance because of a high throw to third base or the plate. (An exception occurs when the runner on third base tags-up on a short fly ball in back of the infield, because it might be impossible to reach second base if the ball falls safely.) The runner on first base is told to tag-up on foul flies for a similar reason.

AIDING THE RUNNER ON SECOND BASE

If first base is unoccupied, the coach warns a runner on second base when the shortstop or second baseman nears the bag. He does so from an erect position, with his hands cupped around his mouth. However, because it is the duty of the third-base coach to guide the runner, unless there is immediate danger the first-base coach does not call. This permits the runner to hear the voice of the third-base coach distinctly at all times.

THIRD-BASE COACH

The third-base coach has duties similar to those of the first-base coach. In addition he shoulders the responsibility of the base runner after first base has been passed. This includes indicating to the runner whether he should continue on to third base or stop at second, if he should stay on the bag at second (which is only necessary when the ball is hit to right field, because the runner is able to use his own judgment in other instances), and whether it is advisable for him to continue on to the plate, or stop after rounding third base. Other duties are to inform the runner approaching third base when a slide should be made and, if so, to which side of the bag, and whether it is necessary to stay on the bag in instances where a throw is likely to be made to third to catch the runner rounding the bag.

AIDING THE RUNNER ROUNDING SECOND BASE

There are ways for the coach to help a base runner in the above situations. The coach's informative actions to the runner are illustrated in Fig. 18–3. For example, when a single is made to right field, or when a ball is fumbled by the first or second baseman with first base occupied and it is apparent that the player will be unable to reach third base safely, the coach stands erect and holds the palms of his hands toward second base. (The coach points to second base if the ball is near the bag or a throw is coming toward second.) If the runner can reach third base, the coach stands similarly and waves his left or right arm toward his chest, using only forearm action.

AIDING THE RUNNER APPROACHING THIRD BASE

Once the runner continues on to third base, he must be guided into the bag. If the play is likely to be close, the coach indicates to the runner to slide. When the throw is to the plate side of the bag,

a. Stopping a player rounding second or approaching third.

Fig. 18–3.   Third-base coach.

the coach crouches to the opposite side and holds the hands low—palms down (Fig. 18-3b). A similar position is taken on the other side of the bag if the throw arrives on the left-field side of the base. These positions indicate to the runner on which side of the bag to slide. If the throw in the above situation is exceptionally wide or is intercepted by another infielder, it may not be necessary for the runner to slide. The coach gives the runner his information by

b. Indicating for the runner approaching third to slide to the left-field side of the bag.

c. Indicating for the runner approaching third to stop on the bag.

Fig. 18–3. *(Continued)*

Fig. 18–4. Stopping a player rounding third base.

standing as is shown in Fig. 18–3a. Similar help is necessary if a runner on second base attempts to advance to third base on a ground ball to the shortstop or on a fly ball to the outfield. In some instances an attempt is made by an infielder to catch a runner after he has rounded third base. The coach then points to the bag to indicate to the player to stay on the bag, and yells, "Stay on the bag" (Fig. 18–3c).

AIDING THE RUNNER ROUNDING THIRD BASE

When a definite scoring opportunity presents itself, that is, when a single is made with second base occupied, or a two-base hit with first base occupied, the coach runs to a point about halfway between

a, b. The position up the base line which permits control of the runner after he has rounded the bag.

c. The hands raised to stop the runner.

d. The runner turns to the left to locate the ball.

e, f. The runner retreats and slides.

Fig. 18–4. *(Continued)*

third base and the plate, and faces the player rounding third base, meanwhile watching the ball so that he can judge whether or not the player can score. If he can score, the coach waves his left hand toward his chest, preferably using only forearm action. In some instances it is advisable to yell to the player to take his time. This often happens when the runner can easily score. On the other hand, it is necessary to urge the player to run in other situations. This is sometimes important even though the ball may not be thrown to the plate, because occasionally a run fails to count because the third out is made at another base before the runner reaches the plate. The coach indicates this by slow and fast arm action, slow action meaning to ease up slightly, and fast action to run hard all the way. If the player is unable to score, the coach raises his arms overhead with the palms of the hands toward the runner.

The position of the coach is especially important when the scoring opportunity is the result of a relay from the outfield or a fumble by the outfielder, because it permits the runner to be turned back even though he has rounded the bag at full speed. As soon as the coach sees that the runner will have to be checked at third base, he runs back toward the bag with his hands in the stop position (Fig. 18–4). This permits the runner to return to the bag without danger of being put out. The coach also runs back to his regular position in the coaching box after having sent a runner to the plate, because help may be given to another runner approaching third base.

In order to make the correct decisions at third base, it is necessary for the coach to know the speed of his players, the throwing ability of the opposing outfielders, the throwing ability of infielders who act as relay men, and the defensive positions of the outfielders prior to the ball being hit. It is also important to consider the speed with which the ball reaches the outfield, the speed and direction of the wind, the condition of the field and the ability of the following batter. Other factors include the number of outs, the score, and the stage of the game. A rule which is almost accepted as standard for third-base coaches is to always send the runner home from second base on a single to the outfield with two out because this hit may be the last scoring opportunity in the inning. For this reason, as well as other scoring situations, it is advisable for the coach to stand at the plate end of the coaching box. This enables him to quickly reach the proper coaching position, if a single goes through to the outfield.

AIDING RUNNERS ON SECOND AND THIRD BASES

After a runner has reached second base and cannot advance, the third-base coach informs him to "Find the ball," as at first base, unless, of course, he knows the pitcher has the ball. (This also applies to the runner on third base.) He also relates the number of outs, and tells the player to remain on second base if a ground ball is hit hard toward or to the third-base side of the shortstop with first base unoccupied and less than two out. If third base is occupied, he is told what the runner intends to do. Of course, with all the bases occupied all runners have to move on a ground ball regardless of the number of outs. However, with only second and third bases occupied, none out and the infield in, the runners on second and third bases are always told to make a ground ball go through the infield before attempting to advance. (Most teams have the runners ad-

Fig. 18–5. Watching the shortstop and second baseman to prevent a pickoff play: the hands cupped at the mouth ready to warn the runner.

vance with one out.) In a similar situation, with the infield back, the runner on third is told to score on a ground ball to the second baseman or shortstop, and in some cases to a first or third baseman who plays very deep, when there is no danger of being thrown out at the plate. (The first and third basemen normally play in to guard against a squeeze play.) The runner on second base is also given this information, but he must use his own judgment in attempting to advance to third base under such circumstances.

Another important duty of the third-base coach is to watch the shortstop and second baseman to prevent a runner on second base from being caught off base (Fig. 18–5). The third baseman is watched with third base occupied for the same reason. If both the shortstop and second baseman play in their regular positions, the coach continually calls, "All right." However, if either of them moves toward the bag, he yells, "Look out" or "Get back." The second baseman is less likely to make the pickoff play successfully because the runner can watch both his movements and those of the pitcher from the regular base-running stance. Because the shortstop cannot be seen from this position, he is the logical player to attempt to catch the runner. Therefore the coach concentrates on this player and warns the runner accordingly.

On fly balls the practice is the same as that followed by the first-base coach. On short or moderately deep fly balls the coach generally calls, "Halfway," and on long fly balls, "Tag-up." If the catcher or an infielder is likely to catch the ball while running away from the infield, the runner on third base is told to tag-up. The runner is also told to tag-up on some long foul flies.

When a double steal is to be attempted with first and third bases occupied, the coach tells the runner on third base to try to score if the catcher throws to second base. He merely says, "Regular double steal" or "Delayed double steal." For this reason he keeps as close to the runner as possible to prevent the third baseman from hearing his conversation. Standing in such a manner also makes it less likely that other players on the opposing team will know such a play is to be attempted because a quick change of position is not necessary. Moving close to the runner from a deep position in the coaching box may tip off the double steal.

The coach also tells the runner to remain at third base if the runner on first base has been given a single-steal sign. A similar warning is given prior to the runner starting for second base on a hit-and-run play because the batter often misses the ball or is unable to reach the pitch. In this case the runner on third base maneuvers as if the runner on first was attempting a steal of second. The runner is also told to be especially alert when the batter might attempt to score the runner with a bunt. If a running squeeze play is to be used, the coach tells the runner to watch the batter for the squeeze sign so that both the batter and runner know that the play will be tried on the ensuing pitch. The runner on third base is also reminded to break for the plate on all ground balls with first base occupied. This frequently draws a throw and prevents a double play by way of second to first. It also enables the runner to score with none out even though a double play is made; likewise with one out when only the runner on first base is forced at second.

SUMMARY

FIRST-BASE COACH

1. Encourage the batter to hustle down the base line and to keep his eyes on the bag, not the ball.
2. Advise the batter to round the bag if possible by waving the left arm and pointing toward second base with the right hand.
3. Inform the batter to round the bag and continue his advance by pointing toward second base with both hands.
4. Remind the runner to stay on the bag until the pitcher stands on or straddles the rubber—to prevent a hidden ball trick.
5. Yell words of encouragement and information to the runner, remind-

ing him of the number of outs and also of the throwing ability of outfielders.

6. Warn the runner on attempted pickoff plays by the first baseman, the second baseman, and the catcher.

THIRD-BASE COACH

1. Guide the runner rounding second base on a ball hit to right field. Swing the arm for an advance. Raise the hands to stop the runner.
2. Advise a runner on second base not to advance on a ground ball toward or to the shortstop's right (or toward the pitcher) with less than two out and first base unoccupied, unless there is an error or the ball goes through.
3. Remain near the bag to stop a runner approaching third base. Get up the base line if there is a possibility the runner might score.
4. Know the speed of base runners and the throwing ability of the infielders and outfielders on the opposing team.
5. Inform base runners about predetermined strategy, when to tag-up and play halfway on fly balls.
6. Watch the shortstop and second baseman for pickoff plays and yell, "Look out" or "Get back" to warn the runner.

DISCUSSION QUESTIONS

1. Describe the duties of the first-base coach with (a) all of the bases occupied and two out; (b) first and second bases occupied and none out.
2. When the third-base coach stands approximately halfway between third base and the plate, what does it indicate to the runner rounding third? Give the two circumstances that make it necessary for the coach to alter his position.
3. How can a first-base coach give assistance to the batter after the ball is hit?
4. What instructions are helpful to a player who is on base or has just reached base?
5. Demonstrate the three basic hand signals which the third-base coach gives a runner approaching third. What are some of the factors which determine the strategy in coaching third base? Include offensive, defensive, and physical factors in your answer.
6. Discuss the strategy of the third-base coach on ground balls when (a) second and third bases are occupied with none and one out; (b) first and third bases are occupied with none or one out.
7. Why is it important for the third-base coach to stand near the runner

when a double steal is to be attempted with first and third bases occupied? How does this become a factor if a single-steal signal is given to the runner on first with the same bases occupied?

8. Explain the actions of the third-base coach in the following situations: (*a*) a runner on second scores on a line single directly toward the left fielder, the batter reaches second base on the throw to the plate and continues on to third as the catcher fumbles the ball; (*b*) a batter hits a two-base hit down the right-field line, then advances to third when the ball bounces away from the right fielder.

TRUE–FALSE QUESTIONS AND ANSWERS

T F 1. Coaching strategy on ground balls is frequently predetermined for base runners by the position of infielders.

T F 2. An alert coach continually yells "All Right" when defensive players are not maneuvering into position to catch the runner.

T F 3. If the third-base coach points his finger toward the bag, the approaching runner knows he must stay on the bag.

T F 4. Failure to warn the runner on third base of a hit-and-run play between the batter and the runner on first is poor coaching strategy.

T F 5. On an advance from first base after a single to left field, the runner looks toward the third-base coach for instructions as he rounds second.

T F 6. Runners on first and second bases are the responsibility of the first-base coach with all of the bases occupied.

T F 7. A smart third-base coach always makes the runner on third tag-up on fly balls in back of the infield.

T F 8. The lead which a runner takes is not the concern of the coach.

ANSWERS

F F F F T T T T
8 7 6 5 4 3 2 1

19

Methods of Giving Signals

The sets of signals or signs in this chapter show the simple, as well as the complex, methods of giving catching, coaching, and batting signals.

Individuals have varying degrees of intelligence and different emotional reactions; therefore it is important to devise a simple set of signals. This gives a reasonable guarantee that all players will understand the signals under game conditions.

SIGNALS OF THE CATCHER

The catcher gives five signals. Three of these indicate the pitcher's assortment of pitches, and the other two involve an attempt to catch a runner off base, one sign being designated as a pitchout signal to the pitcher, and the other as information to a certain infielder to cover the base he defends. The latter is given as the catcher takes his signal position, and if the infielder responds with a prearranged acknowledgment, such as touching the peak of his cap, the pitchout sign is flashed to the pitcher.

SINGLE-DIGIT METHOD

The most simple method for giving signs involves the showing of one signal, one finger indicating a fast ball, two fingers a breaking ball, three fingers a slow ball, a clenched fist a pitchout, and the throwing hand on the end of the glove for an infielder to cover (Fig.

19–1). Since there are four infielders, the catcher often has four signs similar to that of placing the hand on the glove, so that if more than one runner is on base each player will know when to cover. In order to make it easy for the catcher to remember the signs, he gives the signs to the first and second baseman with his right hand, and those to the shortstop and third baseman with his left hand. For example, the signs for the first baseman, second baseman, shortstop, and third baseman could be, respectively: placing the hand on the end of the glove, removing the glove, permitting the glove hand to hang to the inside of the left leg and holding the glove similarly to the outside of the left leg. Another method is to pick up dirt and toss it underhand toward the player expected to cover. This, of course, means only one sign for all players, but if very many pitch-outs are used such a sign is likely to be discovered by the opposing team. In the above signal system the wiggling of one finger and two fingers is often used to indicate a let-up fast ball and slow curve, respectively.

A more complicated method of giving signals is generally used in professional baseball, since the runner on second base often attempts to steal the sign and inform the batter by a prearranged signal the type of ball that is to be pitched. There are many ways to do this. Two of the common methods employ one finger for a fast ball, two fingers for a breaking ball, and three fingers for a slow ball, as in the single-digit method, but include the signal as part of a series of signs.

SINGLE-DIGIT COMBINATION METHOD

Three signals are usually given in the single-digit combination method, and one of these is designated as the actual sign, usually the second showing of the fingers. For example, one finger followed by *one finger* and then two fingers would indicate a fast ball; one finger, *two fingers,* and one finger a breaking ball; and two fingers, *three fingers,* and two fingers a slow ball (Fig. 19–2). The pitchout signal with the pitcher may be designated by showing one or two fingers three times. In this case one finger can be used to indicate a fast ball, and two fingers a curve. The sign for an infielder to cover may be the same as that previously described under the single-digit method of giving signs.

It can be readily seen that there are various ways to signal a fast ball, a breaking ball, and a slow ball in this method of giving signals,

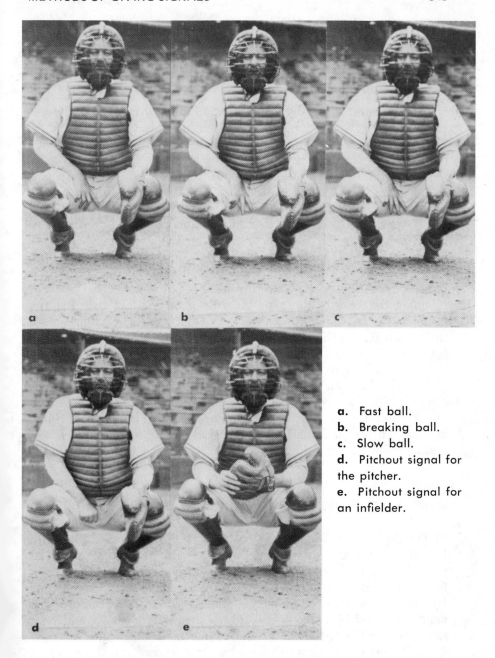

a. Fast ball.
b. Breaking ball.
c. Slow ball.
d. Pitchout signal for
the pitcher.
e. Pitchout signal for
an infielder.

Fig. 19–1. Signals of the catcher: single-digit method.

since the first and third signs may be one, two, or three fingers. The following combination of fingers shows how this may be done:

Fast	1	1	3	Breaking	3	2	2	Slow	1	3	2
Ball	2	1	2	Ball	1	2	1	Ball	2	3	2
	3	1	1		2	2	1		1	3	1

Although the single-digit combination method is a fairly complicated way to give signals, some runners are able to steal the signs. For this reason the catcher may employ a switch signal, such as holding the right hand on the knee with the fingers together, to shift the sign from the second to the third showing of the fingers. A second switch changes the signal to the first showing of the fingers, and a third switch changes it back to the original second sign. Key hand actions prior to the manipulation of the fingers may also be used to indicate whether the first, second, or third showing of the fingers will be the signal, thus making a switch unnecessary. If a switch signal is used, the pitcher generally indicates to the catcher that he has observed the switch by returning a prearranged signal, such as touching the peak of the cap. Another good method is to use the switch signal to change from a curve to a fast ball. The catcher gives the switch signal, then signals for a curve, but the pitcher throws a fast ball. One such pitch will discourage the opposing team from trying to steal signals.

In order to avoid the switch sign, some teams employ a certain showing of the fingers in specific innings. For instance, the first sign may be used for the first three innings, the second for the next three, and the third for the final three. Another variation employs the second sign for the even number of innings, and the third sign for the odd.

MULTIPLE-DIGIT COMBINATION METHOD

The multiple-digit combination method also employs three signs. In this case the first showing of the fingers is a key signal as well as part of the actual sign. Thus if one finger is shown first, the sign is the number of fingers shown once in the signal series; if two fingers are shown, the number of fingers shown twice. For example, *one finger* followed by two fingers and another two fingers would be a fast ball; one finger followed by one finger and *two fingers* a breaking ball; and two fingers followed by *three fingers* and *three fingers* a slow ball (Fig. 19–3). The pitchout with the pitcher may be designated by showing three fingers as the first sign, and the sign for an infielder to cover may be a natural action similar to that in the

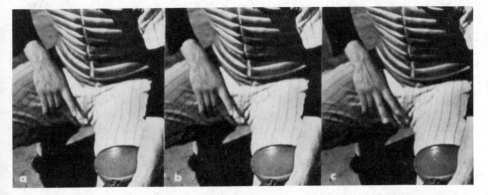

a, b, c. Fast ball.

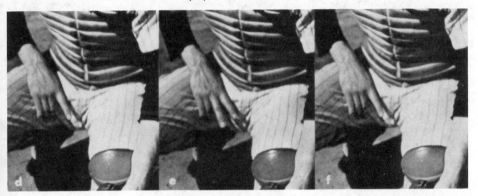

d, e, f. Breaking ball.

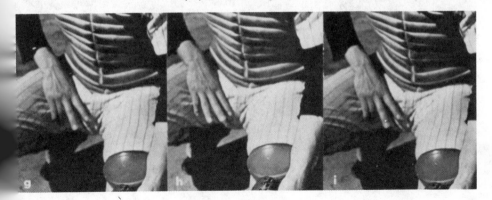

g, h, i. Slow ball.

Fig. 19–2. Signals of the catcher: single-digit combination method.
Signal is second showing of fingers.

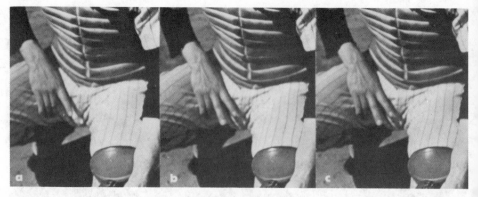

a, b, c. Fast ball.

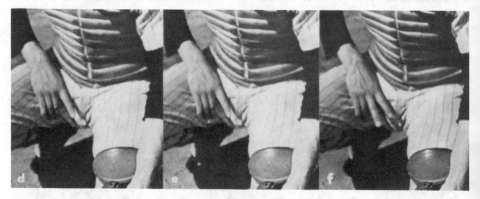

d, e, f. Breaking ball.

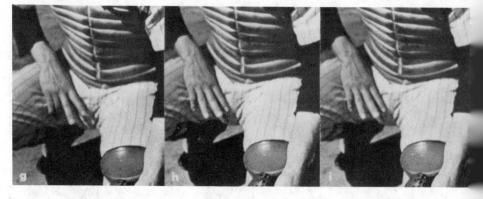

g, h, i. Slow ball.

Fig. 19–3. Signals of the catcher: multiple-digit combination method. Signal is number of fingers corresponding with first showing of fingers; number of fingers shown once in first and second series and twice in third series.

previous description under the single-digit method. In the former case two consecutive showings of one finger following the three-finger sign can indicate a fast-ball pitchout, and two consecutive showings of two fingers a curve-ball pitchout.

The multiple-digit combination method of giving signs also affords numerous ways to signal a fast ball, breaking ball, and slow ball. The following combinations of fingers show these (three consecutive showings of the fingers are omitted as a slow-ball sign because the sign is obvious, and conflicts with a pitchout sign):

Fast	1	2	2	Breaking	2	2	3	Slow	1	3	1
Ball	2	1	1	Ball	1	2	1	Ball	1	1	3
	1	3	3		2	3	2		2	3	3

In a variation of the above method the signal is given after a key or specific showing of the fingers. For example, assume that the key is one finger. Thus in the showing of the fingers under Fast Ball the first sequence would mean curve ball; the second, fast ball; and the third, slow ball. In this case a key signal could be changed from one to two fingers by the use of a switch signal similar to that described under the single-digit combination method.

In a second variation of this method the showing of one finger first would indicate the signal would be the first signal, therefore a fast ball; the showing of two fingers first would mean the second or next showing; and three fingers, the third. Using the showing of the fingers under Breaking Ball in this case the first sequence would mean a curve; the second, a fast ball; and the third, a slow ball.

In still a third variation the signal is a fast ball if the three showings of the fingers total an odd number less than six; a curve, if an even number not over six; and a slow ball, if more than six.

NIGHT SIGNALS

It is usually necessary to employ hand signals in night baseball, since finger signs are often difficult to see under lights. These may be single signs, such as a flat hand, clenched fist, and wiggling the four fingers, because as a general rule no attempt is made by the opposition to steal signals at night. The signals are given from the crotch instead of the thigh. In some instances the call by the umpire determines the subsequent pitch. For example, if the pitch is ruled a ball the next pitch is automatically a fast ball, and if a strike is called the following pitch is a breaking ball. In this case a slow ball may be thrown on a breaking ball signal, and a switch sign, such as touching the mask, is used to change the automatic sign to the opposite sign. (The pitcher answers, as was previously described, by touching the peak of his cap.) A poor lighting system may make it necessary to give obvious signs. This may also be true for day games, if the pitcher does not have normal vision. Some catchers use a flap system, waving the open hand one, two, and three times to indicate a fast ball, breaking ball, and slow ball, respectively.

SIGNALS OF THE MANAGER OR COACH

Batters may be given take, bunt, and hit-and-run and running squeeze signals, and base runners single- and double-steal signals, depending on their batting and base-running ability, the control of the pitcher, the stage of the game, and the type of offense used. These signs all relate to the coming pitch, the take sign meaning not to swing at the ball, the bunt sign to bunt the ball if it is over the plate, and the hit-and-run, running squeeze, and steal signs to execute the hit-and-run play, running squeeze play, and single or double steal if possible. They are usually given after each pitch so that the manager or coach can change his strategy to meet a different count on the batter, an advancement of a runner or runners due to a wild pitch or balk, the failure of a batter to hit or bunt the ball in fair territory on a hit-and-run or running squeeze play, or a shifting of the defense to cope with the sign previously given. However, the sign may remain the same for the next pitch, in which case the rubbing of the uniform in a certain manner is often used to cancel the sign. It may also be necessary to use the rub-off signal if the opposing team anticipates a steal. This may be indicated by an attempted pickoff play or a fake to catch the runner. It is best for the manager or coach to make this decision; otherwise the base runner may attempt to go through with the play and be caught on a pitchout. In some cases he may be caught by a routine throw owing to an inadequate lead.

As a general rule the signs to the batters and base runners originate from the coaching lines. Some high-school and college coaches are required to remain on the bench or in the dugout so they either give the signals directly to players or through one or both coaches. A capable third-base coach may give them, but sometimes the first-base coach gives the signals to right-hand batters, and the third-base coach to left-hand batters. The latter method is commonly employed because the respective batters normally walk toward these coaches as they approach the plate to take their turns at bat. The first-base coach frequently gives the steal sign to the runner on first base, and the third-base coach to the runners on second and third bases. A better method, which is used by some teams, is to have the third-base coach give the signals to all runners because in the case of a double steal with first and third bases occupied both runners are sure of knowing that the sign has been given.

Many managers or coaches go to the coaching lines and give all the signals. This, of course, simplifies the giving of signs. However, if the manager or coach remains on the bench it is necessary for him to have a set of signals with the coaches to inform them of the particular strategy to be used. There are various ways to convey the signs to the coaches from the bench, as well as for the coaches to give signs to the batters and base runners. Touching the peak of the cap, rubbing the uniform in a certain manner, and pulling up the belt are some of the methods employed. Any such signs are workable if they are disguised. This particularly concerns signals given from the coaching lines, because the coach is in open view, and therefore a target for sign stealers on the opposing team. On the other hand, because the manager or head coach is usually in uniform, and difficult to distinguish among other players on the bench, it is not likely that an attempt will be made to steal his signals even though only the actual sign may be given.

SIGNALS FROM THE BENCH

Signals from the bench usually involve some movement of the hand above the belt, since it is often difficult to see the lower part of the body from the coaching lines. The use of one hand is another factor that simplifies the work of the coach. The following set of signs shows how the manager or coach may relay the various signals to the base coaches:

Touching the face with the right hand—*Take*
Touching the peak of the cap with the right hand—*Bunt*
Touching the collar with the right hand—*Hit-and-run*
Touching the letters on the uniform with the right hand—*Single steal*
Folding the arms—*Double steal*
Covering the letters on the cap with the right hand—*Running squeeze play*

These signals are illustrated in the above order in Fig. 19–4.

SIGNALS FROM THE COACHING LINES

The previous set of signals could be used to relay the signs to the batters and base runners from the coaching lines. However, the inclusion of some signals, such as touching the belt or lower part of the

a. Take.   b. Bunt.   c. Hit-and-run.

d. Single steal.   e. Double steal.   f. Running squeeze pla

Fig. 19–4. Signals from the bench.

body, gives more variety. For instance, the first three signs of the set of signals previously described could be combined with three involving the belt. The set of signals below shows this combination:

Touching the face with the right hand—*Take*
Touching the peak of the cap with the right hand—*Bunt*
Touching the collar with the right hand—*Hit-and-run*
Pulling up the right side of the belt with the right hand—*Single steal*
Pulling up the sides of the belt with both hands—*Double steal*
Covering the belt buckle with the right hand—*Running squeeze play*

The signals are illustrated in the above order in Fig. 19–5.

   a. Take.   **b.** Bunt.   **c.** Hit-and-run.

  d. Single steal.   **e.** Double steal.   **f.** Running squeeze play.

Fig. 19–5. Signals from the coaching lines.

GIVING THE SIGNAL

It has been previously stated that the coach must disguise the signals from the opposing team. He does so by including the sign in a series of natural actions. For example, to give a take signal such as is included in the previously described set of signs and properly disguise it, the coach might touch the peak of his cap with the left hand, rub his uniform with either hand, *touch his face with his right hand,* and clap his hands, meanwhile moving around in the coaching box and encouraging the batter to hit the ball. The other signals can be given in a similar manner.

The signals just described may be further complicated to prevent deception. For example, the take sign might be touching the nose, ear, chin, or either side of the face instead of any part of the face, in which case one of the movements not employed could be used to help disguise the sign. Likewise, the bunt signal might be touching the middle or right side of the cap, or two movements combined, such as touching the front and back of the cap. Another variation regarding the take sign involves the direction of the hand. In this case a sideward movement across the chin or forehead could be the sign with a downward movement over the nose or side of the face employed as fake action. The feet can also be used to give signals. In this case the position and angle of the feet in relation to the coaching lines can be employed to indicate specific signals. Another variation involves the use of a key signal. In this method a regular signal is not considered "on" and therefore not carried out unless it is preceded by the key signal.

Some teams employ two sets of signals to minimize sign stealing, one of these being used for the infielders, and the other for the pitcher, catcher, and outfielders. Other teams change signals from day to day, and even during the game if necessary. In rare instances individual signs are used. This system has no weaknesses, but it is difficult to execute, and there is really no need to make signals so complicated.

A few managers or coaches employ, in addition to the usual coaching signs, hand or word signs to inform the batter when a runner or runners will attempt to steal. In the latter case the player's name is frequently used, being preceded by certain word combinations such as, "Get a hold of one" and, "Make it be over." The batter may then stand erect to the rear of the batting box, fake a bunt, or he may deliberately miss a first or second strike to aid the steal.

SIGNALS OF THE BATTER

The batter gives two signals, a hit-and-run sign and a running squeeze sign, depending on his batting and bunting ability, the score, the number of outs, the control of the pitcher, the stage of the game, and whether or not the manager favors the plays.

HIT-AND-RUN SIGNAL

The hit-and-run may be given several times during the game. Therefore individual signals, rather than a team sign, are used for this play, because they make it more difficult for the opposing team to steal the signal. Thus each player has a sign with the three players who precede him in the lineup, and he must know the signs of the three players who follow him in the batting order. This ensures an understanding between the batter and base runner who may be involved in such a play. Some teams, in addition to individual signs, have a team sign to guarantee a similar understanding with a player who might enter the game as a substitute batter. If a runner is substituted for a player on first or second base, with the base ahead unoccupied, the signs of the batters must be determined, provided, of course, a hit-and-run stage may develop. However, since there is little usage of the hit-and-run under these conditions, it is better to omit such a sign, have the runner request that the umpire call time, if necessary, and find out the sign of the player in the batter's box. In high schools and colleges there are few players who can successfully hit and run. For this reason a team sign will suffice, in which case it can be assumed that the batter and runner will get the sign. The batter, however, can repeat the signal to the runner so that both players are together on the play.

RUNNING SQUEEZE SIGNAL

The running squeeze play, which is omitted from the strategy of some managers or coaches, is used very little by those who favor it. For this reason a team running squeeze can be employed with very little risk of detection. This is a common play in high schools and colleges, and a team signal is usually adequate. In this case it is important for the batter to inform the runner by signal that he intends to bunt the ensuing pitch. Failure to use such a signal might lead to the runner being an easy out at the plate (in cases when the batter missed the signal and was not aware that the squeeze play was on).

GIVING THE SIGNAL

The actual signal, whether for a hit-and-run or for a running squeeze play, is a natural action, such as touching the collar with the right hand, and is included in a series of natural actions to mislead any members of the opposing team who attempt to steal signs. It is usually given before the batter steps into the batting box so that there is time for him to convey the signal to the runner. Using the previous illustrations to give a hit-and-run signal, the batter could touch the peak of his cap, rub his uniform, touch the collar with the right hand, and tap the plate with the bat. The sign for a running squeeze play can be given in a similar manner. For example, in this case the signal might be covering the belt buckle with the right hand.

The batter alternately looks toward the coach giving the sign and the runner to whom the signal is given during the process of the natural actions, always making sure that the runner is looking toward the plate when the sign is given. This procedure further disguises the signal, and is practiced regardless of the count, because it makes it more difficult for the opposing team to steal the sign.

There are other ways to give signals. For example, a combination of signs is often used, such as touching the front and back of the cap, or rubbing both the shirt and pants. In the latter case the sign may be two separate rubs or a continuous movement of the hand over the belt. An automatic signal is also employed. This is occasionally used by players who execute the hit-and-run play well. For example, the hit-and-run signal is always considered "on" until a specific sign, such as rubbing the uniform, removes it. A definite hit-and-run signal may be used with this method and the rub of the uniform have a similar meaning.

Some players prefer to use a simple sign, then change to another signal after they have started the runner. This makes it easy for the runner to get the sign, and in addition it prevents the catcher from successfully combating the hit-and-run play on a subsequent turn at bat.

SUMMARY

SIGNALS OF THE CATCHER

1. Use a single-digit method of giving signals for normal conditions. In this and other signal systems one finger indicates a fast ball; two fingers, a curve; and three fingers, a slow ball.

2. Employ a single-digit combination method of giving signals if the opposing players attempt to steal your signals from second base. Three signals are usually given and the first, second, or third showing of the fingers is designated as the actual sign (second in this case). Fast ball—1 *1* 3; breaking ball—3 *2* 2; slow ball—1 *3* 2.

3. Switch to a multiple-digit combination method of giving signals if you want to make your signals more complicated. Three signals are also given in this system with the first signal acting as a key signal.

	Fast Ball			Breaking Ball			Slow Ball		
a) Signal is number of fingers shown which correspond with first signal.	1	2	2	2	3	2	1	3	1
	2	1	1	1	2	1	2	3	3
	1	3	3	2	1	2	1	1	3
b) Signal is first showing of fingers after key signal (using one finger as key).	1	1	2	2	1	2	2	1	3
	2	1	1	3	1	2	1	3	1
	3	1	1	1	2	2	3	1	3
c) Signal is designated as first, second, or third showing by first showing of fingers; one finger indicates first; two fingers, second; and three fingers, third.	1	3	1	2	2	1	2	3	1
	2	1	2	3	1	2	3	2	3
	1	2	1	2	2	3 .	2	3	2
d) Signal is fast ball if three showings of fingers total odd number less than six; curve, even number not over six; slow ball, number over six.	1	2	2	1	1	2	3	2	2
	2	1	2	2	2	2	2	3	2
	2	2	1	2	1	1	2	3	3

4. Develop a simple set of hand signals for night baseball because finger signals may be difficult to see. For example, a flat hand may indicate a fast ball; a closed fist, a curve; and the hand on the glove, a slow ball.

SIGNALS OF THE MANAGER OR COACH

1. Formulate a set of signals which can be easily relayed to both coaches and players. A suggested set of signals follows.

Signal		*Strategy*
Touch face	(Do not swing at coming pitch)	Take
Touch peak of cap	(Bunt coming pitch if it is over plate)	Bunt
Touch collar	(Give runner on 1b hit-and-run sign and hit coming pitch on ground)	Hit-and-run
Pull up right side of belt	(Attempt to steal on pitch unless you fail to get a good start)	Single steal
Pull up both sides of belt	(Work double steal)	Double steal
Cover belt buckle	(Give runner on third base squeeze play sign and bunt coming pitch)	Running squeeze play

2. Disguise the actual signal by including it as part of a series of natural actions.

SIGNALS OF THE BATTER

1. Establish a policy relative to the hit-and-run and running squeeze plays as not all players can successfully execute them.
2. Adopt a team signal for the hit-and-run and running squeeze plays, if these plays are used, to insure that both the batter and base runner will get the sign.

DISCUSSION QUESTIONS

1. What does the showing of one finger, two fingers, and three fingers indicate if the catcher uses a single-digit method of giving signals?
2. Why is it advisable for the catcher to have separate pitchout signs with each infielder? Suggest several ways to give pitchout signals.
3. Explain the single-digit combination method of giving signals. How does the catcher switch the sign from the second to the third showing of the fingers?
4. State several factors which must be considered in the giving of coaching signals.
5. What information is conveyed to the batter by the following signals: (*a*) take, (*b*) bunt, (*c*) hit-and-run? Explain fully in relation to the ensuing pitch.
6. Suggest a practical set of catching and coaching signals. What fundamental principle is characteristic of any successful signal system?
7. Why is it better for the third-base coach to relay the strategy of a double steal to both runners with first and third bases occupied?
8. How do some coaches inform the batter that a runner or runners intend to start on the pitch? Why is this done?
9. Describe a combination batting sign. What is an automatic batting signal?

20

Control of
Game Situations

The success of a manager or coach, if he has a reasonable amount of talent, depends on an intelligent use of the offensive and defensive tactics described throughout the text. This assumes that a manager or coach considers the fact that some players do better when they are prodded, whereas others play best if they are complimented and encouraged.

OFFENSIVE STRATEGY

An intelligent use of offensive tactics may best be explained by considering the methods of attack employed by major-league teams. For example, the New York Yankees of the Babe Ruth era, with four or five long-distance hitters, played a straightaway hitting or slugging type of game, rarely using any definite strategy because it was seldom needed. The St. Louis Cardinals of that day, having perhaps the greatest combined speed of any major-league team, were successful with a run-and-hit type of offense. This is frequently termed a running game because the runner's attempted advance is not necessarily dependent on the batter hitting the ball. The Chicago White Sox, with a minimum of both speed and slugging power during the same period, used the hit-and-run extensively, since this type of play permits the batter to protect the inability of the runner to steal. Most teams favor the New York type of offense in the early innings and a combination of bunting and the various batting and base-running tactics in the latter part of the game. This depends, of course, on the score, the ability of batters to bunt and hit, and the speed of runners on the bases.

It is frequently good strategy to start a runner on first base, or runners on first and second bases, when the count on the batter is three balls and one strike or three balls and two strikes. (A runner on first base is occasionally started with two balls and no strikes charged against the batter.) These are considered natural run-and-hit situations because if the ensuing pitch is a ball, the batter walks and all players running automatically advance. A missed second strike by the batter, of course, makes it possible for the catcher to retire a runner when an attempt is made to advance. A missed third strike with less than two out provides a similar opportunity. For this reason the ability of the batter is considered before runners are started in these situations. (All runners are started when first and second or all of the bases are occupied with two out and the count three balls and two strikes.) The score is also considered, because if a line-hit ball is caught with runners attempting to advance, a double play or even a triple play may be completed. This is a questionable tactic when the opposing team has a substantial lead.

John McGraw popularized starting runners, and called this type of offense the *run-and-hit*. He employed it against pitchers with good control, preferring to start the runner any time he thought the pitcher would attempt to pitch a strike. Though it primarily concerns starts from first base, it also includes those from second base under the conditions previously described.

THE BATTING ORDER

The batting order is arranged so that the best hitters appear in the first five positions. These players then come to bat more often than the weaker hitters and make possible a maximum of scoring. As a general rule the first batter is able to work the pitcher for walks, and the second is able to hit behind the runner. The ability to run and bunt well are also desirable qualities of first- and second-place hitters. The third, fourth, and fifth batters are the distance hitters because they usually have the greatest opportunity to drive runs over the plate. The remaining batters follow according to their ability to hit, the catcher hitting eighth and the pitcher last. However, a good-hitting catcher may be moved higher in the lineup. Roger Bresnahan, for example, was a lead-off man, and Mickey Cochrane batted second. A good-hitting pitcher may also be moved higher on some teams. If a "designated hitter" is permitted for the pitcher, he may be placed anywhere in the batting order.

In order to prevent batting out of turn, it is advisable to post the lineup on the clubhouse bulletin board and on the bench before each game. Two similar lineups must be prepared and, if these are not done in carbon duplicate, the manager or coach has the captain read back the names for any discrepancies. The captain then presents these to the umpire-in-chief, who keeps one and gives the other to the captain of the opposing team. This is normally the rule in all forms of baseball.

There are frequently involvements when a player fails to follow the right batting order. The usual penalty is loss of a time at bat for the player whose batting position was taken. This assumes that the wrong batter successfully reached base. A smart coach or manager waits until this occurs, then informs the umpire of the infraction. The umpire makes no ruling on the matter until an appeal is made even though he may know an incorrect order is being followed. A manager or coach is more likely to observe an incorrect batting order if he keeps score. In scoring it is usually advisable to keep only the record of the opposing team because a coach has enough to do when his team is at bat. These records are valuable in case the team is played again, and the scorecard can be used to give signals, if desired.

DEFENSIVE STRATEGY

In order to form the best possible defense, a team usually holds periodic clubhouse meetings to discuss the ability and tactics of opposing batters and base runners and the manner in which these are incorporated into offensive strategy. The ability of the pitcher on the defensive team is also given consideration in this discussion, and for the purpose of planning offensive strategy, opposing players are studied to determine defensive strengths and weaknesses. Many questions can be answered. Are the opposing players pull hitters, opposite-field hitters, or straightaway hitters, and what players are likely to hit for distance? Do any players prefer certain pitches, and do they have specific weaknesses? How many players are fast and do any of them attempt to beat out bunts? Is there a particular type of team strategy used and does the manager favor certain tactics? What are the strong and weak points of defensive players, particularly the pitcher and the outfielders and the double play combination with respect to handling the ball on relays and double steals?

When specific information is available about the opposition, certain defensive tactics may help to decide some close games. These include the intentional pass, the movement of the defense, and the throw on the double steal.

a. Give batter an intentional pass. (Signal is given to catcher who relays strategy to pitcher.)

b. Walk batter if necessary—first base is open (unoccupied). (Signal is given to catcher who relays strategy to pitcher.)

c. Infield: play back.

d. Infield: play in halfway position.

e. Catcher: attempt to catch runner off third base (if double steal is attempted with first and third bases occupied).

Fig. 20–1. Signals for defensive strategy.

THE INTENTIONAL PASS

An intentional pass is frequently used as part of defensive strategy when only second base or second and third bases are occupied with less than two out, if the batter is not the potential tying or winning run or unless a left-hand pitcher is facing a left-hand batter. (This is also done with two out.) This is particularly true if the following player in the lineup is a right-hand batter and less likely to hit the ball safely. It is then possible to start a double play at second base when the infield plays back in either of the above situations, as well as to the plate if the infield moves in with all of the bases occupied. An intentional pass is also employed when the batter hits for two bases with the score tied and none out in the last half of the last inning. This creates a force-play situation at third base, thereby necessitating a better-placed bunt to advance the runners. If a three-base hit is made under similar circumstances, two passes are given so that a force play is made possible at the plate.

The manager or coach calls to the catcher and informs him by a prearranged signal when he wants the batter purposely walked. Most managers give this information by pointing toward first (Fig. 20–1a). In some of the above situations it is good strategy to have a control pitcher attempt to make the batter hit a low outside pitch. The manager frequently calls "Base open" in this case, or gives a sign such as clenching the fist (Fig. 20–1b). A sign is preferred because it prevents the batter from knowing what the pitcher intends to do.

Fig. 20–1. *(Continued)*

To thwart a squeeze play (with second and third bases occupied) the manager or coach may have the catcher point his index finger toward first base from the regular signal position. In this case the catcher takes his normal stance behind the batter and the pitcher makes a high outside pitchout. This may be done on succeeding pitches.

Generally speaking, the use of the intentional pass is confined to the latter part of the game. Runs resulting from such strategy in the early innings are actually gifts. Furthermore, such runs often build an insurmountable lead.

MOVING THE DEFENSE

The infield is played back or in when third base is occupied with less than two out, according to the score and the stage of the game. As a general rule the deep position is favored during the first five innings unless the opposing team is ahead more than one run. This is particularly true if first base is occupied, because a double play is then possible. Playing the infield in this manner, of course, concedes a run on a ground ball with none out and permits a run to score with one out if a double play is not completed. However, it prevents many balls from rolling to the outfield and lessens the chances for a big inning.

If second base is unoccupied in the above situation and the count on the batter reaches three balls and one strike or three balls and two strikes, the shortstop and second baseman are often moved in several steps because the runner on first base is usually running on the pitch and cannot be forced at second base. This is called a halfway position and is particularly effective if the runner on third base is slow and a weak batter is at the plate. It is also effective with none out, since a runner on third normally does not advance unless the ball goes through the infield.

The position of the infield is especially important late in the game because there may be little or no opportunity to overcome runs scored by the opposing team. In this case the infield is always moved to the short position when the winning run is on third base (also a run that will increase a lead). The infield is also brought in with the tying run on third base in some of these situations. This strategy is usually practiced by the visiting team because the home team has a slight advantage when the score is tied in the late innings.

The manager or coach moves the infield forward and backward with hand signals. These are given in front of the chest and involve both position and movement of the hands. For example, when the manager or coach wants the infield to remain back, he holds his hands with palms toward the infielders (Fig. 20–1c). If he wants the infield to move to the short position, he waves his hands toward his chest. A similar waving of the hands toward the infielders with the infield in means to take the deep position. A halfway position is denoted by placing the hands at right angles (Fig. 20–1d). By crossing his hands in a similar manner, the manager or coach can inform the first baseman to play slightly behind the runner rather than remain at the bag. This is frequently done when the pitcher or a slow runner is on base and a left-hand batter is at the plate.

A sign such as three fingers can also indicate "Attempt to catch the runner at third" in sacrifice situations. This usually follows the reasoning in shifting the infield: conservative play in the first five innings of play, and an attempt to catch the runner later on in the game.

The signs for team strategy are generally given to the captain (if a player on the infield is so designated) or to the nearest infielder, and he in turn relays the information to the other players. The latter method is frequently employed because the yelling of spectators often makes it impossible to attract the attention of a player any great distance from the bench. If the winning run is on third base with less than two out in the last half of the last inning, the manager or coach moves the outfielders in with the infielders because the run will score even though a long fly ball is caught. In this case he has the infielders relay the information to the outfielders. Prior to any change in strategy, he indicates to the catcher to have the umpire call time so that the pitcher will not deliver the ball until the proper defense can be formed. He does this by shaking the hands parallel to the ground with the palms down.

DOUBLE STEAL

The manager or coach also informs the catcher whether or not to throw to second base on a double steal with first and third bases occupied. No sign in this case means "Throw to second," and a sign such as touching the ear means "Attempt to catch the runner off third" (Fig. 20–1e). Some managers or coaches also inform the shortstop or second baseman whether or not to throw home in this situation if the runner on third attempts to score. No signal in this case means, "Use your own judgment on the throw to second," and a definite signal, "Try to catch the runner advancing from first." A signal is also given to the catcher for a throw to the pitcher.

SPECIFIC SITUATIONS

It is also advisable for the manager or coach to have signals with the catcher and other players for specific situations. This may involve a certain pitch or a pickoff play. These may all be actions with the hands which conform to the usual method of giving signals. In the case of pitches, one finger pointed up means a high fast ball and one, two, and three fingers pointed down indicate a low fast ball, curve, and slow ball, respectively. Delivery can also be suggested by sideward and downward action of the hand. For pickoffs, a pitchout signal can be given to the catcher, or to the pitcher or shortstop for an attempt to catch a runner off second base. Calling, "There he goes," or "Second base" may also help the catcher in a steal situation. "No, no," and "Plenty room" are guides when players pursue fly balls near the bench.

SUBSTITUTIONS

Substitutions are usually made as needed, but an exception occurs when there is a possibility that the opposing pitcher might be removed. In this case a manager or coach often delays the substitution of a pinch hitter. During the time lapse the rival manager may definitely decide to change pitchers; once a new pitcher is announced, he must pitch to one batter unless a runner is caught off base for the third out. This permits the selection of a pinch hitter who is most suited to bat against the incoming pitcher. If the decision is made before the change of pitchers, it may be necessary to substitute a second pinch hitter, in which case the original player is lost for the remainder of the game. For a similar reason, a manager or coach frequently delays the replacement of a pitcher, for the rival manager or coach may be eager to substitute a batter. The substitution of a base runner or defensive player at the right time is also important. A smart coach or manager foresees all game developments and always has the necessary players warming up. For this reason it is important for all extra players (except those assigned to the bull pen) to be on the bench so that they can be easily found for an emergency. This is where they belong anyway to vocally and morally support their team.

When a pitcher is in trouble it is often good strategy to request the umpire to call time and go to the mound. This frequently gives the pitcher confidence. It also permits the player in the bull pen to complete his warm-up in case a pitching change is made. Most teams prohibit a player from leaving for the bench until a relief pitcher arrives on the mound. This provides a cooling-off period. It is always advisable for the manager or coach to go to the mound regardless of whether or not the pitcher is allowed to remain in the game. However, it is wise to avoid excessive delays. Normally conferences are covered by rule, two trips to the mound to talk to the same pitcher in an inning or three trips during the game (except in the case of an injury) automatically removes the pitcher (but he may play another position).

THE CAPTAIN

If the game is away, it is important for the captain to learn of any specific rules when he presents the lineups to the umpire-in-chief and to relay the information to the team and to the manager or coach if he remains on the bench. The captain is the only player with authority to discuss matters with the umpires. For this reason it is advisable for him to intercede in any disputes during the game. In such situations he has an opportunity to show real qualities of leadership, and he must always remember that his actions will reflect both upon his team and upon his school.

SUMMARY

OFFENSE

1. Employ an offense that corresponds with the batting, bunting, and running ability of your personnel.
2. Arrange a batting order to give the greatest run potential. Post the order before each game and prepare duplicate copies for the umpire and visiting team.
3. Try for a big inning early in the game, and sacrifice in the late innings.
4. Start the runner on first base on the count of 3–1 and 3–2 with less than two out unless the batter strikes out frequently.
5. Permit players to hit with the count 2–0 and 3–1 when runs are in scoring position; in other words, play offensive baseball.
6. Stress the importance of the sacrifice, and practice this type of bunt.
7. Encourage fast men to bunt for a hit, because even a failure to bunt will force infielders in, thereby weakening the defense. Employ the sacrifice and bunt for a hit when the ground is wet.
8. Use the steal according to the speed of runners. Steal second with one and two out; steal third with one out except with a left-hand batter at the plate. Refrain from using the steal if the ground is soft or wet.
9. Endorse aggressive base running. It pays dividends in the scoring of runs, and develops a spectator interest.
10. Employ a minimum of strategy, for it is better to do a few things well than to execute a variety of tactics poorly.
11. Plan a simple set of signals that can be understood by all players.
12. Substitute when necessary, but before making a substitution think how the opposing manager will counteract your move.

DEFENSE

1. Employ the intentional pass sparingly and preferably late in the game, because the run, if scored, is a gift run.
2. Move the first baseman from the conventional position on the bag to a position slightly in back of the runner if a steal is not likely to be attempted, particularly with a left-hand batter at the plate.
3. Keep the infield back in the first five or six innings; bring the infield in near the end of the game.
4. Shorten the position of outfielders with the winning run on third base and less than two out in the last half of the final inning.
5. Warm up a pitcher, as well as other players, if a replacement might be necessary, but do not cause unnecessary delay to attain a complete warm-up.
6. Take the responsibility for deciding whether the catcher should throw to second base in double steal situations with first and third bases occupied.
7. Be alert for pickoff possibilities and signal the defense if you think a runner might be caught off base.
8. Emphasize speed and performance in pregame fielding practice, for many spectators come early to watch this phase of the game.
9. Make players run to and from the diamond at the end of each half-inning, to speed up the game, and around the field when they report for a game or practice.
10. Discourage conferences and avoid discussions with umpires, for delays upset both players and spectators.
11. Keep the batting record of the opposing team during the game as this will give you information about the various batters and enable you to discover if a player bats out of turn.
12. Call a meeting to discuss pregame strategy if you have specific knowledge about the opposition, particularly if your starting pitcher has control.

DISCUSSION QUESTIONS

1. What are generally considered desirable characteristics of first- and second-place batters?
2. When does a manager or coach make his appeal to the umpire, if he knows an opposing player batted out of turn?
3. Discuss the strategy of an intentional pass. To whom does the manager or coach give the intentional pass signal?
4. State the four ways to combat a double steal (first and third occupied). What defensive alignment requires a pitchout?

5. Describe the three basic methods of attack in baseball, and state the reason for using each.
6. When is the logical time to issue an intentional pass? Give your answer from the viewpoint of strategy and the progress of the game.
7. Designate the position of each infielder in the following situations: (*a*) first half of third inning, the opposing team behind two to one, bases filled, and one out; (*b*) last half of eighth inning, score tied one to one, first and second bases occupied, and none out; (*c*) first half of ninth inning, the opposing team ahead one to nothing, second and third bases occupied, and one out.
8. In cases wherein the batter may be walked if necessary, why is it important for the manager to give a hand signal rather than a verbal signal to remind the pitcher that first base is open?
9. Discuss shifting the infield in relation to early and late stages of the game. Why is this done?
10. Plan the defensive strategy in the following situation: Last half of the ninth inning, score tied one to one, third base occupied, and one out. What if the situation occurred in the first half of the inning?

21

Analysis of World Series Game

The mastery of technique and strategy reaches its most advanced stage in the major leagues. Its final culmination occurs in the World Series when outstanding teams of the American and National Leagues play.

A good example of this display of mastery occurred in the fifth game of the 1942 World Series played in New York between the St. Louis Cardinals and the New York Yankees. Because this game offers many strategic situations, it is analyzed to show not only the managerial strategy of Joe McCarthy (Yankees) and Billy Southworth (Cardinals) but also strategy as it is employed by individual players and in team play. The game is scored on pp. 381 and 382.

PREGAME BRIEFING

For this game the author assumes that managers McCarthy and Southworth in a pregame meeting briefed their teams on the strengths and weaknesses of the opposing team members. An outline of the briefing follows:

OFFENSE

CARDINALS (by McCarthy)	YANKEES (by Southworth)
Pull Hitters	*Pull Hitters*
Moore: line-drive hitter, may try to hit behind runner	Rizzuto: line-drive hitter with power

Slaughter: line-drive hitter with power

Hopp: line-drive hitter with power

Kurowski: power hitter

Marion: occasional power

Cullenbine: switch hitter with good left-hand power

DiMaggio / extra power to all
Keller { fields, hit breaking
\ balls well

Gordon: power hitter

Priddy: occasional power

Selkirk: power hitter, likes low ball

Straightaway Hitters

Brown: switch hitter, no power

Musial: power to all fields

Cooper: line-drive hitter with power, likes ball away

Beazley: no power

Straightaway Hitters

Rolfe: line-drive hitter with some power, may try to hit through short on hit-and-run

Dickey: line-drive hitter with power

Ruffing: line-drive hitter with power

Bunters

Brown

Slaughter

Hopp

Bunters

Rizzuto

Rolfe

Fast Men

Brown

Moore

Musial

Slaughter

Hopp

Fast Men

Rizzuto

Keller

Stainback

Team Strategy

Run-and-hit with frequent bunt

Team Strategy

Straightaway hitting with occasional bunt

DEFENSE

Pitcher

Beazley: good fast ball, curve, and slow ball; good control; pitches mostly low, likes to throw curve; average move to first

Pitcher

Ruffing: extra-good fast ball, fair curve, good slow ball; excellent control; likes to throw fast ball, preferably high inside; average move to first

Catcher

Cooper: good arm—likes to throw

Catcher

Dickey: excellent arm

Second-Base Combination

Marion: stronger arm

Second-Base Combination

Gordon: stronger arm

Outfield

All outfielders throw well

Outfield

All outfielders throw well; DiMaggio has extra-strong arm

THE STRATEGY OF THE GAME BY INNINGS

The following is the author's inning by inning analysis of how the strategy of managers, coaches, and players developed throughout the game.

The batting order of both teams follows:

CARDINALS	YANKEES
Brown, 2b	Rizzuto, ss
T. Moore, cf	Rolfe, 3b
Slaughter, rf	Cullenbine, rf
Musial, lf	DiMaggio, cf
W. Cooper, c.	Keller, lf
Hopp, 1b	Gordon, 2b
Kurowski, 3b	Dickey, c
Marion, ss	Priddy, 1b
Beazley, p	Ruffing, p

FIRST INNING

Cardinals

1. Ruffing walked Brown on four pitches.

Batting Strategy: Brown took Ruffing's first and succeeding pitches for balls because it is usually advisable for the lead-off man to make the pitcher throw a first strike (a second strike when the count goes to 3 balls and 1 strike). This is particularly true in the early innings, and also in the late innings if the opposing team has a substantial lead.

Managing Strategy (offense): Southworth instructed Brown on his way to the plate to make Ruffing get the ball over for a strike before swinging. Therefore he did not give any signs after each of Ruffing's pitches. However, in order to disguise later signals, he moved around in the coaching box, clapped his hands, touched his cap, and so on, to make the Yankees think he was giving Brown take signs.

Pitching Strategy: Ruffing really anticipated what Brown intended to do the moment he stepped into the batter's box. Furthermore, it is the strategy of every pitcher to attempt to get ahead of the batter unless a base on balls is warranted. Under the circumstances, Ruffing was definitely trying to get the ball over the plate; but, as frequently happens in pitching, he was encountering a streak of wildness. This was short-lived, however, since the pass to Brown was the only one Ruffing issued during the entire game.

Managing Strategy (defense): McCarthy reminded Ruffing to keep ahead of the batters before the start of the game. Since four consecutive balls indicated that Ruffing might not have his usual control, McCarthy informed his bull pen to go into action so that another pitcher would be ready to relieve.

2. Moore struck out.

Batting Strategy: Ruffing pitched two more balls, but he recovered control and put over two called strikes, then Moore swung and missed for strike three.

Ordinarily, a batter swings on the count of 2 balls and 1 strike, but Moore failed to do so because Ruffing fooled him with a low outside curve.

Managing Strategy (offense): Southworth's plan with Moore was the same as that for Brown. In other words, when Ruffing continued to be wild, Southworth thought that Moore might also beg his way to first.

3. Slaughter hit Ruffing's second pitch to Gordon for a double play, Gordon to Rizzuto to Priddy.

Pitching Strategy: Ruffing kept his pitches low to Slaughter to try to make him hit the ball on the ground for a force play at second base.

Infielding Strategy: Gordon fed the ball carefully to Rizzuto shoulder-high, because the rule of every good double play combination is to make sure on the first throw for a possible double play. This enabled Rizzuto to complete the force-out and maneuver away from Brown's slide for a quick throw to first.

Base-Running Strategy: Brown slid to the right-field side of the bag because he knew Rizzuto's fast approach would make it necessary for him to throw from that side of the base. He tried to touch Rizzuto's stepping foot to hinder the throw for a double play but failed to arrive in time to do so.

(No runs, no hits, no errors, none left on base)

Yankees

1. Rizzuto drove a home run into the lower left-field stands.

Batting Strategy: Rizzuto, following the strategy of Brown, let the first pitch go by, and it was over for a strike. He took the second pitch for a ball, then made his hit on the third pitch.

Pitching Strategy: Beazley, like Ruffing, knew that Rizzuto was very likely to look at a strike, so he came right over the plate with a fast ball. Because he realized that Rizzuto might swing, he put plenty of stuff on the ball. This is generally good strategy with the bases unoccupied because the percentage is very much against the batter getting a home run or even a single. Beazley next tried to make Rizzuto hit a bad pitch, and missed the low outside corner for ball 1. The count now being 1 ball and 1 strike, Beazley knew that rather than work the corners, he should try to get the ball over the plate. When a pitcher works too cautiously, he frequently gets into trouble, and either gives a base on balls or gets behind so that the batter eventually gets the ball he wants to hit. The latter method of pitching also upsets the defense and uses energy which the pitcher often needs in the late stages of the game.

2. Rolfe grounded out, Brown to Hopp.

Infielding Strategy: Prior to Beazley's first pitch, Brown and Hopp moved in about two steps, since Rolfe occasionally employed the drag bunt.

3. Hopp took care of Cullenbine's grounder unassisted.

Infielding Strategy: Cullenbine's grounder was a hard-hit ball along the first-base line. Hopp blocked it, then picked up the rolling ball and won the race to the bag. It is important for both the first and third basemen to block hard-hit balls along the foul lines, because when the normal fielding position is used, the ball frequently goes through to the outfield for extra bases. In addition, if the ball is blocked, these players can usually recover the ball if it is fumbled and still retire the batter. The third baseman can do so because he plays nearer the plate than the other infielders, and the first baseman because of his nearness to first base plus the fact that he may receive help from the pitcher.

4. DiMaggio flied out to Moore in short center field.
            (1 run, 1 hit, no errors, none left on base)

	1	2	3	4	5	6	7	8	9
Cards	0	x	x	x	x	x	x	x	x
Yanks	1	x	x	x	x	x	x	x	x

SECOND INNING

Cardinals

1. Rizzuto caught Musial's pop fly in back of third base.

Infielding Strategy: Rizzuto called for the fly ball because the shortstop is in better position to make such catches than the third baseman. For the same reason the second baseman takes fly balls in back of first base.

2. Cooper lined the first pitch through the mound for a single.

3. Hopp also swung at Ruffing's first offering and popped to Rizzuto.

Pitching Strategy: Ruffing was now in excellent pitching form; and in spite of the fact that Cooper singled on a first pitch, he put the first ball over to Hopp, thus using only two pitches to two batters, one of whom was retired.

Batting Strategy: Generally speaking, it is good strategy to hit first pitches if it works in your favor. Hopp's swinging at the first pitch was not considered bad strategy, since Cooper reached base. However, if Cooper had been put out, his swing would not have been sound baseball.

4. Kurowski flied to Gordon in short right field.
            (No runs, 1 hit, no errors, 1 left on base)

Yankees

1. Keller's easy grounder went directly to Brown, who tossed to Hopp for the out.

2. Marion grabbed Gordon's grounder near second base and threw to first for the second out.

3. Dickey also grounded out, Brown to Hopp.

Pitching Strategy: It is interesting to note in the above inning that all Cardinals were retired on fly balls and all Yankees on ground balls. Actually, this characterized the two pitchers, Ruffing specializing on high inside fast balls, whereas Beazley favored mostly low balls, and particularly slow balls and curves. This is proved by the box score (page 382), which shows, exclusive of hits and bunts, that the Cardinals hit 17 fly balls and only 4 ground balls as against 17 ground balls for the Yankees and 8 fly balls.
            (No hits, no runs, no errors, none left on base)

	1	2	3	4	5	6	7	8	9
Cards	0	0	x	x	x	x	x	x	x
Yanks	1	0	x	x	x	x	x	x	x

THIRD INNING

Cardinals

1. Priddy raced toward the Cardinal dugout and made a great glove-hand catch of Marion's foul.

2. Beazley fanned on three pitches.

Pitching Strategy: Ruffing continued to use very few pitches. In the case of Beazley, he threw three consecutive fast balls over the plate. It is a good policy to follow this rule when most pitchers are batting because they are seldom good hitters, and to try to fool them generally invites trouble.

3. Brown singled over second.

4. Cullenbine took Moore's easy fly near the foul line.
(No runs, 1 hit, no errors, 1 left on base)

Yankees

1. Priddy walked.

Batting Strategy: Again the plan of attack favored waiting to work the pitcher, because it was still early in the game. Although Beazley understood this, he was unable to keep ahead of Priddy. This was his lone walk.

Managing Strategy (offense): McCarthy now elected to sacrifice because Ruffing was pitching well and because indications were that he might hold the Cardinals scoreless or perhaps allow only one run. A further consideration was the fact that Ruffing batted right-hand and was not a very fast runner; if he were to hit a ground ball it might result in a double play. Since it was only the third inning, McCarthy might have permitted a left-hand batter to swing in the same situation to try to build a commanding lead. He very possibly would have used similar strategy with an established hitter like DiMaggio. In the former case he would have been influenced by the fact that Hopp had to hold Priddy on the bag, thus weakening the defense in the direction in which a left-hand batter naturally hits.

Infielding Strategy: Because the Cardinals anticipated a bunt, Kurowski moved in from third, and Brown moved in and over toward first so that he would be in position to get to the bag to take the throw.

Coaching Strategy: Earl Combs, coaching at first base, relayed McCarthy's bunt sign to Ruffing. The Yankees used the conventional method, wherein the first-base coach gives signals to right-hand batters, and the third-base coach to left-hand batters, since McCarthy remained on the bench. Southworth, on the other hand, gave all signs for the Cardinals from his coaching position at third base.

2. Ruffing bunted toward Hopp, and speedy work by the Cardinal's infield turned it into a double play, Hopp to Marion to Brown, who was covering first.

Pitching Strategy: Beazley, realizing that Ruffing would probably sacrifice, pitched high inside fast balls because they are difficult to bunt on the ground.

Batting Strategy: Ruffing stayed fairly erect at the plate, since he knew Beazley would probably pitch high inside. He was therefore able to make his intended sacrifice on the ground. However, he put too much stress on hiding the fact that he was going to sacrifice, and brought his bat into bunting position late, thus causing the ball to roll too fast toward Hopp. Actually, the

Cardinals anticipated a sacrifice, so it was more important for Ruffing to get into a good bunting position than to try to fool the defense.

3. Moore took Rizzuto's fly in deep left-center field.

Outfielding Strategy: Musial let Moore take Rizzuto's fly because the center fielder has the right of way.

(No runs, no hits, no errors, none left on base)

	1	2	3	4	5	6	7	8	9
Cards	0	0	0	x	x	x	x	x	x
Yanks	1	0	0	x	x	x	x	x	x

FOURTH INNING

Cardinals

1. Slaughter smashed Ruffing's first pitch into the lower right-field stands for a home run to tie the score 1 to 1.

Managing Strategy (offense): Southworth observed that Ruffing's control was now good and that he was keeping ahead of the Cardinal batters, so he told Slaughter to swing at the first pitch if it was to his liking.

Batting Strategy: Slaughter, you will recall, took a strike in the first inning, then hit the first pitch in this inning. All batters vary their strategy of hitting and taking first pitches in order to keep the pitcher under continual pressure. This is particularly true in close games.

Pitching Strategy: Ruffing with a 1-run lead could well afford to continue his practice of trying to keep ahead of Cardinal batters. After all, even a home run would not put the Yankees behind, and if he could get the first pitch by Slaughter for a strike the chances of his making a hit would be reduced. Because Ruffing was aware that Slaughter might swing at the first pitch, he put plenty on the ball. Slaughter, however, timed the swing perfectly, just as Rizzuto did on the 1 and 1 pitch in the first inning.

2. DiMaggio took Musial's fly.

3. Priddy fielded Cooper's grounder and stepped on first for the put-out.

4. Hopp grounded out, Gordon to Priddy.

(1 run, 1 hit, no errors, none left on base)

Yankees

1. Rolfe made first on a drag bunt, and took second when Beazley threw wild for an error.

Batting Strategy: It was Rolfe's idea to make Hopp field his bunt so that Beazley would have to cover first. However, the bunt was not quite hard enough, and Beazley had to come in to field the ball, then made a poor throw to Hopp.

2. Cullenbine flied to Moore in deep right-center field, Rolfe taking third.

Base-Running Strategy: As the ball neared Moore's hands, Rolfe, who was tagged-up, shifted his weight to the foot extended toward third. This enabled him to make his first step with the rear foot.

Batting Strategy: The Cardinals did not anticipate a sacrifice this early in the game with a left-hand batter at the plate, so Hopp played deep. Cullenbine, noticing this, tried to bunt toward first, but the ball went foul. Some managers play this type of strategy during the first four or five innings if either the first or third baseman plays back, hoping the batter may beat out the bunt. After the foul, Cullenbine worked the count to 3 and 1 before flying out.

Managing Strategy (offense): McCarthy did not attempt to sacrifice because he felt that Cullenbine could hit the ball to the right-field side of the diamond and advance Rolfe. Furthermore, DiMaggio and Keller, his two power hitters, were next up. He permitted Cullenbine to swing on the 3 and 1 pitch, since he knew Beazley had good control. The fact that Rolfe was in scoring position and represented the winning run further influenced his decision. This is basic strategy for most managers.

3. DiMaggio rifled a line-drive single to left, scoring Rolfe.

4. Keller drove a single to right, DiMaggio taking third.

Managing Strategy (defense): Behind 2 to 1, with first and third bases occupied and one out, Southworth motioned to the shortstop, Marion, and second baseman, Brown, to remain deep for a double play, indicating that he felt confident the Cardinals could score runs. In addition, even another score by the Yankees at this early stage of the game might not be too difficult to overcome. Furthermore, playing the infield back was the best guarantee against a big inning.

Coaching Strategy: Third-base coach Arthur Fletcher reminded DiMaggio to be sure to break for the plate if Gordon hit the ball on the ground, because he knew the Cardinals would try to make a double play, second to first. Failure to do so would then enable DiMaggio to score. Breaking for the plate in some cases draws a throw and thereby prevents a double play. These are both obvious reasons for not holding third.

5. Gordon struck out on a low outside curve. The strike-out occurred on a 2 and 2 pitch. If the count had reached 3 and 2, Southworth might have brought Marion and Brown in to counteract the fact that Keller would be running on the pitch. In other words, because a double play was not likely under these circumstances, it might have been better to try and head off DiMaggio at the plate.

Pitching Strategy: The real test of a pitcher developed in this inning. With Gordon up and first and third occupied with only one out, a hit could put the game out of control for the Cardinals, whereas retiring Gordon without permitting DiMaggio to score might well save the game. Beazley rose to the occasion and fanned Gordon for one of the two strike-outs he recorded during the game. This is one of the few situations wherein a pitcher should definitely try for a strike-out.

6. Dickey forced Keller at second, Marion to Brown.
(1 run, 3 hits, 1 error, 2 left on base)

	1	2	3	4	5	6	7	8	9
Cards	0	0	0	1	x	x	x	x	x
Yanks	1	0	0	1	x	x	x	x	x

FIFTH INNING

Cardinals

1. Kurowski flied to Keller on the second pitch.

2. Marion's drive to short center was captured by Cullenbine after a hard run.

3. Beazley looped a single to right.

Managing Strategy (defense): Because McCarthy knew Beazley would not try to steal, he had the first baseman, Priddy, move off the bag to strengthen the defense. Priddy in turn informed Ruffing so that he would not attempt to catch Beazley.

4. Rolfe took Brown's pop fly.
   (No runs, 1 hit, no errors, 1 left on base)

Yankees

1. Marion made a glove-hand catch of Priddy's sharp grounder and threw to Hopp for the out.

2. Ruffing's slow roller to third put him on first when he beat out Kurowski's throw.

3. Rizzuto's hot grounder went to Hopp, who with an easy double play in sight, made a bad throw to Marion at second for an error, both Ruffing and Rizzuto being safe.

Infielding Strategy: It was previously mentioned that handling of the ball on the first part of a double play must be well executed, otherwise an adequate pivot cannot be made for the second out. In this case even the first out was missed, thereby putting the pitcher, Beazley, in a hole.

4. Brown fumbled an easy grounder by Rolfe for an error which filled the bases.

5. Cullenbine ran the count to 3 and 1, then popped to Marion in back of third.

Pitching Strategy: Beazley pitched curves until he got in the hole, hoping that Cullenbine would hit the ball on the ground.

Managing Strategy (defense): Southworth again played his shortstop and second baseman deep for a double play because even though Cullenbine was batting left-hand, he lacked speed, so it was possible to double him on a grounder. Kurowski and Hopp both played short to guard against a squeeze play until the count reached 3 and 1. Southworth then moved both players back, particularly Hopp, since Cullenbine normally hit in his direction.

Managing Strategy (offense): McCarthy did not employ a take sign with the count 3 and 1 because the proper time to hit in baseball is when the pitcher is in the hole and runners are in scoring position. Furthermore, Beazley continued to have good control.

Base-Running Strategy: Because Marion was directly in front of Cullenbine's fly, the plate umpire declared "Infield fly," since all the bases were occupied with one out. Cullenbine was therefore an automatic out. Players on the bases, however, were alert, because if an infield fly is dropped, base runners can run at their own peril.

6. DiMaggio grounded to Kurowski, who stepped on third to force Rizzuto. (No runs, 1 hit, 2 errors, 3 left on base)

	1	2	3	4	5	6	7	8	9
Cards	0	0	0	1	0	x	x	x	x
Yanks	1	0	0	1	0	x	x	x	x

SIXTH INNING

Cardinals

1. Moore singled to center on the first pitch.

2. Slaughter got his second hit, a long single to right center that put Moore on third.

Batting Strategy: Slaughter faked a bunt on the first pitch to make the defense think he might sacrifice, thereby increasing his chances of driving a ball through the infield. Bluffing to beat out a bunt prior to hitting is also good strategy for the same reason.

Base-Running Strategy: Moore knew that he could reach third safely. This must be a sure play with none out. The best time to take a chance is with one out, but never when there are two outs because a single will usually score the run from second.

Pitching Strategy: Ruffing raced toward third on Slaughter's hit, and took a position about 50 feet in back of the bag in line with DiMaggio's throw for Moore. It is important for the pitcher to be at least this distance from the intended receiver. Otherwise it may be difficult for him to retrieve an over-throw.

Infielding Strategy: Shortstop Rizzuto played in front of third in the cutoff position. When he saw that Moore would be safe, he intercepted the ball and attempted to catch Slaughter rounding first. He was unsuccessful, but the cutoff play often works whether the throw goes to third base or to the plate.

3. Rizzuto took Musial's pop fly in short left.

4. Cullenbine made a fine catch of Cooper's fly inside the right-field foul line. Moore scored easily after the catch to tie the score, and Slaughter moved to second and continued to third as Priddy threw wild. (Under present day rules, this is a sacrifice fly.)

Base-Running Strategy: Moore knew that he could score easily on Cooper's fly, but he hustled over the plate because he realized the possibility of Slaughter being thrown out at second for the third out. If this occurred before he crossed the plate, then his run would not have counted. Slaughter also considered this point, but he was sure he could reach second safely.

Coaching Strategy: Southworth made a coaching error at this point that might have cost the game. Actually, Slaughter could have scored easily had Southworth taken a position up the base line, but instead he stood near the bag, thus giving no indication of a chance to score. After the game Southworth stated that he stopped Slaughter because he was afraid of DiMaggio's great arm, but if Slaughter had been permitted to round the bag several steps he could have almost walked over the plate, for DiMaggio had to make two grabs for the ball.

5. DiMaggio caught Hopp's fly in deep center field.
                    (1 run, 2 hits, 1 error, 1 left on base)

Yankees

1. Musial chased back for Keller's long drive.

2. Gordon grounded out, Kurowski to Hopp.

3. Slaughter took Dickey's fly ball in front of the right-field stands.
                    (No runs, no hits, no errors, none left on base)

	1	2	3	4	5	6	7	8	9
Cards	0	0	0	1	0	1	x	x	x
Yanks	1	0	0	1	0	0	x	x	x

SEVENTH INNING

Cardinals

1. Kurowski flied out to DiMaggio in left center.

Outfielding Strategy: The ball was hit high in the air, and DiMaggio flipped his sun glasses as he left his starting position. He stepped with his left foot first, since he had to run forward and to his right.

2. Marion popped to Rizzuto in short left.

3. Beazley fanned.
                    (No runs, no hits, no errors, none left on base)

Yankees

1. Priddy grounded out, Marion to Hopp.

2. Ruffing struck out.

3. Rizzuto singled to center after working the count to 3 and 2.

Batting Strategy: Rizzuto took hard swings at both the 3 and 1 and 3 and 2 pitches, apparently with the idea that he might make a long hit. This is good strategy with two out because with a runner beyond first a single might score a run.

Base-Running Strategy: In running to first, Rizzuto kept his eyes on the bag, then located the ball as he made his turn. This enabled him to get the greatest speed from his running ability, and by rounding the bag in stride he was ready to advance if Moore did not handle the ball properly. With two out, a base runner should try to advance to second on the slightest hesitation or omission by the defense for the same reason that a batter attempts to make a long hit with two out.

4. Slaughter caught Rolfe's fly for the third out.
        (No runs, 1 hit, no errors, 1 left on base)

	1	2	3	4	5	6	7	8	9
Cards	0	0	0	1	0	1	0	x	x
Yanks	1	0	0	1	0	0	0	x	x

EIGHTH INNING

Cardinals

1. Brown singled sharply to left.

2. Moore sacrificed, Priddy to Gordon, Brown moving to second.

Managing Strategy (offense): Brown represented the winning run, so Southworth elected to sacrifice. It is a general practice to play for one run in the late innings and to hit straightaway in the early part of the game. You will note in the first six innings that the lead-off batter reached base safely four times and that in only one instance was a sacrifice attempted, and that was with pitcher Ruffing. This is also a general practice, since pitchers are not usually good hitters. In addition, bunting keeps pitchers off base, thereby saving energy. Southworth could have instructed Moore to hit behind the runner had he decided not to bunt, since this method of attack usually makes it possible for a runner on first to reach second. However, this was a definite bunt situation, and he knew Ruffing would try to pitch high fast balls inside. Under the circumstances it would have been difficult for Moore to hit the ball on the ground toward right field.

Base-Running Strategy: Moore's bunt was along the first-base line, so he ran in the three-foot lane, as prescribed by the rules, to avoid interference with Priddy's throw.

3. Rizzuto took Slaughter's pop fly.

4. Musial grounded out, Gordon to Priddy.
        (No runs, 1 hit, no errors, 1 left on base)

Yankees

1. Beazley rushed to first to take Hopp's toss on Cullenbine's grounder.

Pitching Strategy: Beazley broke from the mound as soon as the ball was hit. Since the grounder rolled near the bag, he circled along the line, taking Hopp's toss just before he reached the base, then continued over the bag into fair territory to avoid contact with Cullenbine. If the ball had been hit away from the line, Beazley would have run straight to the base and reached into the diamond for the throw.

2. Musial took DiMaggio's liner.

3. Beazley made a running catch of Keller's bounder, and crossed first base ahead of him to end the inning.

(No runs, no hits, no errors, none left on base)

	1	2	3	4	5	6	7	8	9
Cards	0	0	0	1	0	1	0	0	x
Yanks	1	0	0	1	0	0	0	0	x

NINTH INNING

Cardinals

1. Cooper rifled a single to right center.

2. Cooper took second on Hopp's sacrifice, Ruffing to Gordon covering first.

3. Kurowski fouled a pitch, then blasted a low outside pitch into the stands just inside the left-field foul line for a home run, scoring Cooper ahead of him and putting the Cardinals ahead 4 to 2.

Managing Strategy (defense): Ordinarily, McCarthy would have walked a hitter like Kurowski to set the stage for a double play, then pitch to Marion, a weaker batter. However, on six appearances in previous games, Ruffing had struck out Kurowski three times and forced him to hit harmless flies the other three. Furthermore, Kurowski had looked very weak each time, so McCarthy assumed Ruffing could dispose of him easily again.

Pitching Strategy: From a pitching standpoint, Ruffing pitched well to Kurowski. His first delivery, a high inside fast ball, was actually not over the plate, but Kurowski swung and pulled it foul. The next pitch was a low outside curve, and this, too, did not appear to be a strike. However, Kurowski got out in front of the ball well, and provided the necessary arm power to lift it into the stands. Ruffing was apparently trying to make Kurowski hit a bad pitch, or a pitch outside the strike area. This is frequently done in such circumstances, and if the batter fails to swing and gets the pitcher in the hole, an intentional pass is given. In swinging at the first two pitches, Kurowski was in reality doing just what Ruffing wanted him to do, but a pair of strong forearms enabled him to do what would be impossible for most players.

4. Marion popped out to Dickey in front of the plate.

5. Beazley flied to Rizzuto in short left.
(2 runs, 2 hits, no errors, none left on base)

Yankees

1. Gordon lined a single into left field.

2. A grounder by Dickey to Brown seemed destined to kill the Yankees' last chance to tie or win the game; but with an easy double play in sight, Brown fumbled the ball for his second error of the game. Gordon reached second and Dickey first. The tying runs were now on base with no outs. Beazley was in another trying spot; and the Yankees appeared destined at least to tie the score.

Managing Strategy (offense): Because the Yankees had to tie the game at this point or lose, McCarthy substituted Stainback, a very fast runner, for

BOX SCORE OF THE GAME

St. Louis Cardinals

	AB	R	H	TB	2B	3B	HR	RBI	BB	SO	SH	SB	PO	A	E
Brown, 2b	3	0	2	2	0	0	0	0	1	0	0	0	3	4	2
T. Moore, cf	3	1	1	1	0	0	0	0	0	1	1	0	3	0	0
Slaughter, rf	4	1	2	5	0	0	1	1	0	0	0	0	2	0	0
Musial, lf	4	0	0	0	0	0	0	0	0	0	0	0	2	0	0
W. Cooper, c	4	1	2	2	0	0	0	1	0	0	0	0	2	1	0
Hopp, 1b	3	0	0	0	0	0	0	0	0	0	1	0	9	2	1
Kurowski, 3b	4	1	1	4	0	0	1	2	0	0	0	0	1	1	0
Marion, ss	4	0	0	0	0	0	0	0	0	0	0	0	3	5	0
Beazley, p	4	0	1	1	0	0	0	0	0	2	0	0	2	0	1
Totals	33	4	9	15	0	0	2	4	1	3	2	0	27	13	4

New York Yankees

	AB	R	H	TB	2B	3B	HR	RBI	BB	SO	SH	SB	PO	A	E
Rizzuto, ss	4	1	2	5	0	0	1	1	0	0	0	0	7	1	0
Rolfe, 3b	4	1	1	1	0	0	0	0	0	0	0	0	1	0	0
Cullenbine, rf	4	0	0	0	0	0	0	0	0	0	0	0	3	0	0
DiMaggio, cf	4	0	1	1	0	0	0	1	0	0	0	0	3	0	0
Keller, lf	4	0	1	1	0	0	0	0	0	0	0	0	1	0	0
Gordon, 2b	4	0	1	1	0	0	0	0	0	1	0	0	3	3	0
Dickey, c	4	0	0	0	0	0	0	0	0	0	0	0	4	0	0
a Stainback	0	0	0	0	0	0	0	0	0	0	0	0	0	0	0
Priddy, 1b	3	0	0	0	0	0	0	0	1	0	0	0	5	1	1
Ruffing, p	3	0	1	1	0	0	0	0	0	1	0	0	0	1	0
b Selkirk	1	0	0	0	0	0·	0	0	0	0	0	0	0	0	0
Totals	35	2	7	10	0	0	1	2	1	2	0	0	27	6	1

a Ran for Dickey in ninth.   *b* Batted for Ruffing in ninth.

St. Louis Cardinals	0	0	0	1	0	1	0	0	2–4
New York Yankees	1	0	0	1	0	0	0	0	0–2

Earned runs—Cardinals 4, Yankees 2.

Left on bases—Cardinals 5, Yankees 7. Double plays—Gordon, Rizzuto, and Priddy; Hopp, Marion, and Brown. Struck out—By Beazley 2, Ruffing 3. Base on balls—Off Beazley 1, Ruffing 1. Umpires—Magerkurth (N.L.), plate; Summers (A.L.), first base; Barr (N.L.), second base; Hubbard (A.L.), third base. Official scorers—J. Roy Stockton, *St. Louis Post-Dispatch;* Ed T. Murphy, *New York Sun;* Al Horwits (chief), president Baseball Writers Association. Time of game—1:58.

CARDINALS

Player	Pos	1	2	3	4	5	6	7	8	9	10	11	12	RBI	AB	R	H	PO	A	E
Brown	4	4-6 W		-8		5			8 -7						3	0	2	3	4	2
Moore	8	K		9		9 2-8		3-4 s							3	1	1	3	0	0
Slaughter	9	6-3			≡9	E3-2 -9			6					1	4	1	2	2	0	0
Musial	7		6		8		6	4-3							4	0	0	2	0	0
Cooper	2		-8	3-U		9			3 5-8					1	4	1	2	2	1	0
Hopp	3		6	4-3		8			3 s						3	0	0	9	2	1
Kurowski	5		4			7		8	≡7					II	4	1	1	1	1	0
Marion	6			3-F		9		6	2						4	0	0	3	5	0
Beazley	1			K		-9		K	6						4	0	1	2	0	1
RUNS		0	0	0	1	0	1	0	0	2				4	33	4	9	27	13	4
HITS		0	1	1	1	1	2	0	1	2				9						
LEFT ON BASE		0	1	1	0	1	1	0	1	0				5						
ERRORS		0	0	0	0	0	1	0	0	0				1						

PITCHERS	IP	R	H	BB	WP	HB	B	SO
Ruffing	9	////	/// ////	/	0	0	0	///

YANKEES

Player	Pos	1	2	3	4	5	6	7	8	9	10	11	12	RBI	AB	R	H	PO	A	E
Rizzuto	6	≡7		8	5-U E3	5		-8						1	4	1	2	7	1	0
Rolfe	5	4-3			9 E1 8-1	E4		9							4	1	1	1	0	0
Cullenbine	9	3-U			8	6		3-1							4	0	0	3	0	0
DiMaggio	8	8			7 -7	F-C		7						1	4	0	1	3	0	0
Keller	7		4-3		6-4 -9		7	1-U							4	0	1	1	0	0
Gordon	4		6-3		K	5-3			2-6 -7						4	0	1	3	3	0
Dickey (R-9 Stainback)	2		4-3	F-C		9			E4						4	0	0	4	0	0
Priddy	3		3-6 W		6-3		6-3		4						3	0	0	5	1	1
Ruffing (B-9 Selkirk)	1			6-4 s	5-6 -5		K		4-3						3	0	0	0	0	0
RUNS		1	0	0	1	0	0	0	0	0				2	35	2	7	27	6	1
HITS		1	0	0	3	1	0	1	0	1				7						
LEFT ON BASE		0	0	0	2	3	0	1	0	1				7						
ERRORS		0	0	0	1	2	0	0	0	1				4						

PITCHERS	IP	R	H	BB	WP	HB	B	SO
Beazley	9	//	//// //	/	0	0	0	//

Dickey. He realized that a not too well placed bunt with Dickey running might result in a force play at second.

Fielding Strategy: The Cardinals, of course, knew that the Yankees would probably bunt. Early in the game sacrifice bunts are generally thrown to first, at least when there is the slightest doubt about catching a runner on base. However, late in the game an attempt is usually made to prevent the success of a sacrifice. In this particular situation the logical play was for Gordon at third. For this reason Hopp protected the area from the first-base line to the mound; Beazley took care of the area from the mound to the third-base line; Kurowski covered third, and Marion held Gordon close to second. The short-stop moves away from the bag as the pitcher delivers the ball so that he can cover his position if the ball is hit. However, he keeps alert for a throw from the catcher if the runner advances too far on the pitch. This factor changed the course of the game, because when Beazley's first pitch was a little inside, Priddy, after indicating that he might bunt, backed away from the plate and Gordon was an easy out at second, Cooper to Marion.

Base-Running Strategy: In sacrifice situations the responsibility rests with the bunter. It is not advisable for the runner to take a long advance; he should take a walking advance so that he can either start for the next base if the ball is bunted, or retreat if the pitch goes by the batter. Gordon was overanxious, and as a result became an easy out.

3. Brown atoned for his costly error by racing in front of second to make a diving catch of Priddy's low pop fly for the second out.

4. Brown also took a grounder from George Selkirk, batting for Ruffing, and fired the ball to Hopp to end the game.

(No runs, 1 hit, 1 error, 1 left on base)

	1	2	3	4	5	6	7	8	9	R	H	E
Cards	0	0	0	1	0	1	0	0	2	4	9	4
Yanks	1	0	0	1	0	0	0	0	0	2	7	1

APPENDIXES

A

Scoring, Diamond Layouts, and Practice Aids

METHODS OF SCORING AND OF DETERMINING PERCENTAGE RECORDS

SCORING

One of the numerous kinds of score sheets is exhibited in Fig. A–1. Each of the various types has the following functions in common: when the team is on the defense, to record fielding plays (put-outs, assists, and errors); and when the team is on the offense, to record batting and base-running action.

Each team has its own score sheet. The players' names appear according to the batting order. Next to each player's name is a number representing the defensive position he plays.

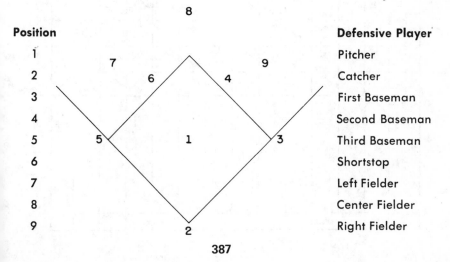

Position		Defensive Player
1		Pitcher
2		Catcher
3		First Baseman
4		Second Baseman
5		Third Baseman
6		Shortstop
7		Left Fielder
8		Center Fielder
9		Right Fielder

Fig. A–1.   Score sheet.

The score sheets of the two teams are marked simultaneously—defensive action under the inning and fielding columns and offensive action in the inning and batting columns.

Fielding Blocks. On the line with each player's name under the fielding columns the number of errors, put-outs, and assists he makes in defensive action throughout the game is recorded by means of dots, the amount to be totaled at the end of the game.

Batting Blocks. On the line with each player's name under the batting column appear dots indicating:

AB	Times at bat
R	Runs
H	Hits
2B	Doubles
3B	Triples
HR	Home runs
RBI	Runs batted in
SO	Strike outs
W or BB	Walks or base on balls
SH	Sacrifice hits
SB	Stolen bases
HP or HB	Hit by pitch or hit batsmen
I	Interference

Inning Blocks. On the line with each player's name his batting and base-running action is recorded by inning in the inning blocks. On the score sheet reproduced in this book each inning block is divided into five parts.

A diamond is in the center of the inning block. The remaining area of the block is divided into four parts by lines drawn from the points of the diamond to the four sides of the block.

A dot is placed in the diamond to indicate the player has scored a run. Numbers 1, 2, and 3 can also be placed in the diamond to indicate the 3 outs.

The lower right corner of the inning block represents first base, the upper right corner, second base, the upper left corner, third base, and the lower left corner, home plate. Batting, base running, and defensive action is recorded in these corners by the following symbols.

——	Single
=	Double
≡	Triple
≣	Home run

• Run (placed in the center of the diamond)
BB or W Base on balls
S Sacrifice
K Strike out
WP Wild pitch
PB Passed ball
E Error
B Balk
SB Stolen base
FC Fielder's choice
U Unassisted

Beginning in the lower right space and reading counterclockwise, the marks in the player's inning block record how he got on base and, once on base, which member of his team enabled him to advance, or, if he did not get on base, which member or members of the opposing team put him out.

Getting on Base. If the batter hits to center field and gets on first base, $- 8$ is recorded in the lower right space of his inning block; if he hits to center field and gets on second, $= 8$ is recorded in the upper right space of his inning block. The 8 represents the position of the defensive player who fielded the ball. At the same time, batting action is recorded for the player in the columns under batting. A batter is not credited with a time at bat if he sacrifices, reaches first base by a walk, is hit by pitch, or interference occurs. In each of these instances the event is recorded under the appropriate column on the line with his name.

Advancing Around Bases. When the player on first base is advanced to second on a hit by the third baseman of his team, a 5 (the third baseman's position number) is placed in the upper right space of the player's inning block. If the player is then advanced to third base by a hit of his team's pitcher (1), a 1 would appear in the upper left space of the player's inning block. If the player is batted home by the catcher (2), a 2 would appear in the lower left space of the player's inning block and a dot would be placed in the central diamond to indicate the player scored a run.

Put-Outs. If the batter hits to the first baseman (3) and is put out by him, a large 3 is written in the batter's inning block. On the line with the first baseman's name, credit for a put-out is also simultaneously recorded. If the batter hits the ball to third baseman (5), who throws the ball to first baseman (3), large numbers 5-3 would appear in the batter's inning block. Simultaneously the credits for an assist by the third baseman and a put-out by the first baseman would be recorded in the fielding blocks on the line with their names. A large F-C in the batter's inning block indicates fielder's choice, or that the batter caused another player to be retired for the third out of the inning. An F-C in a base area likewise means fielder's choice, and also that the batter reached first base as a result of an out or attempt to make an out at another base. In both cases a line is made from the out to F-C.

Outs that result in double plays are circled and connected. Routine outs can be made more detailed by the use of additional letters. For exemple, the letters F, L, or P after a number mean foul fly, line drive, and pop fly respectively. A number after E denotes the player who erred. As an aid in scoring, lines are crossed in the inning area below a third out. This prevents entering the first batter of the next inning in the wrong area.

In the case of unusual developments, such as a base runner being hit by a batted ball, or interference by either the offense or defense, asterisks may be used. One of these can be placed in the area of the batter or base runner involved, and the other with a footnote, at the bottom of the score card. On a catcher's interference an error is charged. A batted ball that hits a runner is an automatic hit, and the fielder nearest the runner receives a put-out. When a runner interferes with the defense, the fielder receives a put-out unless in the act of throwing when the interference occurred. In this case an assist is given, and the player for whom the throw was intended receives a put-out.

Proving the Box Score. A box score is in balance (or proved) when the total of the team's times at bat, bases on balls received, hit batters, sacrifice bunts, sacrifice flies, and batters awarded first base because of interference or obstruction equals the total of that team's runs, players left on base (lob), and the opposing team's put-outs.

$$\text{Total:} \quad AB + W + HP + S = R + \text{lob} + PO$$

DETERMINING PERCENTAGE RECORDS

To determine the *percentage of games won and lost,* divide the number of games won by the total games won and lost.

To figure a player's *batting average,* divide the total number of safe hits (not the total bases on hits) by the total times at bat.

To find a player's *slugging percentage,* divide the total bases of all safe hits by the total times at bat.

For the *fielding average,* divide the total put-outs and assists by the total of put-outs, assists, and errors.

In cases where the remaining fraction is one-half or over, a full point is added to the average.

To determine a *pitcher's earned-run average*, divide the total earned runs charged against his pitching by the total number of innings he pitched (average runs per inning), and multiply by 9 (average runs per game).

An earned run is charged against the pitcher every time a player scores by the aid of safe hits, sacrifice bunts, sacrifice flies, stolen bases, put-outs, fielder's choices, bases on balls, hit batsmen, balks, or wild pitches (even though the wild pitch is a third strike, which permits a batter to reach first base) before fielding chances have been offered to retire the offensive team.

DETERMINING WINNING AND LOSING PITCHER

There are numerous considerations in deciding the rightful winning and losing pitcher when a team uses more than one pitcher in a game. In this case four basic points must be followed:

1. The starting pitcher is credited with the victory only if he has pitched at least five complete innings and his team is in the lead when he is replaced and remains in the lead for the remainder of the game. This applies to games of six or more innings.

2. In a five-inning game the starting pitcher is credited with the victory only if he has pitched at least four complete innings and his team is in the lead when he is replaced and remains in the lead for the remainder of the game.

3. The starting pitcher is charged with the loss of the game if he is replaced when his team is behind in the score, and his team thereafter fails either to tie the score or gain the lead.

4. Whenever the score is tied the game becomes a new contest as far as determining the winning and losing pitcher is concerned.

Special rulings include the removal of a pitcher because of an injury or a commanding lead, or because a manager or coach predetermines that several pitchers will work an equal number of innings.

DIAMOND LAYOUTS

Special care must be taken in laying out a baseball field. This pertains to both measurements and location. The diagrams (Figs. A–2, A–3) show the official measurements for a field, and detailed layouts for bases, base and foul lines, and batter's, pitcher's, and catcher's boxes. It is desirable that the line from home base through the pitcher's plate to second base shall run east-northeast. This means the afternoon sun will be located behind the catcher; therefore the sun will not be in the batter's eyes.

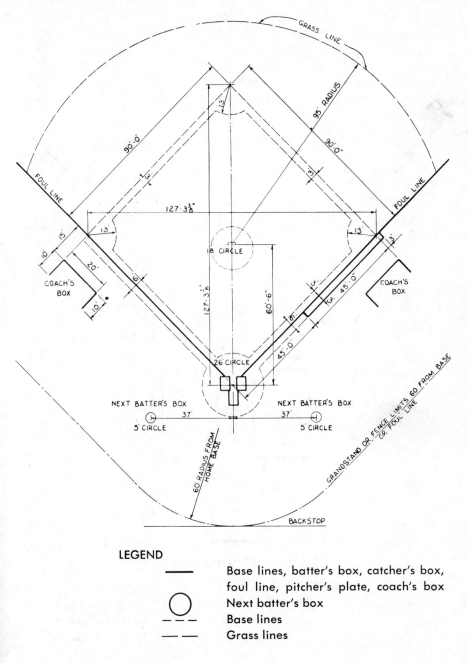

Fig. A–2. Official measurements for laying out a baseball field.

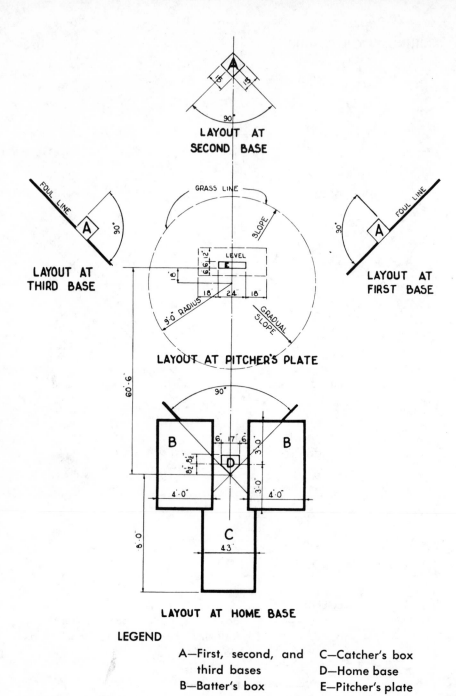

LAYOUT AT
SECOND BASE

LAYOUT AT
THIRD BASE

LAYOUT AT PITCHER'S PLATE

LAYOUT AT
FIRST BASE

LAYOUT AT HOME BASE

LEGEND

A—First, second, and   C—Catcher's box
    third bases   D—Home base
B—Batter's box   E—Pitcher's plate

Fig. A—3. Detailed layout of bases, base and foul lines, and batter's, pitcher's, and catcher's boxes.

Framework, approximately 4′ × 5′, covered with netting or canvas; and base.

Fig. A–4.   Protective screen for pitcher.

Framework, approximately 5′ × 7′, covered with netting; and support.

Fig. A–5.   Protective screen for first baseman.

Place standards on sides of plate or drive poles into ground. Then form strike zone with string. Use rubber at points indicated by heavy lines to provide tension. Very practical because catcher can be used.

Fig. A–6.   Pitching target a.

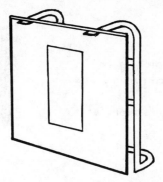

Padded canvas or netting (approximately 3½' × 5½' with hems on all sides) which can be suspended on a metal framework (approximately 3' × 6'). Hollow aluminum pipe is inserted in top hem and rubber hose in bottom and side hems. Pipe rests on arms supported by means of two openings along seam of canvas. Strike zone is painted on canvas or hung from top.

Fig. A–7.   Pitching target b.

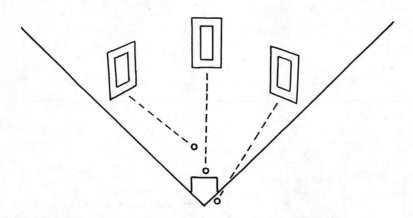

In a restricted area the target may be placed 30 or 40 feet from the plate. It can be placed just inside either foul line or directly in front of the plate. Both left- and right-hand batters may then alternate the position of the tee so that they can practice pulling inside pitches, driving outside pitches to the opposite field, and hitting pitches over the middle of the plate straightaway.

Fig. A–8.   Use of pitching target b with batting tee.

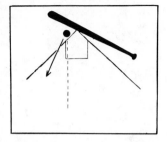

a. Angle of bat for hitting an outside pitch to opposite field.

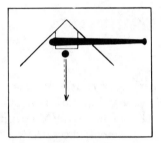

b. Angle of bat for hitting a pitch over middle of plate straightaway.

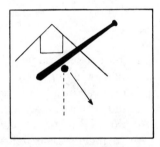

c. Angle of bat for pulling an inside pitch.

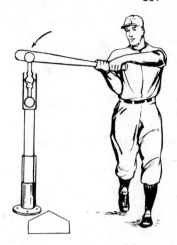

d. Angle of swing for a high outside pitch.

e. Angle of swing for a low inside pitch.

In using the batting tee it is advisable for a player to maintain the normal position of his feet and move the tee to the respective positions (shown to the left). Note in the top diagram (a) that the outside pitch is hit behind the plate. This varies with the position of a player's feet in the batter's box. For example, if a batter stands close to the plate he may hit an outside pitch in front of the plate. In this case the ball is more likely to be hit to center field.

Fig. A–9.   Use of batting tee.

B

Team Organization

The main function of a coach (or manager) is, of course, the teaching of baseball and all its related strategy. However, there are many other areas with which he must be concerned. This includes the preparation of a budget and schedule, the purchase of equipment, the selection and handling of personnel, the election of the captain, and the selection or election of a student (or team) manager. Some knowledge about normal baseball injuries and the care of a diamond may also be necessary.

BUDGET

The first order of business in baseball is to prepare a budget. This should include separate funds for both equipment (including repair and cleaning) and travel. Normally this is compiled a year in advance so it is advisable to learn if the previous prices will hold or whether to expect increases and to what extent. Actually an approved budget is only a guide since a year hence it may be necessary to juggle some items in relation to the inventory at the end of the season. However, purchases for the succeeding season must not exceed the original budget. The system employed may prohibit spending more than the budget but if this ever occurs, whether for equipment or trips, a future budget may suffer. The coach may also be looking for another job.

Normally a school has a specific fund allotted for the various sports. However, it is not unusual to raise money for special projects. There are many ingenious ways. This may take the form of dances and other types of social promotions. The players of some schools handle concessions at games during the fall and winter seasons to finance spring trips and tournaments. Specific promotions may also create fan interest.

SCHEDULE

A schedule is usually predetermined a year in advance the same as a budget. Generally two games per week are satisfactory for a team, three games at the most. Some schools restrict activity the first four days of the week to one game, then permit several games on Friday and Saturday. Sunday is being used by a few schools since this is the most satisfactory date. In addition Monday can then be a non-practice day.

The problem of home and away games is often established by athletic policy. A team should have more home games but this means some teams must have more away games. Schools which are in leagues or conferences usually have rotating schedules so any additional games must be dovetailed around these. Normally an away game is more expensive, particularly if extensive travel is involved. It is best if overnight trips can be avoided. Different food and water plus a strange bed and unusual noises may all affect the performance of some players. A spring trip or a special trip is another matter and may have to be handled exclusively by the coach.

When a budget and schedule are planned well in advance the only real problem relative to games is the weather. To cover this matter it is always important to have the names and telephone numbers of the umpires so that they may be called if there is a postponement. A visiting team should also be advised well in advance so that it will not have to make an unnecessary trip. Other offices concerned with the game should also be given the information, if the game has been cancelled or a date has been rescheduled. This includes the ticket office and the various news medias. As part of over-all planning for rainy days it is advisable to get the latest report from the weather bureau before making a final decision relative to postponement.

EQUIPMENT

The purchase and care of equipment is a very important phase of a baseball program. Quality products will normally pay dividends because they will withstand wear and cleaning better than less expensive merchandise. They will also make the team more presentable. The basic items are, of course, the uniforms, including belts, outer stockings, caps, shoes, and jackets.

UNIFORM

Pants are usually made heavier than shirts because of sliding but even so one shirt will outwear three or four pairs of pants. This immediately creates a problem relative to matching old shirts with new pants. Some prepractice in the new pants may help to solve this problem. On new orders for shirts it is advisable to match numbers and sizes according to the previous order. This is particularly true if there are two sets of uniforms.

BELTS

A supply of various sizes of belts should be available. The belt should be light and preferably wide enough to fit the loops of the pants.

OUTER STOCKINGS

A fine knit lightweight stocking is best although a heavier stocking may be desirable in cold climate. Many stockings have elastic tops insuring that the stockings will stay up.

CAPS

There are many types of caps. Although a good cap is an important part of the uniform, it is better to have two reasonably priced caps for each player, or one of this type or a cheaper cap for practice and a good grade cap for games. Some satisfactory caps of variable sizes can be purchased with embroidered letters, good sweat bands, and elastic backs. The latter are very practical since fitting is simplified. The fact that many players fold a cap and put it in their back pocket before going to the plate has a way of equalizing the looks of all caps. A few players wear inserts and some teams wear protective helmets all of the time. This is a better solution but an insert in a regular cap does not really give adequate protection.

SHOES

There are many satisfactory shoes on the market. A solution to this problem is to give a credit for shoes and the player pays the difference in price. In this system the shoes become the property of the player and the school pays for repairs and toe plates. Shoes that are furnished are often beyond repair at the end of the season and those that are renovated are not always satisfactory, particularly if they have to be used for another player's feet.

Shoes should fit snugly because leather stretches. Normally the correct size is about one size less than street shoes. Pitchers should, of course, have toe plates. These may be obtained from a sporting goods store or a shoemaker can sew a piece of leather over the front and side of the toe. There should be a pan of waterproof oil with accompanying brushes in the dressing room so that the shoes can be treated occasionally. This is very important if the shoes have become wet.

JACKETS

Many types of jackets are available. Lined jackets are often used in cold climates. There is some sentiment for a light, unlined jacket in all climates. It is easier to throw while wearing a lightweight jacket, and a heavier undershirt can always be worn if the temperature is low. Jackets should be numbered.

Many other items should be included in the budget such as white T shirts, undershirts (light and heavy), white sanitary stockings, supporters (including cup supporters and cups, for the pitchers, catchers, and infielders), sliding pads and/or pants, inner soles, black shoelaces, elastic bands, sun glasses, catching equipment, and gloves. The latter may only apply to catching gloves which require a great deal of pounding to prepare and maintain a pitching staff. There will also be a need for suit rolls or duffel bags and perhaps a bat bag for extra bats if a spring trip is taken or if bats are transported separately on trips.

Jackets should be assigned by numbers; and caps, undershirts, and bats should be marked with the numbers of the players' shirts. It is advisable to wash the T shirts, sanitary stockings, and supporters every day and undershirts occasionally. Some teams do this service through a centralized equipment room, clean garments being returned for soiled ones. Uniforms should, of course, be dry cleaned or washed as needed.

In some schools the centralized equipment room handles all equipment. A checkout system is required in this case so that players can be charged with or credited for a return of equipment. If such a system is employed the attendant and his assistants see that the proper mending, cleaning, and identification measures are performed and at the end of the season make a final inventory of all equipment.

BATS

Every player should be allotted at least two bats. Most coaches order bats for the entire team. Before the order is placed it is advisable to ask players for their preference. This is only a guide because spring desires often change. This occurs simply because the feel of similar models often differ. It is therefore important for the coach to concentrate on bats which are more inclined to have good balance, consequently can be more easily swung. Weight and length are other matters to be considered and, of course, they will vary with the strength and the ability of players.

Once a player has made his selections he should mark the handle end of the bats with his shirt number. There is nothing more disconcerting than to have one of your bats broken by another player so it is advisable to establish a rule whereby no player may use another player's bat except by permission.

PROTECTIVE HELMETS

There are several types of protective helmets. These are, of course, requirements for batters in all levels of baseball. They can be ordered with the school letter the same as a regular cap, or the letter can be painted on or decals can be ordered for this purpose. Decal letters or numbers can also be obtained to indicate sizes. These may be S—small, M—medium, L—large, and XL—extra large, or numbers 1, 2, 3, and 4 can indicate these sizes respectively. The letters or numbers can be mounted on the back of the helmets. The batboy should be advised to place the helmets near the bat rack so that the letters or numbers face the field for quick reference. (If there are dugouts or covered benches, hooks and tapes bearing players' names or numbers can be combined to quickly locate gloves at the end of an inning.)

When a batter reaches base the helmet should be slid in the direction of the plate or toward the coach or batboy retrieving it. This may be done by gripping the peak and swinging the helmet, top down, along the ground. If the helmet is thrown it may land on its peak or edge and be damaged. A protective helmet should also be provided for the catcher.

GETTING INTO UNIFORM

A neatly worn uniform is an integral part of baseball. It gives a player confidence and earns the respect of the spectators.

Many schools provide cotton T shirts to wear under the undershirt. Some players prefer these because their skins may be allergic to the wool or partial wool of most undershirts. In warm climates a light cotton or synthetic undershirt may suffice. The undershirt is normally tucked in and around the supporter so that the shirt rests against the skin. If sliding pants are worn these come next. The regular uniform shirt is then put on.

The player now sits down and pulls on his sanitary hose and regular stockings. Some players place their regular stockings above the knees then pull elastic bands or garters over the knees (this may have to be a prepared piece of elastic to avoid the hindrance of the circulation). The pants are then turned inside out and the ends of the legs are pulled over the knees. The elastic bands or garters are now placed over the pants below the knees. It may be necessary to do a fold-over with the ends of the pants and stockings to make a comfortable fit.

Now the player stands and ties on the sliding pads (if he does not use sliding pants). These may fit under or over the regular shirt. He next pulls up his pants and puts on his shoes and cap.

There is another way to put on the pants if the pants are about the right length and stockings are used with elastic tops. In this case the pants may be pulled on in regular fashion. To get the proper fit, it may be necessary to fold the top of the stocking to the desired knee length. This fold may be either toward or away from the leg to provide a pad on which to slide. The former method will prevent the pad from rolling as a result of a slide.

The first of the two ways of putting on the pants may also be used with elastic stockings if the pants are about the desired length. In this case the ends of the pants are placed below the knees and the elastic is rolled over the pants. Some players twist the top of their sanitary stockings, then tuck them in for the desired stocking tension.

PERSONNEL

The main qualification for selecting a squad is, of course, baseball-playing ability. Attitude is another factor because every player must obey the rules and work in the interest of the team. This includes behavior on the playing field as well as on trips. There is a time for fun in both places but there should be no indulgences that reflect on the team or school. This includes off-the-field behavior at any time and particularly during the baseball season. In this connection it is advisable for the coach to offer some advice about proper dress and acceptable manners pertaining to both eating and personal conduct. The former includes shaving and getting the hair cut. A word about overexposure to the sun is also in order.

THE COACH

Granted that a team has a reasonable amount of talent, the coach becomes the focal point of success or failure, for he must have the ability to analyze the various personalities and get the most out of them. This may require counseling and a pat on the back or reprimand at the proper time. There are really no major problems in coaching but many decisions which have to be made may be important to a player or players, and consequently they affect the entire team.

Although winning is the main objective in a given game, many teams are often unevenly matched. The prime objective must be a sound baseball program. This implies well-organized and informative practice sessions—sessions that keep players busy and interested. If this is done then a team can expect a fair share of victories. Some coaches anticipate success at any cost. However, if a squad plays up to its potential as individuals and as a team, that is about all a coach can expect; therefore if his team loses he should be willing to gracefully congratulate the winning coach at the end of the game.

Confidence and enthusiasm are requirements of a successful coach. The same qualifications are desirable in a captain. If these are lacking then it is important to include a "holler guy" or two on the squad even though they may not become regular players. Such individuals usually provide the spark which every team needs. The same players may make ideal base coaches and, of course, "holler guys" on the infield stimulate all players to a maximum effort.

Patience is another very important asset of a coach because all teams make mistakes. Errors of omission can be handled constructively by individual conferences and sessions with the entire team. However, there seems to be no cure-all so about all a coach can hope for is that similar mistakes will not be made in future games.

The qualifications of each position must, of course, be considered in selecting a squad. These appear as introductions to the individual chapters. A simple screening process may also be found in the introduction to the chapter on practice techniques. After the squad is selected it is advisable to discuss the basic rules with the team and inform the players that current rule books and literature about baseball are available in the baseball office. Important rules should also be posted in the locker room with other material which might prove helpful. The summaries at the ends of the various chapters and articles and photographs from publications come under this category.

STARTING PITCHERS

Most players will fit into the various infield and outfield positions but pitchers are a special breed of personnel. Very often natural ability is not too much different so that a final judgment must be based on control and poise and the degree a pitcher progresses in early training. Once this is done a rotation of starting pitchers can be planned. The remaining pitchers must then be considered for long and short relief assignments.

RELIEF PITCHERS

Good relief pitchers may become almost as valuable as starting pitchers. They have special qualifications. These may be listed as: 1. a rubber arm, implying a strong, flexible arm which can stand lots of use; 2. the faculty of being able to warm up quickly; and 3. the ability to hit the strike zone consistently and particularly low. An effective relief pitcher must be mentally and physically conditioned to save games because he is normally called from the bull pen hastily and with runners on base. A regular pitcher may also be an effective relief pitcher between starts.

In order to meet every emergency it is advisable for a bull pen to be designated before the game. There should be a catcher assigned for this duty, properly equipped with a baseball. It is important to identify pitchers as first relief and second relief, otherwise the bull pen may be worn out. The first relief should be loosened up at the start of the game. If the first relief is called into the game, the second relief should begin to loosen up. In more advanced stages of baseball both left- and right-hand pitchers may warm up simultaneously late in the game, to counteract left- and right-hand batters.

When a relief pitcher goes to the mound he should know the game situation relative to the score, number of outs, runners on base, and the ball and strike count, if any, on the batter. If it is necessary to pitch from a set position he should throw his preliminary pitches from this position.

RULE COVERING REPLACEMENT OF PITCHER

A starting pitcher must pitch to the first batter or any substitute until such batter is put out or reaches first base (unless the pitcher sustains injury or illness). The same rule applies to a relief pitcher; that is, he must pitch to the player then at bat or any substitute batter until such player is put out or reaches first base, or until the team at bat is retired. This means that the relief pitcher may not have to make a pitch if a player is picked off base for the third out.

BATTING SLUMPS

The inability of players to consistently hit during a series of games is another matter that is related to personnel. Basically a slump is a slump but each player must be handled differently. Some faults may be observed but generally speaking the problem results from a lack of confidence; consequently a player develops an unnatural approach to batting.

More batting practice is the common remedy for a batting slump. Rest may be another although this may do just the opposite, if there is an adequate replacement. If at all possible the individual should be kept in the lineup because confidence in a player's defensive ability is bound to eventually bring back confidence in the batter's box.

Perhaps a slumping player's greatest weakness is overeagerness. With each failure at bat he becomes more anxious for a base hit. Using a wider stance and becoming more conscious of the opposite field may overcome the problem of impatience. A slight recoil of the hips accompanied by a deeper position of the hands may also be helpful. Selecting a lighter or heavier bat, choking the bat, and moving closer to the plate, are other corrective measures. Then some coaches feel that bunting practice will enable a player to find his normal batting eye. Any of these points may result in improvement but the best solution is a return to fundamentals plus concentration on a late step and swing.

THE CAPTAIN

The captain is, of course, an integral part of the personnel complex. A good captain is an invaluable asset for both the players and coach so his election should be a serious matter. Some coaches prefer to name a captain for each game, then have an election at the end of the schedule. However, rules for the election are often traditional and must be followed. On occasion the right man is not elected but generally speaking the team knows best.

The main job of a captain is to provide a liaison between the players and coach. In this way the coach can solve small problems which might otherwise get all out of proportion to their importance. Such problems, of course, vary with the different levels of baseball. A baseball coach will always have a few personnel problems because only the nine players he selects for a given game can play and these selections cannot be determined by a yardstick or a stop watch as in some other sports.

A phase of the captain's duties is to take duplicate lineups to the plate before the game and explain any unusual ground rules (unless the coach or manager goes to the plate). If the game is away he must learn if there are any special ground rules. These rules may be contested. The umpire-in-chief arbitrates any such discussion and resolves the matter, normally according to the rule book. The captain then wishes the opposition good luck and returns to the bench and relays information relative to rules to his team.

On some teams the coach or coaches (and trainer) are given a small token at the end of the season. The captain and team manager combine on this project, then make the presentation at the team banquet. It is a small matter but it has become conventional in some schools.

The captain is usually elected after the last home game or at the team banquet. It is best if he is a senior and this too is often covered by rule.

THE STUDENT (OR TEAM) MANAGER

In recent years the manager's chores have changed. He and his assistants formerly did about everything, including getting all equipment on the field, collecting laundry, tidying up the locker room, shining shoes, cleaning and tagging equipment, and making an inventory at the end of the season. (Some managers continue to perform such assignments but they are student employees.) Players are able to do many of these things and should. This includes taking their own bats (also catching equipment) to the field, exchanging soiled white T shirts, understockings, and supporters for clean equipment if there is a centralized equipment room, or placing the soiled whites and towels in bags marked for this purpose, and caring for their shoes.

On game days the manager has the responsibilities of towels and drinking water (unless there is a convenient fountain or fountains) for both benches or dugouts and towels for the visiting team's dressing quarters, the helmets for his own team, rosin bags for the mound and batting circles, and often fees for the umpires after the game. In addition he normally provides chewing gum. It is better to parcel this out rather than have players repeatedly request gum, otherwise certain players will get most of the supply. The manager also records attendance for games and practice sessions although on some teams individual players check their own attendance on a bulletin board and the manager tabulates this at the end of the week.

The manager has important duties relative to the playing of the game. He must score the game and report the final result to the press or to the publicity office of the athletic department. If there is a specific office for publicity it is also necessary for him to prepare a special statistic sheet for this office. He must also transfer game statistics to a master sheet so that a running game-by-game account can be kept of both batting and pitching statistics. These should be posted and given to the press periodically. If the coach charts pitchers for control and uses a rating system to determine the potential of individual players for getting on base, advancing base runners, and driving in critical runs, the manager assists in compiling these statistics and posts them. Statistics are an incentive for most squad members to improve and for outstanding players to excel. Taking notes for the coach during the game is another job.

Two other chores for the manager pertain to office work. One of these involves the final compilation of statistics for the season. This includes both freshman and junior varsity baseball. In addition he should deposit a list of team letter winners in the director's office, properly signed by the captain, manager, and coach, and make sure same has been done for other teams, if numerals or other awards are given. If a special newsletter or publication is circulated he should also help to compile this.

The second of the two office jobs involves trips. He should make all of the necessary arrangements for transportation, sleeping quarters (if required), and meals, all based on the budget. If cash is needed, it is drawn as specified. Then at the end of the trip a financial report must be made to the business office. This should be accompanied by receipts for any services paid by cash.

Once a game trip is finalized the manager should prepare an itinerary, including a listing of the traveling squad. Excuses for players must also be submitted to the proper academic office. It is advisable to post the itinerary and copies should be given to individual players. Then several days before the contemplated trip he should confirm details of the date, time, and meeting place with the transportation company. If the travel and game occur on the same day and lunch is necessary, he should arrange for box lunches and make the arrangement for the pickup. This, of course, depends on the desire of the coach. Lunches can, of course, be eaten enroute to the destination. They offer a second advantage since all players eat a satisfactory lunch. Two sandwiches, some fruit, and iced tea (or a liquid meal) provide an adequate lunch approximately three hours before the game. The manager must also check the traveling list for all departures. In addition he should make a final check of the bench for equipment left after both home and away games, and also the locker room after away games.

This does not, of course, limit a manager's efficiency. He can assist during batting practice, chase foul balls, chart pitchers and batters, and pick up loose equipment after both practices and games. During batting practice it is the responsibility of both the coach and manager to see that balls are quickly retrieved and returned to the feeder behind the pitching mound. Balls and bats should also be picked up around the plate area. These may become hazards in a variety of ways. This applies to other articles such as catching equipment, helmets, batting tees, and a pitching protector which is not being used. All players should be advised to perform these duties in the interest of safety.

A manager must also run a campaign to create an interest in managing unless paid managers are employed. Posters, notices in the school publication, and personal contracts usually bring the desired results. Sophomores who are unable to make the grade as varsity players are also possibilities for the managing department.

The manager is also elected at the team banquet and he too should be a senior. However, a dearth of managers may make it necessary to select a junior. A paid system of managers, of course, has no such weakness.

The manager's first duty is to get organized for the next season. He helps to plan the first squad meeting, prepares and distributes the final schedule, if it is ready, and distributes any forms which have to be filled out. He will also have to begin early correspondence relative to plans for away games.

To simplify the team manager's duties as well as assist the coach and/ or trainer in seeing that the various responsibilities are carried out, a check list is valuable. This can be applied to both home and away games.

Home Game	*Away Game*
Ball (chasers)	Balls (practice)
Balls (practice and game, 8–12 rubbed with dry dirt to remove gloss)	Bag (bat)
	Box (for caps)
Bases (extra or straps)	First aid (kit)
Dressing facilities (for umpires and visiting team)	Itinerary
	Lineup (card)
Field (preparation)	Money (meal, etc.)
First aid (kit)	Reservations
Greeter (for visiting team)	Roster (team)
Lineup (cards)	Rule (book)
Rosin (bags)	Schedule (pregame)
Rule (book)	Scorebook (and pencil)
Scorebook (and pencil)	Suit (rolls or bags)
Sun glasses	Towels (on bench)
Ticket (takers)	Transportation
Tickets (complimentary)	Undergarments (sanitary)
Umpires (notices to)	Uniform extras (belts, caps, stockings)

INJURIES

First aid is the immediate and temporary need of an injured player until the services of the team physician can be obtained. Very often adequate first aid minimizes the aggravation of the injury and permits a quicker recovery.

When a player is injured there are three steps to take:

1. Examine for obvious deformity and any deviation from the normal structure.

2. Listen for a complete description of the complaint as to how the injury occurred.
3. Administer first aid when the injury is not of a serious nature and arrange for the proper procedure in obtaining medical care.

The most common injuries in baseball are strains, sprains, and contusions. Immediate first aid consists of ice, compression, and elevation, after which the player should be referred to the team physician for diagnosis and further treatment.

Blisters and sliding burns should be cleansed with soap and water and a sterile compress applied. If the injury is extensive, refer the case to the proper medical authority.

In order to give the necessary first-aid treatment it is advisable to have a first-aid kit on the bench. It should contain the following:

Adherent	Liniment
Ammonia inhalants	Ointment (for dressings)
Antiseptic	Sling
Aspirin	Splints (arm and leg)
Cotton-tipped applicators	Sponge rubber (various thick-
Elastic bandages	nesses)
Felt	Sterile compresses
Gauze	Tape (several widths)
Ice bags (or equivalent)	Tongue blades

Extras

Elastic straps (for shin guards)	Rosin
Elk hide laces (for gloves)	Rule book
Eye black	Shoe laces
Pine-tar cloth (for bats)	Spike cleaners

Salt tablets should be provided in the locker room.

MAINTENANCE OF FIELD

Preparing and maintaining a proper playing surface is an important aspect of baseball. The grass of the field can be treated like most grass areas. It needs periodic watering and rolling and it must be fertilized and seeded occasionally.

The soil on the skin part of the infield is a subject in itself. It is difficult to give an exact formula to fit different soils which are native to the various parts of the country. One authority recommends 65–75 per cent sand and 25–30 per cent silt and clay (of approximately equal proportions). This area needs continuous raking and dragging with a mat, and some water to settle the dust. Some groundskeepers add loam to harden the infield—sand if the infield is dry. Some fill is also needed along the first- and third-base lines to prevent lips and ridges. This is also important around the grass lines of the infield. Any such fill should, of course, be screened.

Both the pitching mound and plate are critical areas because they require solid footing for pitchers, catchers, and batters. Clay loam consisting of a mixture of 40 per cent clay, 40 per cent sand, and 20 per cent silt is recommended for the area in front of the pitching rubber (also for the bull pens). Slightly dampened unbaked brick clay provides a good footing for the plate area. Both of these places require daily filling, tamping, and watering, unless the fill is damp. They should be covered with tarpaulins after practices and games unless the ground is wet.

In order to properly protect the pitching area, it is wise to cover the front part with a piece of canvas or rubber (approximately 3 × 5 feet). The back edge can be spiked down just beyond the pitching rubber, thus enabling batting practice pitchers to step on the canvas or rubber when delivering the ball. This is especially practical before games because it minimizes the work of the groundskeeper after regular infield practice.

The field should, of course, be properly marked with white lime or a comparable material before games. This includes the foul lines, the two batters' boxes, the catcher's box, the two circles for on-deck batters, and restraining lines (beyond which a ball is out of play).

An adequate fencing and visible scoreboard also improve a baseball field. Any shrubbery should be placed behind the fence, and the scoreboard should be located so that coaches can see it without changing their position on the bench. It is also advisable to have a ball and strike arrangement because strategy is based on the ball and strike count of the batter.

WET FIELD

Tarpaulins should be available to completely cover the dirt of the mound and plate areas if rain occurs before or during a game. In removing these, the corners of one end should be pulled over the tarpaulins so that the water will roll off into the grass or less used areas. There should also be some dry sand and dirt on hand so that wet spots may be covered if resumption of play is possible. Small wet areas can be first broomed. Brooming may also be necessary along the first- and third-base lines where water often collects. Sponging the base lines may also help. Driving stakes into extra wet areas, then removing same is another means of getting quick drainage.

A box of sawdust (or some comparable drying material) should be kept on the home bench on wet days. Balls which have been rejected by the umpire can then be rolled in the dust. This absorbs the external moisture and enables the balls to be put back in play.

SCOUTING

There seems to be a minimum of scouting in baseball below professional level. The most important reason is financial, because it costs money to travel. No team really has any secret weapons but it is, of course, helpful to know just what tactics the opposing team will use and the various abilities of its players. Some of this subject has been covered in the text under offensive and defensive strategy in Chapter 20. There is also an individual breakdown of players for the Major League game analyzed in Chapter 21. These do not cover all of the aspects of scouting but if you get too detailed your own team may suffer. It must be remembered that not too many players below the professional level are capable of putting scouting information into practice. This might even be said for some professional players.

FALL BASEBALL

Fall baseball can be very beneficial to screen players for spring. This particularly concerns sophomores because very often the varsity coach rarely sees the freshmen perform as a team.

In some areas a schedule of games is played. However, these are mostly institutions which do not play football. Schools with a full sports program have less locker space and time, equipment is difficult to obtain or administer, and usually all of the trainers are assigned to regular fall sports. The baseball coach may even be the problem himself since he might have to coach a fall sport or work in some other department of the athletic program.

Although many baseball players participate in fall intercollegiate sports or intramural activities, enough players will usually be on hand for the first two or three weeks of fall practice when the weather is usually ideal for baseball. There is generally enough enthusiasm generated to have some practice games, or at least have a rotating system of players on the defense under game conditions. This alone will make a fall program worthwhile.

C

Preseason Training

PRESEASON PLANNING

Approximately a month before the start of baseball practice correspondence should be sent to the members of the squad. This should advise them that a meeting will soon be held in the interest of the coming season. A specific date for the meeting may be given, or this can be relayed later through bulletin boards and announcements in the school paper. It is advisable to mention something about the importance of conditioning in the correspondence so that players will not come to the first practice session without having had any previous exercise. Badminton, handball, squash, and volley ball are good off-season activities. However, participation should end as soon as baseball practice begins.

It is advisable to hold the meeting about a week before the first practice session. The matter of team policy, the planned practice schedule, and various other matters can be discussed at this time. If the academic schedule overlaps the baseball-practice time the players should be requested to submit their class schedules. It is usually advisable to have each player fill out a publicity sheet at this time, unless one has already been prepared for another sport. Eligibility forms can also be completed or brought up to date, although the team manager can collect these later when the final squad is picked.

FIRST PRACTICE DAY

In order to begin practice without delay lockers should be properly identified and stocked with practice uniforms, undershirts, and jackets. Such items as belts, outer stockings, and caps can be issued separately. These and sanitary articles can be placed around the locker room, unless all equipment is distributed from a centralized equipment room.

Shoes can be furnished by individual players unless leftover or renovated shoes are tagged. If new shoes are needed these can be supplied according to policy. In this case the shoes should be obtained or ordered well in advance. They should also be broken in gradually because new shoes which are worn for long periods frequently cause blisters.

Since pitching is the most important phase of baseball, a pitching staff must be carefully nursed at the start of the season. Light throwing can be combined with running and pepper games during the first two weeks of practice. Spinning the curve ball is not necessarily out of order during this period if only a roll-over curve is employed. Starting with the third week of practice pitchers should throw only every other day, gradually stepping up the speed of their fast balls so that at the end of the fourth week of practice they are throwing at maximum speed. The curve ball (and other breaking pitches) should follow the same pattern. Six weeks is a more realistic period for reaching a peak in pitching. However, unless inside facilities are available, or the team plays in a warm climate, the shorter period might have to be followed, or even less. In this case prepractice conditioning becomes more important. The following schedule is planned for a complete infield. All drills except those involving cutoffs and relays (1a, 1b, 2, and 3) c⌐n be practiced on an infield. The latter can be delayed until the outfielders and relaymen are ready to make long throws.

SCREENING AND EARLY PRACTICE

It is important to conduct tryouts and begin preseason training with a workable squad as soon as possible. An ideal preseason plan involves seven weeks; tryout and regular players report on a staggered schedule:

	Tryouts	*Regular Players*
First week	Pitchers, catchers	————
Second week	Infielders, outfielders	Pitchers, catchers
Third week	————	Infielders, outfielders

At the end of the third week, tryouts are selected or rejected, thus leaving four weeks for intensive practice with the final squad. The advantage of such a schedule is that tryouts are given an adequate screening period, and regular players get enough preliminary conditioning to begin intensive training at the start of the fourth week. In addition, the absence of regular infielders and outfielders the first two weeks simplifies the screening operation.

For the practice routine during the first three weeks refer to the introductory paragraphs of Chapter 16, "Batting and Fielding Practice," p. 279. Players on tryout status will, of course, have to display their talents within this time. The main objective is to judge talent and pick the final squad. However, the third week can be a period of individual instruction for regular pitchers and catchers, using in particular Drills 12, 13, and 14 (pp. 306–08). If desirable, the Pitching Control Drill, p. 322, can also be performed. In this case emphasis should be placed on delivery of the ball in relation to the two pitching stances, not on control. The latter can be checked later when pitchers are deeper into the training program.

SIX-WEEK PROGRAM FOR PITCHERS

There are so many hidden factors in coaching that it is difficult to establish a specific schedule for pitchers. For example, some pitchers can do more work and need more work than others; the weather and failure to make practices may throw a pitching plan completely off schedule. The same factors may also affect team planning, and a coach should therefore keep his schedule flexible. An ideal six-week program for pitchers is outlined below; this represents the final weeks of the seven-week plan previously mentioned. Numbers following days of the week indicate approximate time in minutes to be spent in throwing; numbers in parentheses indicate approximate time to be spent on specified drills. Infielders and outfielde.s should report at the start of the second week so they may be used as batters, runners, and defensive players in the various drills.

FIRST WEEK

Light throwing combined with running and pepper games. Running to be light at start of practice, intense at end. When pitcher has completed his throwing, he should play pepper, then do his intensive running, and shower.

	Plan 1		Plan 2	
Monday	5 minutes		5 minutes	
Tuesday	—		5	
Wednesday	5		—	
Thursday	—		10	
Friday	5		—	
Saturday	10		5	

SECOND WEEK

Infielders and outfielders report. Continue light throwing, running, and pepper games.

	Plan 1		*Plan 2*
Monday	5	minutes	10 minutes
Tuesday	10		—
Wednesday	—		5
Thursday	10		10
Friday	—		—
Saturday	10		10

Signals should be posted so players learn signals in relation to plays and situations which occur in drills.

THIRD WEEK

Pitchers are now put on an every-other-day throwing schedule.

Plan 1	*Plan 2*		
Monday	Tuesday	5 minutes	Throwing with a gradual increase of speed. Continue running and pepper games.
Wednesday	Thursday	10	Drills 12, 13, and 14 can be performed (20 minutes).
Friday	Saturday	15	Pitching Control Drill, p. 322, if desirable. Catcher may umpire and manager may chart, or manager may do both.

Regular players do Drills 19 and 20 when pitcher is on mound; pitchers perform drills on day they are not scheduled to throw.

FOURTH WEEK

Pitchers and catchers have now had three weeks of conditioning and infielders and outfielders two weeks. They are thus ready for more intensive drills. It is recommended that the explanations of the specific drills listed below be reviewed (see Practice Drills, pp. 288–322).

Plan 1	*Plan 2*		
Monday	Tuesday	10 minutes	Drill 10 on day pitcher throws (15 minutes).
Wednesday	Thursday	15	Drill 11 on day pitcher throws (20 minutes).
Friday	Saturday	Practice game	Pitchers work three innings (nine consecutive outs if weather is cold). If pitchers have control trouble or labor through their innings, get the next pitcher warmed up.

Batting and base-running drills should be started the fourth week. If batting cages and pitching machines (and batting tees) are available, some players should be assigned to these. Other players report to the field for Drills 15 and 16. Drills 7 and 8 can also be performed. These drills can be practiced the first four days of the week when the pitchers are throwing, and are therefore beneficial to pitchers and other defensive players. Pitchers can act as runners on days they are not scheduled to throw. Credit players for completing drills satisfactorily so that they understand the techniques and strategies of plays and maneuvers (see pp. 321–22).

Fielding practice should also be started during the fourth week of practice. This gives the opportunity to perform Drills 1a, 1b, 2, and 3. Pitchers and extra players can run bases for these drills. Drills 4a, 4b, 5, and 6 can also be executed during fielding practice. All players should participate as runners. It is best to do all of these drills at the start of the fielding practice so that pitchers can leave the field after the drills.

FIFTH WEEK

Up to the sixth week of practice the conditioning and training of pitchers and the various pitching, catching, and base-running drills should be given precedence over batting practice. This is why special batting cages are so important in preseason practice.

During batting practice, players can work Drill 17. Have half the squad do Drills 21, 22, and 23 after batting practice on Wednesday, the other half after batting practice on Thursday.

Plan 1	*Plan 2*		
Monday	Tuesday	Practice game	Pitchers work 5 innings (15 consecutive outs if weather is cold).
Wednesday	Thursday	Batting practice (10–15 minutes)	Drills 9a, 9b, 9c, and 18 on day pitcher throws (20 minutes).
Friday	Saturday	Practice game	Starting pitchers work 6 innings. At this stage in schedule, practice game should be played like a regular game.

If you have the time, chart pitchers for control during fifth and sixth weeks. This can also be done during batting practice or practice games, and on the side lines.

SIXTH WEEK

During batting practice Drills 24 and 25 can be executed. Drill 17 can also be repeated at this time. Although some coaches may not want to use these plays or maneuvers as part of their offense, the drills provide good training.

Plan 1	*Plan 2*		
Monday	Tuesday	Batting practice (10–15 minutes)	Pitchers do intensive running the day they throw batting practice.
Wednesday	Thursday	Practice game	Wednesday pitchers work 3–4 innings; Thursday pitchers work 2–3 innings. All pitchers do intensive running after pitching. Pitchers not scheduled to pitch do intensive running early.

Assuming the first game is to be played on Saturday, pitchers are to rest on Friday. Others may engage in light running and throwing on this day.

PLANNING DAILY TIME SCHEDULES

The foregoing recommendations are only patterns. Any two coaches may, of course, have entirely different viewpoints on the subject of conditioning and training. This difference might also include the matter of technique and strategy in relation to both offense and defense.

In any practical schedule, batting and fielding practice must dovetail into the planning. These are both beneficial and interesting to players and should be indulged in almost daily, beginning with the fourth week of practice. Generally speaking, approximately an hour should be devoted to batting; about a half hour to fundamentals or drills, or brushing up on some phase of the game that has not been executed properly; and 20 to 30 minutes to fielding. If the ball is fungoed to infielders and outfielders during batting practice, regular fielding practice may be shortened or performed every other day. In this case it is best to have the practice on days when the fungo bat is used sparingly during batting practice. Too much throwing by regular players can be just as harmful as overindulgence by pitchers.

Planning must obviously take into consideration the number of games scheduled, when games are played, and what pitchers are used in a given game. It must also take into account what pitchers have warmed up (and how much) during a game. Pitchers who have not participated in the game should normally do some throwing and running after the game, unless a game or practice game is scheduled for the next day. Some running should also be done by pitchers who have been used during the game, with the exception of a starting pitcher who has pitched six to nine innings or who has thrown almost enough pitches for a complete game. The responsibility is necessarily that of the coach. These matters, as well as the repetition of certain drills during practice sessions, must always be carefully thought out, so that all players will have the required conditioning and know-how for their responsibilities.

Some of the important details about strategy and tactics can be covered in team meetings. However, no amount of talk can ever be a substitute for the actual doing.

SUGGESTED DAILY PRACTICE SCHEDULE FOR TEAM

	Hours	
Preseason	2½	(maximum)
Regular schedule	2	(maximum)
Pregame day	1½	(maximum; off-day for starting pitcher unless he wants to follow the practice schedule below)

SUGGESTED DAILY PRACTICE SCHEDULE FOR STARTING PITCHER

First day (after pitching 9 innings)	Stretching exercises, pepper game, light running
Second day	Pepper game, short batting practice session, extensive running
Third day	Pepper game, short warm-up, light running
Fourth day	Start another game

Matured pitchers are usually able to work with a three-day rest according to the above schedule. However, some pitchers may need four days rest between games. For this reason it is necessary to make an analysis of each pitcher before preparing a schedule. It may even be necessary to bow to certain idiosyncrasies or desires of some players relative to a between-games work schedule, particularly if this results in effective pitching.

Sample stretching exercises for increasing the strength of the back, shoulders, abdomen, hands, wrists, and arms:

1. Feet together, hands on hips. Bend the knees and stretch the arms forward and return to the original position. Build up to 20.
2. Feet apart. Extend the arms sideward with the palms down. Rotate the trunk to the left and back, then to the right, keeping the legs straight. Build up to 20.
3. Wider stance. Same starting position. Bend forward, swing the trunk left and touch the left foot with the right hand, keeping the legs straight. Return to the starting position, then bend forward, swing the trunk to the right and touch the right foot with the left hand. Alternate. Build up to 20.
4. Lie on back. Extend the arms behind the head with the palms up. Bend the trunk and touch the toes, keeping both the arms and legs straight. Return. Build up to 20.

5. Grasp any parallel support that will permit the body to extend down with the feet off the ground. Suspend briefly. Repeat 5-15 times, depending on the length of the hang.
6. Grip a small rubber ball with the arm extended and the palm down. Bend the wrist down. Return the wrist. Now rotate the arm a half-turn outward; then open the hand, stretching the fingers. Again grip the ball and return the arm to the original position. This can be done on a count of 6, beginning with the down flex of the wrist. Build up to 20.

Sample drills for the development of endurance and stamina:

1. Two players. Players face each other (3 to 4 feet apart). Player number 1 tosses the ball high or low and to either side of player number 2. Player number 2 returns the ball belt high to player number 1 then the process is repeated. Continue for several minutes then player number 2 gives player number 1 the workout. Players continue to alternate.
2. Two players. Player number 2 takes a defensive position on a marked spot. Player number 1 rolls the ball to the left or right. Player number 2 fields the ball and tosses it back then resumes his original position. Additional tosses are made and players change positions.
3. Two players. Eggs-in-basket relay. Two parallel lines are formed by placing three gloves in each line—about 25 feet apart. Three baseballs are placed in each line, 25 feet from the first glove. On a starting signal each player takes a ball to the first glove, then returns and takes a second ball to the second glove, etc. The action continues after returning to the starting mark by retrieving the balls in the same order to their original positions.
4. Line of players. Each player has a ball. A coach stands a few feet from the line. The first player gives the coach the ball and sprints in the direction of his approach and receives a lead throw. He then returns and starts the formation of another line. After the last player has performed the drill is done in the opposite direction. Repeat 10-20 times.

SUGGESTED PRACTICE SCHEDULE FOR A 3:00 P.M. GAME

Up to 2:00	Visiting team batting
2:00 to 2:30	Home team batting
2:30 to 2:40	Visiting team fielding
2:40 to 2:50	Home team fielding
2:50 to 3:00	Groundskeeper prepares field for the game

At 2:55 the umpires, coaches, and captains meet at home plate. The captains present their lineup cards then there is a discussion of the rules. The game begins promptly at 3:00 P.M.

The above schedule is fairly uniform for most schools. It is planned so that players of the home team may be able to attend a class after 12 o'clock.

D

Code of Ethics *

1. It is the duty of the coach to be in control of his players at all times in order to prevent any unsportsmanlike act toward opponents, officials, or spectators.
2. Coaches are expected to comply wholeheartedly with the intent and spirit of the rules. The deliberate teaching of players to violate the rules is indefensible.
3. Coaches should teach their players to respect the dignity of the game, officials, opponents, and the institutions which they represent.
4. Coaches should confine their discussion with the game officials to the interpretations of the rules and not constantly challenge umpire decisions involving judgment.
5. Whereas friendly banter between players is not to be prohibited, cursing, obscene language, malicious or personal remarks to opponents or spectators should not be tolerated at any time. Rather the players should spend their energies toward encouraging their teammates to better efforts.
6. Coaches should emphasize the fact that their base coaches must confine their remarks to their own teammates and not to "ride" the opposing pitcher.
7. Coaches, themselves, should refrain from any personal action that might arouse players or spectators to unsportsmanlike behavior.
8. Coaches should expect from the umpires a courteous and dignified attitude toward players and themselves.
9. Coaches should seek help from school administrators in controlling unruly students and spectators.

*As compiled by the American Association of College Baseball Coaches.

E

Alphabetical
List of Illustrations

F

List of Illustrations
by Page Number

Glossary

Advance—Move toward the next base. To reach a base nearer the plate.

Assist—A fielding credit for a player who throws or deflects a batted or thrown ball in such a way that a put-out occurs or would have occurred except for a subsequent error by a teammate.

Assortment of pitches—The fast ball, breaking ball, and slow ball of a pitcher.

Backstop—The screen or stands in back of home plate. The catcher.

Back-up position—The point behind a defensive player fielding a hit or thrown ball where a missed ball may be recovered.

Bad ball (or pitch)—A pitched ball outside the strike area.

Balk—An illegal action of the pitcher which permits base runners to advance one base.

Ball—A pitched ball ruled outside the strike area by the umpire.

Baseball—The round object with which the game of baseball was invented or evolved. It shall weigh not less than five or nor more than five and one-fourth ounces and measure not less than nine nor more than nine and one-fourth inches in circumference. A game invented by General Abner Doubleday in Cooperstown, New York, in 1839 (or evolved by combining characteristics of other games such as cricket and rounders).

Base hit—A fair batted ball which permits the batter to reach first base without the aid of an error by the defense (not at the expense of a runner being retired at the next base).

Base line—The direct line between bases.

Base on balls or walk—Four pitches ruled outside the strike area by the umpire.

Base open—First base unoccupied with second base or second and third bases occupied.

Base runner—The batter running to first base. Any offensive player on base.

Points involving rules have been interpreted from the Official Rules adopted by the American and National Leagues and the National Association of Professional Baseball Leagues. These may be found in the *Official Rule Book*, published by **The** *Sporting News*.

Baseman (first, second, and third basemen)—An infielder covering a definite area around a base.

Bases—Three bags and a rubber plate at the extremities of the base lines; namely, first base, second base, third base, and home.

Bat—The wooden stick with which the batter hits the ball. It shall be entirely of hard, solid wood in one piece and measure not over two and two-thirds inches in diameter at the thickest part nor more than forty-two inches in length. (A laminated bat of several pieces may be used if it meets specific requirements.)

Batter—The player hitting.

Batter's box—The area within which a player must remain while batting.

Battery—The pitcher and catcher.

Batting order—The order in which players appear at the plate to bat.

Bench—The location of members of a team when not on the field.

Blocked ball—A batted or thrown ball touched, stopped, or handled by a person not engaged in the game (ball is dead).

Blocking ball—Obstructing the path of a thrown or hit ball.

Break—The start of a player. The change in direction of a pitched ball.

Bull pen—The warm-up area of the pitcher during a game.

Cat (old)—A game of ball, called, according to the number of batters, one old cat, two old cat, and so on.

Catcher—The player behind home plate to whom the ball is delivered by the pitcher.

Change of pace—The variation in speed of pitches. A slow ball.

Choke grip—Holding the bat several inches from the end.

Coaching lines—Areas for performing coaching duties.

Control—The ability of a pitcher to reach the strike area with his assortment of pitches.

Count—The number of balls and strikes charged against the batter.

Cover—To protect a base from an attempted advance by a base runner.

Cross-fire delivery—A pitched ball delivered by stepping in the direction of the foul line instead of toward the plate.

Cutoff position—A point in front of a base where a throw from the outfield may be intercepted.

Cutting corners—Pitched balls passing over the inside or outside edge of the plate.

Dead ball—A ball not in play. A ball not likely to carry far.

Delivery—The complete pitching effort of a pitcher.

Diamond—The playing field. The infield.

Double play—A play retiring two base runners or the batter and a base runner. There must be two successive put-outs between the time a

ball leaves the pitcher's hand and is returned to him while he is standing in the pitcher's box.

Double play combination—The shortstop and second baseman.

Double steal—The advance of two base runners to the next bases unaided
by a hit, put-out, error, balk, base on balls, or hit batsman.

Drive—A long-hit ball. To hit the ball hard.

Earned run—A run which scores as the result of safe hits, sacrifices, stolen
bases, put-outs, bases on balls, hit batsmen, balks, or wild pitches (even
though the wild pitch be called a third strike) before fielding chances
have been offered to retire the side.

Error—A misplay by the defensive team which aids the team batting.

Fair ball—A legally batted ball that settles on or between the foul lines or
touches an umpire or a player within this area, or a ball that is on or
over fair ground when bounding to the outfield past first or third base.

Fake bunt—Bluffing to bunt the ball (also catch, throw, or swing).

Fat fast ball—A moderate-speed fast ball thrown belt-high over the center
of the plate.

Feeder—A player or coach who stands behind the mound and supplies the
pitcher with baseballs during batting practice. A player tossing or
throwing the ball to another player.

Field—The playing area. To catch the ball.

Fielder—A player fielding the ball. An infielder or outfielder.

Fly ball—A ball hit in the air.

Follow-through—The continuation of the arm and body in the direction of
a throw. The pivot of the body after swinging at the ball.

Force-out or **force play**—The retiring of a base runner by touching a base
to which he is forced to advance.

Forfeited game—A game awarded to a team because the opposing team
delays the game or refuses to continue play. The score of a forfeit
game is 9–0.

Foul ball—A legally batted ball that settles on foul territory before reaching first or third base, or that bounds past first or third base on or over
foul territory, or that first falls on foul territory beyond first or third
base, or touches the person of an umpire or a player or any object
foreign to the ground while on or over foul territory. (The batter is
out if he bunts the ball foul on a third strike.)

Foul tip—A ball that goes sharply and directly from the bat to the catcher's
hands and is legally caught. It is not a foul tip unless caught, and any
foul tip that is caught is a strike and the ball is in play. It is not a
legal catch if the ball rebounds from any part of the catcher's equipment other than the catcher's glove or hand.

Fungo—A ball hit to a player during practice. The act of hitting the ball to a player during practice. A light bat used in practice.

Good ball—A pitch in the strike area.
Ground ball—A ball hit on the ground.

Halfway—The approximate position of a base runner between bases when a short fly ball is likely to be caught with less than two out. The moderately deep position of the infield with a slow runner on third base and a weak batter at the plate.
High sky—A sky which bothers a player's vision. A cloudless sky.
Hit—A fair batted ball permitting a player to reach base without the aid of a misplay by the opposing team (not at the expense of a runner being retired at the next base). When a fair ball strikes the person or clothing of the umpire, or a base runner on fair ground before touching a fielder other than the pitcher (except when an infield fly hits a runner on base). To bat the ball.
Hit-and-run—An offensive tactic in which the batter starts the runner, then attempts to hit the ball through an opening in the defense.
Hit straightaway—To hit the ball where it is pitched. Take a natural swing at the ball.
Hitch—A faulty movement of the bat just prior to swinging (usually dropping the hands to the belt line).
Hitter—The player batting. Designated hitter—Player batting for pitcher.
Home plate—The fourth base.
Home run—A safe hit resulting in a complete circuit of the bases.
Hop—The bounce of a ground ball. The rise of a fast ball.

In the hole—The pitcher is in the hole with two balls and no strikes, three balls and no strikes, or three balls and one strike on the batter. The batter is in the hole with two strikes and no balls, or two strikes and one ball, charged against him.
Individual offensive bunt—A ball placed by the batter to thwart the defense. A bunt attempted for the purpose of reaching first base.
Infield—The area around the bases covered by the pitcher, catcher, and infielders. The infielders.
Infield fly—A fair fly ball (bunted and line-hit balls excepted) over the infield which automatically retires the batter whether or not it is caught, if the fielder is in a reasonable fielding position (normally facing the infield) and the following conditions prevail: first and second bases or all the bases occupied with less than two out. When a runner off base is hit by the fly, both the batter and runner are out; if a runner on base is hit by the fly only the batter is out; and in both cases the ball is dead.

Infielder—A player covering a definite area on the infield.

Inning—That portion of a game within which the teams alternate on offense and defense and in which there are three put-outs for each team.

Intentional pass—Four deliberate pitches outside the strike area.

Interference—An illegal act. Offensive interference: The team at bat interferes with, obstructs, impedes, hinders, or confuses a defensive player who is attempting to make a play. Defensive interference: The catcher interferes with the batter's right to hit the ball. By umpire: Interfering with the catcher's throw to prevent a runner from stealing; also when a batted ball hits an umpire before touching a fielder.

Key (signal)—A signal which reveals the pattern or character of a subsequent signal.

Lead—The distance a base runner stands from a bag. The advantage in runs scored by a team.

Lead-off man—The first batter in the line-up. The first batter in an inning.

Line-hit ball—A hard-hit fly ball that travels close to the ground.

Lines—The boundaries of the field and areas involving the catcher, base runner, and coaches.

Line-up—The nine players composing a team.

Mask—The protection for a catcher's face.

Move of a pitcher—The speed and deception of a pitcher in throwing to first base from a set position.

Obstruction—An illegal act. A defensive player who, when not in possession of the ball and not in the act of fielding the ball, impedes the progress of any base runner.

Offer at the ball—Swing at the ball.

One-base hit (single)—A safe hit resulting in the batter reaching first base.

Opening (or hole)—An unguarded area of the defense.

Opposite-field hitter—A right-hand batter who hits to the right-field side of second base, and a left-hand batter who hits to the left-field side.

Out—Retired. Not safe.

Outfield—The area in back of the infield covered by the outfielders. The outfielders.

Outfielder (left, right, and center fielders)—A player covering a definite area in the outfield.

Passed ball—A pitched ball which the catcher fails to stop and which permits a base runner to advance.

Pepper game—One player bunts to several players.

Pinch hitter (or runner)—Substitute batter (or runner).

Pitch—A ball delivered to the catcher. To deliver the ball.

Pitcher—The player who starts the game or who puts the ball in play. The player who delivers the ball to the catcher.

Pitcher's mound or **box**—Elevated area in the center of the infield from which the ball is delivered to the batter (15 inches above base lines and home plate).

Pitching rubber—The rubber plate from which the ball is delivered to the batter.

Pitchout—A ball pitched outside the strike area for the purpose of catching a base runner off base.

Pivot man—The player who makes the force-out for the first part of a double play.

Pop fly—A short fly.

Pull hitter—A right-hand batter who hits to the left-field side of second base, or a left-hand batter who hits to the right-field side.

Put-out—A play retiring the batter or a base runner.

Questionable pitch—A pitch that may be ruled either a ball or a strike by the umpire.

Rebound—The bounce of a ball away from a wall or fence.

Receiver—A player catching the ball. The catcher.

Regulation game—When the home team scores more runs in eight innings than the visiting team scores in nine innings. May be five or more innings if inclement weather or other causes force termination of play, or four and one half innings if the home team scores more runs in four innings or before the completion of its fifth inning than the visiting team scores in five complete innings.

Relay position—A point in the outfield where a throw may be received from an outfielder and a subsequent throw made to a base.

Retire—To put out a batter or base runner.

Run—A complete circuit of the bases. The act of moving fast.

Run-and-hit—An offensive tactic in which the batter hits the ball while a base runner is attempting to steal. (Because the manager assumes that the pitch will be over the plate, he signals to the runner to start.)

Run-down—The movement of players when a base runner is caught between bases.

Run batted in (RBI)—A run which scores because of a safe hit or sacrifice hit, an infield put-out (but not a force double play nor one started by the first baseman by fielding a ground ball and stepping on first base) or outfield put-out, or which is forced over the plate by reason of the batter receiving a base on balls, getting hit by a pitched ball, or being awarded first base because of interference or obstruction. The batter is also credited with a run batted in if, with less than two out, an error is made on a play on which a runner from third base would score and does score.

Sacrifice bunt—A ball placed by the batter to advance a base runner or runners.

Sacrifice fly—A fly ball which enables a base runner to score after the ball is caught.

Safe—Not retired. Not out.

Sailer—A fast ball that sails to the side of its original path.

Score—A complete circuit of the bases. The number of runs scored by each team.

Scoring position—A base runner on second or third base.

Screen—To evaluate the ability of players. A device to protect the pitcher and first baseman during practice.

Set pitching stance—The position from which the pitcher delivers the ball while holding base runners on base.

Shortstop—An infielder covering a definite area between second and third bases.

Signals or signs—Actions or words to convey information between the manager, coaches, and players.

Single steal—The advance of a base runner to the next base unaided by a hit, put-out, error, balk, base on balls, or hit batsman.

Sinker—A fast ball that goes down. A line-hit ball that drops quickly.

Slider—A fast ball that slides to the side of its original path.

Slugging-type game—Hitting straightaway.

Slump—A period of inefficient batting, pitching, or fielding which may be caused by illness, a lack of confidence, or the development of improper batting, pitching, or fielding habits (often the result of experimenting or trying too hard).

Spit ball—A formerly legal pitch which was delivered with slippery elm (produced by chewing the bark) on the index and middle fingers.

Squeeze play—An offensive tactic in which the batter attempts to score a base runner on third base with a bunt.

Start a runner—Give the base runner a steal, hit-and-run, or run-and-hit sign.

"Stay up"—Refrain from sliding.

Stolen base—The advance of a base runner to the next base unaided by a hit, put-out, error, balk, base on balls, or hit batsman.

Straightaway hitter—A left- or right-hand batter who hits in the territory between left-center field and right-center field.

Strike—A pitch ruled in the strike area by the umpire. A pitch which the batter misses or fouls. (A missed or fouled third strike which is caught by the catcher retires the batter.)

Strikeout—Three strikes. Three pitches ruled in the strike zone by the umpire (called strikes) or a combination of called strikes and swings by the batter. A bunted third strike which is declared foul.

Strike area (or zone)—The area (or zone) over the plate and between the batter's arm pits and top of his knees, when he assumes his natural stance.

Stuff on the ball—The speed and action of fast balls and breaking balls.

Swing—An attempt by a batter to hit the ball.

Tactic—An offensive or defensive maneuver. Strategy.

Tag—Touch a base runner with the ball. Touch a base with any part of the body while in possession of the ball.

Tag-up—Position of a base runner for an attempted advance on fly balls with less than two out.

Take a strike—Permit one strike to be called before attempting to hit the ball.

Target—The position of the catcher's hands prior to the release of the ball by the pitcher. The position of the first baseman when throws are received from near the plate.

Technique or fundamental—Any action essential to the playing of the game.

Texas Leaguer—A short fly ball which falls behind the infield for a hit.

Three-base hit (triple)—A safe hit resulting in the batter reaching third base.

Thrown out—The retiring of a base runner by a tag or force-out.

Tip-off—An individual mannerism revealing an individual or team tactic.

Toss—A short underhand throw.

Trapped ball—A batted ball that is caught near the ground on the first bounce.

Trapped runner—A player caught between bases.

Triple play—A play retiring three base runners or the batter and two base runners. There must be three successive put-outs (as in the two successive put-outs for a double play).

Triple steal—The advance of three base runners to the next bases unaided by a hit, put-out, error, balk, base on balls, or hit batsman.

Two-base hit (double)—A safe hit resulting in the batter reaching second base.

Umpire (arbiter)—An official of the game. *Note:* If a ball hits an umpire before passing a fielder other than the pitcher, the ball is dead; when the ball hits an umpire after having passed a fielder other than the pitcher, the ball is in play.

Waiter—A batter who attempts to reach first base by obtaining a base on balls.

Warming up—Throwing the ball in practice or before the game starts.

Waste pitch—A ball pitched outside the strike area to determine the batter's intentions.

Wild pitch—A pitched ball which the catcher is unable to block and which permits a runner to advance.

Windup—The preliminary action of the pitcher prior to pitching the ball when it is not necessary to hold a base runner on base.

Sample Tests

For self-testing or use in the classroom, two sets of sample test questions have been prepared for Part I, Defensive Baseball; and for Part II, Offensive Baseball; Part III, Practice Techniques; and Part IV, Game Strategy. These consist of Discussion Questions and Multiple-Choice Questions and Answers.

PART I: DISCUSSION QUESTIONS

1. Suggest the correct pitch and location of the ball in the following situations (specify high inside, low outside, etc.): (a) Score tied, eighth inning, first base occupied, none out, (b) the infield plays in to cut off a runner at the plate, (c) first base is occupied with a left-hand batter up, (d) a squeeze play is anticipated with a right-hand batter up.
2. Describe some specific batting weaknesses and suggest ways to exploit them.
3. Discuss the two methods of blocking ground balls in the outfield. When is it advisable to block the ball?
4. How does a catcher conceal his signals from the opposing team? Suggest two ways to give signals.
5. Which foot is moved first if an outfielder starts in and toward the left-field line for a ball? Back and toward the right-field line?
6. State two occasions when the first baseman tosses the ball to the pitcher covering first. When is the ball thrown?
7. What are some of the points infielders must take into consideration in fielding ground balls?
8. Suggest the proper way to step from the rubber after taking a set pitching position. What is the important thing to keep in mind with regard to the action of the hands?
9. State several ways a second baseman might pivot on a double play. Do the same for the shortstop.
10. Describe the two pitching positions. Which of these is employed with the following bases occupied: (a) first and second bases, (b) second and third bases, (c) first and third bases?

11. Why do most catchers give a target in foul territory when waiting for a throw from the second baseman to complete a force play?

12. What are considered general batting weaknesses? Give your answer in relation to the location of the three basic pitches; that is, a fast ball, a curve ball, and a slow ball.

13. Suggest a tactic for a right-hand pitcher which might catch a runner off first base. How does a left-hand pitcher prevent the runner from getting a fast break for second?

14. State the duties of the shortstop and second baseman if the batter, (a) singles sharply to left field with second base occupied, (b) lines a hit between the right and center fielders, (c) sacrifices with first and second bases occupied.

15. What frequently helps a pitcher whose fast ball is consistently (a) below the strike area, (b) above the strike area, (c) to either side of the strike area?

16. Plan the defense to prevent the batter from sacrificing a runner from second base to third.

17. Under what circumstances does the third baseman act as the cutoff man? How does he assist the cutoff man on throws to third?

18. If an intentional pass is being given to a right-hand batter which member of the double play combination covers second base? Why is this done?

19. Recommend several ways to determine the direction and velocity of the wind. Which of these are preferred?

20. What does it mean to trap a ball? If a trapped ball is thrown to second base with first and second bases occupied, how would you handle the play if:
   (a) the runner on second remained on the bag;
   (b) the runner on second broke for third?

MULTIPLE-CHOICE QUESTIONS AND ANSWERS

1. A pitcher commits a balk if he:
   (a) Steps toward second base and fakes a throw to catch a runner from a set pitching position;
   (b) Straddles the rubber without the ball;
   (c) Steps toward third base and attempts to catch a runner from a windup pitching position.

2. On a single to left field with second base occupied, the shortstop:
   (a) Runs to the outfield;
   (b) Covers second base;
   (c) Covers third base.

3. The infield fly rule may be declared with less than two out when:
   (a) First and third bases are occupied;

(b) Second and third bases are occupied;

(c) First and second bases are occupied.

4. If a left-hand batter hits a low line drive between the left fielder and the left-field foul line, the ball:

(a) Curves toward foul territory;

(b) Curves toward the left fielder;

(c) Sinks after it passes over the infield.

5. In sacrifice situations the pitcher delivers:

(a) A high fast ball;

(b) A belt-high slow ball;

(c) A low curve.

6. The logical order of signals for a pickoff play by the catcher is:

(a) Pickoff signal to infielder, pitchout signal to pitcher, acknowledgment signal by infielder.

(b) Pitchout signal to pitcher, pickoff signal to infielder, acknowledgment signal by infielder.

(c) Pickoff signal to infielder, acknowledgment signal by infielder, pitchout signal to pitcher.

7. When the batter bounces a single through the infield on the count of three and two with two out and first and second bases occupied, the outfielder usually throws:

(a) To the plate;

(b) To third base;

(c) To second base.

8. The accepted method for catching a routine ground ball stresses:

(a) One foot ahead of the other;

(b) One knee on the ground;

(c) Both feet together.

9. In taking a throw from the catcher on an attempted steal the defensive player tries to catch the ball:

(a) In front of the bag;

(b) Over the bag;

(c) In back of the bag.

10. If the batter bunts the ball toward the third baseman to sacrifice a runner from first to second base, the catcher:

(a) Backs up first base;

(b) Covers third base;

(c) Guards the plate.

11. The batter may run on a dropped third strike:

(a) With first and third bases occupied and one out;

(b) With second and third bases occupied and none out;

(c) With all of the bases occupied and one out.

12. After a player has assumed a natural batting stance his strike area is

considered the space over the plate between:

(a) The letters of the uniform and the knees;

(b) The shoulders and the knees;

(c) The armpits and the top of the knees.

13. A preplanned play to catch a runner at third base on a sacrifice requires teamwork between:

(a) Pitcher, second baseman, and third baseman;

(b) Pitcher, catcher, and third baseman;

(c) Pitcher, shortstop, and third baseman.

14. When the manager or coach signals the first baseman to play off the bag with a slow runner on first, the first baseman relays the signal to the pitcher, then takes his position:

(a) In front of the runner;

(b) Behind the runner;

(c) In the base line.

15. A right-hand batter with average running speed is at the plate with first and third bases occupied and one out. The team on the defense is ahead 10 to 3. A hard-hit ground ball goes directly toward the third baseman. The ball is fielded cleanly. To which base is the throw made:

(a) Second base;

(b) First base;

(c) The plate.

16. The pitcher runs straight to first base and takes the first baseman's throw from a stretch position on the bag, when the first baseman:

(a) Is playing deep and fields a hard-hit ground ball along the foul line;

(b) Is playing deep and fields a hard-hit ground ball toward his right;

(c) Is playing in and fields a ground ball away from the bag.

17. In fielding bunts which are rolling away from the plate, the catcher:

(a) Picks up the ball with his bare hand;

(b) Keeps to the right of the bunt and scoops up the ball with both hands;

(c) Keeps to the left of the bunt and scoops up the ball with both hands.

18. When first and second bases are occupied in a sacrifice situation, the second baseman:

(a) Holds the runner on second;

(b) Covers first base if the ball is bunted;

(c) Backs up first base if the ball is bunted.

19. The third baseman bluffs or fakes a runner back to second base after fielding a hard-hit grounder in the following situations:

(a) Second base occupied with one out;

(b) Second and third bases occupied with none out;

(c) Second base occupied with two out.

20. In a preplanned play to catch a runner at third base on an attempted sacrifice, the shortstop drives the runner back to second when the pitcher:

(a) Gives a signal;

(b) Is bringing his hands down to the set pitching position.

(c) Looks toward second from the set pitching position.

ANSWERS

1	2	3	4	5	6	7	8	9	10	11	12	13	14	15	16	17	18	19	20
b	c	c	a	a	c	c	b	a	b	b	q	c	a	b	c	c	b	a	c

PARTS II, III, AND IV: DISCUSSION QUESTIONS

1. Does the batter have to turn into foul territory after passing the bag on a straight run to first? Give the reason for your answer.

2. Why is it inadvisable to slide into first base? When is there an exception to the rule?

3. Name the various types of bunts. Describe two different ways to make a sacrifice.

4. Discuss the strategy of a base runner advancing from first base if the second baseman is fielding a ball in the base line. What base running rule must be remembered?

5. Explain the action of the hips and arms in hitting both inside and outside pitches.

6. When is the logical time to attempt to beat out a bunt? Explain your answer in relation to the type of bunt to be made (long or short) and the ball and strike count at the time of the execution.

7. What does the statement "Hit behind the runner" imply? How does this offensive maneuver differ from the hit-and-run?

8. Why is it inadvisable to break for the next base when a batter indicates he will sacrifice? Describe the proper footwork in this situation.

9. How can a player be rewarded for a successful performance of batting? Explain this point in relation to regular batting practice and intersquad games.

10. When is the best time to use the squeeze play? What is the difference between the safety squeeze and the running squeeze?

11. In coaching third base, would you normally give a stop or go signal

in the following situations: (a) a hard-hit single to right field with a fast runner on first base and one out, (b) a hard-hit single to left field with a moderately fast runner on second base and two out.

12. Why is it advantageous to hit the first pitch (if it is a strike) in a sacrifice situation? Explain your answer in relation to the position of all infielders.

13. On a throw to the plate from the outfield after a single, the batter's advance past first depends on what two factors with respect to the defense?

14. Describe the difference between a regular double steal and a delayed double steal with first and third bases occupied.

15. How does the first-base coach assist a batter running from the plate? Give your answer in relation to both a ground ball to an infielder and a hit to the outfield.

16. Outline a routine for infield practice. State the sequence of throws after the ball has been returned to the catcher by the first baseman.

17. Suggest a method for charting pitchers to improve control. What is considered a reasonable ratio of fast balls to other pitches during an average game?

18. What modern devices are employed to facilitate batting practice? If balls are being hit to the infielders during batting practice what must the fungo hitter keep in mind?

19. Give the number of the defensive position for each player as it applies to the scoring of a game.

20. In an intentional pass situation why is it best for a manager or coach to use a hand signal rather than a verbal signal to relay his strategy to the catcher.

MULTIPLE-CHOICE QUESTIONS AND ANSWERS

1. The majority of players favor bats which combine length and weight of:
   (a) 33½ inches and 36 ounces;
   (b) 35 inches and 34 ounces;
   (c) 34½ inches and 32 ounces.

2. On a hit-and-run play the runner on first:
   (a) Watches the entire flight of the ball as he breaks for second;
   (b) Starts for second then glances toward the plate after two or three steps;
   (c) Breaks for second the same as on a steal.

3. The three-foot line appears:
   (a) The first half of the distance to first base;
   (b) The last half of the distance to first base;
   (c) All the way down the base line.

4. In running out of the base line to avoid being tagged, a player can run:
   (a) 5 feet out of line;
   (b) 3 feet out of line;
   (c) 4 feet out of line.

5. When only second base is occupied with less than two out it is advisable for the runner to break for third if a hard-hit ground ball goes:
   (a) Directly to the shortstop;
   (b) To the shortstop's right;
   (c) To the shortstop's left.

6. Most players are classified as:
   (a) Straightaway hitters;
   (b) Opposite-field hitters;
   (c) Pull hitters.

7. In sacrifice situations the main objective of the batter is to:
   (a) Make a good bunt;
   (b) Disguise his intentions;
   (c) Get away from the plate fast.

8. The easiest double steal can be executed with:
   (a) First and third bases occupied;
   (b) First and second bases occupied;
   (c) Second and third bases occupied.

9. When a running squeeze play is employed, the runner on third breaks for the plate as:
   (a) The pitcher starts his windup;
   (b) The pitcher is about to release the ball;
   (c) The pitcher steps to throw.

10. The best all-purpose slide is:
    (a) The hook slide;
    (b) The head-first slide;
    (c) The bent-leg slide.

11. On a delayed steal from first base the runner:
    (a) Stops, casually fakes going back to first, then breaks for second;
    (b) Continues his advance and breaks for second;
    (c) Comes to a flat-footed stop, then breaks for second.

12. The main objective in using the batting tee is to:
    (a) Perfect the angle of the swing;
    (b) Learn to hit fast and slow pitches;
    (c) Coordinate the stride and swing.

13. When two base runners are tagged while standing on third base:
    (a) The runner who originally had possession of the bag is out;
    (b) The runner who advanced from second base is out;
    (c) Both runners are out.

14. If a batter triples in the last half of the final inning with the score tied and one out, the manager of the defense:
    (a) Walks the next batter to set up a double play;
    (b) Walks the next two batters intentionally and brings the outfield and infield in;
    (c) Moves the infield to a halfway position and pitches to the next batter.

15. The greatest emphasis in coaching should be placed on:
    (a) Batting;
    (b) Pitching;
    (c) Base running.

16. When a manager or coach knows an opposing player is batting out of turn he makes his appeal to the umpire after the player:
    (a) Steps into the batter's box;
    (b) Hits the ball;
    (c) Reaches base safely.

17. If the second signal is used in a single-digit combination method of giving battery signals, a curve is indicated by:
    (a) One finger, two fingers, and one finger;
    (b) Three fingers, one finger, two fingers;
    (c) Two fingers, three fingers, one finger.

18. The qualities for a good second-place hitter include the ability to:
    (a) Run, bunt, and hit to the opposite field;
    (b) Run, bunt, and hit behind the runner;
    (c) Run, bunt, and hit for extra bases.

19. When a manager or coach wants an intentional pass issued, it is best to:
    (a) Signal to the catcher;
    (b) Signal to the pitcher;
    (c) Call "intentional pass" to the pitcher and catcher.

20. In selecting a defensive team the first five players should include:
    (a) Pitcher, shortstop, first baseman, center fielder, and catcher;
    (b) Catcher, pitcher, second baseman, right fielder, and third baseman.
    (c) Second baseman, pitcher, center fielder, catcher, and shortstop.

ANSWERS

1	2	3	4	5	6	7	8	9	10	11	12	13	14	15	16	17	18	19	20
c	b	b	b	c	c	c	a	a	b	b	b	b	c	b	c	a	b	a	c

Index